THE CITY ASSEMBLED

The Elements of Urban Form Through History

SPIRO KOSTOF

THE CITY ASSEMBLED

The Elements of Urban Form Through History

With the collaboration of Greg Castillo

Original drawings by Richard Tobias

With 346 illustrations, 40 in color

Thames & Hudson

Frontispiece 1 *Frankfurt-am-Main (Germany), looking from the Römerberg toward Alter Markt and the cathedral, before the Second World War. On the right is the late medieval Haus zum Engel; on the left, with a typically Germanic projecting oriel, the Renaissance Haus der Zwölf Himmelzeichen, displaying the signs of the zodiac. The area beyond, long since encroached on and built over, was originally a large open marketplace. Its memory lived on in the name of the narrow street, Alter Markt ("old market").*

Published in 2005 in paperback in the United States of America by Thames & Hudson Inc., 500 Fifth Avenue, New York, New York 10110

thamesandhudsonusa.com

Library of Congress Catalog Card Number 2004102924
ISBN 0-500-28172-6

Printed and bound in China by C&C Offset Printing Co., Ltd.

CONTENTS

INTRODUCTION

A city is said to be an assembly of people, a congregation drawn together to the end they may thereby the better live at their ease in wealth and plenty. And the greatness of a city is said to be, not the largeness of the site or the circuit of the walls, but the multitude and number of the inhabitants and their power. Now men are drawn together upon sundry causes and occasions thereunto them moving: some by authority, some by force, some by pleasure, and some by profit that proceedeth of it.[1]

The definition is that of the 16th-century Italian philosopher Giovanni Botero, penned under the heading "What a city is, and what the greatness of a city is said to be." Given its late Renaissance time frame – an era remembered for its commitment to city building as a studied art – his disregard for the ennobling power of physical form seems a calculated affront. Botero insists that the message of the city lies in its human activity: in processes political, military, recreational, and economic. The idea must have shocked contemporaries used to assuming the primacy of built form, whether that of the solid vernacular or the pedigreed urbanism of radial avenues and grand plazas. I admit to finding both versions of the urban artifact seductive. *The City Assembled: The Elements of Urban Form Through History* is an exploration of their overlap.

From this book's inception – now more than ten years ago – I had always thought of it as half of a larger study. The first part would look at city form in complete patterns, the way we see it in town plans or from the air. That was the method employed by the companion to this volume, *The City Shaped: Urban Patterns and Meanings Through History*. There I discussed five approaches to urban form used throughout history in a variety of cultures. A chapter on "'Organic' Patterns" examined the non-geometric configurations often romanticized as "natural" modes of building and dismissed abiding myths about the ways in which such cities come about, emphasizing their premeditation and artificiality. "The Grid" examined a form ubiquitous in both time and place and presented an account of its brilliant variations, ranging from communitarian experiments like that of Salt Lake City all the way to the standard blueprint of land speculation and the matrix for colonial settlement. A third chapter, entitled "The City as Diagram," looked at those precise urban geometries created as a depiction of some presumed or promulgated order, from concentration camps and model company towns to built cosmologies like Beijing. "The Grand Manner" explored the urbanism of political triumph. Its design vocabulary is heroic, theatrical, and above all else selfconscious, relying on vistas, splendid tree-lined thoroughfares, and a repertory of accents like commemorative columns, obelisks, and triumphal arches. A final chapter was devoted to "The Skyline," because it too is a way of seeing the city whole. As an urban signature, the rise of a privatized skyline of business above the previous silhouette of faith and governance forces us to question the legitimacy of accumulated capital to crown our civic horizon.

The second part of my examination of urban forms and meanings is this volume. We now focus on the constituent elements of city building common to all settlement patterns, independent of the modes of classification distinguished in *The City Shaped*. Every city has an edge which changes over time – whether it has an "organic" pattern or is laid out as a grid or a triumphant city in the Grand Manner. Every city has internal divisions, public places, streets. These are the subjects of the following chapters. I wanted to explore here the urban geographer's concept of the urban fringe belt; the role of the parish in the spatial structure of the Christian city; the origin of the residential square; the nature of the bridge-street; and other such familiar devices out of which urban form assembles itself with verve and imagination and mischief. Finally I conclude with a chapter on urban process, which, used here to refer to the transmutations of cities both forceful and incremental, embraces all of the topic areas previously discussed.

I did not start this work to advance a great hypothesis or promote a new kind of urban history. The categories I propose here are, as all classifications of settlement form must be, essentially arbitrary. Cities are too particular as phenomena – specific to moments in time and to the vicissitudes of site and culture – to be pinned down by absolute taxonomies. Urban observers devise various approaches to their quarry, each attuned to a specific interest. Mine has remained throughout these two volumes the same: to render accessible the universal experience of making cities, and to do so within the legitimate parameters of my discipline – architectural history. I have emphasized urbanism as *process* – the many ways in which the city's physical frame is adjusted to changing exigencies.

Urban form is never innocent of social content: it is the matrix within which we organize daily life, and all of us have strong opinions about it. In every instance, sometimes repeatedly within one chapter, I have followed the narrative through to the present to reveal that the discourse engages our own time in unexpected ways. Modernism is a harsh intrusion in the development of almost every theme in these two volumes, and the current recovery from the less tolerant aspects of its doctrine has made us consider what it is we treasure about the traditional city. A new generation of urban designers – Ricardo Bofill, Rob and Léon Krier, Elizabeth Plater-Zyberk and Andres Duany among others – are helping us in this effort by elegantly recharging old urban forms with present-day common sense. Their participation in the continuous rebuilding of our global constellation of towns and cities is already shaping the next episode of an ongoing story.

SPIRO KOSTOF
Berkeley, July 1991

In June 1991, with the first four chapters of *The City Assembled* in draft form, Spiro Kostof was diagnosed as having cancer. For the next three months he marshalled his energies to sketch out "Urban Process," the book's last chapter. He died on 7 December 1991 at his home in Berkeley, California.

As his research assistant of five years' standing, I was called on by Professor Kostof to help in the preparation of the final text and to see his manuscript through to publication. The task would have been impossible without extraordinary assistance provided by the impeccably professional staff at Thames and Hudson. Once again, as with *The City Shaped*, great support came from Richard Tobias, Spiro Kostof's longtime collaborator in matters pictorial. Much of the ancillary work on the present volume – compiling notes and bibliography, and tracking down some of the illustrations and caption material – was taken on by Kai Gutschow, who performed with unswerving competence despite rapid-fire deadlines. I am additionally grateful to Mr. Gutschow and to Johan van der Zande for their collaboration in producing the index.

This book has benefited greatly in substance and style from the involvement of many individuals. Diane Favro was generous in sharing her scholarship concerning Roman urbanism with Professor Kostof. Ken Caldwell of ELS Architects in Berkeley, California, Jan Bowman of the City of Eugene, Oregon, Mary Louise Days of the City of Santa Barbara, California, and Linda Tigges of the City of Santa Fe, New Mexico, contributed their professional expertise and provided research documents. Nezar AlSayyad, Dora Crouch, and Steven Tobriner were instrumental in polishing the text through their advice and encouragement. For their help in procuring photographic illustrations I must thank Maryly Snow of the Environmental Design Slide Library at the University of California, Berkeley, and Laurie Haycock Makela of the Walker Art Center in Minneapolis, as well as Diane Favro, Paul Groth, Donlyn Lyndon, and Marc Treib. As with *The City Shaped*, Elizabeth Byrne of the College of Environmental Design Library at Berkeley was extremely helpful. Finally, I must voice my gratitude to my partner, Georg Raffelt, for his support through the stormy unfolding of my charge in this publication, and to my mentor, Spiro Kostof, for having entrusted it to me.

GREG CASTILLO
Berkeley, February 1992

1 · THE CITY EDGE

PRELIMINARIES

FROM the awesome specter of a ring of walls rising sheer in the countryside, to signs that read "Berkeley City Limit" or "You are Now Entering Muncie, Indiana," circumscription is a principal characteristic of city-form.

The linguistic and iconographic support is various. The traditional Chinese words for "city" and "wall" are identical; the character *ch'eng* expresses both of them. The English word "town" comes from a Teutonic word that means hedge or enclosure. The Old Dutch version, *tuin*, means fence; the Old High German *zun* means a rampart. Mural crowns on city deities were common to more than one culture. Hellenistic *tyche* figures like that of Antioch are one example.

To be sure, there is a big difference between a fortified barrier, with towers and elaborate gates, and a mere sign. Things have changed in the modern period: we no longer think of the city as a closed form with hard edges. But one thing has not changed. When we cross a city's boundary, then as now, we accept certain legal restraints, and local rules of conduct; and if we make the city our place of residence, we also agree to be taxed, to use our property in some ways and not others, and to expect a range of services in return. Belonging is a privilege, and has its price. All this is determined by an arbitrary line. What is the nature of this line? How does it change over time? These are the questions I am concerned with in this chapter.

Delimiting a city may precede settlement or follow it. This of course depends on whether the city is created as a fresh plantation or is carved out of prior settlements. The latter can come about through some form of *synoecism*, or else through *incorporation*, that is, the official designation of a rural settlement or a suburb as an independent municipality.

Whether the city boundary was established prior to settlement or afterward, it was, in the past at least, a solemn occasion. There are founding rituals in almost all cultures. Plowing furrows where the city boundary is to be, after a ritual examination of the site, figures in both Indian and Etruscan traditions.

The *Manasara* instructs the architect in charge of the limitation procedures to "meditate on the two oxen as the sun and the moon, on the plough as the boar-god [Vishnu] and on the builder as Brahma." And the Etruscan cutting of the *sulcus primigenius*, the initial furrow, was performed with a bronze plough to which an ox

2 *opposite Amersfoort (The Netherlands) shows a number of faces of the city edge. The core is still circumscribed by the traces of its early wall, demolished in the 15th century and replaced by the muurhuizen, or "wall-houses," built from the rubble. The medieval gate at this end of the main street was left standing. Outside the core, early linear suburbs grew up along the main roads. Gradually the intermediate spaces were filled in, with houses, schools, and industry; then suburbs developed beyond the railroad (upper right). A ring-road skirts the planted line of the later wall.*

3 *above The* tyche *(literally "luck") or city goddess of Antioch, crowned with a ring of walls: Roman copy of an original of the 3rd century BC.*

and a cow had been yoked, both white. The founder would lift the plough off the soil to mark the city gates. The furrow itself was sacred and could not be crossed. When Remus tauntingly stepped over his brother Romulus's furrow for the new city of Rome, Romulus killed him, "for that he presumed to leap over an holy and inviolate place," Plutarch writes—that is, for committing sacrilege.[1]

This line demarcated the *pomerium*, a strip of land associated with the walls and lying both inside and outside of them, bounded by stone markers, on which no building was allowed. Only conquerors who had added new territory to the Roman state were permitted to extend the *pomerium*. Within this urban boundary, neither burials nor military activity could take place. And the city could be unmade with a counter-furrow. When Scipio took Carthage and destroyed it, the site was plowed, or rather unplowed. As one ancient source, Herennius Modestinus, makes clear, this had legal implications. "If revenue was due to a city, and the city had been plowed over, this city had no further legal existence. So Carthage ceased to exist and its revenues were treated as those of someone dead."

The record of delimitation is often colorful. In the founding rite of Antioch, for example, elephants from King Seleucus's army were stationed to mark the sites of towers in the city wall, and the city limits and streets were traced with wheat. Baghdad's famous circle was drawn with ash. Invariably there were sacrifices or similar ceremonies before and after the act of marking. For the medieval *bastides* in Gascony, the ceremony of the raising of the stake or *palum* carrying the flag with the emblems of the founders preceded occupation. We also have clear evidence from more than one region for the continued ritual commemoration of the city boundary. In Rome, the *pomerium* was celebrated in February, when *Luperci* (priests of the deity Lupercus) ran along its length clad in goatskins, striking women to make them fertile. In Hinduism, the rite of *pradakshina*, or delimitation of sacred space, involved the circumambulation of the capital city by its god, and therefore by the king at the time of his coronation. This rite is recorded for Madurai and several other Southeast Asian cities. And in the Kathmandu valley up to the present time, on the twelfth day of the month of Bhadra, in the evening hours, the population circumambulates the town of Bhaktapur, following the city boundary as it was established in the late 18th century.

The city bounds are not revised lightly, but are not ordinarily frozen in perpetuity. They have to be adjusted as the settlement grows or shrinks through time. Even when there is no actual redefinition, the boundary may subsequently lose some of its significance. Overflowing cities, for example, might create such a blanket of settlement outside the walls that their visual impact would be undermined. Conversely, a city like Rome which kept her Classical walls all through the Middle 4 Ages came to occupy a small fraction of the urban land they enclosed. The customs line was a much more realistic circumscription of the *abitato*, or built-up area.

THE CUSTOMS BOUNDARY

The customs boundary did not always correspond to the city limits as defined by the walls, precisely because the walls did not remain true to the actual extent of the urban fabric. Since the customs barrier was there to regulate the collection of tolls, its location had to be reasonably coordinated with the physical limits of the built-up area. At Bordeaux, the medieval walls did serve as the official customs barrier all the way to the Revolution. Gaps were filled with iron grills; even the river frontage of the Pl.4 Place Royale was closed in by a great ironwork screen. Indeed, in many medieval towns where defensive walls were not an urgent necessity, some sort of barrier,

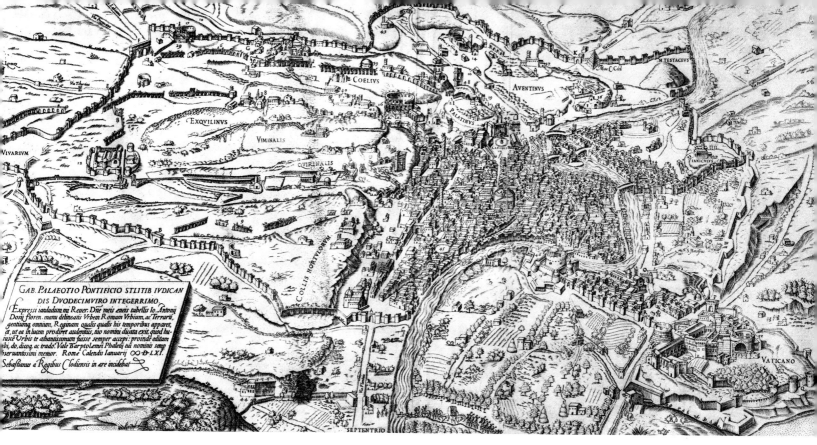

4 *Bird's-eye view of Rome from the north by Antonio Dosio, 1561. Within the great circuit of the Aurelian Walls, built in the late 3rd century A D, the city has shrunk and shifted its center of gravity northwestward. To the east and south, Roman ruins survive amid fields. Exceptions are the Early Christian shrines of S. Maria Maggiore and the Lateran (between the word "Viminalis" and the distant wall).*

The living city is concentrated to the west, in the Tiber bend and the antique left-bank district of Trastevere. Between the two lies the Tiber Island. The city is entered from the north through the Porta del Popolo (A). A new northwestern extension (right foreground) grew up with the rise of Christianity: here the Vatican, clustered around the church on the site of St. Peter's extramural burial, was linked to the city by the suburb of the Borgo, fortified in the 9th century.

however flimsy, was nonetheless undertaken at great cost, in order to protect the town's rights of tollage and to control access to its markets. At the very least, there would be simple bargates at major points of access.

But in many important cities, walls and customs barrier became disengaged more than once. In ancient Rome, the Republican (so-called "Servian") walls of the 4th century B C, a tight fit for their time, had been vastly outgrown by the reign of the first emperor, Augustus. In order to reduce smuggling, a customs boundary was then drawn farther out along a limit fixed by peripheral building—what Pliny calls *extrema tectorum*, the limits of the built, and what the Roman citizens themselves called *continentia*, or the continuous fabric of the city as far out as it stretched. The Aurelian Walls of the later 3rd century A D may have followed closely this Augustan barrier. Then, as the city shrank after the fall of the Roman Empire, the customs line had now to be moved back well inside the Aurelian Walls, once again to correspond to the reality of the urban situation.

We know something of the Augustan customs barrier. It was meant to facilitate the levying of a tax on market goods being imported into the city; items brought in for personal use were exempt. The tax was assessed according to piece or bulk, and it was collected at thirty-seven gates or customs stations placed critically along the consular highways that converged upon the city from all directions. Besides the stations, we can also expect that the barrier would have developed its own related land use. There is evidence that large magazines and depots for wine, and perhaps also animal pens, were built intentionally just outside this boundary. The wholesaler would thus escape paying customs, passing on this financial burden to the local retailer who had to bring the goods inside the *continentia*.[2]

When the stations along the incoming roads, supplemented by an impermanent barrier of some sort, did not prove adequate, the city had to go to the expense of building more permanent customs walls. In 1734–36, when Berlin enlarged the boundary of Friedrichstadt, one of the five separate units of which the city was made up, it put up a new wall pierced by monumental gates. One of these, the Brandenburg Gate, was both a customs station and a grand entry into the city.

We might recall here two other 18th-century customs barriers. One is that of Moscow, called the Kamer-Kollegia Wall, established just before mid-century. The other is that of Paris, famous for its toll gates or *barrières* by Claude Nicolas Ledoux.

The last city walls of Paris had long proved an inadequate barrier. Until 1780 smuggling into the outer districts was restricted only by temporary barriers across all roads and streets that crossed the customs boundary, including a great ironwork grill across the Champs-Elysées known as the Grille de Chaillot. That year the tax farmers, the group of financiers which leased from the king the profitable collecting of taxes and fees on state monopolies, determined to extend the customs boundary, build a proper wall, and punctuate it with manned stations. Ledoux received the commission for these stations, and he designed over fifty massive, fortress-like pavilions of which six survive today. They were instantly unpopular, and were furiously attacked during the Revolution. In the 1860s they were permanently abandoned by the State. Ledoux also proposed inns in connection with the *barrières*, where those who arrived late, after the gates were closed, could spend the night.[3]

Customs barriers remained in place even after the obsolescence of city walls in modern times. At Brussels, for example, the *fosse de l'octroi* remained as a barrier after the town walls themselves were torn down on the order of Napoleon I and converted to tree-lined boulevards by 1840. The customs barrier's ditch was filled up and its wooden palisade demolished only in the 1850s and 1860s.[4]

The customs house was an important architectural element of the city edge, especially in cities built along rivers or on the sea where it gained prominence as a skyline feature. Venice's Dogana da Mare (customs house for goods arriving by sea) stands at the tip where the Grand Canal meets the Giudecca Canal; the complex included ranks of warehouses. Rome revamped its Porto di Ripetta, the northern of two customs stations on the Tiber, in the early 18th century. The Ripetta was a rutted unstable bank near the Aurelian Walls where cargo boats drifting down with the current from Tuscany and Umbria had landed since antiquity. Pope Clement XI (1700–1721) had it embanked and terraced by means of ramps and a flowing set of stairs, designed by Alessandro Specchi. Wren designed an impressive customs house for London in 1671 (it burnt down in 1718), and Dublin's domed customs house on the banks of the Liffey, of 1781–91, designed by James Gandon, has itself a Wrenlike grandeur.

5 *Barrière du Trône, Paris, by Ledoux, 1784–87; engraving by Mercier after Courvoisier. The columns and the double pavilions (characteristic of entrances on main roads, here to the northeast) survive today.*

6 *The citadel and town of Aleppo (Syria), as illustrated by Alexander Drummond in the mid-18th century.*

THE MULTIPLE EDGE

The shift of the city edge is not always a simple matter of peripheral growth or shrinkage. Equally pervasive is the multiple city edge, that is, those cases where the city comes to be composed of two or more independently outlined units in close proximity.

The citadel and the walled suburb are common enough in every culture to need 57 little comment. The citadel is obviously poised for defense; it occupies high ground when it can, and overlooks the town proper. This arrangement holds in the Middle East from the earliest phases of settlement history down through the Islamic period. Hittite Hattusas (Bogazköy) and medieval Aleppo are versions of this millennial model. So is the acropolis/outer town arrangement of Mycenaean and early Greek cities.

The relation of the citadel to its town will depend to a large extent on the topography, as well as the political and military situation. It might be helpful to identify two phases in this Middle-Eastern model—without necessarily implying an evolutionary pattern. In the first phase, the citadel *is* the town. There is only one circuit of defense. To the degree that this citadel-town attracts people to itself, there will develop a settlement on the adjacent sloping site, which in time will have to be contained within its own ring of walls. This is the second phase. The lower town will now become the main residential core, and the citadel will be restricted to the role of an administrative center—or, in the case of the Greek *polis*, a religious center— exclusively. It will now be a tight, well-defined unit at the edge of a sprawling urban form, the main portion of which is the low-lying residential and commercial quarter. Eventually, as in Hittite Carchemish, an outer town may develop as a third walled unit.

Concentrating on ancient Anatolia for the moment, we encounter perhaps as many instances where the citadel is an edge unit of a larger urban fabric as we do of the citadel as a fortified unit in the center of town. I would be tempted to explain this latter type as a third phase of development, wherein suburban activity manages to engulf the citadel on all sides. The process is in fact demonstrable in sites of long continuous occupation like Aleppo. The stark contrast of the fortified natural 6 outcrop and the settlement on the flatland between this rocky mound and the small river Kuwayk, a contrast evident at least since the Hellenistic town of Beroia occupied the site, had become muted by the 16th century when Ottoman Aleppo had managed to engulf the citadel mound.

It is, however, also possible for the citadel to be imbedded in the urban fabric from the start, as a matter of policy. A number of Urartian and Neo-Hittite towns in Anatolia, e.g., Zincirli (Sam'al), show this arrangement. The two types—the citadel at the city edge and within the fabric—are encountered again in the West during the Middle Ages. The lord's castle at the edge of town can be either incorporated in the perimeter of the city wall or altogether separate from the city, as were Anglo-Saxon *burhs* providing protection to unfortified towns like Hamwich. When the fortress is on an eminence in the center of town, it may signal an original accommodation or a later development whose motivation is not always straightforward (see "Urban Divisions," below, pp. 76–77).

The other variant to these dualisms of town and citadel/fort has to do with cases where the two entities are less distinct, more parallel. At Beycesultan in Asia Minor, close to the source of the Meander, the Bronze Age settlement consisted of two citadels on parallel mounds on either side of a main road.

The incidence of twin *cities* is more widespread than one might suppose. The pairing of a city and its port becomes relevant to this discussion when the two are intentionally conjoined, as were Athens and the port of Piraeus in the 5th century B C by means of the famous Long Walls. Other pairings are more conceptual than physical. The association of a civil with a religious city can be instanced by Hattusas/Arinna. In the proximity of Antioch and Apamea we have the interdependence of a civil capital and a military base. Another instance of this arrangement is the relation of Roman legionary camps and adjacent civil towns, as in Mainz (where the two overlap), York (where the two are on either side of the river), and Bonn (where they are separate but on the same side of the river). The connection is sometimes achieved by having one of the two main streets of the camp continue into the civil town.

Medieval Europe supplies a number of instances of cities made up of two or more independent towns. One of them may have developed out of the original castle enclave, but more properly they would be adjacent administrative units, sometimes having different ethnic origins. Examples are Gdańsk, which until the mid-15th century consisted of Altstadt and the gridded Rechtstadt; and Berlin, where the oldest settlement, going back to 1237, comprised Coelln (later Insel) on the Spree island and Berlin proper to the north of the island.

THE CITY EDGE

The enduring contrast of town and countryside was sustained through much of history by a fortified wall. Representing an enormous financial burden for its builders, emphatic bounding was undertaken only when vital for military and economic protection. Access to town and market was controlled at the city gate: a memorable threshold for travelers, and the basic instrument of customs collection. Where the walled frame opened to embrace a working harbor, quays and protruding docks feathered the margin where town and water meet. The industrial era proved to be the unmaking of insular city form. Circuits of defense and customs assessment pushed out to distant national frontiers. Factories and suburbs leapt the constricting bounds, bringing down city ramparts and with them the fundamental notions of urbanity these had contained.

Pl. 1 The wall of Siena divides the well-governed city from its countryside. Ambrogio Lorenzetti's fresco in the Palazzo Pubblico, painted c. 1340, shows tightly packed houses and shops (three cloth workers are busy on the left), which had already crept up to the wall by 1262. The gate bears the city's emblem, the wolf with Romulus and Remus, borrowed by the Sienese from Rome. Outside, as the banner proclaims, people work the fields and travel in safety; note the paved high road and the fortified villa-farm on the hill.

Pl. 2 *Turin (Italy) from the northeast,*
c. 1750. The city rises above a broad band
of bastioned walls, moat and earthworks.
In Bellotto's view we see two of the
arrowhead bastions and the stretch of wall
between them, by the Royal Palace, which
had been built in 1646–58 by Amedeo di
Castellamonte as part of the 17th-century
town extension beyond the area of the
ancient Roman city. Repairs are under
way on the Bastion Verde; the extramural
wasteland serves for the workmen, as well
as for laundresses and idlers.

Inside the walls, on the left is the palace
with its garden and a corner belvedere.

Beyond are Guarini's fantastical dome over the Chapel of the Holy Shroud and the cathedral campanile. Further away, near the second bastion, two crenellated turrets stand out: this is the Porta Palatina, *one of the Roman city gates, later incorporated in the medieval fortifications. It and the stretch of wall here, now part of the royal gardens, survived Napoleon's order to raze Turin's defenses.*

Meeting the water

Pl. 3 opposite, above *Seville in the 17th century controlled all Spanish trade with the New World, but its port was informal. Ships simply moored beside the broad banks of the Guadalquivir, edged raggedly by houses. Far right is a gate in an altered stretch of wall; in the distance, the towers of the Alcázar. The city is dominated by its cathedral belltower, originally the minaret of the Great Mosque.*

Pl. 4 opposite *Bordeaux was similarly the premier colonial port of France. Its waterfront was transformed, shortly before Vernet painted it in 1759, with a view to grandeur rather than efficiency. The Garonne was lined with houses and public buildings, most notably in the Place Royale (de la Bourse), center, marked by an equestrian statue of Louis XV and an iron grill to the fenced-in quay.*

Pl. 5 above *At Boston (Massachusetts), Atlantic Avenue marks the original shoreline. An early waterside scheme was Alexander Parris's Quincy Market of 1825 (right center, just above this caption). After almost two centuries of growth and decay, SOM's Rowes Wharf (lower left) is restoring grandeur to the harbor.*

UNDERGROUND

THE SOONEST REACHED AT ANY TIME

GOLDERS GREEN
(HENDON AND FINCHLEY)
A PLACE OF DELIGHTFUL PROSPECTS

Pl. 6 left Cologne in 1886, six years after Joseph Stübben started planning the Ringstrasse with its majestic boulevards, "a chain of festive rooms," encircling the dense old city. In this bird's-eye view from the southwest traces of the 12th- and early 19th-century fortifications can still be seen. The main roads have been laid out—the trident intersections mark the sites of gates—and the space is beginning to be filled in by parks, railroads, factories, and other institutional buildings. Within a decade the "Neustadt" would be almost complete. (Watercolor by Jakob Scheiner)

Pl. 7 above London's Golders Green offered an idyll of country living farther afield, made possible—and encouraged— by the Metropolitan Railway, whose station opened in 1907.

Pl. 8 Highrise slabs and farm fields are primary elements of the suburban landscape north of Frankfurt-am-Main (Germany). Here, as elsewhere in Western Europe, the exorbitant cost of inner-city land and the expansive scale of public-sector housing schemes have pushed these projects to greenfield sites at the city edge.

Pl. 9 The opposite extreme—a patchwork of detached houses—is the common pattern for suburbs in the United States, here exemplified by balloon-frame housing tracts in San Fernando (California), 1986. The development of cheap nails and pre-cut "two-by-four" studs in the early 19th century made the light, efficient, mass-producible balloon frame possible; that, and the encouragement of the Federal Housing Administration in the 1930s, led to the situation where some two-thirds of American families now live in their own houses.

In China the administrative headquarters of different bureaucracies, in those cases where the capital of a prefecture doubled as a provincial capital or a county seat, were sometimes housed in completely separate, adjacent cities. This is the case with the twin cities of Fengyang in Anhui Province. The twin city was also one of several models for the Chinese imperial capital. The model appears in the later first millennium B C in towns like Xindian (Shanxi province), Handan (Hebei province), and the Yan capital Xiadu (also Hebei). These have a face or a corner shared by the two enclosures. The twin type, when used by non-Chinese dynasties like Liao and Jin, serves for population control—Chinese citizens in one, the natives of the ruling dynasty in the other.[5]

The line between a "multiple city" and a city with one or more walled suburbs is of course a fine one. In Chinese cities, many of which had a square or rectangular shape, the four cardinal gates that pierced the town wall spawned four unequal suburbs with their own defenses. Since the suburb, here as everywhere else in the world, usually starts as a linear development outside the city gate, a long narrow strip was a recurrent shape for these Chinese satellite settlements.

One of the most telling cultural chapters on the subject of the multiple city is Islam. Throughout its history, the Islamic city has given proof that it was conceived not so much as a tidy walled package contrasting with the open countryside, but as a composite of walled units. Twin cities, initially separated by open space, were not uncommon. Isfahan in Iran and Raqqa in Syria are two such cases where the twin settlements slowly came together across the intervening space. At other times, the twin cities would be separated by a canal or a river, as was the situation for Adana and Gurgan in Iran. Ports in Syria were composed of two separate entities: the town proper and the fortified anchorage and landing facilities.

With Baghdad and Cairo, the configuration has a different rationale. Here it is a matter of the development over time of a succession of palace centers and military encampments, each growing into a town and adjusting its relationship to the others. The cellular growth had dynastic motivation, commonly buttressed by sectarian or ethnic distinctions.

Cairo began with the military camp of Fustat planted by the invading Muslim armies in 641 outside the small Byzantine town of Babylon on the east bank of the Nile, opposite and to the north of the ancient capital of Memphis. This camp transformed itself in a decade or two into the capital of the province of Egypt and the seat of the Umayyad governor. The Abbasids forced out this first major dynasty of Islam, took Egypt in 748, and set their own encampment, El Askar, northeast of Fustat; thereby, they repeated the pattern, begun by Fustat, of juxtaposing an administrative center to a prior town. When in the next century a rebellious governor of Egypt, Ahmed ibn Tulun, broke with the Abbasid caliph in Baghdad, he built his very own princely settlement, al-Qata, north of El Askar. And when adherents of a radical Muslim sect, the Shiite dynasty of the Fatimids, marched on the city in 967 from their headquarters in Mahdiya, Tunisia, they built yet another walled enclosure further north—al-Qahira, "the Victorious," whence we derive the name Cairo—while the earlier settlements merged into the "old town." Finally, an orthodox savior from Syria terminated Fatimid rule in 1169, and built a formidable citadel east of this long string of towns, against the rocky spur of Muqattam, as al-Qahira itself fell back with the older core.

There are Western parallels of this serial layout, Cracow for example. The city rebelled against royal authority in the early 14th century, and in the decades that followed, as deliberate punishment for this defiance, the kings proceeded with the creation of a series of cities between Cracow and the river which were intended to weaken it. Of these—New Cracow, Kleparz, Stradom, and an independent settlement for Jews called Casimir—only the last was walled. The sequence was completed when the Austrians laid out, on "their" side of the river, the new community of Josephstadt (Podgorze in Polish) late in the 18th century.

THE WALLED EDGE

To look in any detail at defensive walls as an urban edge would entail a brief world history of military architecture. For my purposes, it will be sufficient to consider the nature of the walled edge as this is defined by the protective curtain itself, and by the land uses immediately within and without.

ALTERNATIVE BOUNDARIES

Many cities made do without walls. Sometimes this was because the natural site was defense enough, as in the case of Akhenaten's Amarna on the east bank of the Nile, where the cliffs pull back to form a huge half-circle some 6 miles (10 km.) long; or Nabatean Petra, which lodged in a crater. Or else the larger frame of nature or of the State made defense unnecessary. Minoan Crete relied on its navy to keep itself free from invasion, as did Venice. Japan also trusted the sea to protect its cities, which as a rule were unfortified. In the history of the United States, only eleven cities were ever fortified for a short period of their early existence—and that flimsily.

During the Middle Ages, the great bulk of towns in England accepted the fact that, as the Venetian visitor Girolamo Lando was to put it appreciatively in the 17th century, the country had "the sea as its wall and moat."[6] Towns with defensive circuits in the manner of Europe were rare. Most were on the medieval English "frontiers": Dunbar on the Scottish border, with its curtain wall and incomplete Elizabethan bastioned circuit; and Conwy and Caernarvon, fortified against the Welsh. Otherwise walls were not a matter of defense, but of allegiance: thus, privileged royal boroughs were defended, while seigneurial boroughs were often
73, unwalled.[7] The old city walls of London, dating back to Roman times, had only an
164, administrative function by the Middle Ages. In the Netherlands, by contrast,
246 defense was so very essential that without a wall a city could rarely qualify for a charter.

Beyond the presence of natural defenses, cities dispensed with walls when they felt confident that the political system they were a part of was too strong to fear attacks. The Ottoman Empire, confident of its military power, fortified cities only on threatened frontiers, through Hungary and along Armenia. Its great predecessor, the Roman Empire, was unassailable enough in the first and second centuries A D to allow the old cities within its boundaries to neglect their defenses, including its own Servian Walls, and the newly founded cities to have an open periphery. But beginning in the 3rd century, provincial cities, unable to rely on the central protection of Rome, threw up new defenses, usually around a small part of the
4 sprawling fabric. Rome itself hastily built the great circuit of the Aurelian Walls in the 270s taking in as much of its vast metropolitan fabric as possible.

Sometimes conquerors would insist on defenseless cities, in order to display their own control over the conquered territory. Napoleon I forced some European cities he took, like Turin, Frankfurt and Brussels, to pull down their defenses. The Mongols, similarly, forbade the building of city walls throughout China in the

7 Ruins of Aztec, near Chaco Canyon (New Mexico). Built in the 11th century by the Anasazi, this is one of several "great houses" where kivas (circular rooms for social or religious purposes), dwellings, and plazas were contained within a single outer wall. In each settlement the Great Kiva (up to 63 feet/19 m. in diameter) served for communial meetings.

1280s, and ordered the leveling of many extant walls (e.g., those of Suzhou) to prevent their cities from serving as bastions of Chinese resistance. With the weakening of Mongol power in the 1350s, the cities were ordered to rebuild their dismantled walls in order to protect the Mongols from Chinese rebels.

In the absence of their own defenses, settlements sometimes had to depend on a central fortified space to withdraw their population in time of danger. This is the role of the *Fluchtburgen* or *Volksburgen* in the Germanic area of medieval Europe—great round enclosures, not regularly inhabited, surrounded by earthworks and a palisade. In other instances, as with Anglo-Saxon England and the Inca in the New World, unwalled cities sometimes had a fortress nearby to ensure their defense.

Without a pronounced physical barrier of any sort, the city ends with its last straggling buildings, and the fields begin. A simple way to get some protection for the city without the major investment of resources which a defensive circuit calls upon is to build the outermost houses in a tight ring with contiguous walls, as a 8 windowless periphery. The practice is widespread. It is shared, for instance, by the Neolithic settlement of Çatal Hüyük in central Turkey, by Avola in Sicily as rebuilt after the earthquake of 1693, and by the "great houses" of the Chaco culture in New 7 Mexico. In antiquity, the period of the 11th–10th centuries B C in Syria/Palestine and Anatolia knows the systematic application of this kind of defense, e.g., Bethshemesh and Debir in south Palestine.[8] At times the houses are built directly against a thin, continuous wall, as happens in the mid-2nd millennium B C at Malthi, in southwest Greece, which began as an unfortified settlement.

With a definite physical barrier of any kind, from the simplest to the most elaborate, the settlement is locked in place. Expansion is possible only through the construction of ever larger concentric circuits; otherwise growth is forced to remain internal. Contact with the world outside is focused at the access points of these defenses. This hard edge must be effective both in siege warfare and in protecting a city's market privileges.

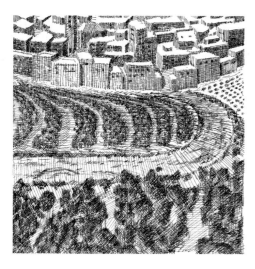

THE NATURE OF CITY WALLS

Pl.2 Walls need room. They may appear as a thin single line on a city plan, but in reality they occupy enough space to be represented instead as a wide band. In the technically least sophisticated barrier, the ditch and bank with or without a palisade, this band may be 30 feet (9 m.) across—or more. The addition of water turns the ditch into a moat, and increases its effectiveness. Since the earth excavated in making the moat goes to build up the rampart, the proportions of the two are closely related.

9 To save labor, and to take advantage of the defensive possibilities of the site, the walls often trace land contours, incorporating natural features into their design. Indeed, the presence of such features affects the initial choice of the site. Topography, then, is a major determinant of the shape of the city edge. The reason we have so many roughly circular cities is that hilltops were a favorite location for settlements worried about their defenses; such sites also afforded a stretch of negotiable slope for expansion when the need arose. At the same time the circular or semicircular circuit, in the centuries before artillery and other far-reaching firearms, was the most efficient in terms of manpower: it was the shortest defense line around a maximum area, and so required fewer defenders than right-angle or broken outlines.

13 Early wall systems in rugged terrain, throughout the Mycenaean and Hittite empires for example, used local boulders in a thickset construction of cyclopean masonry. Wooden walls also represent an extensive primitive tradition. The *ostrogi* of Siberia were towns protected by one or two lines of stockade—large pointed stocks, usually oak, with intermittent embrasures; the later circuits were provided with towers for cannon at the corners and at the gates. The stockade of 17th-century Tobolsk was initially a dense row of fir trees which grew close together like palisades.[9]

Masonry walls are often a later consolidation of earth ramparts. This is the case in China, where early walls of pounded earth were later faced with bricks, ceramic blocks and ashlar. Surviving brick and stone walls do not predate the late 14th century. The circuit is most commonly rectangular here, and only on rare occasions circular. There are a few exceptional cases where the outline of the walls represented "certain auspicious creatures in a geomantic effort to secure prosperity and good

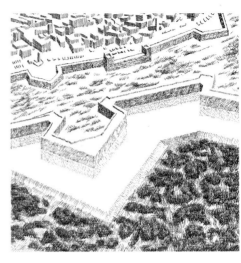

fortune for the city." An example is Ch'uan-chou-fu in Fukien province, where the walls resembled a leaping carp.[10] This sort of wall symbolism is not unknown in the West: the 16th-century fortress town of Willemstad, for example, had seven bastions intended to represent the seven united provinces of the Netherlands.[11]

Masonry walls may consist of a single or a double curtain, of varying thickness *10, 11* and design. Median cities like Ecbatana, Herodotus tells us, had as many as seven concentric rings, each out-topping the other. An Assyrian relief of the 8th century B C depicting the Median city of Kishesim conforms to this description.

In medieval Europe the idea of the double curtain becomes current in the 14th *14* century. The addition of a second wall created a sheltered belt which could be used by the besieged to gather and stage unexpected sorties.[12] The moat would still be part of the arrangement in the system of masonry walls, but it is now commonly accompanied by the glacis, sometimes referred to as the "killing ground"—an inward-sloping artificial bank that would improve the defender's vision, expose the enemy to fusillades, and impede the movement of heavy siege machinery.

13 below Novgorod (Russia), ca. 1635; from Adam Olearius, Beschreibung der Muscovitischen und Persianischen Reise *(1656). On this side of the Volkhov River is the brick-walled kremlin, a fortress containing the cathedral and administrative headquarters. Opposite lies the wooden-walled "Market Side," crammed with merchants' homes, warehouses, and churches founded by individuals or local communities. An extramural monastery is also protected by log walls.*

26, The land walls of Constantinople, built under Theodosius II in the 5th century,
114 doubled the defensive circuit for added security. Invaders traveling overland would
have first to traverse a wide moat, faced with stone and subdivided by right-angle
spurs. A terrace some 50 feet (15 m.) in width separated the moat from a low outer
wall. Beyond that lay a similar terrace, called the *peribolos*, and then the high inner
circuit of walls.

The point about defensive curtains, whether of masonry or not, was, in fact, that
they be free-standing, so that they would have on either side of them room for
maneuver. In China, for example, wide ramps from within gave access to soldiers
and horsemen, so that they could get up easily to the top of the ramparts. The
"pomerial" street of Roman cities, whatever its ritual associations, served
essentially the same function of facilitating troop movement. In Classical antiquity
this feature seems to have been an exclusively Western, Italian element; it is not
found in Greek cities. But then the very loose fit of the defensive curtain in ancient
Greek urbanism, with ample unbuilt space between the walls and the inhabited area,
made this official rampart road unnecessary.

One of the earliest and sternest provisions of urban law had to do with
maintaining an intramural zone free of building. Since property values decreased in
walled towns as one moved away from the center, the immediate intramural area,
being farthest from the center, was the least desirable—and so it was customarily
underbuilt. At the same time, this was an ideal area for squatters who could prop
makeshift shanties against the wall. In China, the poor not only built dwellings up
against the wall but scooped out caves within it to use for shelter, at Chengtu for
example. We must remember here that the early earth ramparts of Chinese cities
15 were massive affairs. At Han Chang'an, the 40-foot (12 m.) high circuit of rammed
yellow earth was 40–50 feet (12–16 m.) wide at the base.

14 *The sheltered zone within the double
walls of Carcassonne (France). The inner
wall (right) was originally built in the
5th/6th century. In two 13th-century
campaigns it was first modernized and
enlarged and then given a protective outer
wall. (To create level ground between the
two, soil was cut away, leaving the early
foundations exposed.)*

Compromises between the military necessity to keep the defensive zone wide and clear and the temptation to use it for makeshift shelter were common. The statutes of 1262 in Siena seem resigned to usurpation, and insist only that houses along the city wall be fitted with merlons. In the 14th century the city taxed abutting houses, and legislated where windows could be opened in order to assure the wall's integrity. *Pl.1*

Others drawn to the walled city edge were the powerful and the rich. Here they could stake out pleasure gardens in the ample open spaces of the fortifications. This *Pl.2* as especially so when, with the advent of the cannon-ball at the end of the 15th *62* century, the curtain wall with its high towers and machicolated galleries became obsolete. Once before, in the Hellenistic period, the development of the catapult principle had occasioned the far-spreading carapaces of moats and outworks that we see installed in the ruins of the castle of Euryalos in Syracuse, Sicily. But the bastioned wall of the Renaissance altered the nature of the city edge in unparalleled *16,* ways. *17*

To minimize the impact of artillery on the stone curtain, the walls were now lowered, and the towers brought down to a corresponding height. Some of this wall mass was further reduced by being concealed in the broad ditches that were meant to keep cannon at a distance, and so dull their aim. In order to use the same weapon effectively against the attacker, spacious artillery platforms had to be created at the top of these stubby towers, and earth ramps had to be provided within the walls for easy access to the platforms. All this vastly expanded the size of the unbuilt area between the outer limits of the residential fabric and the wall proper. The space *36,* given over to the wall system now commonly exceeded the area of the town fabric. *Pl.6* To make room, suburbs or rural settlements were razed, as in the case of Turin's suburbs and extramural monasteries in the 1530s.

Not everyone was in favor of this modern system of defense. The citizens of Bologna, for example, refused to update their simple 13th/14th-century curtain (what John Evelyn called "a trifling Wall") despite pressure from their papal over-

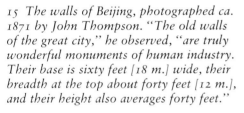

15 The walls of Beijing, photographed ca. 1871 by John Thompson. "The old walls of the great city," he observed, "are truly wonderful monuments of human industry. Their base is sixty feet [18 m.] wide, their breadth at the top about forty feet [12 m.], and their height also averages forty feet."

lords to do so. They objected to the enormous expense of constructing a bastioned wall, and the even larger open-ended burden of maintaining it in good shape and investing in military hardware and personnel. They reminded the papal administration of the destruction of private property that would be entailed. They pointed to the merits of an open city which would allow the formation of an army in the field.

But the core issue was political. The fiercely independent subject municipality resisted being encircled because to allow this physical circumscription was to make public their acceptance of papal rule. Their ambassadors in Rome argued diplomatically in 1561 that "This city should have no need of fortification in that the citizens, the people and all of the magistrates are so devoted, faithful and obedient to His Holiness and to the Holy See, that in every eventuality they are enough to defend and preserve this state, as they have done on many occasions in the past."[13] The argument was not original with the Bolognese. The doctrine of the open city, the notion that the strength inherent in true political unity makes walls unnecessary, had been put forth by Machiavelli earlier in the century.

At any rate, this republican sentiment did not carry the day. The bastioned wall became universal military dogma. By the end of the 17th century there spread, beyond this line of primary defense, a panoply of outworks—semi-independent units like pincers, lunettes, and ravelins—and the fortified counterscarp. The city, from one point of view, was never more decisively cut off from its countryside. Viewed another way, however, the city edge swelled into an enormous area of open space that lay idle for long stretches of time between hostilities.

Already at the end of the 16th century, in cities like Antwerp and Lucca, the idea took hold of landscaping this open space for pleasure. The most adroit modification

17,
19

Pl.2
Pl.16

16, 17 *below Dunkirk (France) in 1650 and 1701. These two views graphically display the difference in structure and in spatial demands between a medieval single-curtain wall and the most sophisticated form of Baroque bastioned fortifications, vastly extending the city for purely military purposes.*

18 *opposite Mural traces and boulevards in Paris, from Turgot's plan of 1739. The parallel straight streets mark the site of the 14th-century city wall (the inner one on the rampart and ditch, the outer one on the counterscarp). Running diagonally across at the left (north), and planted with trees, is the line of the 1640s wall, taking in a larger area. It is punctuated by the ornamental Porte St.-Martin and Porte St.-Denis, both of the 1670s. Outside the latter is the beginning of a linear suburb, the Faubourg St.-Denis. At the far right is the circular Place des Victoires, begun in the 1680s.*

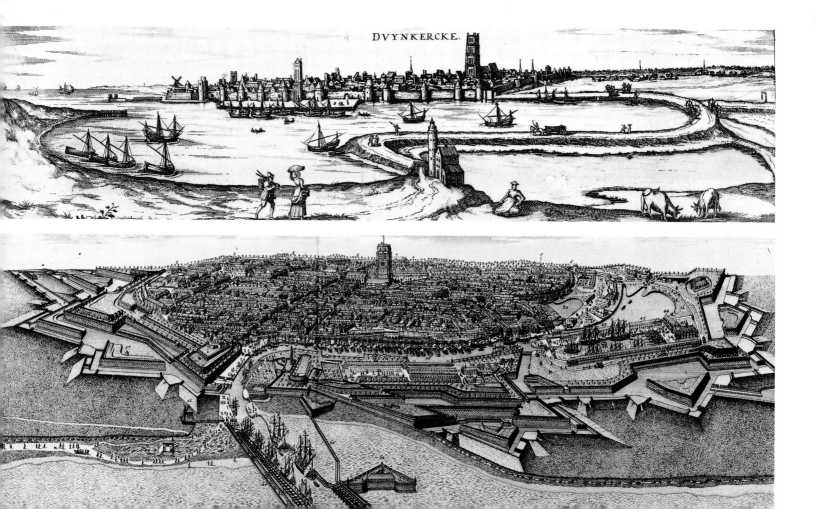

DVYNKERCKE.

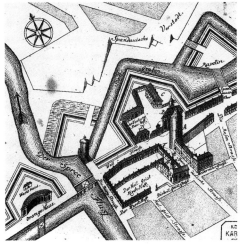

19 Berlin, Heilig-Geist Viertel (Quarter of the Holy Ghost), 1720. Inside the wall east of the river are the church and hospital of the Holy Ghost, and a garrison area, including a school, church, and powder tower. The Spandau suburb lies outside to the north (cp. Ill. 36). Note the ravelins—semi-independent arrowhead fortifications—to left and right.

came in Paris following the authorization by Louis XIV in 1646 to abandon the city's new but obsolete defensive walls and to transform them into tree-lined promenades. Along the ramparts on the northeast side of the city, pleasure parkways called "boulevards" were fashioned, and two triumphal arches—the Porte St.-Denis of 1672–73, and the Porte St.-Martin of 1674–75—replaced the old town gates. Commercial traffic was banned from these parkways, which received a broad raised drive for carriages—the cours—flanked by shaded sidewalks. Indeed, the word "boulevard" has a military derivation: the French word boulevart, meaning a large bastion, is a corruption of bulvirke, a Nordic word for palisade or bulwark. When in the 18th century Paris outgrew this ring of rehabilitated walls, the parkways were lined with cafés and other places of amusement.[14]

Other French cities followed suit. Bordeaux filled up its ramparts and built cours over them in the 1740s and '50s under the Intendant of the province, Aubert de Tourny. Berlin civilized its walls in 1734, Hanover in 1763, Graz in 1784. Brussels got its peripheral boulevards—a circuit of 5 miles (8 km.)—courtesy of Napoleon, who had decreed the destruction of its walls in 1810. The work was finished in 1840, but "the salubrity of the boulevards as promenades was vitiated by the foul water of the Senne and by the appalling tenements alongside it."[15]

Long before then, a whole range of uses had been found for the bastioned defense zone, some of them military and some recreational. A bastion in Berlin's obsolete circuit of defenses was put to good use for the local garrison in the Quarter of the Holy Ghost. In Dresden, the Zwinger palace was built on one of the city's bastions. So at Würzburg the Residenz and its gardens were fitted into the eastern range of the city walls, under the general direction of Balthasar Neumann.

A late example of this playful conversion of the defensive belt is Copenhagen's Tivoli gardens. The city walls were maintained there as a functioning circuit until the 1840s at the service of one of the last absolute monarchies in Europe. When George Carstensen, soldier, author and bon vivant, proposed to transform a bit of the glacis into a pleasure ground, Christian VIII overruled his army officers and signed the lease in 1843. The area was a 15-acre (6 ha.) spot outside the city's west gate, and included three points of the star-shaped fortifications.[16]

THE FRINGE BELT

17 The girdling of the city form with the sort of formidable anti-artillery defensive system that gave the names of Vauban and of lesser figures like Menno van Coehoorn their luster in the later 17th century made expansion beyond it difficult.

16, In cities with the old-fashioned curtain walls, the edge was usually limited enough
Pl.1 to be considered traversable. The extramural zone attracted, first of all, urban uses requiring plenty of cheap space, e.g., horse and cattle markets, and water reservoirs; and also noxious manufacturing processes like tanning, recalled to this day in street names like Skinners Lane at Caernarvon, or Tanners (*Garbarska*) Street in Cracow. Potters, fullers, blacksmiths also plied their business out here. In one of the oldest Chinese cities, Shang (or Yin), there are remains of artisans' workshops outside the earth walls. This component is also there in later cities, when strong guilds kept certain artisan elements from establishing themselves in the city proper.

Secondly, institutions deemed a health hazard found acceptance in this no-man's-land. Leper houses were a common fixture of the suburban periphery of London, Leicester and Stamford.

Finally, there were religious houses that arrived on the scene too late to be lodged in the old walled core. In the 13th century, with the rise of the Mendicant Orders, it is common to find the Franciscans establish themselves on one side of a city just
20 beyond the walls, the Dominicans on the other side, and the lesser orders like the Servites and Augustinians in the intervening spaces of the periphery (see also p. 129). Medieval Florence shows the classic distribution of these friaries. In England the Blackfriars (Dominicans) and the Greyfriars (Franciscans) are often on the same side of the city's edge, in the direction of growth. A Scottish example is St. Andrews in the mid-15th century.

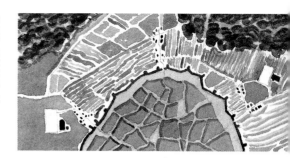

20, 21 *Two Mendicant Orders establish their churches and preaching grounds outside the walled city. The area is gradually built up and the churches enlarged, leaving the preaching grounds as public spaces in the urban fabric.*

22 *The process of leapfrogging, as the built-up area expands, leaving gaps and zones of varied use that are modified in subsequent phases.*

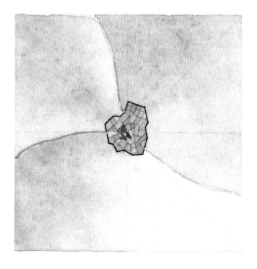

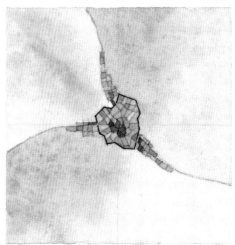

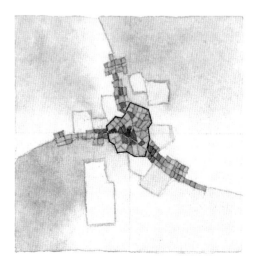

23 *The edge of Essen, the great steel town in the Ruhr Valley (Germany), 1910. Just to the right of center, a half-timbered farmhouse can be seen, stranded as a vestige of the area's rural past.*

Geographers call this extramural zone the "urban fringe belt." It contains a heterogeneous collection of land uses, and shows a large-scale, low-density building pattern that contrasts with the thickly woven fabric of the core. In time the city may 2, incorporate and leapfrog over its first fringe belt, alter some of its character with an 22 overlay of residential development, and give rise to a new fringe belt further out. Alternating irregular rings of fringe belts and residential districts can be detected on the plans of many European cities.

Each successive fringe belt embodies some distinct land uses consonant with the period in which it was formed. Parks do not pre-date the Baroque centuries. The tradition of locating colleges at the edge of town is at least as old as Abelard's university on the Left Bank of Paris, unless one chooses to go back to Plato's Academy on the outskirts of Athens. Planned cemeteries are likely to signify a late phase of the pre-industrial era, say the 18th century, when church graveyards were becoming obsolete, and Enlightenment thinking insisted on the more decorous and sanitary disposition of the dead in the open margins of the city-form. In more recent times, the fringe belt would accommodate heavy industry and working-class 23 housing, sports grounds, and in the outermost rural-urban fringe, slaughter-houses, junkyards, sewage plants and oil refineries. In the United States, the most notable planned units of the latest urban fringe are industrial parks, shopping centers, corporate campuses, and of course the ubiquitous tracts of suburban homes discussed later in this chapter.

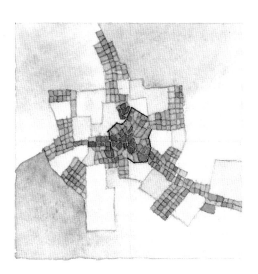

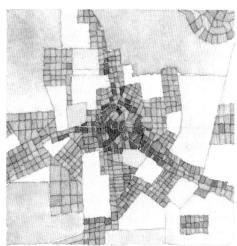

24 *Porta S. Giovanni, Rome, through which travelers from the south entered the city at the Lateran. The gate was built in 1574; this photograph of the 1860s records a customs booth just inside it on the left.*

CITY GATES

As long as the wall remained a valid boundary for the city, the building of much of the fringe belt was concentrated outside the gates, leaving the in-between land to agriculture. The gates were of critical importance in a walled city. They funneled highway traffic into the city, and were often named after major centers that lay at the other end of the highway. In the ancient Middle East, gateways were used as the meeting places for the governing and judicial authorities, and markets were often located near them. Names might also refer to extramural cult centers (for instance the great pilgrimage basilicas of Christian saints outside the gates in Rome), or they might be honorific (as in the case of Rome's Porta Appia, named after its builder, the censor Appius Claudius). There were also names that were simply descriptive, like North Gate and New Gate, or lofty ones like Cairo's Bab an-Nasr (the Gate of Succour).

During the Middle Ages in Europe, guilds were commonly associated with city gates and towers. There were also looser neighborhood associations that derived their identity from adjacency to a city gate, whose defense depended upon them. These Societies of the Gates are well attested to in 13th/14th-century Italy, where they were organized into militias of foot soldiers, the *fanti portes*.

The other medieval affiliation was that of noble families. Those among them who owned fiefs and lands on both sides of the city wall would build fortified residences in an adjacent tower or gate, which was an effective way to exert power by controlling the urban approaches. In Bordeaux the *ostaus* or noble houses stood next to the ramparts, and the families appropriated the closest towers. This was a challenge to one of the most coveted privileges of a city charter, the building and maintaining of defensive walls, which traditionally was everywhere a princely prerogative; and the seizure of the gates occurred precisely where city authorities were weak and unable to shake the yoke of landed gentry.

In the case of cities of Roman origin, it is possible that this usurpation may have been linked to the Roman imperial tradition. We know, for example, that in Constantinople throughout the Middle Ages the ninety-six towers of the Theodosian Walls were entrusted to the powerful owners of adjacent land.[17] But by the 15th century, in cities like Bristol, occupancy of rampart towers had even devolved upon the merchant class.

It is probably with this long tradition of popular and noble abuse of the pomerial margin in mind that Alberti demands "a very handsome open space both within and without the walls, and dedicated to the public liberty; which should not be cumbered up by any person whatsoever . . . under very great penalties."[18]

As official entrances of the city, the gates received architectural care. They were often monumental, with spacious passages at ground level and rooms above. From the 17th century onward the triumphal arch as city gate suited the formality of the *18* Grand Manner. Colbert's plan for Paris showed grand approach avenues ending in triumphal arches. Even without any other defenses, free-standing gates might be set up to play their assigned role in urban life; this was the case at places in Britain like Glasgow, New Aberdeen and Tewkesbury. When walls were superseded by a newer set, the old gates were often retained as monuments within an extended town. There are examples at Amersfoort in the Netherlands, Rothenburg in Germany, and *2,* Auxerre in France. *27*

Ceremonies at city gates, especially for arriving princes or other important visitors, have a long history in more than one cultural sphere. Memories of these arrival rituals still survive. When the king or queen of England comes to the City of London on an official function, the Lord Mayor stands on the spot where the appropriate city gate used to be, and hands the sovereign the key to this non-existent gate.

In the design of gates, this welcoming function was frequently in conflict with the needs of defense. The medieval gateway was flanked by strong towers and protected by mechanisms like the portcullis and the barbican. A popular convention in antiquity which survived into the Middle Ages was the so-called bent entrance, or bent approach. Two gates were arranged off-axis behind one another, so that it was *25* necessary to make a sharp turn to pass through the second. An L-shaped passage within the main mass of the gateway, or else an L-shaped approach into the gate from the outside, exposed the invading enemy to the fire of the defenders.

The conflict between access and obstruction also shows up in the relation of city gates to the internal network of streets. Where defense is a primary concern, gates at opposite ends of the city might not be directly connected with through-streets. In some historic cities of China, two of the four gates of a normal gridded plan—and sometimes all four of them—are arranged on a bent axis, so that the connecting streets will form "T" intersections (e.g., the towns of Shanhsien and Ninyang in Shantung province). This design also conformed to the ancient Chinese belief that ghosts and other evil spirits (*kuei*) always traveled in straight lines and were unable to turn corners.

MURAL TRACES

How do walls disappear, and what takes their place? The answer is partly contained in how they are built. Ditches or moats with wooden palisades, or other systems of impermanent materials, are the most vulnerable. The citizens themselves were a main threat to the wooden picket walls of American cities like New York, Albany and New Orleans. Even before the boards rotted away, which came within four or

25 Detail of the walls of Beijing in the early 18th century, showing the bent entrance system. The outer gate leads into a courtyard; from there, a second gate at right angles leads through the inner wall.

26 In Istanbul, market gardens occupy the moat of the double walls built in the 5th century to defend Constantinople (see p. 30 and Ill. 114).

five years, they would be cut up by miscreants for firewood. A report of 1654 reveals that certain Dutch burghers of New York were required to cut and haul one hundred palisades as replacement of those they burned.

18   The memory of these defenses is often preserved, in name or shape, even when they have long vanished. Many cities have their Wall Street or Linienstrasse. New Orleans has Rampart Street, which is in the tradition of the Parisian boulevard. Diagonal streets at the edges of an all-pervading grid sometimes attest to a replaced fragment of a city wall. The general outline and change of level of old bastions may still be evident in the urban fabric. An example is Vienna's Mölkerbastei, with the Albertina at the top.

Clues to vanished systems of fortification are ring lanes which tended to develop on either side of the wall course, and cul-de-sacs which may signify original streets that ended at the wall. Moats were commonly filled in and turned into a thoroughfare. The line of town ditches may sometimes be traced "by strips of open ground which were shunned by later builders or by lines of buildings with subsidence cracks."[19] In Amsterdam, where the early fortifications were ditches without walls, the ditches were converted to urban waterways. In Bruges too, when the then extant wall was brought down in 1297, the moat was not filled in, but became part of the city's extensive system of waterways.

Pl.6   In cities where growth has been aggressive, the bastioned curtain ends up as a
39,   ring-street or a system of boulevards, as we saw, which becomes the locus of offices
51   and other commercial functions around the inner city, or is left open for recreation. Where towns were too small or insignificant to have much demand for building land, the fortifications were re-used for agriculture. The practice here is to have the wall pulled down, fill the ditch, and then reparcel the land so created. Bourtange in the Netherlands is a good example.

Otherwise the land is leased or sold for construction. In Siena, the so-called *carbonaie*, huge trenches beyond the walls in which wood fires would be set in order to prevent besiegers from attaining and scaling the ramparts, were rented out to individuals when later walls enclosed the suburban fringe, and became the cores of new neighborhoods. This is probably what explains some of the straight streets at the edges of the built-up areas in an otherwise "organic" city form. During the 15th century in the Dutch town of Amersfoort, the city council divided into lots and sold the land of the demolished inner wall. The resultant *muurhuizen* (wall-houses) can
2   still be seen lining a gently curving street in the center of the modern town.[20]

27 The Tour de l'Horloge at Auxerre (France) is a surviving gate from an earlier wall, left standing when the city expanded. It was built in the 15th century, with a belfry and clock symbolizing civic liberties granted to the community by its lord, the Duke of Burgundy. (The spire was rebuilt after a fire in 1891.)

When the walls are simply abandoned, they become host to a number of mixed uses. In Istanbul, the Ottomans allowed the old ditch to be filled in and turned into 26 fertile market garden plots, conveniently located for the demands of the inner city. The space between the double walls has been used sporadically for squatter housing, including gypsy encampments, and for the city's most important uncontrolled market, at Topkapi gate.[21]

Retained walls have two modern functions. They can serve to regulate traffic, as they do in Rome, where the gates funnel incoming vehicles, or Siena, where they 24 define what has recently become a car-free inner core. Or else the walls themselves can serve as pedestrian routes, as at York and Canterbury. To the extent that they are well-preserved and interesting, walls can also turn into "heritage," that is, a monument catering to tourism. Often the wall defines a protected conservation zone which it separates from the new town.

In cities with "organic" plans, gates are frequently the converging point of several interior streets. The point might be met on the other side of the walls by two or more country roads. Such irregular constellations on modern maps might well reveal the site of an old city gate, long after the disappearance of the defensive circuit.

MEETING THE WATER

A great many towns are built on water—along rivers or on their delta, or at the meeting of two or more rivers, or on the edge of lakes and seas.

One characteristic of waterfront cities, as Braunfels has pointed out, is that when we arrive by boat, we enter them "not on their periphery but in their center."[22] In some, we would land right in front of residential buildings intermixed with business structures and warehouses. Amsterdam and Lübeck, Hamburg and Dubrovnik are examples. In others—Naples, Marseilles, Genoa—port life is distinct from the well-to-do residential districts further up.

RIVER TOWNS

In China, a river bank was the most favored place for a town. The word *p'u* which means "the bank or reach of a river" is often found appended to town names, as in Chang-p'u (Fukien province), "on the bank of the Chang River." Again, the name might refer to the specific location of the city in relation to a river, as in Fen-hsi (Shansi province), "west of the Fen River." Or else there are generic names like "river city" (Chiang-ch'eng, Yunan province), and "the mouth of the river" (Chiang-k'ou, Kweichow province).[23] In Europe, river names are commonly attached to city names—La Charité-sur-Loire, Alfeld-an-der-Leine, Bradford-on-Avon.

The particularity of the site, and the way the settlement meets the water, give character to the city form. Aligning growth with the river is a common response. In central Sweden, for example, the original settlements stretched long the water—a street parallel to the stream, and narrow passageways leading down to it. Frequently the town was sited where a raised ridge was cut by a stream, as with Enköping.[24]

The wedge between two rivers was chosen by cities as diverse as Basel, whose medieval nucleus was the long narrow hill where the little river Birsig meets the Rhine; and Moscow, with the Kremlin at the confluence of the Moscow and Neglinnaia Rivers. Berne is on a ridge of hills surrounded on three sides by the Aare, and there are other medieval towns that lodge in the horseshoe bend of a river. Strasbourg had its beginnings on the many islands formed by the tributaries of the Ill and the Rhine. New Orleans developed between a lake (Pontchartrain) and a river (the Mississippi), having started out on a restricted strip of natural levee at the mouth of the river. Contrary to the very common situation of cities at the mouths of embayed rivers (London, Hamburg, Old Quebec), here there is no embayment at all, the Mississippi being uniformly wide for hundreds of miles upstream.[25]

Many river towns stayed put on one bank. In some cases—Cologne is a familiar instance—this was because the river was too wide to bridge until modern times. The choice of bank was conditioned by a number of practical factors. The direction from which local products enter the river traffic, the patterns of water flow, the relative productivity of the basin land, considerations of defense—these are all commonsensical issues to take into account. But there were also ritual considerations. In ancient Egypt the preference for the east bank of the Nile had a religious dimension; and facing south was important in Chinese cosmology.

The incidence of cities growing on both sides of a river is limited, and usually
57 requires special pleading. In cases like Prague on the Vltava, the narrow east-west ridge on the left bank made sense as the location for the fortress of the Hradčany; the medieval burgher town spread out on the flat land of the right bank. Buda and Pest were really separate towns, incorporated into a single municipality only in 1872.

River towns often took advantage of the presence of a small island to get across, for one of the characteristic impulses of river towns is to span the water before them and make contact with the land routes on the other side.

4 Rome and Paris are famous cases of the island crossing. The Tiber Island comes at a point where the river constricts and the rough, sharp banks slope down without leaving too much flat area for alluvial deposits; and since further inland the river becomes broad and shallow and harder to cope with, sea traffic stopped at this island crossing.

226 In Paris, the original Gallic inhabitants had occupied the Ile de la Cité, one of two strategic islands on the site. The Romans, when they came to found Lutetia, preferred the higher ground on the left bank, just south of the island. After the collapse of Roman dominion, the town withdrew to the island once again and walled itself there. Its subsequent history would be a progressive spilling out of this insular boundary to both south and north. The other island, the Ile St.-Louis, was not developed until the 17th century.

During the Middle Ages, one of the commonest city-forms all over Europe was precisely the *ville-pont* or bridge-city: the main settlement built on a river bank, with one or more bridges crossing to a district, itself walled, but smaller and of less consequence. This almost always originated as a populist suburb across from a main city gate. Its subservient standing is implied in names like Oltrarno or Trastevere, signifying "the other side of the Arno" or "across the Tiber." The bridge between
225 the two settlements was critical; it was sometimes fortified, or at least given a tower, lined with houses and shops, and was continued at either end with main streets.

Now the river was a convenience—principal highway, source of drinking water, and power for industry (e.g., to operate grain or timber mills): it was not exploited as something pretty to look at and enjoy esthetically. There were some exceptions. Islam, always enamored of water, made playful incidents of crossings. And in Europe, Florence started exploiting the picturesque aspects of the Arno as early as
224 the 14th century, when the middle of the Ponte Vecchio was left open to the view. In the 1560s Vasari's Uffizi was endowed with a colonnade and upper-floor belvedere from which to enjoy the river.

28 *The river front of Vasilievsky Ostrov in St. Petersburg, opposite the Admiralty. Veldten's granite quays controlled the river, resisting its floods, its winter ice, and the spring onslaught (seen here) when Lake Ladoga upstream releases its floes. The low buildings far left predate the embankment, as does Mattarnovi's Kunstkamera of 1718–34 on the right. Quarenghi's Neoclassical Academy of Sciences (1783–89) was purpose-built for its enhanced site.*

In Paris in the next century, thanks to the presence of the royal palace of the Louvre along its edge, the Seine on both sides began to be regularized. The Grande Galerie of the Louvre (1603–6) extended 500 yards (450 m.) along a riverside quay, and in 1662 the Collège des Quatre Nations became the first monumental building in Europe designed to face on to a river. The Invalides met the river with a broad garden, and in the 18th century the Ecole Militaire reprised this arrangement.

St. Petersburg followed suit. The quays of the Neva were faced with granite in the 1760s and 1770s, and on them rose the monumental buildings of the central district. The monumentality of the new stone quays also affected civil architecture. Building height was raised to an obligatory 70 feet (21 m.) or so, and architectural details like cornice lines were carefully controlled. Florence and Rome did not get their embankments until the later 19th century, even though both suffered terribly from floods.[26]

PORTS AND RESORTS

The issue of monumentalizing the water's edge is complicated by functional arguments. To the extent that a river is a working watercourse with a port, there is a definite conflict between those who make use of it for trade-related activities and those who would turn it into a work of art. As Joseph Konvitz puts it, "those who operate the maritime world and those who grant cultural significance to its artifacts . . . belong to two separate cultures . . . which have little to say to one another."[27]

This is especially true for port facilities linked to a busy pattern of long-distance trade—which often means sea ports. With rivers we would be dealing by and large with barges and small vessels that are able to go under bridges and dock in shallow water. With maritime ports, the entire waterfront is armed with docks, berths, warehouses, shipyards and all their coincident clutter. To civilize Ostia in the second century, Amsterdam in the 17th, or Liverpool in the 18th was not only a formidable task, it was also seen by most as counterproductive.

Esthetically unified designs for sea ports clearly ran foul of the myriad activities that were dependent on access or proximity to water. At best, one could dramatize or accent with architectural effects certain features of the waterfront, or else create landmarks on the skyline immediately behind the edge of the water to impress incoming vessels with an initial, striking picture. Temples on high ground, church towers and high domes did well for the distant view, discounting such exotic devices as the Colossus of Rhodes, one of the Seven Wonders of the ancient world, standing astride the harbor and scaled to the vastness of the sea. Within the actual working repertoire of the waterfront, some building types lent themselves to a measure of monumentality, without sacrificing their functional adequacy. Lighthouses, for example: the Pharos of Alexandria was celebrated in antiquity.

29 Artificial harbors under the Roman Empire could be treated as architectural programs cut of whole cloth. Ostia could boast the harbor of Claudius and the hexagonal harbor of Trajan lined with uniform porticoes. In other Roman cases along the Mediterranean, moles and jetties were given colonnades or arcades, and sometimes triumphal arches. Warehouses were often made externally fancy, or could command attention because of their requisite solidity and their serial massing.

To study the port facilities of Leptis Magna in North Africa, or Caesarea, the seaport of ancient Judaea, is to appreciate the scale and splendor of the planned Roman waterfront. Caesarea's, undertaken by Herod the Great, was the first major harbor to be built in the open sea, without benefit of a protective bay or peninsula. Sheltered by huge breakwaters of concrete, the inner mooring, overlooked by a temple dedicated to Roma and Augustus, was kept free of silting by means of sluices. There was room for a hundred ships at a time. Also of concrete were the lighthouse and the foundations for the monumental statues that flanked the harbor entrance.[28]

The likes of this self-conscious monumentality we will not witness again until the 18th century. Certainly not in the Middle Ages. Not in the Renaissance either, despite ideal port town schemes concocted by people like Francesco di Giorgio and Pietro Cataneo, with the harbor laid out as a watery plaza, or the designed urban rivers of Francesco de Marchi. In fact, the actual apparatus along the waterside remained simple, even provisional, until modern times. (The first commercial dock was built at Liverpool in 1710-15, open to the town. It would be another century or more before the enclosed systems of basins and warehouses were developed in London and Hull, secure behind strong walls.) In the 17th century, which witnessed the first universal spread of Baroque design, calls for its application to the waterfront had no takers. John Evelyn's 1666 plan for London envisaged among other things the redoing of the main stretch of the Thames in grand style, ridding it of landing stages and yards, putting warehouses beneath beautiful palaces on the embankment, or better still, banishing them altogether to the south side of the river, so that the north embankment could be given entirely to decorous buildings, triumphal arches and the like. This in effect would have meant the suppression of the vitality of London as a production center—a center for the manufacture and movement of goods.

Far from heeding such wholesale beautification of the waterfront, the 17th century marked the emergence of rational port-city planning in Western Europe—in France, Sweden and the Netherlands. This is the time of permanent commercial and naval fleets, a consequence of the establishment of farflung colonial empires that stretched the boundaries of Europe to Southeast Asia and the Americas. The aim of this planning was to produce an urban framework suitable for the exploitation of the sea. The four new port cities founded under Louis XIV to serve the overseas interests of France—Brest, Lorient, Rochefort on the Charente River, and Sète— were centers where the royal fleet could be built, and land bases provided for overseas trade companies. The waterfront had to be planned around arsenals and armories and warehouses and housing for the workforce, not representational public buildings.

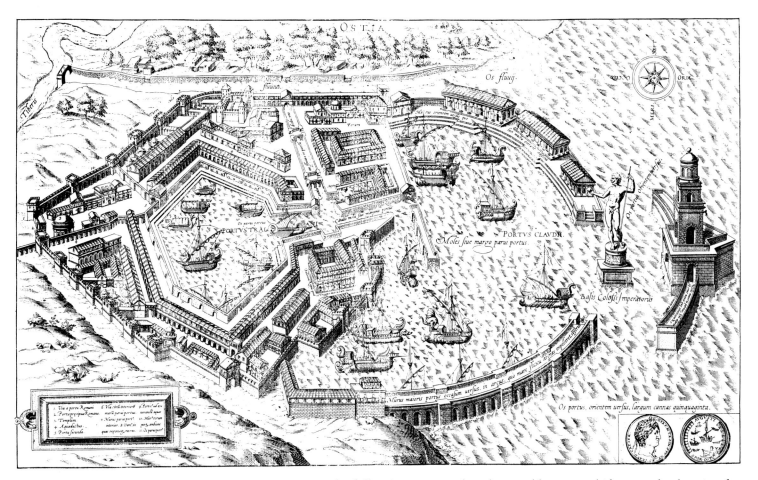

OSTIA

29 *The walled port of Ostia, as somewhat fancifully reconstructed in Braun and Hogenberg's* Civitates Orbis Terrarum. *The harbor of Trajan is on the left, that of Claudius on the right, with a lighthouse and monumental statue. The porticoed buildings served as storehouses and as accommodation for the navy. The town of Ostia lay to the left.*

It was in the following century that the trend began to shift towards planning for its architectural value alone—towards monumental and, from the viewpoint of port activity, impractical, solutions. Bordeaux, on the Garonne River, is famous for having realized the most ambitious of these proposals. A center for trade in wine, *Pl. 4* manufactured goods, sugar and slaves, it was a significant and busy port all through the later Middle Ages and the Renaissance. Now a splendid series of formal squares took over the waterfront, combining housing and public buildings like the *127b* Bourse, the hall for tax authorities, etc. The leading designer was Jacques Gabriel, Louis XV's Chief Architect. All this did very little for shipping.

London also saw one grand scheme after another, proposed by the architects of the later 18th century like the Adam brothers and George Dance. One of these was executed—the Adams' Adelphi Terrace, between the river and the Strand. Taking its cue from Evelyn, the scheme combined unified blocks of four-story houses over two basement stories of warehouses opening out to docks. The warehouses turned out to be subject to flooding and were consequently rejected by the authorities. The houses, on the other hand, were very successful.

In some ways, this brilliant double-decker invention is the first shot in a succession of sweeping waterfront designs that will culminate in Le Corbusier's unexecuted Algiers project—the "viaduct city" following the beautiful coastline or corniche, with six floors beneath the motorway and twelve above. They all tried, in one way or another, to encase the needs of a working harbor in a magnificently orchestrated ensemble where city and water met.

30　None did so more triumphantly than French Algiers itself—in the 1860s. There, the steep drop from the level of the old city to new port facilities at sea level was negotiated by a double set of ramps, and an avenue above running parallel to the ridge that formed the city edge. Into this avenue, the Boulevard de l'Impératrice, the ascending ramps of the port opened. The ramps and boulevard were supported on vast arcades, arranged in terraces and sheltering storage vaults and other port amenities. What had been the walled edge of a city-fortress under the Turks was thus composed into an open urban elevation through the most accomplished conventions of the Grand Manner.

In America too, this trend toward the monumentalizing of the waterfront began to be felt at the very end of the 18th century. The locus was Boston; the guiding vision, that of the architect Charles Bulfinch and his merchant clients. At his time the harbor had a ragged look—with wharves built into it on the east side of the Shawmut peninsula, and the waterfront fringed with warehouses, ropewalks and shipyards. In 1710 King Street had been extended into the water for half a mile (800 m.) by the Long Wharf, a broad causeway lined with rows of shops and warehouses providing the first deepwater anchorage in Boston.

Bulfinch started regularizing the waterfront to the north and south of the Long Wharf with continuous blocks of uniform design, changing the nature of the soft and squishy marshes to hard, flat working surfaces. His India Wharf, with a long tier of five-story warehouses upon it, civilized a clutter of docks and rundown buildings. When the domed and temple-fronted market by Alexander Parris was put up in 1825, Boston seemed poised to project the dignity of a Roman imperial harbor.

There were no followers. American river towns continued in that lively improvised chaos described so well by Mark Twain, and illustrated in those bird's-eye city views popular in the second half of the 19th century. And by then it was mostly too late. New transportation technologies had ensured the decline of ports. The railroad brutally severed cities from their waterfront, and ended that informal, easy access of the city dweller to this improvised theater of coming and going. In Boston the railroad path (now Atlantic Avenue) connecting North and South Stations sliced a number of warehouse buildings down the middle. The tracks and

30 *Algiers, seen from the jetty at the turn of the century. The redesigning of the waterfront was achieved in 1860–74 by the civil engineer Raffeneau de L'Isle: the Boulevard de l'Impératrice was terraced out over the decayed Turkish fortifications, and a double ramp led down from there to the port (out of the picture to the right).*

31 *Boston (Massachusetts), Quincy Market, by Alexander Parris, 1825. The land in front was later reclaimed, and the buildings now lie inland (see Pl. 5).*

massive staging yards mechanized the waterscape. At its technological best, there was a precise interlocking of the tracks with buildings and piers. But in the 1950s, after the demise of the trains brought on by long-distance trucking, even this coordinated system lost its urgency. The dismantled tracks offered a readymade path for the later motor corridors, which confirmed in concrete the gash between the *Pl. 5* city center and the waterfront.

In the 1960s, Americans had some second thoughts about these waterside wastelands. Since it was not realistic to revive the old rituals of sea trade, the only option was to find some new purpose for the waterfront. There was one early, and extraordinary, try: the gigantic stainless steel arch of the Jefferson National Expansion Memorial in St. Louis, commemorating the city's role as the gateway to 32 the western frontier. To make room for the new park at the river's edge, forty city blocks of the original waterfront were cleared of their derelict warehouses, many pioneering cast-iron structures from the mid-19th century.

Nearby, past the Eads Bridge, at Laclede's Landing, we have the evidence of the most recent phase of thinking about the landscape of the old riverfronts—adaptive re-use. There is now hardly any American city on the water that does not have its converted warehouse district with cute eateries and clever things to buy, and a kind of dogged amusement park mood that brings in tourists and creates an illusion of

32 St Louis (Missouri), looking from Laclede's Landing toward the Gateway Arch of 1962–65. A historic warehouse district is being converted to provide office and commercial accommodation.

urban vitality. Isolated luxury-housing projects put up by developers tend to emphasize the alienation of the common citizenry from its own waterfront.

These townscapes of leisure emulate an urban prototype far removed from that of the working waterfront. I am thinking of the seaside resort, which gained acceptance beginning in the late 18th century. The idea here was to unwind and take the sea air, so the designing of the shoreline with impressive promenades was perfectly
33 consonant with the main purpose of such places. Brighton was first. That is where Londoners started going, in the words of Marc Girouard, "to knock back glasses of disgusting sea water and be dipped into salt baths by formidable bathing-women." In the 1790s the Marine Promenade was laid out as the first attempt at grand design. It was a smashing success. Fifty years later the pedestrian and carriage promenade swept past miles of terraced summer residences, some arrayed in sinuous crescents
146 framing private seaside parks.

Tourists brought the resort townscape to the Riviera as well. The Promenade des Anglais in Nice was built in 1822–24 by the community of English visitors as a route for seaside strolls and to provide employment for the locals. It was soon shaded by palms and bordered by villas and palatial hotels.

A new vocabulary of building types specific to seaside towns emerged in the course of the century. The most startling was the pier, its spidery iron legs supporting a pedestrian boardwalk and entertainment pavilions above the waves. Again, the prototype was English. Brighton had three piers of which two still stand: the West Pier of 1863–66 and the Palace Pier of 1898. At Nice the Jetée-Promenade of 1890 replaced an earlier structure destroyed by fire. The luxurious casino, another seaside phenomenon, was a French specialty. Monte Carlo's extravagant example was created by Charles Garnier in the 1880s.

Beaux-Arts formulas for the design of an elegant recreational waterfront came to America with the "White City" of the World's Columbian Exhibition, held in Chicago in 1893. Daniel Burnham, the Fair's chief designer, incorporated these principles in his 1909 Plan of Chicago. It was America's first modern exemplar of what it would be like to design a city from the shoreline inland. He proposed opening the entire lakefront to recreational use, scenic promenades, and parks. A measure of this was in fact realized—which is more than can be said of dozens of other projects during the height of the City Beautiful movement for riverfront improvements, like Edward Bennett's for Minneapolis and Elgin, Illinois, or Charles Mulford Robinson's for Cedar Rapids, Iowa.

Today we are getting a fresh glimpse of the rediscovery of the waterfront—an effort to bring city and harbor together in a more intimate relationship reminiscent of these older ways. Pleasantly designed esplanades for bicyclists and strollers, like those planned for London's Docklands redevelopment, encourage the townfolk to explore their urban shoreline. The dismantling of expressways along the water's edge is now no longer rejected out of hand. Portland, Oregon, and San Francisco, California, did it not long ago, and Boston is proposing to put its elevated highway underground.

There in Boston, plans are also afoot to regenerate stretches of Boston Harbor with development that mixes commercial, residential, and maritime functions.
Pl.5 Rowes Wharf, named after a dilapidated 18th-century pier, centers on a vast 80-foot (25 m.) high coffered arch capped by a circular public observatory. With its sheaths of traditional masonry and its Classical evocations of form, the project, and others of the same breadth that are likely to follow, may yet give us a modern taste of the great waterfront scenes at Leptis and Caesarea.

33 Brighton (England), Marine Promenade and Chain Pier, 1832. The publisher of this print, J. Bruce, hailed the pier as a "brilliant piece of modern architecture."

ON THE PERIPHERY

The phenomenon of suburbs is almost as old as cities. Where there is tight circumscription, there will be spill. Where people live in close quarters, they will be tempted to rid themselves of noxious but necessary activities and some forms of low life, or else move away from them. To the degree that a city is prosperous and resourceful, it will attract to its periphery outsiders who wish to share its advantages.

EARLY SUBURBS

It is not now possible, and perhaps not very important, to know if the history of suburbs started as an extrusive process from within, or as deliberate accretion. In the ancient Middle East, towns as far back as the 3rd millennium B C had, outside their walls, a suburban area combining clusters of houses, farms, and cattle stalls surrounded by fields and gardens. In Mesopotamia this suburban belt contained a commercial center—a harbor settlement on a river or a canal—and a secondary temple, sometimes linked to the city proper by an elaborate processional way.[29]

One of the earliest cases of an external group attaching itself to the body of an old city is the institution of the *karum*—a colony of Assyrian merchants who would settle just outside an already flourishing town in a neighboring state like those of Anatolia, and entrap the town in a network of long-distance trade. The site of Kanesh (Kültepe), near Kayseri, has yielded the remains of the most important *karum* in this chain of Assyrian trading posts; but the excavations have also revealed that the walled town had a suburb of its own making even before the advent of the Assyrian merchants, and that it was this suburb which the colonizers occupied and replanned.

This was in the Bronze Age, about two thousand years before Christ. But the example of Kanesh would prove commonplace throughout antiquity and the Middle Ages, indeed even beyond (see below, pp. 93–94). The most intensely researched chapter in the history of these extramural trading colonies has concerned the growth patterns of the medieval city in Europe. We have long been familiar with the concept of the *faubourg*, a French word derived from *forisburgus* or "outside of town." Passing tradesmen, the theory goes, attracted to a stable settlement with buying power, in time would plant themselves permanently astride the highway, in the shadow of the city gate, and develop their own organization, their own life. Artisans prevented by guild restrictions from living in the city, and others like innkeepers and horsetraders anxious to serve this prosperous extramural community, would join in. When it became counterproductive for the city to continue to exclude this suburb administratively, it would be embraced and incorporated, even if that entailed the major expense of enlarging the city defenses to include the suburb within their circuit.

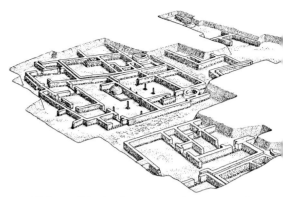

34 *Kültepe (Turkey), excavated remains of the Assyrian* karum *or trading colony on the edge of the ancient town of Kanesh. Low courtyard houses were divided into various quarters by squares and streets. The early suburb and the* karum *proper were occupied only from ca. 1950 to ca. 1750 BC.*

As Henri Pirenne first gave it its classic formulation in 1922, this dualistic genesis of medieval cities assumes that the older fortified nucleus was either an episcopal city or a lord's *castrum*. The new commercial settlement, called *forisburgus*, *novus burgus*, and more tellingly *portus*, had a market; this was usually an elongated space amounting to nothing more elaborate than a widening of the main road that ran through the nucleus. On this public space rose the church, the *ecclesia mercatorum*. The earliest trace of the *portus*, it would now appear, is in the Carolingian period. From the 10th century onward the *portus* begins to sport its own defenses. When the fusion occurs with the older urban core, the common term for *portus* residents, *burgenses*, begins to be applied to the residents of the old core as well, who had previously been known as *cives*, *castellani*, or *castrenses*. That is the root of our own modern terms *bourgeois*, *Burger*, "burgage," etc.

At the same time, there were a great number of settlements founded in Germany by kings or lords in the period from Charlemagne to Otto I—towns like Bremen, Hamburg, Verden, Paderborn, and Magdeburg—for which the *portus* was initially a separate settlement, across the river or down below in the valley, economically independent, and oriented instead principally toward the trade of the highway.

In the towns of Old Russia, the relation of town (*gorod*) and suburb (*posad*) does not parallel the European models. The suburb was not an association of free traders and craftsmen, but an extraurban unit that served exclusively the needs of the leading classes of the *gorod*—the princes, boyars, and their courts. Movement in and out of this unit was strictly controlled by the city authorities. Only much later did a third outer zone of "free districts" (*slobody*) develop beyond the restricted suburb, where traders and craftsmen settled in response to princely promises of non-interference and a degree of self-government.

It is now clear that a number of medieval cities grew out of several distinct elements, each with a different origin and history, and that the Pirenne thesis of the merger of a defensive nucleus and a suburb of merchants is only one limited explanation of urban process in the Middle Ages. Ghent, for example, was born out of *two* independent *portus*, related respectively to a count's castle enclave and to the old Roman fortress transformed into an abbey.

The processes at work in the evolution of medieval city-form have much wider validity. The ribbon development outside the city gates finds ample demonstration in Chinese cities, and so do satellite communities. Attenuated roadside suburbs beyond the walls affected Roman imperial cities as widely spaced as Timgad in Algeria and London. The fringe belt in their case included army barracks, large

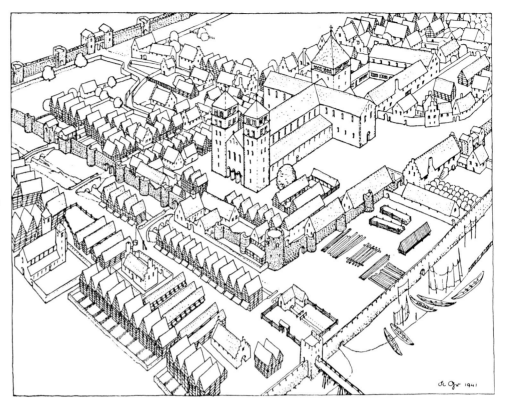

35 *An episcopal city and its* faubourg: *a reconstruction of Strasbourg ca. 1100. The core is the rectangular, walled Gallo-Roman city, which lay on two major trade routes at an important river crossing. Here the cathedral was established. Gradually a trading suburb grew up outside the walls to the southwest (bottom left), centered on a major market-street. This* faubourg *was annexed by the bishop and enclosed ca. 1000 by a wall (bottom right). In 1262 the citizens of Strasbourg shook off episcopal rule, and erected their new town hall in this former suburb, facing the main gate of the inner city. (From Gruber)*

establishments of leisure like baths, amphitheaters and circuses, burial monuments, and the suburban villas of the rich.

At the very least we have to distinguish, then, between suburban extensions that never lose direct contact with a prior city—typically attenuated settlements starting at the gate and lining the road that leads away from it—and others that in effect start as new centers without being physically contingent upon the city, and behave rather as satellites around it. We have also to distinguish between spontaneous extensions of the city form like the ribbon development on main roads, and intentional, planned additions. 164

PLANNED EXTENSIONS

The incidence of planned units, well known in the West since the Renaissance, is much commoner in earlier centuries than may appear. Medieval towns of an "organic" plan which seem cohesive and of a piece can often be shown to have grown in planned increments. A method has in fact been advanced by geographers like M. R. G. Conzen to identify successive planted units on the basis of the direction of the plots and the level of the streets, and documentary evidence can then be used, where it exists, to date some of these phases. The method has been fruitfully applied to medieval towns in Britain, including Eynsham in Oxfordshire, Ludlow, Pembroke, and Conwy. Earlier still, Roman Pompeii is as susceptible to an urban geographer's dissection as is Ludlow. Later, in the much cited instance of Turin we can enumerate several enlargements to the original Roman colony, especially between the 16th and 18th centuries.[30]

Until then, there was relatively slow urban growth in Europe: towns of the 12th century were not too different in the 16th. Where self-assured cities advisedly overreached the bounds of the built-up area when enlarging their enceinte—providing for future growth while enclosing arable land used in the meantime to secure their food supply in time of war—they would need a long time to fill this expansive girth. Both Florence and Siena, in the confident mood of the 13th century and on the basis of past increases in their urban population, built ambitious rings of new walls around 1300. But the next century, the century of the Black Death, of famines and internecine warfare, was disastrous for European cities. Florence would not fill its walls until the second half of the 19th century, when, for a brief spell, it served as the capital of the new Kingdom of Italy. Siena never managed to go the limit. In other cities the built edge crept outward at a snail's pace. Barcelona took two centuries to reach the ramparts of 1359. Prague, Delft, Toulouse and Milan had similar experiences.

Beginning in the 17th century came large leaps in area and scale. This was the time when municipal independence, in decline since the 14th century, had reached its nadir. The towns of Europe were firmly under the thumb of the State. Commentaries on statecraft like those of Giovanni Botero now stressed the strategic and symbolic importance of size. New princely quarters began to be added to old cities, quarters often large enough to overwhelm the historic core. These methodical extensions, employing broad avenues, impressive squares, parks, and appropriate monumental buildings, were often intended to drown out municipal government and transform the old cities into princely capitals.

German cities are most conspicuous in this regard. We can list Kassel, Karlsruhe, 36 Mannheim, among many others. In Berlin, the first westward extension came in 1674; that was the small grid of Dorotheenstadt, laid out by the Electors of Brandenburg next to the old medieval town. Fifteen years later came the carefully planned suburban grid of Friedrichstadt, further extended in 1721.[31]

The State-sponsored planned extensions for the ruling classes, motivated by iconographic programs rather than any practical urgency, contrasted with the unsanctioned, spontaneous, tawdry development beyond the walls for which there was no official tolerance. In Paris, the Crown forcefully discouraged suburban spread. A law of 1548, renewed in 1644, forbade new construction in the extant 18 *faubourgs*, and also emigration beyond the line of the new boulevards. In London, large outlying estates belonging to prominent noble families or to corporations were being platted as independent residential quarters for a genteel clientele, even while royal edicts repeated warnings against suburban construction. In fact, neither the draconian proclamation of Elizabeth I in 1580 that prohibited the construction of any houses within an area 3 miles (5 km.) wide around London except where there had been a building within living memory, nor the later attempt of the Commonwealth Parliament in 1657 to contain the City, proved effective.[32]

Where the privileged sort refused to be lured away from the historic center, which was the case in much of Continental Europe, the urban periphery beyond the broad 39 insulating belt of the city walls turned into a zone of exile for the working classes and the industries that employed them. The threat of such an encircling mass to the center itself was not lost on the members of the French court. A few months before the Revolution of 1830, the King was warned in plain terms: "Your prefects of the police are allowing the capital to be blockaded by a girdle of factories. Sire, that will be the cord that will strangle you some day."[33]

36 *Berlin in 1723. The medieval town is confined within a bastioned wall. Among the suburbs developing around it, the princely creations of Dorotheenstadt (northwest) and Friedrichstadt (southwest) stand out with their orderly grids. They are separated by Unter den Linden (marked by two heavy black lines).*

INDUSTRIAL EXTREMITIES

It was at the zenith of the absolutist epoch, in the light of State-organized standing armies and navies and the decline of siege warfare, that the walled edge had first come to seem militarily anachronistic. And it was during the Enlightenment in the second half of the 18th century, when the first strains of a Romantic interpretation of nature were being heard, that the separation of town and country ensured by that bristling regiment of bastions and breastworks, ravelins, forts, half-moons, and *17* pincers, began to be viewed as socially intolerable.

An uncurbed migration toward the big cities made the constraint all the more unnatural. There was dire talk of urban pathology. Jean-Jacques Rousseau wrote that he left Paris in 1756 "never to live in a town again." The proper environment for a natural society, as he saw it, must be Nature itself. Men were "not meant to be crowded together in ant hills, but scattered over the earth to till it."

And there was a political side to the argument. Cities hogged the resources of the country. They kept the peasant down, and deprived him of the fruit of his labor. Again Rousseau:

> People the territory evenly, extend the same right to everyone, carry the same abundance of life into every quarter—it is by these means that the state will become at once the strongest and the best governed that is possible. Remember that the walls of towns are made only from the debris of rural houses.

Communism would later give its own gloss to this indictment: cities behind their walls artificially segregate the urban from the rural proletariat. The fear of a conspiracy to disempower the masses by dividing them is behind Marxist doctrines of disurbanization.

In reformist urban discourse, the ultimate enemy was the developing industrial environment. The rate of congestion was frightening. Manchester, to take one dramatic case, had 12,000 inhabitants in 1760, 400,000 in 1850. While every available hole in the old core was being filled in with makeshift accommodation for the immigrant working class, profit-driven jerry builders put up, as fast as they could, minimal rental housing quarters on the periphery where land was cheapest. The city edge pushed out helter skelter and without any effective public control, either beyond a still extant defensive zone, or in the case of unwalled edges, filling and overreaching the fringe belt of the pre-industrial era. Here is how Friedrich Engels describes this new suburban edge in his book of 1845 entitled *The Condition of the Working Class in England*:

> Single rows of houses or groups of streets stand here and there, like little villages *37* on the naked, not even grass-grown, clay soil . . . the lanes are neither paved nor supplied with sewers but harbour numerous colonies of swine penned in small sties or wandering unrestrained through the neighborhood.

Squatter settlements were a common edge fixture of newly-industrialized suburban landscapes. For rural newcomers, the self-built shanty was often the housing of last resort. The blossoming of capitalism under Japan's Meiji government at the turn of the century brought with it a proliferation of shanties that suddenly appeared on suburban marshlands and river shores and in the vicinity of Tokyo's cemeteries and isolation wards: in other words, on the least desirable unbuilt sites. The simple wooden structures disappeared just as quickly, their inhabitants displaced by fires, or when changes in neighboring land uses made demolition and redevelopment profitable.[34] The shanty-towns that sprang up

37 *A group of cottages with open cesspit on the outskirts of industrial Preston, from a British Government report of 1844—one year before the publication of Engels's* Condition of the Working Class in England.

around German and Swedish industrial centers during the same period were equally ephemeral, while those of Rome, Barcelona, Madrid, and Lisbon survived into the second half of the 20th century.

38   The shanty-towns of Paris were to a large extent the legacy of demolition and renovation of the city core. Escalating land values and rents prompted by Haussmann's *grands travaux* pushed the homeless to vacant land on the periphery, where a wretched expanse of constructions provided a stark contrast to the studied elegance of central Paris. One of the most enduring encampment sites was the zone *non aedificandi*, where building was supposedly prohibited, that was attached to the obsolete fortifications marking the city limits. Its inhabitants, nicknamed *zoniers*, still numbered more than 40,000 in the mid-1920s.

In part to prevent this low-grade, random sprawl from overwhelming the core, many cities on the Continent held on to their fortifications long after there was any justification for them in the traditional terms of warfare. This was especially so in capital cities where the national government resided. A conservative military, always certain of the inevitability of insurrection, held on to the defensive circuit and its extravagant open land, while city agencies saw this military zone as an invaluable chance for bringing order to the periphery. In the Netherlands, the large commercial cities scored early victories: Haarlem pulled down its walls in 1820, Utrecht in 1824, Amsterdam in 1837. Border towns here and elsewhere in Europe held on to their fortifications until after the war of 1870–71, and in some cases even as late as 1918.[35]

39   In Vienna the medieval walls around the historical city, modernized with bastions, were declared redundant in 1857. Already in 1704 an outer rampart and ditch, the Linienwall, had been installed a good distance away from the fortified nucleus to give some protection to a huge suburban zone much larger than the inner city itself. By the mid-19th century there were more than thirty distinct working-class suburbs between the glacis of the old circuit and the Linienwall. Keeping the imperial court and the upper classes isolated from this volatile social element was considered essential, and the army stubbornly opposed all plans to raze the inner defenses. And when the imperial decree of December 1857 signed by Franz Joseph which ordered "the abolition of the enclosure and fortifications of the inner city,

38 A shanty-town on the eastern edge of Paris, photographed by Charles Marville between 1856 and 1865. The area, near the present Rue Champlain, just outside the Boulevard de Belleville, was beginning to be developed at the time; the squatters would be driven further out.

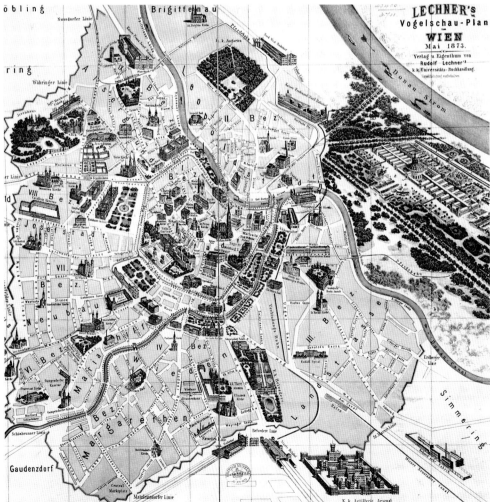

39 Vienna in 1873. The old city, dense with monuments, is in the center. The suburbs, mainly working-class, are confined within the Linienwall of 1704. Between the two areas, the bastioned wall has been replaced by the wide, open-textured Ringstrasse. Here major civic and national administrative buildings (upper left), cultural institutions, and a few elegant residential blocks islanded in space (see Ill. 116), interspersed with public gardens, provided a protective zone between classes.

together with the ditches thereof . . . for the purpose of the suitable connection of the same with the suburbs" made further opposition futile, the army insisted on an enormously wide girdle street so as "to maximize mobility for troups and minimize barricading opportunities for potential rebels." The result was the great *116* Ringstrasse, which for all its urbane civility did not in fact unite the center and the periphery. As Carl Schorske put it, "What had been a military insulation belt became a sociological isolation belt."[36]

THE OPEN CITY

The bursting of the city edge, whether with upper-class enclaves or lower-class improvisations, had one underlying cause—and that was the change, under a system of capitalism that was in full swing by the 17th century, in the concept of land and its disposition. Traditionally, land had always been tied to the specific uses the owner made of it, and the alienation of land was subject to severe restrictions. The new system began to see land as a speculative commodity, and to divide it into abstract units for buying and selling.

The major resistance to this open-market policy came from ancient feudal rights and royal prerogative, and from municipal authority to hold some land in public custody. But sovereigns, always in need of money, were not averse to alienating their patrimony, and cities were equally tempted to translate public lands to revenue. The selling of Paris began in the early 16th century with François I, who parceled royal properties like the Hôtel St.-Pol and distributed them to his favorites. In England, the contemporary dissolution of the monasteries under Henry VIII gave the Crown lavish riches of land and property; within a century most of it was leased or sold to *164* private users, or alienated as reward to court favorites. The Dongan Charter of 1689 gave the city of New York general ownership of all of Manhattan except the little that was then under private ownership; almost immediately the city fathers set about to sell this patrimony, as a painless replenishment of the treasury coffers. With large publicly held sections of edgeland placed in the hands of private interests, the war of containment was lost, and the right of government to control the pace and pattern of growth was seriously compromised.

The object of suburban development was not so much to respond to an actual demand brought on by swelling urban populations as it was to create and encourage this demand. The real object was to make money for developers and the people they employed. John Nash could see this clearly, even as he helped the profiteering along *45* with his development of Regent's Park in north London early in the 19th century:

> The artificial causes of the extension of the town [he wrote] are the speculations of builders encouraged and promoted by merchants dealing in the materials of building, and attorneys with moneyed clients, facilitating and indeed putting into motion, the whole system.[37]

So the new quarters had to be made attractive enough for the better sort to draw them away from the old core. The belief had to be instilled—and sold—that the move to the suburbs represented a search for a better life. At the same time one had to fight official prejudice against growth. As early as the 17th century, in treatises like Nicholas Barbon's anonymously published *An Apology for the Builder*, attempts were made to justify suburban expansion on rational grounds. In John Summerson's words, Barbon set out to show that suburban building, far from being a menace to the public welfare, is a healthy and necessary development, which enhances existing land values near the centre of the town, provides new markets, settles the equilibrium between town and country, and creates revenue and potential cannon-fodder for the Government.[38]

CONTROLS AT THE FRINGE

The public struggle to regulate the impulses that spawned the open city has been spasmodic and often ineffectual. In terms of reasserting a new city edge, the bravest initiatives included the concept of the greenbelt and the legal instrument of the regulating plan. The annexation of surrounding communities extends such controls to the far reaches of the urban fringe.

Greenbelts and allotment gardens

The greenbelt was a means to arrest sprawl by designating a wide zone *non aedificandi* all around the urban core. This open land, used for agriculture and general recreation, was to be the natural counterpoint of the old defensive walls, in that it would limit the size of the city and discourage expansion beyond it. For the concept to work the city must have total control of the land in question, and thereby be empowered to determine its uses.

A reserved zone of open land on which no permanent building would be allowed was not a particularly new idea. The Roman *pomerium*, the pasture lands of ancient cities, and the English common lands all had the effect of limiting their cities' growth and keeping the built center within a practical distance from the countryside. But only with the unwalled open city of the industrial era, and the unchecked stretch of its periphery incident to mass transportation, did the greenbelt acquire reformist urgency. Indeed, it was those 19th-century idealists like Robert Owen and Ebenezer Howard, intent on turning their back on the industrial metropolis and installing a fresh settlement pattern of self-sufficient country towns, who first considered the device of the greenbelt obligatory.

Ledoux's design for Chaux with its perimeter belt of playing fields may well represent the first actual use of the greenbelt in a new town.[39] More relevant to the English urban experience, however, was the example of the parkland towns in Australia and New Zealand, beginning with the design of Adelaide by Colonel William Light in 1837. The colonization of these distant territories, which was advanced to alleviate the persistent unemployment in Britain in the wake of the Napoleonic Wars, gave license to try out town-planning formulas; and the threefold scheme of townland, parkland and suburban land, introduced at Adelaide and repeated in scores of government-sponsored new towns up to and beyond the First World War, especially in South Australia and less pervasively in Victoria and New South Wales, proved the most tenacious.[40]

The towns were simple grids. The suburbs beyond the town parkland had their own encircling green. Roads radiated "in all available directions from the centre of population to the extent or confines of the land proposed to be sold," as the Surveyor-General G. W. Goyder first instructed in 1864. After about 1880, railroad lines and yards usurped one side of the greenbelt.

The parkland principle came under attack from Charles C. Reade, who was appointed town-planner of South Australia in 1919. He noted that the parklands locked up the urban center "as completely as many of the European towns were once upon a time hemmed in by fortifications," and advocated "continuous growth and contact between the central and suburban areas." By this time, Howard's Garden

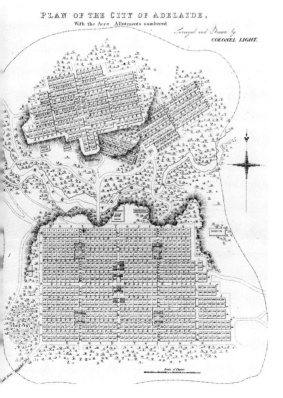

40 *Adelaide (South Australia), site plan by Colonel William Light, 1837. The main city, to the south, and its suburbs lie on either side of the River Torres, surrounded and separated by parkland.*

PLAN OF THE CITY OF ADELAIDE,
With the Acre Allotments numbered.

Surveyed and Drawn by
COLONEL LIGHT.

41 *Rustic summer-houses complement modern allotment garden plots outside Bratislava (Czechoslovakia). Unlike British allotments, which have declined in number by half after a Second World War peak of 1,400,000, those on the Continent have remained popular as warm-weather leisure retreats.*

City, which recognized an indebtedness to Adelaide, had had its first installation at Letchworth in England, prescriptively bounded by a broad agricultural greenbelt, and the earliest of many projects to "girdle" London in the same way had made their appearance.[41]

The London proposals were for anything but a uniform zone of unbuilt green. Their inspiration came rather from the American parkway system. Nurtured by Frederick Law Olmsted and others, and developed with some success in cities like Boston, Minneapolis and Chicago, the system entailed the linking of peripheral open spaces with landscaped boulevards to create an irregular but continuous ring of green around the town. The ring made no pretense to support agriculture. It was exclusively recreational, and both residential and institutional building was permitted.

The London and Home Counties Green Belt Act was passed in 1938; land began to be acquired at a slow pace. In 1955 the principle was generalized for all of England, one aim now stated as being "to prevent neighboring towns from merging into one another."[42] At the same time, the New Towns Act of 1946, which embraced the model of the Garden City as national policy, made the greenbelt commonplace in the settlement pattern of post-war England.

Some form of containing green, kept more or less free of building in the public interest, is an established notion of present-day city-making theory. A handful of cities like Ottawa have creditable greenbelt systems, while others rely on legal instruments to coax one into place over time. In most cases, however, the greenbelt is reduced to a series of non-contiguous segments. In German land-use patterns, for example, the common practice was to introduce green wedges between built-up areas, or ribbons of landscape along major transit arteries.[43] This is clearly a more flexible arrangement in terms of growth, and has more to do with the Modernist concept of the linear city, spearheaded by theorists like Spain's Arturo Soria y Mata and Soviet planner N. A. Miliutin, than the English love affair with Garden Cities.

A faint echo of this particular doctrine of urban limitation can be detected in the institution of the allotment garden. This was an English thing in the beginning. It can be traced there to the dawning of the Industrial Revolution in the late 18th century, and to cities that were most affected by it. Citizens there, mostly working-class folk,

42, 43 *Laying out new streets and rearranging property boundaries in the Kienheide area of Frankfurt-am-Main; from J. Stübben,* Der Städtebau *(1924). The system applied is the* Frankfurter Umlegegesetz, *which became Prussian law in 1918. Farmland is acquired by the city through eminent domain (compulsory purchase). Streets are laid out, and the thin strips of land are combined into usable building plots, which are then redistributed according to the size of an owner's previous holding. Building designs are drawn up and executed by city commissions.*

could rent for a token sum small gardens at the edge of town, where they could be out in the fresh air with their families, and incidentally raise food to supplement their diets. In early 19th-century Birmingham, which had no parks or other public open spaces, many thousands took advantage of this wholesome excursion. As an observer remarked in 1833:

> It is the custom of Birmingham for working men to have gardens at about a guinea a year rent, of which there are a great number round the town, and all of the better parts of the workmen spend their leisure hours there . . . they have little summer-houses where they spend their evenings and Sundays.[44]

41 By the end of the century the allotment garden had taken hold on the Continent as well. The only problem with this ragged green belt was its impermanence: it was simply eradicated or pushed forward as the city needed the space to expand. Only in relatively recent times did some countries begin to recognize the allotment garden as an integral part of the city-form.

The regulating plan

The regulating plan, or *piano regolatore*, was precociously introduced in Italy with a law of 1865 in connection with the rebuilding of Naples. It established that every city with a population of 10,000 or more could, "for the sake of the common good determined by existing need to provide for the general health and requisite communications," draw up a legally binding master plan enforceable through the right of eminent domain. Once approved by the State, the plan would be valid for twenty-five years, and would be the guiding blueprint for the pattern of urban changes during that time. This plan was to be distinguished from the separately approved *piano di ampliamento*, which would apply to the expansion of the residential core beyond the limits of the master plan. It would set norms to be followed by developers in suburban construction, in order "to ensure the proper sanitation of the new development, and its safe, convenient and decorous disposition." Alas, this commendable legal apparatus did little to curb the licentious spread of cities, either in Italy or in other countries that instituted similar procedures of public review.

Germany was exceptional. There, cities dealt with the key issue of private speculation, and the self-serving, random fluctuations of the city-form it caused, through municipal ownership of large tracts of land which could be developed in the public interest. The municipality of Ulm, for example, at one point owned as much as 80 per cent of the greater urban area. Historically, a critical factor was the passing of princely lands to municipal control when the centrality of Baroque absolutism eased, during the 19th century, into the modulated power structures of the Liberal State.

42, 43 Along with the lands came the legal rights to lay down the street network (*Fluchtlinien*) in extension plans, not only for the development of this public domain, but also for privately owned parcels. The critical instrument was the Prussian Building Land Act of 1875. It imposed the cost of building, draining and lighting the streets of planned extensions on the owners of frontage sites. Construction could also be prohibited on green-field sites lacking streets and public utilities—which is why German cities remained relatively free of the squalid belts of privately-owned shanties the French call *lotissements*. In laying out orderly suburban plans over private land, the municipal authorities were empowered to erase the extant pattern of property boundaries, and assign owners new lots in proportion to their original holdings.

Annexation

To prevent the growth of a confining perimeter of industrial slums, or worse yet, exclusive residential enclaves in neighboring communities that would siphon away wealthy taxpayers, German municipal administrators embarked upon an urgent program of annexations. Between the 1880s and 1910, Frankfurt and Düsseldorf doubled the area under their respective city jurisdictions. Cologne incorporated nine communities in a single leap in 1888, increasing its expanse more than tenfold. Berlin's attempts to do the same were for the most part blocked by an ongoing administrative battle with the State of Prussia. The extended city that finally emerged in 1920 consolidated seven neighboring towns and fifty-nine rural parishes into a single metropolitan district covering 878 square kilometers (335 sq. mi.).

This swallowing of peripheral communities by an adjacent city was sometimes more than a simple act of predation. Annexation was actively pursued by many suburban German towns. It provided the benefits of a planned street network and coordinated systems of transit and public utilities, often without an increase in local taxes. Opposition, when it was present, usually came from communities with an established historical identity, as in the case of Deutz and Mülheim, two of Cologne's old rivals.[45] But in most cases the particularity of annexed communities had already been dissolved in a slurry of industrial suburban expansion, with many residents dependent on the neighboring metropolis for employment.

The precedent for all this was provided by Paris during the prefecture of Baron Haussmann. Eleven independent communes that ringed the city beyond the limits of the late 18th-century customs boundary were first enclosed within a new set of walls built in 1841, and then legally annexed in 1860. This created the so-called "petite banlieue," while the "grande banlieue" referred to the post-1860 ring of built-up suburbs. Haussmann's replanning of the newly annexed zone, as François Loyer points out, stamped a new urban identity on these quasi-rural settlements by purposely obliterating their former structure.

That this particular strong-arm technique of submerging individuated communities within the identity of the greater metropolis smacks of a program of urban colonization—albeit justified by rational city planning—was not missed by contemporaries. An 1865 prediction of the condition of Paris a century hence reported that the city

> had successively broken its new walls and spilled out over all parts of its surroundings, absorbing them into its body. It was now more than one hundred kilometers [62 mi.] around and in itself filled the Département de la Seine. Versailles was its royal vestibule; Pontoise was proud to form one of its suburbs. Each day the citizens of Meaux climbed the towers of their cathedral to see if Paris had reached them yet. . . . The monstrous cancer, always expanding, had chewed up all the flesh around it, and, annexation by annexation, all France had become its suburb.[46]

Los Angeles, California, figures large as a 20th-century instance of such aggressive annexation. The city extended over an area of 43 square miles (111 sq. km.) at the turn of the century; by 1930 it had grown to 442 square miles (1,145 sq. km.). Once it had installed the Owens River Aqueduct, and a court decision had confirmed that the municipality alone controlled the water of the Los Angeles River, the fate of adjoining communities was sealed. The city would provide water to these communities only if they agreed to be "annexed" (the term applies technically to communities that were unincorporated, that is, rural enclaves under county supervision) or "consolidated" (if they were already incorporated as towns).

Growth fever struck America between 1950 and 1970. City administrators like those of Houston, Texas, annexed vast suburban tracts "to avoid strangulation by neighboring populations which earn livelihoods in a city, but do not contribute proportionately" to the tax base.[47] That city's incorporated area more than doubled in a single year, 1956. Other examples from a 1972 study by Richard Forstall are amazing. In those two decades Jacksonville, Florida, grew 25-fold; Nashville, Tennessee, 23-fold; Phoenix, Arizona, 14-fold. The backlash was a revival of incorporation, most stridently again in California. By defining themselves as independent communities, wealthy suburban enclaves escape the formidable tax burden of supplying public services to adjacent metropolitan areas bloated with annexations and beset by the problems of inner-city poverty. It is suburb reinvented as city; pristine and problem-free.

44

44 *Houston (Texas) at six stages of its spectacular growth: between 1836 and 1904; in 1920; in 1940; in 1954; in 1957; and since 1957, as the city greatly exceeded the 12–mile (19 km.) span covered by this drawing.*

THE SOFT EDGE OF SUBURBIA

With the important exception of the developing world, where migration into metropolitan centers continues unabated, the 20th century has brought us to the end of the age of centripetal cities. Both in Europe and in the United States many of the largest urban cores are declining in population. Meanwhile, their outlying regions are flourishing—in the case of the U.S., at a punishing cost to the inner city. This redistribution of urban vitality has initiated what could be called the era of the middle landscape: that synthesis of city and country which is quickly becoming more populous than either.

TRANSPORTATION AND THE CITY EDGE

The modern suburb, in the sense of a residential settlement for commuters, was from the very start the child of fast transportation. This is what distinguishes the modern episode of the periphery from all previous suburban activity. Prior to 1800 the maximum girth of a city was influenced by walking distance. In ten minutes a pedestrian can cover about half a mile (0.8 km.); horse-back riding and wagons moving through narrow streets set a comparable pace. Certainly, residences at distances from the city center that would prove inconvenient for pedestrians were always accessible to the wealthy through private transportation. There was no difficulty connecting Florence on an infrequent basis with the rich estates that occupied the extramural land, Giovanni Villani tells us in the 14th century, for a radius of 3 miles (5 km.). The Baroque period saw a vast increase in coaches. In Paris there were 12,000 of them by 1700. In addition, those who could afford to availed themselves of pre-taxi hackney service or the sedan chair.

But the modern suburb conceives itself as a dormitory community, that is, one to which you can repair at the end of every working day in the city, and get back to work in the morning. In London it was not unknown in the early 18th century for the well-to-do to live in peripheral villages like Streatham, riding into the city every day to work. By century's end a new pattern of residential settlements was transforming the more remote communities of Putney, Hampstead, and St. John's Wood. However, as a mass phenomenon suburban commuting really had to await the revolution of modern transport systems—turnpikes, railroads, streetcars, subways, buses, and ultimately the automobile.

45

It is of course not at all accidental that the earliest planned suburbs, developed by estate owners for prosperous merchants of George III's London, should coincide with the arrival of the first credible mass transportation system—horse-drawn stages that ran on an extensive system of paved highways built by authority of successive Turnpike Acts. Estate development often occurred between arterial roads, along which a different, linear suburb was very much in evidence. In fact, a peculiarity of England with respect to the Continent was precisely the coexistence of these planned estates with the roadside ribbon development which we encountered in the Middle Ages.

Continental suburban sprawl, both of the rough and of the genteel sort, was not contiguous or uniformly extensive. It occurred most characteristically in pockets between the tentacular pattern of transportation routes emanating from the city center. This phenomenon stood out most clearly in a city like 19th-century Turin where the original gridded city-form had earlier been maintained through several extensions of the fabric. Now, beyond these grids, the working-class suburbs or *barriere* created by private enterprise occurred on sites along the radial thoroughfares, marking a sharp break with the long history of State-controlled rectangular planning. The suburbs (Barriera Nizza, Borgo S. Paolo, etc.), forming a crescent around the western half of the city with the Po describing the eastern half, were separated from each other by fields and farmland. Each district had its own identity, its fairs and festivals, its own sports groups. Far from cohering socially as a unified zone, the *barriere* ranged as unreconciled adversaries.

The real suburban boom began with the steam railroad. The suburban villa districts serving Stockholm and Vienna sprang up after the inauguration of suburban rail services there. Tokyo's Meiji-era interurban lines had established the future direction of suburban expansion by the 1880s.[48] The Harlem River line out of New York reached neighboring Westchester County as early as the 1840s, and in the ensuing decade real estate developments popped up in Rye, Tarrytown, and New

45 *London's northwestern edge in 1834; detail of a map by Benjamin Davies. Development is concentrated to the east of Maida Vale, which follows the straight line of a major Roman road to the Midlands. West of it are the village of Paddington (extreme south) and fields belonging to the Church of England. The built-up area to the east lies just to the north of the "New Road," a mid-18th-century urban bypass. At first, suburban building kept to the traditional pattern of terraces. Then, on the Eyre Estate in St. John's Wood, villas with gardens suddenly appeared. At about the same time (ca. 1815–25), Regent's Park was laid out to the east.*

Rochelle.[49] Since stations were some distance apart, American railroad suburbs were deployed like beads on a string. Furthermore, since the station was their true center, and since most commuters had to walk to and from the station, they tended to be compact. For a time at least natural greenbelts surrounded these small pockets of suburbia.

The high price of fares and the speculative nature of development made early railroad suburbs exclusive havens for the well-to-do. The collusion of developers and transportation companies in perpetuating this has been amply documented, both in America and Europe. Berlin's peripheral and east–west rail lines were built in the 1870s and 1880s by the Prussian State. Where new routes traversed open land it was snapped up by speculators without State intervention: development assured riders, hence revenues, for the State-owned railway. The largest of the city's private streetcar operators was involved in land development as well. Through such arrangements Berlin's exclusive southwestern districts were superbly served by transit lines, including subways and elevated railroads, with fares affordable only 46 to the better-off.[50] London's Metropolitan Railway nudged this tradition into the 20th century with its development of company-owned land north of the city. Promotional material extolled the scenic charms of what it called "Metroland," and Pl.7 touted its investment potential as a "rare opportunity for small capitalists."[51]

Proponents of housing reform saw mass transit instead as an opportunity to benefit the working class. London's City Solicitor, Sir Charles Pearson, had championed the first underground railway line as a salvation for the laborer. "The passion for country residence is increasing to such an extent," he maintained, it is "impossible for persons who do not mix with the poor to know."[52] With the Chatham Act of 1860 most of London's new rail lines began to offer reduced fares to workers and clerks on "workmen's trains" that ran early mornings and late nights. The new policy was not the only factor in the enormous working-class migration out

46 Berlin, Reichskanzlerplatz (now Theodor-Heuss-Platz), in the Charlottenburg district; photograph by Waldemar Titzenthaler, 1909. The subway station had opened a year earlier. All around are building lots for sale; in the background, Heerstrasse is being pushed out into the country.

of the city in the final quarter of the century. In the rush to construct new lines into London, demolitions displaced more than 76,000 people between 1853 and 1901.[53] Working-class colonies grew in the southern and northeastern suburbs close to the railroads. Few laborers settled before 1900 in West London, which was not served by "workmen's trains."[54]

The correlation between mass transit and suburban growth was made frustratingly clear to German city administrators in the 1870s, when horse-drawn tram franchises were granted to private companies. The profit-minded operators hesitated to open any route that could not guarantee a steady clientele capable of paying steep ticket prices. As a consequence, needed connections to developing or less affluent districts were shunned as bad investments. With the advent of the electric trolley a decade later transit entrepreneurs balked again, this time at the high cost of installation. Many municipalities seized this opportunity to take over the lines, using them as tools to direct the course of urban growth. Düsseldorf and Frankfurt began subsidizing fares for working-class riders in 1903, again with the hope that access to cheap, low-density accommodation outside the city would contribute to housing reform. But in Germany, as almost everywhere else, the periphery was cheap only as long as it remained inaccessible. The new streetcar lines brought to the suburbs not just commuters, but land speculation and rising prices.

With the advent of the car and its establishment as a private mode of mass transportation—in the United States as early as the 1920s—the nature of urban growth and urban form changed radically. Simply put, this vehicle allowed an
47 unparalleled stretch of the city, since more people could move farther away on their own than was ever the case with public transportation.

The most obvious result is that the motorcar suburb is not bound by the linear logic of train or tram. It can be located anywhere around the edge and can spread out mindlessly, since it is not restrained by the focal anchor of a station or a streetcar stop. So the star-shaped city of the trolley days oozed into an amorphous blob. Ribbon development did not, of course, disappear. It was reaffirmed in America by the "strip"—that city edge extension of the old main street, geared to a car-buying and servicing culture. To the extent that the first urban freeways, chiefly in Los Angeles, followed along earlier track lines, they could become the new directional forces of the automotive age. The 1950s marked a noticeable return to the linear pattern in American suburbs, with development this time following existing or projected freeways and paved rural roads. But again, since there is nothing that prevents commuters from driving ten minutes or more beyond their freeway exit, these linear bands could be very thick indeed.

A SPECTRUM OF SUBURBS

The protean guises of suburbia reflect differences in local culture, banking systems, transport, building technique, and administrative authority. At its broadest, the spectrum of suburban residential form spans two poles: from the diffuse patchwork
Pl.8, of detached houses at one extreme, to the sharp juxtaposition of high-density
Pl.9 apartment blocks and open expanses at the other. These diametric settlement patterns are typically aligned with the extremes of another continuum, ranging from the laissez-faire to the centrally planned.

Beginning with the Georgian prototypes, English suburbs were built at densities that might seem more appropriate in the urban core. The common housing unit was
45, the crescent or the terrace—rows of identical attached houses. This particular
167 housing formation would remain a fixture of the English city edge. Building

47 *Grand Central Parkway in Queens, 1937, looking toward New York City; small suburban developments of varied shape are hooked on to the highway.*

48 Bedford Park, London: a variety of
house types in Blenheim Road, by Norman
Shaw, 1880s.

societies, which originated in the 1730s and were standardized as regulated
mortgage institutions by an Act of 1874, helped to install single-family terrace
housing as the norm for the class of family headed by a shopkeeper, small
tradesman, or well-off artisan. Detached villa residences set in their cozy arcadias
remained the prerogative of the well-heeled. Villas were, however, sometimes
placed alongside refined terrace designs within a single community, as in London in
St. John's Wood and, later, in the "aesthetic" residential developments of Bedford 45,
Park (1875) and Hampstead Garden Suburb (1906). Not until the widespread 48
introduction of the semi-detached house during the inter-war period did an
alternative more like the leafy, green-lawned suburbs of middle America come into
currency.

Earlier, British terrace housing traditions had been carried to America's Atlantic
seaboard, where tidy brick rows became a mainstay of residential blocks built in the
late 18th and early 19th centuries. But the building type fell largely out of favor by
1900, a victim both of changing fashion and of an association with immigrant
crowding in New York, Baltimore, and Boston. Only in one region, centered around
Philadelphia, did the row house retain its popularity among suburban builders and
residents through the early 20th century.

A number of special circumstances distinguish urbanization in the United States.
The cities were newer, of course. There was an early and enduring obsession with
the detached house. The individual share of urban space, generally speaking, was
profligate by Old World standards. In 1899, A. F. Weber calculated that a
comparable selection of American and German cities would yield densities of 22
persons per acre as against 157.6 persons per acre. And the resistance in the U.S. to
large-scale planning, to public policy about housing, or to any curbs on speculation
is proverbial. Land, beyond being a profit-turning commodity, had little social
meaning.

Speculation in land values is what urban process has always been about in America. Many cities were born as speculative ventures, and grew the way they did from the same motive. Without defensive walls to fight against, and with farmers roundabout not unduly loyal to the traditional uses of their land, cities spread out impetuously and in incoherent spurts. Subdivision had its own logic, unrelated to orderly growth or predetermined need.

49

The central premise that allowed for this erratic urban process was the right of landowners to develop their property as they saw fit. In the period until the Second World War, speculative greed was all-consuming, and the ways of satisfying it almost entirely unimpeded by public pressure. The developer subdivided where he wanted to, and as soon as he staked the lots, the host city was obligated to bring in the major utilities. All the developer had to do was sell the lots and make money. Buyers would build on their own, as and when they could. Especially in the 1920s and '30s, one could find many cities whose edge showed miles of streets with sidewalks and expensive utilities, but no houses. Many of these unused building lots—"dead land," as they were aptly called—remained tax delinquent or abandoned. In 1928, we are told, 55 per cent of all subdivision lots in Cook County, which encompasses Chicago, and its fringe were vacant.[55]

All of that changed in the post-war decades. An unprecedented rush to the suburbs was fueled by a surge in roadbuilding that put vast tracts of farmland within the commuter's automotive reach, and by new, cost-efficient building methods. But more than anything else, a 1934 decision by the Federal Housing Administration to support low-cost insured loans for single-family houses is accountable for American suburbia as we have it today. In concert with generous provisions for veterans—

47
50,
Pl.9

49 *Grand Island (Nebraska), looking northwest from the courthouse, 1885. The blocks of the grid are built up seemingly at random, and appear to stretch endlessly across the prairie.*

50 *California tract homes under construction at Lakewood in the San Fernando Valley, 1950. The house and garage foundations have been poured; piles of lumber are stacked awaiting erection.*

51 Cologne (Germany), Kaiser-Wilhelm-Ring nearing completion in 1885. On the site of the old fortifications, middle-class apartment blocks, a dense building type, look out across public gardens (cf. Pl. 6).

mortgaging the entire value of the house with no down payment—the policy removed risks for buyer and builder alike. Instead of just subdividing farmlands and selling them off as house lots, developers could increase their profits by taking over the construction side as well. And they did, on a scale that proved fateful. One of the most celebrated developers, Levitt and Sons, was by 1950 producing a four-room house every sixteen minutes.[56] If the results were bland and conformist, consumers seemed not to mind. The suburban environment that was once an exclusive turf for the wealthy is today America's most popular residential pattern.

Latin American cities have witnessed a similar middle- and upper-class predisposition to abandon city for suburb. Mexico City, for example, has in its Colonia Polanco an example of an early 20th-century villa district for the entrepreneurial elite. Cocoyan, Las Lomas de Chapultepec, and El Pedregal are some of the city's elegant post-war suburbs.

On the European Continent, only Belgium can point to an early and sustained tradition of single-family suburban home development—this fostered by the most concentrated road and rail network in the world, government subsidies of private house-building that go back to the 19th century, and a policy of almost always granting the individual permission to build on his land, wherever it might be located.[57]

Other Europeans regarded the suburban villa as a quintessentially English phenomenon—this despite the common heritage of a North Sea culture zone in which single-household urban residences were once predominant.[58] Mid-19th-century planners in Vienna and Cologne lost their battle to include neighborhoods of villas in "the English Style" as part of their cities' Ringstrasse developments. *51* Private initiatives were more successful in this regard. The 1850s and '60s saw the far reaches of what is now the 16th *arrondissement* of Paris become a colony of picturesque retreats graced by Gallic renditions of the *jardin à l'anglaise*. Vienna's first suburban villa precinct, Cottage, began to be built in 1873 along the wooded reaches of the Wienerwald. Similar districts emerged during the course of the decade southeast of Amsterdam in Het Gooi and in Stockholm's suburb of Sundbyberg.

In a very basic sense these communities were failures. Suburban life on the Continent never acquired the social cachet that a luxurious apartment in town held. Villa suburbia was no match for the competition—this being the opulent residential construction associated with Haussmannization and the new Ringstrasse districts— and so was seen by those who could afford it as a landscape of summer residences and second homes. Many of these soon disappeared under the massive apartment blocks of an expanding urban fabric, as was the case along the Avenue de l'Impératrice (today Avenue Foch) in Paris, and in Stockholm's Sundbyberg.

The 19th-century suburbs of most Continental cities, peppered with tenements and smoking factories, remained stretches of an unabashedly working-class edge. These suburban fringes became, in the years preceding the First World War, the stage for a European attempt to install the low-density British landscape of cottages and terraces, here in the service of the proletariat. The model was Ebenezer Howard's Garden City, as demonstrated in projects by Raymond Unwin. European variants, however, were situated on the periphery of existing towns and dependent upon them for employment, conditions directly opposed to Howard's principles.

Unwin's rural townscape ideals were especially well received in Germany, where they meshed with a persistent ideal of single-family housing and the picturesque aesthetic championed by Camillo Sitte. The move for decentralization swept the housing reform movement, resulting in a handful of model towns: Hellerau (1909), to the north of Dresden, and Staaken (1914), just west of Berlin, are two prime examples. The same period in Sweden saw the "garden suburbs period" of Stockholm's development;[59] and outside Paris, a series of *cités-jardins* was undertaken by the Office Public de la Seine, as the start of a French program of decentralization. But in France, as well as elsewhere in Europe, low-density ideals ran foul of the urgencies of a housing crisis. Chatenay and Plessis, two of these towns, show an initial phase planned in the English manner, followed in the early 1930s by a second phase in which individual houses are replaced with blocks of flats, at double or triple the previous population density.[60]

The reform movement for small suburban homes collapsed entirely in the wake of the Second World War, which begat dramatic migrations and cruel housing shortages. City peripheries were now transformed beyond recognition by large-scale public housing estates. Stockholm had been experimenting since the 1930s with highrise suburban flats: the 10-story *punkthus*, or point block, a slim slab that contrasted well with the tossed northern landscape—less so with the surrounding cottage development—was the result. By the late 1940s variants were beginning to go up across Europe. In Scandinavia, in suburban new towns like Stockholm's Vällingby and Helsinki's Tapiola, as well as in Britain, multi-story flats were built to accent lowrise terrace blocks in what was known as "mixed development." This variation on Modernist design, made more palatable by a dose of "townscape," was promoted by the London County Council as an alternative to the "uniform pinkish-grey hell" of suburban cottage estates.[61]

The 1960s saw this mixed aesthetic formula repudiated in Britain by industrial cities like Liverpool, Birmingham and Glasgow, each of which was under pressure to churn out five thousand new units of housing annually. The targets were achieved by abandoning any vestige of Picturesque notions for stark multi-story slabs of Piranesian scale that directed the outward sprawl of the suburbs upward as well. Here as elsewhere the result has been a suburban landscape planted with what are generally perceived as hostile monoliths; growing consumer resistance to this type of housing; and in heavily regulated housing markets like those of France and Sweden, an early 1970s renaissance of long suppressed single-family home construction.[62]

52 *Vällingby (Sweden). Like the two other new towns on the edge of Stockholm begun in 1952, it is small, and planned around a subway station. A commercial center, with shops and offices, aims to give it self-sufficiency. Housing types mix lowrise terraces with highrise towers.*

EDGE CITIES

The post-war decentralization of European capital cities was sometimes further elaborated by a planning policy of satellite towns. London built its compliment in the immediate post-war period; Moscow's date from the late 1950s; and Paris is still developing its five new towns—Cergy Pontoise, St.-Quentin-en-Yvelines, Évry, Melun-Sénart, and Marne-la-Vallée. Like Vällingby outside Stockholm and Tapiola 53, outside Helsinki, all reflect the basic planning aim of sowing outlying residential 52 zones with services and functions that duplicate those found in center-city business districts.

The United States has seen a parallel process in the emergence of what are now called "edge cities." Most started as typical tract-home suburbs with a shopping strip and a regional shopping center. In the 1980s hotels and office parks or towers appeared, sensibly close to white-collar patrons, and new cities were born. They sit in the middle of open landscape, 10 miles (16 km.) or more from the edge of town, places like Cumberland and Buckhead north of Atlanta, Georgia; Bishop Ranch and Dublin in California's San Francisco Bay Area; Westheimer, Greenway Plaza, 54 Greenspoint, and the Galleria area west of Houston, Texas; and most impressively, Las Colinas between Dallas, Texas, and its airport, spread out on more than 18 square miles (47 sq. km.) of land and intended for a maximum population of 150,000.[63]

There has always been some vestigial pretense that suburbia is not complete in itself, that the umbilical cord that ties it to the city center cannot be totally severed. That symbolic bond has become meaningless to the new edge-dweller. Downtown

53 Marne-la-Vallée (France): part of the center of Noisy-le-Grand, one of the nuclei of the new town. On the right is the "Palacio," an apartment block by Ricardo Bofill, completed in 1983. Marne-la-Vallée, founded in 1972, was deliberately established to the east of Paris to balance the natural population movement westward.

54 Greenway Plaza, one of the "edge cities" of Houston (Texas), with its own highrise downtown and peripheral housing.

areas were formerly valuable because of their central location. The network of high-speed roadways that linked suburb to core, and that made a home far from town possible for many, has been slowly equalizing the values of urban and outlying land. Suburban highway crossings have become new economic centers of gravity, duplicating inner-city services and short-circuiting the loathed pattern of rush-hour commuting. Put in the language of a Californian developer: "We can offer a self-contained city, and that's a hell of a selling point."[64]

Life on the edge is self-contained in a second sense as well. As has been pointed out by Robert Fishman, the most cogent observer of post-suburban settlement form, "The true center of this new city is not in some downtown business district but in each residential unit." Automobile drivers—the only fully entitled citizens of edge cities—can now compose their own town "from the multitude of destinations that are within suitable driving distance."[65] Of course the older pedestrian city always offered a similar option, but with an important difference: it was there charted within a landscape of value-laden symbols of urban culture, and conditioned by a spontaneous public life. The edge city's high-speed vehicular promenade, made in isolation through an unbounded settlement, must be seen as a radically new way of experiencing urbanity, stripped clean of the centralizing presence of a civic realm.

Perhaps it is only fitting that at the end of the 20th century the city is without its defining outline—its *limes*, as this threshold is called in Latin—and now becomes diffuse and incorporeal. The ritual tracing of bounds in the soil of what was to become Rome inscribed something that was more than a functional mechanism or a matrix of economic forces. It drew the civic body, and rendered that abstraction in physical form.

Although we abandoned such pieties in more recent times, we still recognized some enduring difference between the urban figure and its surrounds, still endowed it with an individuality celebrated in poetry, proud boast and jokes. The character of our city was relished if we were lucky, endured or escaped if we were not. Today's uncircumscribed settlement patterns and lifestyles make these extremes unnecessary, perhaps impossible. We now choose, if we wish, to live without restriction in fast landscapes that are convenient, efficient and bland. If this city without boundaries is to be faulted, it is for its failure fully to encompass the builders rather than the built.

2 · URBAN DIVISIONS

INTRODUCTION

THE Berlin Wall was a *cause célèbre* of our times. It was a symbol of the bitter 55 contest of two ideological camps that sought to divide the globe between themselves after the havoc of World War II, and proof for those in the Western camp of the brutal suppression of human freedom that reigned on the other side.

The Wall, made of concrete and barbed wire, was real enough. It cut across streets and building complexes, meandered with seemingly random purpose through the 56 old fabric of the city, and was watched over by grim towers at regular intervals. The drunken path in fact represented a line of military reckoning: it ran between the urban areas in the control of the Allied forces and those of Russia during the final days of the liberation of Berlin, after the horrible rain of bombs had done its job.

The Americans, British and French shared twelve boroughs in the west, with about 54 per cent of the city's land; the remaining eight boroughs went to the Soviets. The central sector, the heart, of pre-war Berlin—Mitte—was wholly within the Soviet sector. This had the capital's most prestigious buildings—the city hall, key embassies, the Brandenburg Gate, the university, the state library, the great museums, the cathedral, the national theater. Almost nothing of all this had been left standing intact. The Russians and their East German clients, after twenty years or so of living with the ruins, decided in September 1964 to resurrect this Mitte and focused their efforts on Alexanderplatz. The West Berliners, meantime, had chosen 123 their own administrative center at the borough of Schoeneberg with its old city hall, and had developed a lively, flashy central business district in the Zoo quarter, with the glittering Kurfürstendamm as its shopping spine.[1]

By then the Wall hastily thrown up in 1961 had acquired a brutal finality. It seemed destined to last forever. But in November 1989 a realliance of the major powers made its glowering and deadly presence suddenly pointless. As the world, briefly stunned, turned jubilant, the two halves of Berlin reached out toward each other: within days the Wall began tumbling down.

In contrast to this violent and bluntly physical barrier, there are arbitrated, legalistic, invisible urban divisions which we are not ordinarily aware of at all. They are designated on city maps, and have quite specific consequences. I leave aside

55 opposite Berlin, looking along the Wall from the Reichstag in the West toward the Brandenburg Gate and East Berlin, 1966.

divisions that serve the purposes of private interests—insurance companies, real estate boards, commercial concerns that mean to target their advertising pressures according to the financial implications of our address. What I have in mind are the lines drawn by public authority—wards and parishes and precincts, the *arrondissements* of Paris and the *rioni* of Rome—which for all their intangibility are very much a matter of genuine effect. They are political, or more generally administrative, divisions, and since the beginning of cities they have governed the ways we are managed within the urban order—how we are taxed, serviced, pressed into military service, or kept under control. In other words, the object of these divisions is to design the *population* within the urban form, an arrangement that is either coerced or *de facto*. And because they deal with people, the divisions were often coincident with deep social schisms, and their very existence brought about tensions and open conflict.

Now obviously analogies between the structure of urban form and the social structure of the urban population are not always intentional. Urban divisions can also come about independent of—or even *despite*—the apparent intentions engraved in the city's structure, or can develop within it out of unforeseen social changes, as when a new ethnic ghetto is created within a formerly smart neighborhood, or when the forced departure of a particular group, like the evacuation of the Jews from Alexandria under Nasser, radically transforms the internal makeup of the city. In such cases the disturbance of the human arrangement ends up by rearranging the workings of the city.

Broadly speaking, and by way of organizing the prodigious material, we might recognize four kinds of specialized partition of the urban territory: the administrative district, where the ruling authority resides; the religious district, an absolutely critical one until the laicization of the Western world in the wake of the French Revolution; the district of business and commerce; and, of course, the residential component of the urban structure.

Historical accounts commonly represented the initial triad as the standard jurisdictional divisions of the public domain, and matched them with physical assignments. It was Regensburg in 11th-century Germany, for example, that proclaimed its territory to be composed of three sectors: *pagus regius* (royal district); *pagus clericorum* (religious district); and *pagus mercatorum* (market district).[2]

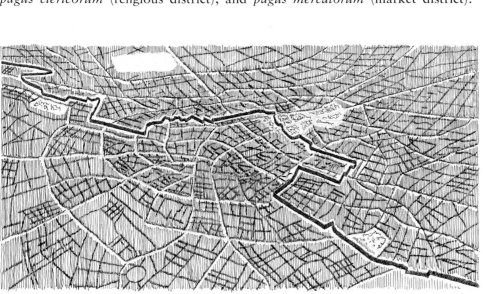

56 The line of the Berlin Wall, seen from the east. The whole of the historic center—the area of the walled city and its early western suburbs (cp. Ill. 36)—lay in East Berlin; West Berlin was left with the vast park of the Tiergarten in the middle.

PRAGA

MVLTAVIA FLVVIVS

57 *Prague, from Matthäus Merian's* Neue Archontologia Cosmica *(1638). The city is divided both topographically and temporally. On a height to the left is the walled citadel-town, the Hradčany, containing the castle and cathedral. Below lies the Mala Strana, a residential and commercial district, with its marketplace. The name means "lesser side," indicating its subordination to the Old Town opposite, to which it is linked by the fortified 14th-century Charles Bridge. The Old Town centers on its marketplace, next to the twin-towered Týn Church. The line of its walls is marked by a leftward diagonal above the island. A diagonal to the right of that is the long Wenceslas Square (cp. Pl. 20), in the New Town. This much larger unit, with its own vast central marketplace, was added by the Emperor Charles IV in the 14th century.*

Some such formula, explicitly set forth or simply implanted in the urban form, applied to most cultures and most periods—until relatively recent times.

The application of this convenient system of four categories (which I propose to follow) is not quite as satisfactory for the modern city as it is for the vast bulk of history before it. Not only is the religious component substantially diffused, if not absent (as was the case with the Soviet Socialist city), but the commercial and business district, combined with a heavy burden of modern industry, is more complex and compartmentalized than in any previous era.

The categories I propose overlap with divisions suggested by the system of *topographical* classification pertinent especially, but not exclusively, to Western Europe. The distinction of hilltop from valley settlements is a common one in the Middle Ages, and it has political resonances. The hilltop is where a town usually begins, with a princely citadel, a cathedral, a basic nucleus of feudal authority. Down in the valley is a civil core of craftspeople and traders. Medieval Basel is just one example that fits the pattern.[3]

A second familiar distinction is of a *temporal* kind: old town/new town—medieval/modern. The city form reinforces the contrast. The old town is often "organic" in layout; the new town, with the railroad station and its crown of hotels, is laid out on a broader, more regular street matrix. The distinction here is between the pre-industrial and the modern industrial city. But the term *Neustadt* (new town) can also have a more ancient application referring to a late medieval addition to the old core, which becomes part of the historic town in later periods, in contra-distinction to the modern quarters.

THE SOVEREIGN DISTRICT

The presence of a ruler, of a ruling elite, is considered a necessary condition of the pre-industrial city, in Sjoberg's classic account of it. The city helps to sustain the ruling elite, and in turn the city's own health, its growth and survival, requires a well-developed power structure. Elites are overwhelmingly urban. "Whoever heard of kings living in villages?" as Sjoberg puts it.[4] He goes on to postulate that "The more potent the elite, the grander the city."[5] This explains, in his view, the pre-eminence of capital cities.

Giovanni Botero, in his 16th-century treatise *The Greatness of Cities*, made the same case 300 years earlier. He wrote:

> It doth infinitely avail to the magnifying and the making cities great and populous the residency of the prince therein, according to the greatness of whose empire she doth increase. For where the prince is resident there also the parliaments are held, and the supreme place of justice is there kept. All matters of importance have recourse to that place, all princes and all persons of account, ambassadors of princes and of commonwealths . . . all such as aspire and thirst after offices and honours run thither amain. . . . Thither are the revenues brought that pertain unto the state, and there are they disposed out again.[6]

58 Constantinople, the Great Palace, an extensive sovereign district set against a closely-built urban backdrop. The hippodrome adjoins the palace wall in the foreground.

The extent of the administrative center will depend on a number of things, and most directly on the size of the palace bureaucracy, and whether or not there is a resident palace guard of any size. Many rulers preferred to be surrounded by their own select troops, which therefore had to be quartered in the palace area. With their barracks and parade grounds, housing for the bureaucracy, workshops for royally protected arts and crafts, and religious buildings, landscapes of state like the Great
58 Palace of the Byzantine emperors in Constantinople, or of its successor the Ottoman Topkapi, could be extensive and populous quarters. The palace grounds in Beijing included vast storehouses for prodigious quantities of dues in kind—rice and corn and salt, cloth, wines, animals and bales of straw.[7] In such places, the palace in fact wags the town.

59 Beijing. The Forbidden City lies in the center of the northern walled enclosure, set within the administrative imperial city. That is in turn surrounded by the residential city of the conquering Tartars. Beijing was divided not only hierarchically but ethnically: the southern walled zone was the Chinese city, for the conquered local people.

PRINCE, COURTIERS, AND PEOPLE

Within this complicated landscape, the ruler's residence was set apart from the functional and bureaucratic spaces of the palace grounds. To secure greater privacy, the prince might even live away from his bureaucrats in a second sovereign zone. In
13 the old Russian towns of Pskov and Novgorod, for example, the walled-in kremlin which held the cathedral and the major public buildings of the administration and the judiciary was not the place of residence of the ruler. In the case of medieval Novgorod, he lived on the other side of the Volkhov River from his bureaucrats.

In the capital cities of China, the administrative and princely components were
59 two adjacent but separate units—the "palace city," called Forbidden City in Beijing, for the emperor and his immediate entourage, and the "imperial city" for the government. Two spatial arrangements were known. In one—T'ang Chang'an is an example—the palace city and the imperial city were two independent entities with a large square between them. Or else the palace city was embedded in the center of the imperial city, which was the case with Khubilai Khan's capital Dadu, and also of course Beijing.

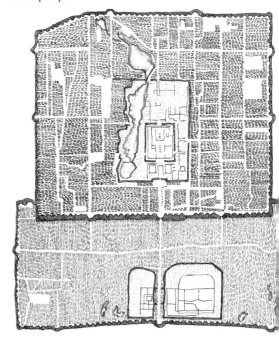

The meeting ground of ruler and people is a critical aspect of the sovereign district. It is usually a large public space where crowds can gather to hear the ruler address them in person, or to petition him. The outermost gate of the palace is the place of direct popular appeal in Islamic capitals, such as the Ali Qapu in Shah Abbas's Isfahan, or the Gate of Justice at the Alhambra. The connection between ruler and people was made in Roman and Byzantine times via sports. The Palatine in Rome set the pattern: the emperor would descend to the Circus Maximus from the imperial palace which overlooked it, to preside over the games and be cheered by the crowd. In Constantinople this pattern of palace and hippodrome was repeated. *58*

A SITE FOR THE PRINCELY RESIDENCE

There are two primary impulses that motivate the sovereign district—the dignity of the ruler, and his safety. Both have a bearing on size.

The first issue has to do with appearances, and especially with the impression the ruler strives to create—of stability, of wealth, of power—for the benefit of his own people and of foreign ambassadors. Since many cultures accepted the principle of the divine right of kingship, or even conceived of the king as being himself divine, the enhancement of that central mystery, the staging of the cosmic ruler as it were, conditioned the extent and complication of the sovereign district.

The ruler's safety is not merely a personal matter, but a matter of state. It ensures the stability of a regime, and the orderly transfer of power. The threat to this safety is seen to come both from within the city and from without, depending on the popularity of the ruler. Alberti was much occupied with this distinction between the benevolent ruler and the tyrant. He writes:

> A good King takes care to have his City strongly fortified in those Parts which are most liable to be assaulted by a foreign Enemy: a Tyrant, having no less Danger to fear from his Subjects than from Strangers, must fortify his City no less against his own People than against Foreigners: and his Fortifications must be so contrived, that upon Occasion he may employ the Assistance of Strangers against his own People, and of one part of his People against the other.[8]

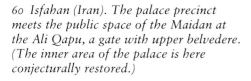

60 Isfahan (Iran). The palace precinct meets the public space of the Maidan at the Ali Qapu, a gate with upper belvedere. (The inner area of the palace is here conjecturally restored.)

61 *Salzburg (Austria), dominated by the medieval castle of the bishops.*

He advises that

> The Palace of a king should stand in the heart of the city; it should be easy of access, beautifully adorned, and delicate and polite, rather than proud and stately. But a lord should have a castle rather than a palace, and it should stand so that it is out of the city and in it at the same time.

What Alberti is suggesting here is that the degree of the ruler's rapport with his people, or the character of the governmental system, can be gauged by the location and architecture of the ruler's residence, and also by the nature of the dividing apparatus. Looking at this border, we have, at one extreme, the model of the walled "Forbidden City." Here the administrative compound is tightly sealed, whether in the center or pushed against the main system of fortications, and rigidly ordered within as a series of units of decreasing accessibility. At the other extreme, we can count many examples, from Minoan Crete to the White House in Washington, where the palace area is not fortified and, as with William the Silent's Prinsenhof at Delft, not even particularly dominant within the urban frame.[9]

Unfortified does not, of course, mean freely accessible. The Palatine had its own natural boundaries in the valleys that separated the hilltop from the Capitoline, the Aventine and the Caelian; and the open streetfront of the White House is maintained only mythically behind diverters put up in stages against modern threats like suicide runs of explosive-carrying vehicles. But the presumption is always there that the less removed the sovereign district within the fabric of its town, the less isolated behind a system of defenses, the more benign or consensual the regime. This dual engagement of the sovereign district—to external foes and to the ruler's subjects within—merits further comment. In relation to the former, one theory holds, for the choices prevailing in antiquity at any rate, that if the palace complex is at the edge of the city, against the city wall, or even astride it as at Khorsabad and Babylon, this fact, far from being a sign of royal worry, may indicate a powerful, inclusive state—an empire that can ensure the overall defense of its territory. By contrast, the location of the princely citadel in the center of town might well represent a weakened, or non-existent authority, when the city is on its own, surrounded by rival provinces, and needs a stronghold of last resort should the main walled settlement be overrun. The contrast would be between, say, Hattusas, when Hittite power was at its peak, and Zincirli during the Neo-Hittite period when small areas had to fend for themselves without the protection of a mighty central authority.

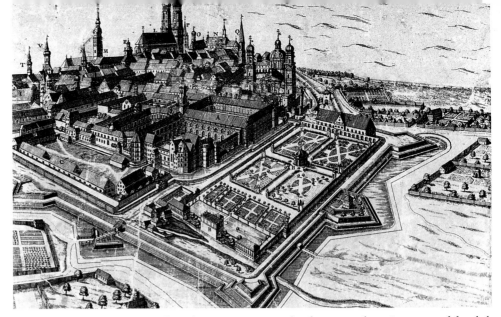

62 *Munich (Germany), bird's-eye view from the northeast; detail of an engraving after M. Wenig, 1701. In the background is the city, with the twin-towered Frauenkirche. In the foreground is the ducal palace, or Residenz, several times enlarged. Its elaborate formal garden occupies a special extension within the bastioned walls.*

The fact that many medieval towns grew in the front yard, as it were, of feudal castles often meant that in its subsequent history the sovereign district would figure at the edge of the urban fabric and high above it. In cases where the relationship of prince and people was an adversarial one, this topographic pre-eminence later attained special importance.

In European history, the contest between burghers and lords in the governance of cities was often physical enough to make the location and defenses of the castle matters of strategic urgency. The more aggressively the town asserted claims of self-governance, the wiser it was for the prince to keep his castle at the periphery of the town. So it is that we find two rival districts of government, with the municipal apparatus in the thick of town and the lord's perch on high, open ground. The town's goal is to overcome the castle through political means, or, failing that, by force. The lord will respond with a vigorous assertion of his sovereignty. Braunfels observes, in relation to the conflict between prince-bishops and burghers in the southern Germanic lands, that "the episcopal seats that survived were those in which the bishop, as ruler, occupied a castle on a ridge in the vicinity of the city." He lists as examples Salzburg, Würzburg, Trento, Bamberg, Eichstatt, Passau and Freising.[10]

But the presence of a stronghold at the edge of town may also be unrelated to this sort of indigenous struggle. It may represent a *post facto* dominion of the city by an alien power. That is the explanation of the Roman fort of Antonia in Herodian Jerusalem, or the Medicean fort at Siena.

There is, finally, in the peripheral placement of the palace, the issue of expansion. It is clearly much easier to acquire extensive gardens and adjacencies at the edge of town. By planting their first castle (*der Alte Hof*) in Munich at the northeast corner of the settlement, the dukes of Bavaria would be enabled to spread extravagantly northward in the 16th and 17th centuries. At Isfahan, similarly, the choice of the city edge for the palace area in Abbas's new town allowed for the possibility of an extensive quarter west and south, with the mansions of the courtiers on either side of a great avenue (the Chahar Bagh), and then, beyond the bridge of Allahavardi Khan, an enormous royal country residence, the Hazar Jarib, at the end of the avenue. Since such far-reaching grounds are one form of defense—the greater the distance that must be traversed to get to the ruler, the better his chance of organized resistance or escape—the location of the palace at the edge of town might well be seen as strategically sensible.

61

Pl.2

62

63 *Continuity in the Kremlin, Moscow: on the left is the Palace of Congresses, of 1960–61 (M. V. Posokhin, designer-in-chief); on the right the Trinity Tower, of 1495.*

There seems to be, then, no easy formula for the disposition of the sovereign district within the city. This should not surprise us. As always in the analysis of urban form one must consider specific circumstances—the context of culture, politics, social change. For this particular topic, the context involves questions of continuity, legitimacy, balance of power, and system of government.

Continuity has to do with the enduring quality of the sovereign district across time. We find, for example, that many law courts in French towns stand on the site of medieval royal palaces: the *palais royal* at some point in time, when major changes in political government had taken place, gave substance through its traditional authority to the *palais de justice*. And by the same token, bishops' palaces of old spawned *préfectures* or town halls.

The legitimacy issue is related to this. Governments that want to be seen as radical and revolutionary will sometimes spurn the official site of the *ancien régime*. They will build their own sovereign district. Muslim and Chinese dynastic behavior moves the royal residence to a different location in the capital if a new regime decides to continue the city as the central seat of power, or else the regime builds an entirely new capital further away. Regimes that seek to convey the reassurance of stability, of total control, of the historical dimension of their country despite changes of governmental structures, will occupy the main setting of the government they superseded—as the Louvre, sacked by the Revolution in 1789, returned to being the residence of the head of state until 1870; or as the Kremlin of the czars continued to house the rule of Stalin, Brezhnev and Gorbachev.

CHANGING THE COURSE OF STATE

The most interesting shifts in the urban geography of government come about when a representational system supersedes an autocracy. In the rise of independent urban communes during the later Middle Ages, especially in Tuscany and Switzerland, princely districts were shunned or even destroyed. Zurich levelled the imperial palace around 1200, and the site, known as Lindenhof, was not built upon. Several Swiss towns razed their Zähringer castles in the late Middle Ages. Communes set up town halls in central locations, in symbolic contrast to royal and lordly palaces at the edge of town. To avoid the princely core north of the river, the city of Bamberg built its town hall at the bridges that united this core with the merchant district on the other bank. 64

Conversely, if the shift was the other way around—from communal power to single-person rule—as was the case in Italy in the 14th–15th centuries, the lord might seek to move into the center of town to signify his control of the communal apparatus and the legitimacy of his rule. At Mantua the Gonzaga palace used an earlier communal building, the Domus Magna, as a legitimizing front. In Ferrara, the Este castle, for long at the edge of town backed against the defensive wall along the canal of the Giudecca, made itself a mid-city presence by the remarkable expedient of doubling the size of town. The filling in of the canal, and the laying out of the so-called Herculean Addition (after its patron Ercole d'Este) on the other side of the castle in the late 15th century, is already in plain sympathy with Renaissance ideal cities like Filarete's Sforzinda, where the lord's residence occupies the center of a radial scheme.[11]

By the 15th century the power of representative governments was on the decline across Europe, and the consolidation of the absolutist state well on its way. The result of was a phase of expansive sovereign districts, beginning with the Louvre in Paris and culminating in the Baroque spreads of Turin, Versailles, Karlsruhe and the like. Pl.2

When a king settled in a new capital, in these late medieval and Renaissance centuries, he would also require the nobles of his realm to reside in that city for at least part of the year, in order to have them under close supervision and avert uprisings. Mostly these nobles would engage or build townhouses close to the court. Again, sometimes the attempt would be made to transport the country manor within the walls. Warsaw is an example. When King Sigismund III moved his court from

64 *Polarities in Bamberg (Germany): upper left, the towered and spired cathedral, with the bishop's palace—rebuilt in the 18th century—slightly below it to the right; bottom right, the town hall, straddling the bridges leading to the burghers' quarter (out of the picture in the foreground).*

Cracow to Warsaw in 1596 and made it the new capital of Poland, the nobility that had to follow him there built manors within the city, which were in effect private mini-cities. The manors had their own courts, and their own craft organizations which were conceived as competitive to the city guilds.

Proximity to the princely palace was a good index of social standing. In old cities abruptly elevated to the rank of a princely capital, the landscape of existing real estate did not always allow for an orderly hierarchical deployment. This hierarchy was more readily staged in planned capitals, as in Shahjahanabad (Old Delhi) with the issuance of land grants to noblemen in the area west of the Red Fort, or better still, with elaborate precision, in Lutyens's layout for New Delhi.

What happens when post-Renaissance absolutism spends itself, and parliamentary states begin to be installed in the 19th century? There are two basic options. One is to try and keep the entire governmental apparatus in one area of the town, preferably grouped with some decorum. London illustrates the pattern, with Downing Street that has served as the prime minister's residence since 1731, the Parliament building at the Palace of Westminster, Whitehall (Cardinal Wolsey's palace confiscated and enlarged by Henry VIII, later the site of government offices), and St. James's Palace forming a fairly compact government district.

The other model is Paris or Rome, where government buildings are scattered all over town. This is usually considered a bad thing—wasteful and a missed opportunity for monumental planning. I am not at all sure. The dispersal of official monumentality is certainly beneficial to traffic patterns, property values, and perhaps even to the dignity of the town as a whole.

There was just such a debate in the 1870s when Rome was selected to be the capital of the united kingdom of Italy. One faction, represented by Quintino Sella, proposed to turn Via XX Settembre (formerly the Strada Pia) into ministry row stretching from the Quirinal to Porta Pia—both symbolic nodes of the liberation of Rome from papal rule. It never worked out. An impressive Ministry of Finance, and a more restrained Ministry of War, were built along the axis; but the government soon set about to occupy and remodel older buildings (the Palazzo Madama became the Senate and the Palazzo Montecitorio was doubled to hold the Parliament), and to erect others in different sections of the storied town as the Liberal State's talismans of appropriation.[12]

The less unified landscape of government is usually the result of a sudden decision to elevate an older town to the rank of capital, as in Rome. Several other examples suggest themselves. Calcutta, the old trading post, was designated the capital of British India in 1773. Sofia was selected as the capital of Bulgaria in 1879, when it was a small unremarkable town of about twenty thousand people. And Prague, formerly capital of the smaller region of Bohemia, was settled upon as the capital of post-war Czechoslovakia in 1918. In these instances, administrative and government offices, at the beginning at least, are often lodged in older buildings which may be scattered across the townscape, palaces are converted to embassies, and the new representational buildings go up where land can be easily procured.

DEMOCRACY AND SOCIALISM

Pl.15 The American concept of the civic center, the chief jewel of the City Beautiful movement, is an interesting modern attempt at a unified administrative scheme, merged here with cultural institutions. The association of government buildings with the monuments of bourgeois culture had European precedent. Vienna's 39 Ringstrasse is an example. But the American civic center, as it was realized in San

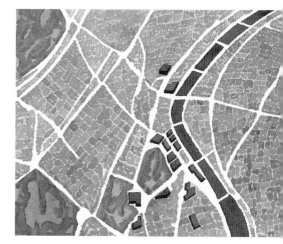

65, 66 Government buildings grouped in London (top) and dispersed in Rome (above). London's concentration centers on the Palace of Westminster (lower right, by the river and bridge), a royal residence since Anglo-Saxon times and seat of parliament and the law since the 13th century. The Houses of Parliament were rebuilt on the site of the palace after a fire in 1834. Not until the later 19th century were the law courts moved, to a purpose-built structure on the edge of the City (farthest north). Whitehall extends north from the Houses of Parliament; Buckingham Palace is to the southwest, between St. James's Park and Green Park.

In Rome, capital of Italy only since 1870, institutions are widely scattered, with the Palazzo Madama farthest west and several ministries strung out along the Via XX Settembre to the east, ending with the Ministry of Public Works.

67 St. Petersburg, Dom Sovetov (by N. A. Trotsky, begun 1936), built as the administrative and Party headquarters of the city. It stands in Moskovskaya Square, planned as a new urban center south of the old czarist capital.

Francisco and Cleveland and proposed for many more, was inspired by the example of the Washington Mall, a feature of L'Enfant's plan for the capital, as reinterpreted by Daniel Burnham and his colleagues in the McMillan scheme of 1902. Administrative and cultural buildings of a uniform Classical design were symmetrically disposed around a mall, creating a formally landscaped monumental core. This grouping, according to John Nolen, a leading planner of the day, was convenient for conducting official business; created "an impression of dignity and appropriate beauty" for citizen and stranger; and formed "a rallying point for the city's life. Here the best impulses may crystallize, inspired by the noble character of the edifice, into devoted action for the public good."[13] Something of that idea still holds in the civic centers of more recent American towns where town hall, fire department, police headquarters and the public library come together in a modest display of civic propriety.

The focus of Socialist cities rebuilt on the Soviet model is a ceremonial center of a different sort. The administrative and other representational buildings preside over a huge open space carved out of what was the old central business district, and overlooked by a grandiloquent monument to Lenin (or, until the mid-1950s, Stalin). Moscow's Red Square is the prototype for these urban compositions.[14] In *122* Leningrad/St. Petersburg, where the historic core was left largely intact, a new Socialist center was created at the city edge in the late 1930s. Baku followed a parallel *67* strategy, building its imposing Government House and Lenin Square—as large as Moscow's Red Square and St. Petersburg's Palace Square put together—on a vacant site in the industrial outskirts.

GOD IN THE CITY

Next to the sovereign district, the most important allocation of urban turf is that of the religious establishment. In the opinion of some students of urban origins, in fact, God had a pre-eminent claim to the city, ahead of kings and merchants. Paul Wheatley, for one, argues that "Whenever in any region of nuclear urbanism in the Old or New World we trace the characteristic urban form back to its origin, we arrive at a ceremonial centre." Beginning as nothing more than tribal shrines, in their classic phase these cities became monumental ritual settings where "a sacerdotal elite, controlling a corps of officials and perhaps a praetorian guard, ruled over a broad understratum of peasantry."[15]

Even without embracing such theories, the evidence for the success and endurance of temple cities is undeniable. In these, economic and political institutions were subordinated to religious norms, which formed the basis for a rigid social structure. At the very least, religion was so predominant in the physical structure of these holy cities that they seemed the exclusive habitat of priests and pilgrims. We think of Benares (India), Anuradhapura (Sri Lanka), and the great landscapes of Angkor Thom. In Greek antiquity Delphi and Olympia were pan-Hellenic sanctuaries, where city-states erected treasuries and competed publicly through their athletes. Mecca to this day is less a city with a resident population than the annual focus of the pan-Muslim pilgrimage, one of the five tenets of that religion. And Mayan centers like Uxmal, Chichén Itzá and Palenque were so carpeted by temple compounds that one school of expert opinion maintained until recently that they were never true functioning cities.[16]

GOD VS. KING

How the ceremonial center was secularized in time (if that is the way we should see the process at work) remains largely speculative. There is, at any rate, no unvarying universal pattern.

The rise of the office of kingship was central to this transformation: that much seems certain. But the relation of the new secular authority to the entrenched sacerdotal elite was shaped in a variety of local efforts—through revolution or in progressive stages—and was subject to readjustments. It is also well to remember that secularization is a relative term, since both king and priesthood were equally bound by the central beliefs of their religion.

We cannot therefore expect to find, at the start, two clearly separate urban divisions housing the secular power (represented by the king, or some form of elected or appointed civic authority) and the sacral power (represented by the priesthood). The settings of the two dominions overlapped or were juxtaposed in accordance with the nature of the internal contest, and changes in these physical arrangements had serious political import.

Crudely, we can distinguish three typical situations:

(1) In the first of these, the secular power might be seen to subsume the religious. In the theocracies of ancient Sumer, Cambodia, Ceylon, various pre-Columbian cultures, the New England township with its meeting house, and until recently in Tibet, the head of state was also chief priest. The pharaoh of Old Kingdom Egypt was himself a god, and Roman emperors, who held the title of *pontifex maximus*, presumed to godhead or were deified after death. God's domain within the city is

68 *Mecca (Saudi Arabia), the Ka'ba. The settlement lay on ancient trade routes, and the site of the Ka'ba was the goal of pilgrims long before the coming of Islam. At first houses clustered close around the shrine; they were later cleared to allow more room for circumambulation. A surrounding colonnade was built in the 9th century by the Caliph, rebuilt with the mosque in the 16th century by the Ottoman Sultan, and rebuilt again recently by the Saudis.*

here nothing other than an extension of the sovereign district—or else the two are coincident. Caligula had method in his madness when he claimed the Temple of Castor and Pollux on the Forum as the vestibule to the imperial residence on the Palatine, and made plans to join the palace by a wooden bridge to the Capitol, the sacred *arx* of the city.

The Chinese emperor presided over a state religion, focused on the official temples of the state gods, most notably the two Confucian "school-temples," the *fu-hsueh* and the *hsien-hsueh*, which were centers for the worship of sages and exemplary officials. "China had no sacred cities or holy public shrines," F. W. Mote writes. "The state cult was the private business of the emperor."[17] The most important monuments of the state cult, the Temple of the Imperial Ancestors and the Altar of Land and Grain, were situated in the palace precincts. There were also temples to famous local men, and temples associated with bureaucratic careers. Temples to city gods were themselves part of the State structure, since these gods were considered the supernatural counterparts of magistrates and prefects.[18] Public religion, both Buddhist and Taoist, had no priestly hierarchy, no bishoprics or parish structure.

Each temple was an independent unit licensed by the State; it "could be closed or required to move by secular authority."[19] The most prestigious of temples were invariably located in the countryside, and had no enduring involvement with city life.

Not uncommonly in theocratic systems or sacral autocracies, the locus of the high priesthood would be embraced in the sovereign district itself. In Minoan Knossos, for example, or at Mycenae, there is no distinct realm of God: formal worship rituals take place in the palace of the ruler. The same was seemingly true in the Harappan cities of the Indus Valley, where no religious buildings as such have been found. In Islam, at the beginning, Friday mosque and ruler's palace were next to one another, since the ruler led the prayers, there being no separate priestly hierarchy. And of course the ultimate assimilation of Church by State is in Socialist countries, where religion is technically irrelevant. In the Soviet Union, prior settings of Christianity and Islam were converted to secular uses, or became officially approved tourist spots, as with the churches of Kizhi in Karelia, the monasteries of Novgorod, and the mosques and *madrasas* of Samarkand and Bukhara.

The obverse of playing host to God within the palace is for the prince to reside in religious surroundings. We recall that the original focus of the Palace of Westminster was an abbey. The practice of establishing the royal household in proximity to a monastery which would also hold, or be close to, the prince's burial place is not unusual for the Middle Ages. It finds a late calculated exemplar in Philip II's Escorial, a day's journey east of Madrid, the last of a long line of Spanish palace-monasteries that starts in the 8th century.[20]

(2) The second possibility is for the priest to lay claim to the temporal realm, by fiat or after the fact. The bishops of Rome armed themselves with the dual authority of *sacerdotium* and *imperium* on the basis of the so-called Donation of Constantine, a document forged in the 8th century to show that the Emperor Constantine, at his conversion to Christianity, passed on to the popes imperial prerogatives, which they could therefore legitimately exercise in the West. To this day the Vatican is an autonomous entity within the Italian State, enjoying privileges of extra-territoriality.

The bishops of the Church and heads of abbeys claimed sovereignty over cities all through the Middle Ages and even later. The incidence of a town growing up around a substantial monastery is common enough in Europe, except Italy. English examples are Battle and St. Albans; the most famous Germanic example is Melk on the Danube, one of the few monasteries in Europe never to have been secularized. Even as the cities ventured to gain a degree of self-determination, the long dependence on priestly governance was reflected in the fact that the nascent city council met for a time in the main church, until an independent city hall made the separation of powers physically evident. In some cases, Lucca for instance, this did not happen until the Renaissance.

(3) The struggle of the secular branch to subjugate this rival power of religion when it asserted independent authority is a common theme of history. The rebellion of Henry VIII against Rome is a particularly blatant case. The resulting confiscation of Church property in the 1530s and 1540s radically, and permanently, altered land uses in London and throughout the realm. It also enabled the sovereigns of England to separate the royal residence from Parliament at Westminster, starting "their strange peregrination through their newly acquired ecclesiastical possessions . . . [which] led across Whitehall and St. James's Palace to Buckingham Palace, having gone farther afield, for a short time, to Kensington Palace."[21]

69 Melk (Austria); bird's-eye view by Leopold Schmittner after Franz Rosenstingl, celebrating the early 18th-century rebuilding of the Benedictine abbey. The dependent town lies below, in every sense in the shadow of the monastery.

The shift of balance from the one authority to the other is sometimes legible at the level of the urban form. Even when the priesthood is dominated by the ruler, the way of expressing this relationship may be quite revealing. Compare Mesopotamian cities with later Assyrian cities. In the first, the temple overwhelms the palace: the king is shown humbly lodged at the shadow of the ziggurat. In Assyrian Khorsabad, on the other hand, the king's palace turns the ziggurat into a mere appendage.

In the Christian world, the medieval examples of Ulm and Pisa illustrate the subversion of priestly rule. At Ulm, the first parish church was outside the city walls, subject to the abbot of Reichenau. But the present cathedral, built in the center of town beginning in 1377, was paid for by the citizenry and supervised by the city council. Unbeholden to abbot or bishop, it stood as the symbol of the city's independence. The famous cathedral complex at Pisa, which replaced the old one beginning in the later 11th century, was a monument to the victories of the maritime republic over neighboring Genoa and Lucca and the Muslims in Sicily, and a statement of the city's pretensions. That the bishop's palace was not integrated into the composition of this "ecclesiastical acropolis" (in the phrase of Braunfels) underscored its close relationship with the city government.[22]

But as a rule, the city had these two poles, the civic and the religious, separate and meaningfully counterposed. Whatever the political struggles that established their interrelationships, the two centers of a Classical city, agora and acropolis, together defined the public realm. In Western Christian cities, similarly, the palace of the king or of his authority and the palace of the bishop next to the cathedral stood as pendants, often at opposite ends of town.

149

TEMPLE AND TEMENOS

The unalterable anchor of the *temenos* or sacred precinct is the house of God—temple, church, mosque, or synagogue. This is rarely a lone building sitting in isolation within the urban fabric, even though skyline features may dramatize its singularity at long-distance. The planning of the precinct itself was usually a matter of organizing sequences of sanctity—entrance architecture, stairs and sacred ways, courts, buildings for various preparatory or complementary rites, the climax of the *sanctum sanctorum*. The grouping of temples in carefully planned relationships (New Kingdom Karnak, Roman Baalbek) recurs in most polytheistic cultures. Since the temple, as the house of God, was not meant to be entered by common folk, public places for open-air services, processions, or just plain gathering were important. Even where services were held indoors, outdoor gathering places like the atria of Early Christian churches or the *sahn* of an Islamic mosque were allowed for, commensurate with the rank of the sanctuary and the numbers of the faithful.

At the same time, more or less extensive facilities of treasuries, storerooms, and repositories indicate the economic and political clout of God's landscape in the city. In fact, God's estate was often prodigious: in Sumerian Lagash, for example, one-fifth of the city-state's territory belonged to the temple.[23] If physical contests and dramatic presentations were associated with the cult, as they were in ancient Greece, we will find settings like stadiums and theaters integrated in the planning of the temenos. The grounds might also include sheltering porticoes and pavilions, rest places, and overnight accommodation for pilgrims and for patients brought to the sanctuary to be healed. The temenos as a whole will often have its own boundary wall, and a series of territorial divisions within.

The Christian cathedral precinct had from the start a complex of buildings surrounding it: belltower, baptistery, bishop's palace, hospital, cemetery, and from the 9th century onward, especially north of the Alps, cloisters inhabited by the cathedral canons in accordance with the rule of Chrodegang of Metz, an uncle of Charlemagne.[24] In early Italian towns like Grado and Torcello, and in later ones like Parma, this loosely but powerfully assembled group is still legible.

Cathedral towns were seats of bishops. In England, in ten of the seventeen dioceses of the country during the Middle Ages, the bishop's residence was attached to a monastery, and his cathedral was at the same time a monastery church (e.g., Canterbury, Ely, Durham—though at Durham the bishop was also a secular ruler), at least until Henry VIII's dissolution of the monasteries. In most cases monasteries were there first, and the bishops came on the scene when the town was firmly established about them.

Christian monasteries were ample establishments, with their cloisters, preaching areas in the case of the Mendicant Orders, kitchen gardens and fields, and adjacent rental property. The origins of most monasteries were extra-urban, or else they could spawn their own settlement independent of a host city. Sooner or later these clusters were integrated into the urban fabric, occupying a generous share of space within the walls in contrast to the congested core. Cologne had no fewer than fourteen of these institutions in the 11th century. The union of a cathedral town with one or more monastery settlements was not uncommon. Reims married the monastic settlement of St. Remy; Augsburg joined the cathedral with the Benedictine monastery of Sts. Ulrich and Afra by means of a ceremonial axis, the Maximilianstrasse, in the late 16th century.

A walled enclosure sets off English cathedral-monasteries from their towns. In contrast, most Continental cathedrals are intimately embraced by the town fabric.

Shops or houses are built against their walls, or between their buttresses. Examples are St. Bavo (the Groote Kerk) at Haarlem and the cathedral of Ferrara. One *Pl.28* exception is Germany, where the cathedral, although in the center, is often walled to form a stronghold;[25] another is east central Europe, where castle *and* cathedral are sometimes joined within one wall on a high well-defended site (e.g., the Hradčany at Prague, Wawel Castle in Cracow). This latter arrangement is also typical in towns *57* established by the Teutonic Order in the Baltic provinces, such as Riga and Reval.

Among episcopal seats of the Christian world it was considered a matter of prestige to have as many churches as possible, dedicated to those saints germane to the city's history and associations. A symbolic arrangement can sometimes be inferred.[26] We are told that at Paderborn Bishop Meinwerk planned to install four religious institutions along the axes of the cathedral compound, which would constitute the four ends of the cross (two, to the east and west, were completed); and in cities like Hildesheim and Utrecht, "the most important ecclesiastical institutions unite into the form of a cross whose beams meet at the cathedral."[27]

GOD AMONG NEIGHBORS

Despite the prominence of the acropolis, the cathedral precinct, or the Friday mosque, the physical presence of God is diffused throughout the city. At the most intimate scale, there are the domestic shrines in every house, and roadside and crossroad shrines.

At a more public level come the buildings dedicated to neighborhood-specific cults. The crowded pantheons of polytheistic state religions allowed different deities to stake claim to individual quarters within the city. In Christianity and Islam, officially monotheistic, a kind of covert polytheism remained in the cult of saints.

70 *Canterbury (England), the cathedral precincts seen from the west. The surrounding enclosure is still clear today, when it consists partly of walls and partly of houses. Within is the cathedral, with the buildings of the former Benedictine monastery on the east and north. The archbishop's palace lay close by to the northwest. The northern end of the precincts is occupied by the King's School, partly re-using monastic and archiepiscopal buildings.*

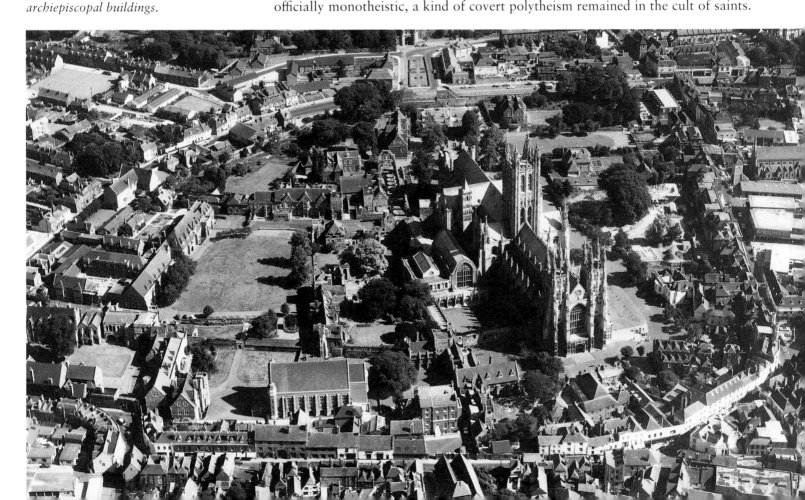

Lesser religious buildings across the city go up where they do for a variety of practical and symbolic reasons. Hephaestus, the god of anvil and forge, presided over the agora at Athens, with the area behind the temple taken up by the houses of his own craftspeople. In Rome, Minerva, the patroness of arts and crafts, was honored in the Forum of Nerva, which straddled the Argiletum, the busy thoroughfare running through the popular quarter of the Subura. Vitruvius goes into some detail on this matter. Mercury should be in the forum, he advises, Apollo and Bacchus near the theater, Hercules at places of physical contest like the circus and the amphitheater, and Venus at the harbor. The temple of Mars should be outside the city, because then, he says hopefully, "the citizens will never take up arms against each other, and he will defend the city from its enemies and save it from danger in war."[28]

In the context of urban divisions, the most useful role of the lesser cult building is to serve as the focus of a worshipping community small enough to be socially cohesive. The power of religion to organize the urban populace at the neighborhood level is a staple of the pre-industrial city. Two coherent systems of this organization are the Islamic neighborhood unit, especially the Ottoman *külliye*, and the Christian parish.

If the large Friday mosque of an Islamic town was the focus of the community as a whole, it was the modest district mosque which held together a group of townsfolk identified by the same linguistic, ethnic, or tribal affiliation. In Bukhara under the Timurids, for example, there were some 200 small mosques for the 200 wards into which the town was divided. Each ward or *guzar* had 30–60 houses, a mosque (often named after its builder), a school, and a water cistern.[29] In Old Delhi, the distinctive neighborhoods were called *mohalla* and were gathered around a mosque or a temple depending on whether the inhabitants were Muslim or Hindu.

The Ottoman *külliye* started as a container of Muslim culture, to be inserted in conquered Byzantine towns like Bursa, Edirne, and Constantinople. It was a way of keeping institutions of Turkish social, cultural and religious life aloof from non-Muslims. The word "*külliye*" means "the whole" or "collectivity." In physical terms, it was an articulated set of buildings—mosque, bath, school, almshouse, inn, hospital, etc. The ruler, and the rich and powerful subordinates, built the public buildings of the *külliyes*, and established endowments of money-making properties in order to maintain them.

THE CHRISTIAN PARISH

The parish is a worshipping community, and a social organization dedicated to the welfare of its members. It serves the need for the faithful to be baptized, hear Mass, and be buried; and for the Church to keep its buildings in good order and its priests supported, and to generate revenues for these purposes and its programs at large.

The origins of the parish are urban, since the Church in its first centuries of triumph was based in cities and governed by its bishops. The cathedral monopolized baptismal and burial functions, but was willing to delegate routine observances—Mass, confession—to subsidiary churches. The parish covered a vast territory, usually coincident with the city. This system survived in Italy until the late Middle Ages, in the sense that the churches of suburban and of rural communities remained directly dependent on the bishops, who had first claim to the tithes and taxes collected.

But with the dissolution of the Roman urban order, the focus in much of Europe shifted to the countryside. To organize the vast rural territories still only tentatively

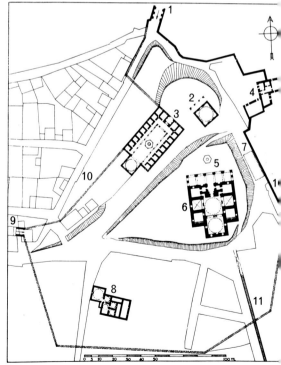

71, 72 *Bursa (Turkey)*, külliye *built by Sultan Yildirim Beyazit, 1398–1403. Above, view from the west, dominated by the twin domes of the mosque. Below, plan. 1 main entrance, 2 türbe (tomb) of Beyazit, 3 medrese (school), 4 palace, 5 fountain, 6 mosque, 7 soup-kitchen, 8 bath-house, 9 second gate, 10 perimeter wall, 11 aqueduct. (From Vogt-Göknil)*

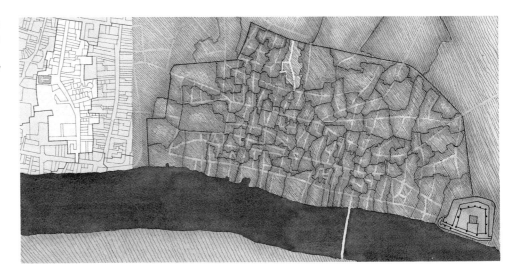

73 *Parish divisions within the walls of the City of London, and enlarged detail of the parish of St. Michael Bassishaw. Each parish is focused on a street; the boundary runs at the back of the properties.*

loyal to Christianity, hundreds of churches were built north of the Alps during the Merovingian and Carolingian eras, the 8th and 9th centuries, each one anchoring a distinct parish. The parish was now a small unit of pastoral care, centered on the church and its graveyard, its priest, and a fixed endowment, usually a *mansus* or glebe of about 30–40 acres (12–16 ha.). The priest was duty bound to keep a school open, for the teaching of religion and morals.

The church was a communal house. Here serfs were liberated to the pealing of bells, here justice was meted out by secular judges. The latter activity was expressly prohibited in France by the council of Liege in 1287, on the grounds that a place of asylum and protection could not reasonably be used to try criminals and assign often corporal, or even bloody, punishment.[30] The area of immunity also extended to the cemetery, and even further into the parish grounds, the limits being marked by crosses at street corners. As the council of Clermont declared in 1095, "If a person, pursued by an enemy, takes refuge next to a cross on the road, he will remain free as if he were in a church."[31] What is more, houses were built on church grounds in troublesome periods, protected by crosses against seigneurial justice.

The parish boundaries were irregular but critically important, since all those born 73 within them were entitled to benefits. The area was commonly the sum total of the lands from which the parish church received tithe.[32] In England, where the civil division into circumscribed villages probably preceded the building of churches, the integrity of the parish was reaffirmed at Rogationtide, the week before Ascension Day, by "beating the bounds"—a procession that made the circuit of the fields, as Elizabeth's order in 1559 makes clear: "The clergy shall once a year at the time accustomed walk about their parishes with the Curate and other substantial men of the parish . . . and at their return to the church make their common prayer."

Central to parish history from the 9th to the 12th century is the resistance of the Church to relinquishing control over this extensive rural network—and the aggressive campaign of feudal lords to secularize it. First in the countryside, away from the urban seats of bishops, and then within the cities themselves, parish churches began to be built by private initiative, as a revenue-producing enterprise; the priest became an employee of the lord. The town with many lords had many churches. This partly accounts for the wide disparity from city to city in the number of parishes. The situation in England is typical. By 1200, York had 40 parishes, Lincoln 50, London 100 within the walls. Some of these were tiny, comprising only a handful of households; others encompassed a huge urban area. John Evelyn wrote that "'tis prodigiously true, that there are some parishes [in London] no less than two hundred times larger than others."[33]

This struggle between the Church and lay communities continued beyond the age of feudalism, when a group of neighbors might be as likely as a castled magnate to own and administer a parish church. The *Kaufmannkirchen*, or merchant churches, of Germany come to mind. At the same time, with the tithes and taxes often diverted to the pockets of parish lords and priests, fraternities were organized to generate welfare funds. In a century or two parish fraternities, with parallel associations in crafts, began to be a potent force in organizing towns. Bakers might be associated with one church, tailors with another, merchants and shipmen with still others. Guild councils met in the church, at least initially. The strong point, however, remained the neighborhood, not the craft connection. Parishioners took part in feast days and processions, attended all burials, extended benefits to destitute members, and helped the unemployed.

It was during the 11th and 12th centuries that the Church launched a concerted, and ultimately successful, campaign to bring the parish structure under its centralized control, and to define its legal status. This happened first in a German city, Worms. It was divided into four parishes in 1016. The more difficult, and slower, task was to end the jurisdiction of lay parishes by persuading the magnates to turn over the churches in their ownership to bishops or well-established monasteries. Paris reorganized its parishes along these lines in the 12th–13th centuries, chiefly on the initiative of Bishop Maurice de Sully. By then a measure of uniformity began to be established by canon law for the entire Christian realm, which held firm until the modern period. This victory of the Church entailed some loss of face, and of power, for the great family communities of the Middle Ages. The memory of lay parishes was henceforth translated into the family chapels attached to the body of cathedrals and other major churches as subject units of God's unchallengeable rule.

THE CONTEST OF RELIGIONS

Changes in the state religion have major consequences for the urban form. The symbolism of conquest may require dramatic supersession. The cathedral of Granada was built on the foundations of the razed Friday mosque; on the other side of the Atlantic during the same period, the Spaniards were also destroying the chief shrine of another culture, the Aztecs of Tenochtitlán, and replacing it on an adjacent 254 site with the cathedral of the newly-named Mexico City.

255 A more level-headed adjustment is architectural conversion—the church becomes a mosque (Istanbul) or vice versa (Córdoba). But urban conversions are rarely that simple. For one thing, the hallowed precincts and rituals of some religions are place-specific and not easily interchangeable. For another, political reality or symbolism may force visible readjustments of accent within the urban fabric.

The promotion of Christianity as state religion of the Roman Empire in the 4th century is a case in point. When that happened, the cathedral often found itself, impractically enough, outside the city walls. This was so because it had to be raised over an empowering locus of veneration, often the tomb of the local martyr; and this martyrium was bound to be in an extramural cemetery, since in Roman times burial within the circuit of walls was proscribed. Or again, special circumstances, like the 4 installation of the bishop of Rome in the peripheral Lateran area by Constantine the Great, might create a disadvantaged urban start for the superseding deity.

74 *Quwwat ul-Islam, the first congregational mosque of the Muslim conquerors in India. It was begun in 1199 to serve their new settlement, Lal Kot, one of many predecessors of New Delhi in the plain near the Yamuna River. The portico is made up of fragments from pre-existing Hindu and Jain temples; the great victory tower, the Qutb Minar, bears inscriptions proclaiming its purpose to spread the shadow of Islam to east and west.*

Two possibilities would then exist for the city form. Either it would reorient itself to accord with the new religious center, as happened in Milan or Trier, or else it would relocate the cathedral in a more central location by solemnly translating the relics of the martyr, or demoting the original cathedral in favor of a newer church in the thick of things.

When takeover is not thorough, as it was from paganism to Christianity, but rather in the nature of coexistence, the city will develop more than one special district for God. Multifaith cultures like India find to their considerable pain that such accommodations are not easy. The same is true with the case of Jerusalem, *Pl.10* which Muslims, Christians and Jews have had to share in the past, and must again now.

The story of this city is especially instructive. We have, at the earliest phase of its history, the hallowed center of the Jewish commonwealth, with the Temple as the only religious focus. Then, the Romans under Hadrian destroy the Temple, and establish the Roman state religion in its place. With the triumph of Christianity two centuries later, the tomb of Jesus, the Holy Sepulcher, becomes the focus of the city. In the 7th–8th centuries, Islam plants the Dome of the Rock and a Friday mosque on the precinct of the Temple Mound. Finally, the Jews return after the Second World War to reclaim a fragment of the Temple grounds, the Wailing Wall, as their legitimate locus of veneration. Today almost the entire town of Old Jerusalem is a carpet of overlapping sanctities.

THE SEPARATION OF CHURCH AND STATE

To approximate in our own times the authority of religion within a pre-industrial context, we would have to single out fundamentalist Muslim states like Saudi Arabia, Iran, and Pakistan. Throughout the modern world, with such rare exceptions, the presence of God has been systematically isolated from the affairs of humans. Religion is now a matter of conscience, not of law.

In spatial terms, the consequence of this radical diversion of God's sway has been to contract the temenos and interiorize the temple. Once, the cult building spawned designs beyond itself. Entire cities, the land itself, formed religious compositions of great force. The account of Etheria, the virgin of Galicia, who visited Jerusalem about 385, vividly conjures how the entire region, with the valley of Kedron and the mountains on the other side and the small towns roundabout, was turned into a sacred landscape during Holy Week. More recently on the North American continent, the same dedication of settlement pattern to a higher design could be felt in the New England township that was conceived in its totality to be the blueprint of a covenant with God, or in Brigham Young's Salt Lake City, laid out as the City of Zion to shelter the Chosen People until the Second Coming.[34]

Modern societies have tended, since the Age of Enlightenment, to turn away from the notion of an extended sacred terrain in favor of a pluralist, laic order. In the industrialized West, the determination to organize human life into isolated functions and assign to each one its own physical setting made God's space a specialized realm, while it separated workplace from residence. The public realm once accented by the cult building saw a spectacular new monumentality of tall office buildings and department stores, massively overwhelming the landscape of God. Where steeple or minaret still rule, they rely on laws to protect their visual prominence—or else they advertise the stubborn backwater remnants of a world that is no longer there.[35]

PAGUS MERCATORUM

One of the most insistent explanations for the existence of the city has been trade. Market theories of one sort or another have buttressed discussions of urban origins, from Pirenne's *faubourg* to Kristaller's central place theory and Jane Jacobs's more recent *The Economy of Cities*.[36] We should therefore expect that where merchants are established in a city, where business is conducted, will be a critical assignment.

Indeed, there is ample proof in history that the merchants' quarter had privileged standing in the urban structure—excellent allotment of land and often substantial accommodations. In new towns of the Middle Ages, for example, the merchants were given the prime lots around the square, before the rest of the urban land was assigned to settlers. Merchant houses were well-heeled, often grand. And a whole range of business-related buildings—guild halls, warehouses, markets, exchanges—survive to prove that even before the modern period those who occupied the city in order to make and sell goods were capable of a monumental celebration of their activities.

Trade was the central economic concern of cities only until the Industrial Revolution; thereafter, manufacturing and service activities become increasingly important, and the nature of the business district changes radically. This is not to say, of course, that there was no other occupational area beyond the commercial in pre-industrial cities. Pottery making, tanning, and the cloth industry had their own areas, usually at the city edge. For the manufacture of textiles especially, entire districts existed in cities of Flanders, North Italy and England. In the 17th-century planning of Amsterdam, a large area in the west (later known as the Jordaan and Leyden districts) was spaciously laid out as a workers' district, with houses and factory buildings like tanneries, mills and dye works.

But the distinction I am making is above all quantitative. As Marc Girouard points out, at its productive peak, in the mid-14th century, Florence was making 80,000 pieces of cloth a year; in the 1850s one warehouse alone in Manchester had a turnover of 100,000 *bales* of cotton cloth.[37] The very rationale of cities changes because of manufacture after 1800; we enter a period based on systematic mechanization, and on mountains of paperwork coincident with this new volume of industrial production. New towns are now born for a specific industrial or manufacturing purpose—mill towns, mining towns and others that are often planned by the company itself.

MARKET TOWNS

For the moment, however, our focus is on the pre-industrial world. And the simplest case for the environment of trade is the unwalled town that was born or created exclusively for the exchange of goods. Market towns were, by their nature, small: if they prospered and grew, they also diversified. In Europe many survive little changed since their origin in the Middle Ages. They are called *bourg* in France, *Flecken* or *Marktstadt* in Germany. The logic of their placement is two-pronged. It responded to local and regional patterns of communication, and to the presence of fortified strongholds, be they ecclesiastical or secular.

Often there was nothing to these towns but a string of houses along a single, wide street expanding in the middle—the marketplace itself. The street market might extend its activities to a secondary street crossing it at right angles; or to streets parallel to it. Or else the market was a triangle or a rectangle of open space at the meeting place of several roads. In the towns of the dukes of Zähringen in Switzerland, the market square stretched the full length of the town, and was extended as the town grew. This elongated marketplace was subdivided by means of public fountains, so that a variety of market activities—the vegetable market, the cattle market, etc.—could take place at the same time, each within one of these frames.

In China market towns developed around temples, the manors of landowners and merchants, and around manufacturing facilities, like ceramics works. They also materialized at important transport nodes like bridges and the crossing of waterways, and where a resident working population at a military camp or an arsenal attracted them. Some were deliberate plantations. Many never amounted to anything more than a handful of houses and a few shops.[38]

In Tudor and Stuart England there were about 760 market towns, 50 more in Wales. Some of them—Gloucester and Bristol for example—were founded well before the Conquest. The towns came at intervals of every few miles, and were centers for the distribution and sale of agricultural produce. Each had its official market day or days, as well as periodic fairs. In the larger market towns, trade was dispersed into specialized areas like the "horse fair" and "cornhill." The towns also possessed shambles, where fish and flesh were sold, and shops with wooden pentices in front stretching out several feet into the street. Under this projection, shoemakers and tailors sat at trestle tables, and worked under the public eye.[39]

HOSTING FOREIGN MERCHANTS

We should, at this stage, distinguish between retail trade and wholesale trade. The first was by and large a center-city phenomenon; it was in the open market of the town, and in shops along streets that emanate from it, that the townspeople bought staples and products of local craft. Special goods—spices and wine and luxury items of various sorts—came from overseas through the agency of merchants who traveled across the country along protected routes. The exchange took place outside the walls, before the city gates; or in specially designated areas within, where the foreigners who managed long-distance commerce found a home away from home.

To the extent that this long-distance trade is geared to port towns rather than the high road, I discussed its waterfront environment in "The City Edge." In such towns urban space is assigned disproportionately in favor of merchants. The strand is their

75 *Chipping Campden (England), a purpose-built medieval market town. An island of buildings gradually grew up in the wider central area, including the market hall of 1627.*

stage. Warehousing districts are a common feature, from the *horrea* of Roman cities to the long, corrugated-iron godowns of Singapore and Haiphong—although between the end of the Roman Empire and the late Middle Ages this building type disappears, and goods are stored in cellars and vaulted ground-floor rooms of merchants' houses, and in inns and consulates.

Cities felt ambivalent about their foreign lot—strangers who were willing to be away from their homeland for long periods of time, and whose ways were alien to the local population. Their activity was openly mercenary, and so gave offense to the pretensions of the nobility, the clergy and the learned class that there is more to life than making money. Christian dogma proscribed usury, and was suspicious of financial transactions. The consequences of this antagonism were exclusionary and restrictive quarters, and special arrangements of self-rule independent of the laws of the host city.

In the Middle Ages, urban territoriality was exceedingly important to foreign groups. These were called "nations," and what they needed was places in which to worship, to warehouse goods, and to arbitrate their own disputes so as not to be bound by local authority—which meant consulates. "Nations" were trade associations and social clubs in one; membership in them was obligatory.[40] For the necessary interaction of merchants and bankers, a place of exchange was often provided. The *loggia dei mercanti* of Italian cities like Bologna or Siena sometimes fronted on a little square. At Bruges it was the Beurseplaats, on which stood inns and consulates.

Beyond this public presence, there was the matter of housing. Separate districts for foreign merchants were intended to insulate the local citizens from unfamiliar customs and habits. The result proved quite the opposite in the case of Russia, where an early 17th-century influx of Protestant merchants and professionals sparked a campaign by Moscow's Orthodox zealots to protect the city from heresy. All foreigners were evicted in 1652 and forced to relocate to a new quarter on the banks of the Yauza River, well outside the city walls. By century's end the contrast with the old town was startling. Instead of Moscow's rustic mix of solid timber houses, muddy lanes, shops and hovels, was a stately town in the European manner. Here young Peter the Great was introduced to broad straight avenues, planned squares, well-built brick homes with large windows and ornamental gardens: a notion of civic order which would be restated in his new capital city of St. Petersburg.[41]

Moscow was not alone in hosting a throng of immigrant businessmen. Merchants of the Hanseatic League had their own distinct, by which I mean legally defined, quarter—in London, Bergen or Novgorod. This, the so-called "steelyard," was outside the taxes and tolls of domestic markets. In Constantinople during the late Middle Ages there were some 60,000 Italians—Genoese, Pisans and Venetians. They had their own district across the Golden Horn, called Pera; it remained the European quarter all the way to the 20th century.

THE MARKET AND THE STATE

Concessions to foreign merchants were anomalous to the ways of local trade, which was conducted under the watchful eye of the State. It supervised where and when business would be conducted, and by whom. Government maintained a strict monopoly on precious commodities like salt and silk; it determined and controlled measures and weights. It regulated guild activity, and set rates for tolls and taxes. In regard to urban form, this zealous supervision proved justified. The fact is that

76 Bruges (Belgium), Beurseplaats, as it appeared ca. 1640; from A. Sanderus, Flandria illustrata (1735 edn.). Inscriptions identify the establishment of the Genoese merchants to the left, that of the Florentines to the right.

77 Como (Italy), Palazzo del Broletto, dated 1215. The name comes from brolium or brolum, *a fenced-in area. The open arcade on the ground floor provided a sheltered trading area within the larger market square; the upper room served as town hall and law court.*

unless regulated, merchants will appropriate any public space for their purposes. The attempt by Christ to rid the Temple grounds in Jerusalem of merchants and their stalls was no senseless display.

In the inner city, a central open space was traditionally set aside for the conduct of business—whether it is the Greek agora, the Roman forum, or the medieval 149 marketplace. The space might be irregularly defined or be given an architectural frame of uniform porticoes. In the early imperial capitals of China—e.g., Chang'an 158 (and following Chinese prototypes, those of Japan, like Nara)—the markets were inscribed rigidly on the two sides of the central ceremonial axis. As commerce grew during the later T'ang and Sung dynasties, from the 8th century onward, a slow revolution can be detected toward a more open system of trading. Some of its features, as Skinner summarizes them, were: (1) a relaxation of the requirement that each county could maintain only one market, which had to be located in the capital city; (2) the breakdown and eventual collapse of the official marketing organization; (3) the disappearance of the enclosed marketplace, along with the walled-ward system (about which more later), and their replacement by "a much freer street plan in which trade and commerce could be conducted anywhere within the city and its 189 outlying suburbs."[42]

Even in more democratic set-ups, the Greco-Roman cities and the medieval communes of the West for instance, the conduct of business was only comparatively free, though the control was supposed to be self-administered. Symbolic of this partnership between the public and the private interest, government and business shared the same open space, the same civic container—even the same building. The message here was that to do business was a privilege of being a citizen. Remember, for example, the medieval combination of town hall and market, a type that takes us from the medieval Broletto in Como all the way to Boston's First Town House. 77

Sometimes the town hall stood in the middle of the public space, creating interconnected market and civic squares (e.g., Como, Siena). In towns where the bishop was lord (prior to the liberation of the burghers), and the market took place before his church and under his jurisdiction, the two institutions often continued to occupy the same public space.

The physical relationship of the civic and the commercial realms was primarily a political and social issue. But there was also the matter of decorum. At certain moments of history, the activities of government and trade were seen as incompatible, and planning decisions were taken to keep them clearly apart. In the Greek world it was Aristotle, in the 4th century BC, who insisted that civic forum and market be separate: the Athenian agora underwent some major tidying up about then to delimit the commercial scene. Rome at this time began to distinguish its Forum Romanum, where the Senate held forth and public meetings took place, from the noisy profiteering of business, and a series of specialized markets—the Forum Boarium, the Forum Pescatorum, etc.—were started some distance away.

The early Renaissance boasts some rare instances in which the town square, which had routinely doubled as the marketplace in many medieval towns, sought a more exclusive dignity. In the new towns it founded in the 14th century, Florence began by establishing market privileges for the town square, but subsequently moved the weekly market to a designated field outside the town walls, the so-called *mercatale*. In the later towns like Giglio Fiorentino the extramural market is part of the original plan, as the town square becomes monumentalized for "functions associated with the administration and representation of the Florentine state."[43]

161 London's authorized markets—as distinct from informal street markets initiated by vendors known as costermongers—were nearly all established by royal charter. The charter for Covent Garden, granted to the Earl of Bedford by Charles II in 1661, defined the market area and what could be sold there, and endowed the Earl's heirs with the right to enjoy the market's profits in perpetuity. By the early 19th century London could boast an impressive array of specialized marketplaces that included Mark Lane for grain; Smithfield for livestock; Aldgate for meat; Billingsgate for fish; Covent Garden, Spitalfields, and Southwark's Borough Market for vegetables; Newgate and Leadenhall for meat and vegetables. This retail structure differed from that found at the time among major Continental cities, and indeed in other English towns, in that there were no large-scale general markets.[44]

THE ENVIRONMENT OF TRADE

What were the appointments of the marketplace? It is possible to recreate the picture for Western Europe in the Middle Ages from documents and surviving artifacts. The *77* town hall with market-related activities on the open arcaded ground floor has already been mentioned. The official market building in the English market towns was, in fact, interchangeably called market hall or town hall; its other functions are indicated in alternative names like guildhall and courthouse. Generally erected in *75* the open space of the market, the multipurpose building would often shelter a row of shops along one end. There was a statutory obligation to provide a "common beam," with the accompanying weights and measures. The architectural accommodation for daily buying and selling was fairly basic. The emphasis was on the temporary installation, or the temporary use of multipurpose structures. In the present town centers, one can sometimes detect an echo of this market structure in a narrow island of row buildings found astride a central stretch of the High Street, adjacent to the market cross.[45]

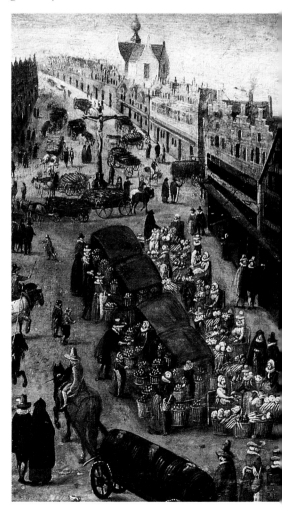

78 Antwerp (Belgium), booths set up in the Meir, the major east-west street of the town, late 16th century. In the background is the market cross—unusually, in the form of a crucifix. Houses fronting this commercial street have shops on the ground floor.

79 *Ypres (Belgium), the Cloth Hall, mainly 13th century. Here market activities were combined with the functions of town hall, law courts, prison and chapel. The building's civic importance is proclaimed by its belfry.*

The market belfry was a separate building that functioned as the rallying point for burgesses in the towns of Flanders. It was an impressive landmark, at times the most prominent of the city. At Ypres the belfry was 70 meters (230 ft.) high, at Ghent 91 *79* meters (298 ft.), and at Bruges 100 meters (328 ft.). A statue of Roland was a common fixture of Germanic town markets, the symbol of the peace of the city (*Stadtfried*); *301* examples are at Riga and Bremen. Among the public buildings of this core of commerce were the merchants' hall (*Kaufhaus*), often combined with the town hall, a corn hall, the cloth hall (*Gewandhaus*), and also sometimes a salt house (since the town held a monopoly of this substance), and a meat hall.

Hygienic conditions in halls used for the sale and storage of foodstuffs were appalling by today's standards. A Napoleonic campaign for sanitary markets transformed the building type in France at the start of the 19th century; the Market and Fair Clauses Act of 1847 did the same for England. The great glass and iron market structures of the latter half of the century were the result. One of the earliest and most imposing examples was the Halles Centrales in Paris, begun in 1853, and *Pl.14* designed by Haussmann's life-long friend Victor Baltard. Of the fourteen pavilions originally projected, twelve were built, the last two in the 1930s. Each was a specialized produce market, linked to the others by a grid of streets roofed by glazed vaulting. This "Exposition Universelle of victuals," as it was described, spawned a legion of imitators throughout the world.[46]

But commercial activity obviously was not confined to the marketplace or the closed market building. Linear extension along adjacent streets was the rule, be it in Pompeii, Ningpo, or Budweis (Česky Budějovice). The common pattern was to have the shop on the ground floor and the shopkeeper's lodging above. Apprentices and *Pl.28* employees used the work- and sales-space as their sleeping room.

Occupational grouping seems to have been standard practice in most cultures. To *Pl.1* this day street names all around the world imply an arrangement of like businesses along the same street or groups of streets—the Rue des Cordonniers (shoemakers' street), the via dei Baullari (trunk-makers' street), Wheelwright Lane, Färbergasse (dyers' street). In medieval Ningpo the colorful street names included "Bamboo-dealers' Alley," "Medicine-shops Lane," and "Southern-style Food Alley."[47]

In the case of Europe, however, current research is suggesting that we may have placed too much faith on toponymy. The tidy functional array of trades might have been reflective more of the wishes of town government (and perhaps the example of the Middle-Eastern bazaar which the Crusaders made known) than of reality. Where documentation has been pieced together, the results are ambiguous. In Kiel during the late Middle Ages, for example, no shoemaker lived on Shoemaker Street: five shoemakers were neighbors in the Hassstrasse, five lived near the city wall, and three elsewhere. Only a few trades were tied to specific locations, and this for reasons having to do with topographic advantage. Proximity to water was essential to fishermen and tanners. Ropemakers used the town moat as ropewalk. The demands for humid storage spaces for wool and fiber, and for ample natural light for weaving, directed weavers to sloping sites, where one side of the house could be dug into the hillside and the other be open to the day. In the words of the best current student of urban toponymy in Germanic lands, Johannes Cramer, "The city at the end of the Middle Ages was ordinarily not physically organized by trades; on the contrary, the majority of trades was arbitrarily distributed over the city space."[48]

224

What is more certain is that during the Middle Ages, especially in northern Europe, the functional specialization of districts was connected to guilds. Members tended to live within the precinct of the guildhall. Guildsmen alone could occupy shops; foreigners and others could trade only in the open market place.

301

Guilds are actually an almost universal feature of the pre-industrial city. We know them in Babylonia and Assyria, in Greece and Rome, in Tenochtitlán and the early Hindu cities. Their concerns were the maintenance of a monopoly over their own economic activity (including the selection and training of personnel, the control of the product, and the fixing of prices); the welfare of members; arbitration in internal disputes; and representation in public ceremonies. At Coventry, for example, the processional order established in 1445 for the Corpus Christi and Midsummer rites was based on occupational groups ranked according to the number of civic offices held by each.[49]

The system of guilds, which was meant to provide solidarity and security for the artisan, craftsman and merchant, could also be a stifling social device. Many new towns in the Middle Ages and later lured merchants and artisans with assurances of a "free" market. Guilds in Moscow's pre-Petrine period lived and worked in the *Chernyie Slobody* or "Black Settlements," from which the modern Russian word for "freedom," *sloboda*, is derived. The etymological associations are somewhat misleading. In fact, the inhabitants of these districts were earmarked for special taxation.[50] Feudal lords who built the castle towns of Japan in the 16th and 17th centuries attracted a business component with the offer of liberal, open working conditions. But it was customary for the *daimyo* to take the merchants with him when he moved the location of his headquarters. This dependence was expressed physically within castle towns, where merchant and artisan quarters were lodged between those of the lord's inner circle and an outer zone of lesser vassals.[51]

Chinese guilds coexisted with, and were arguably less important than, native-place associations. A craft or a business was usually the preserve of people from the same provenance. In the city of Hangchou, for example, carpenters, cabinetmakers and medicine dealers came from Ningpo, tea and cloth merchants from Anhwei, opium dealers from Canton, etc. In Beijing alone in the late imperial period there were close to six hundred native-place associations. Each of them had its own mortuary where bodies were kept until the bones could be sent to the ancestral home for burial; poorer members of the association were buried in ground which was a substitute for native soil.[52]

80 opposite *Isfahan (Iran), plan of the mile-long* suq *connecting the 11th-century congregational mosque at the north to the new Maidan-i-Shah district created in the 17th century. It follows the ancient trade route leading south from the old city toward the river. The circulation spine is domed throughout its length and lined with shops, grouped according to the type of goods sold. At intervals, arches give access to caravanserais, medreses, bathhouses, mosques and storage areas. A cluster of caravanserais borders the Maidan to the north; to the south is the Shah's Mosque; to the west the site of the palace.*

THE CASE OF ISLAM

A dual arrangement of the *pagus mercatorum* was operative in Islamic cities. The town center was the focus of commerce, and there the guilds were in charge. A secondary commercial quarter, known in the Ottoman period as *taht al-Qala* ("under-the-citadel"), developed when power was ensconced in a fortress at the urban periphery. This site was a natural for horse markets and the makers of arms, for transport industries and grain markets.[53]

But the classic locus of trade was the linear market system called the *suq* or bazaar. The *suq* is organized strictly by categories of business, and almost all are encompassed except the selling of fresh food stuffs and livestock, which is done out of doors. From documents, it seems that there was a hierarchy to this organization, in relation to the public buildings the *suq* connected. Beginning at the mosque, you had candle and incense sellers first, along with booksellers, bookbinders, and vendors of small leather goods; then the general textile and clothing markets, except for furs and precious textiles like silks which had their own separate, secure building within the market called the *kaissariya* or, in Turkish, *bedesten* (the Western equivalent may be something like London's Burlington Arcade); then came furniture and household goods; finally, close to the city gates, you had things relating directly to long-distance commerce—ironmongers and smiths, and sellers of saddles and bridles, tents, baskets, and other such necessities for the caravan trade. There were also specialized bazaars for things like grain and brassware. The *bedesten* would be deployed along a main street, as in Algiers, or within a loose business grid of relatively wide, open and regular streets, as in Istanbul. It included the *saga*, or market for currency exchange, situated close to the Great Mosque. This explains the frequently central location of the Jewish quarter.

One of the chief features of the Islamic business district is precisely this coordination of local and long-distance activity and the weaving of it all into the urban fabric. In the main cities, the bazaar complex contained, besides secure strongrooms and occupational *suqs*, *hammams* (baths), *khans* or caravanserais for the traveling merchant, inner mosques, and fountains. The Kapali Carsi (covered market) in Istanbul, for example, had 60 streets, over 3,300 shops, 20 *khans*, a fountain for ritual ablutions, several small mosques, two *bedestens*, and even an open public place or *maidan*. These non-residential business premises, then, were in reality total social entities—which makes a telling contrast to our own shopping malls, where by and large you only shop and eat.

These great systems of trade are now largely obsolete, except as picturesque spots for the tourist in search of native bargains. The bazaar has been superseded by the department store and the shopping district in the modern sections of the old Islamic towns. In the Soviet sphere, the lively bazaar stretches of Samarkand, Khiva and Bukhara were closed down and replaced by government-controlled consumer cooperatives in the 1930s. Only in the *kolkhoz* markets, where farmers with private plots sold their produce in an officially tolerated exception to the principles of Socialist economy, did the bazaar find a sympathetic commercial substitute.[54]

THE BUSINESS DISTRICT OF CAPITALISM

In the Soviet Socialist system, retailing was a State monopoly, and therefore competition, if it existed at all, was perfunctory. The location of the shops was quite unimportant. The limited number of retail outlets and the scarcity of supplies guaranteed that consumers made the rounds of all retailing sites.[55]

The organization of the capitalist business district in the West proceeds from very different premises, and also represents a fundamental shift from the prevailing order of the pre-capitalist city. At issue is the treatment of urban land as a source of income, an attitude that first becomes manifest in the 16th century. Land ownership in the medieval city was mainly functional; the lot was held by the burgher as if in trusteeship, and was intended to provide a living, not to enhance one's personal wealth. Where you were in the city had to do with your guild and other systems of association.

Unfettered mercantilism and industrialism changed the emphasis to an economic view of urban land, which began to be appraised for its rent-productivity. To raise its value, an impression of preferred location had to be created. The merchant might now move his work premises, and even himself, out of his house, and rent the property. His behavior, multiplied a thousandfold, made a suburban location desirable as residence, and a downtown location desirable as workplace. This land-rent gradient, as urban geographer J. E. Vance, Jr. puts it, "ended the idea of the ordered city and economically encouraged the *segregation of uses*."[56]

This grossly synoptic view—one that presumes to encompass several centuries and a world geography—cannot do justice to the range of complicated physical adjustments the capitalist city went through. A fuller history of the modern retail landscape would have to include the great merchandizing revolution of the 19th century that led to the department store. Early models have been sought in the so-called bazaars of London, from the 1830s and 1840s, large buildings where individual retailers could rent stalls; the European and American arcades; and the amalgamation of urban property by individual retailers like Aristide Boucicaut of the Bon Marché in Paris, and in New York R. H. Macy and John Wanamaker. At least in the case of Paris, we have a fairly clear picture of the devastating effect of the *grands magasins*, those resplendent new consumer palaces geared to national and

81 Chicago (Illinois). Commercial vehicles and streetcars tangle at the junction of Dearborn and Randolph Streets in the Loop, ca. 1909.

82 *The towers of Lower Manhattan, New York, ca. 1975.*

83 *The American central business district under attack from expressways, encouraged by the pressure of cars and mid-century policies of "urban renewal."*

international markets, on the traditional *quartier* economy of local making, selling, and dealing.[57]

The triumphant installation of a commercial urban core was nowhere more pronounced than in the American city. As the middle- and upper-middle-class residential component withdrew to quieter sectors further out, their premises were appropriated by business or taken over by those lower down on the social scale. What had been the town itself in earlier days was transformed into an intense and more and more exclusive *pagus mercatorum*, with single-purpose concentrations *Pl.13* like a financial district, a specialty shopping district, and an administrative district.

The phenomenon of the CBD, the central business district, should not be taken for granted, however familiar it has since become. There was nothing quite like it in Europe, especially from the moment when the tall building came of age in the 1880s. Chicago's Loop or the aggregate of Lower Manhattan gave the CBD a sort of *81,* monumentality that rivalled what was once the privilege of the authentic public *82* realm of faith and government. The crude competitive assembly of tall buildings "is not an architectural vision," Montgomery Schuyler wrote in 1899, "but it does, most tremendously, 'look like business'."[58]

If the central business district wore its compactness like a badge of success, it could not indefinitely find room after 1920 for the new automotive shoppers and their vehicles. As a first step CBD streets were widened, to relieve congestion and to increase taxable values. But the more lasting relief came with the strip. The American strip has been described as the "linear disposal area for surplus urban energies."[59] These arterial streets, like *suqs* of the age of Ford, host business machines and equipment, supermarkets and eateries for suburbanites, and, of course, the sale and maintenance of automobiles. The first city and suburban strips followed old commuting routes of trains and streetcars. In the Thirties and Forties the strip hit the highways. Today it settles as well at the freeway interchanges at the city edge, where shopping malls and office parks find congenial posts.

84 *The towers of La Défense, seen from central Paris. This CBD at the city edge began to be developed in 1956, to accommodate post-war growth without destroying the city center. The buildings were to be erected along government guidelines by private enterprise, which has pressed for greater height, density, and freedom from design regulations.*

The city center of office towers is no longer an exclusive North American specialty. But cultural circumstances are sufficiently idiosyncratic wherever the model is being installed to cancel any thoughts of universal urban behavior. The American pattern has been mirrored to a certain extent by London's first generation of office towers which crowd the City's financial center. Continental highrise business centers, on the other hand, have largely avoided monument-laden city centers in favor of sites on the immediate urban periphery, especially those contiguous to railway terminals: Montparnasse in Paris and Vienna's Franz-Josef 84 Terminal are examples. Second-generation European CBDs—La Défense in Paris and London's Canary Wharf—rise beside ring highways, much in the manner of American edge cities. Finally, it must be noted that the passage of pre-industrial, Third World, and Post-Socialist cities to one of these Western configurations is not simply a matter of time. Superficial similarities should not obscure the truth that "both the processes and the forms of urban growth are, to some degree, culturally specific regardless of the rates of growth and modernization."[60]

KEEPING APART

Upon being asked his advice by the Lord of Huan regarding the organization of housing in cities, the Chinese philosopher Kuan-tzu replied:

> The scholar-official, the peasant, the craftsman and the merchant . . . should not mix with one another, for it would inevitably lead to conflict and divergence of opinions and thus complicate things unnecessarily. . . . Let the scholar-officials reside near school areas, the peasants near fields, the craftsmen in the construction workshops near the officials' place, and the merchants in the *shih* (commercial wards).[61]

Two thousand years later—in 1910 to be exact—Viennese architect and planner Otto Wagner wrote:

> We may consider it axiomatic that the administration of a great city [i.e., a metropolis] demands its division into wards. The situation and boundaries of the

85 *An impression of the tower houses of medieval Bologna (Italy). Many were erected in the 12th and 13th centuries by noble families as urban counterparts of their rural castles. They embodied class consciousness, and they also served as fortresses in the struggle between two rival factions in the city. The resulting chaos was eventually controlled after the rise to civic power of the merchants and craftsmen in the mid-13th century.*

86 *The twenty* arrondissements *of Haussmann's mid-19th-century administrative reapportionment of the city. Numbering starts with the Louvre quarter northwest of the Ile de la Cité.*

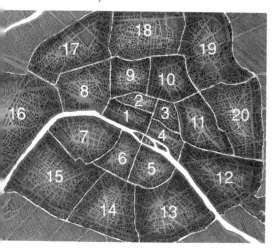

wards or boroughs form the foundation of the systematized regulation of the great city.[62]

These far-ranging prescriptions point up two fundamental truths about the making of cities. One is that some system of division must be installed for the population at large if the city is to function properly. The other is that this system will fulfil multiple purposes—and will be based on a variety of social groupings. The administrative need is obvious: we have to be taxed, policed, counted in time of census, and effectively provided with services. Yet Kuan-tzu's concern is also abiding. Urban divisions segregate groups whose cohabitation might result in serious conflict. He singles out occupational differences. Deeper sources of conflict are likely to be cultural—religious, ethnic, linguistic.

The system of division is rarely simple. Most urban populations are subject to overlapping jurisdictions. Take medieval Siena. The basic tripartite structure, the *terzi*, represented the three settlements that were involved in the synoecism of the 7th century—Città, Camolia and S. Martino. To the extent that topographic features had separated the original villages, the *terzi* might be said to have a physical identity. Each *terzo* was subdivided into overlapping lesser districts—*contrade, popoli* and *lire*. The *contrade* are known outside Siena today for their competition in the Palio, *Pl.18* the famous twice-yearly horserace held in the Piazza del Campo, at the meeting point of the *terzi*. They are territorial divisions, now seventeen in number (of which ten, drawn by lot, compete); originally there were more than fifty, and they had military as well as administrative significance.[63]

And one more introductory point. Administrative arrangements and those that are based on economic or cultural segregation are not always discrete options. It is often the case that an initial grouping of the urban population according to geographic origin, clan structure, or ethnicity may attain in time the legal force of administrative boundaries. But it is also the case throughout history that an administrative reapportionment may be resorted to by urban authorities intentionally to break up and dilute cultural nucleation which may have grown too incestuous or self-sufficient, to the detriment of a general, citywide order.

The Rome of Augustus and the Paris of Haussmann furnish us with two well-known exercises of administrative assertion. Pre-Augustan Rome had a four-part division—Suburana, Esquilina, Collina and Palatina—which ultimately went back to the tradition of the four ancestral tribes. Augustus's promulgation of the fourteen *regiones*, pie-shaped administrative units with the Palatine at the center, had two interrelated aims: to wipe out older, less neutral allegiances; and to annex the suburbs or *pagi*, terminating the semi-independence and inferior status of this large fringe belt.

Haussmann's enemy was the *quartier*, the long-lived, independent-spirited neighborhood fabric of old Paris, several times renamed and regrouped in the 18th century but never dissolved. Even the establishment in 1795 of twelve *arrondissements*, dependent municipalities with their own administrative apparatus, proved innocuous. Haussmann's twenty *arrondissements*, each subdivided into four 86 *quartiers*, encompassed a much broader scheme that took in the suburban belt of the *banlieue*; meantime, the historic neighborhoods were also being strapped together, their involution deflated by ramrod *percées* that yielded spacious boulevards. The city of Paris itself was overwhelmed in the regional frame of the prefecture. To Haussmann this was a critical development. The old city, the commune of Paris, had its own fiercely proud mythology. The new Paris subordinated this independent identity in the name of an administrative superstructure.

BARRIERS VISIBLE AND INVISIBLE

The landscape of urban divisions is in the main invertebrate. Crossing from one borough of a modern city to another, or from one parish to another in pre-modern days, there are no walls to breach, no gates to negotiate. Historically, material enclosure in the design of urban populations has been the exception.

Some instances of walling-in as a physical form of discrimination against ethnic or religious minorities can be cited. In Hellenistic Antioch, for example, there were two separate quarters each with its own wall—one for the Greek settlers, the other for the native Syrians forcibly transferred from their villages to the new city.[64] During the Reconquista of Spain, the Christian liberators, if they did not expel Muslim residents outright, confined them to a walled quarter called the *moreria*. The policies of James I, King of Aragon, as they pertain to Valencia are documented.[65] Upon the city's fall, James designated fifteen urban districts, and a sixteenth for the Jews. The initial plan was for the Muslims to share the town, and a protective wall was resorted to in order to separate them from Christians. The wall ran close to the cathedral and to two public roads. In the end, the Muslims were settled inside a walled suburb, which, James had to make clear, was in fact to be considered as being within the city.

Less justified in terms of inter-ethnic or inter-racial conflict are walled partitions for the urban population at large. The earliest instance I know of is in the Hittite capital of Hattusas. The lower town was divided into three walled neighborhoods, connected to each other through gates, each with a temple and fountain as a civic center.

Two better-known episodes involve the cities of ancient Peru and those of pre-T'ang China. The Peruvian paradox is of orthogonal walled compounds in cities without defensive walls. In the Chimú capital of Chan-Chan, near modern Trujillo, is a loose assembly of eleven unequal residential compounds within high walls of adobe brick, impenetrable except for tiny entrances. At Huanuco Pampa, a walled compound of fifty buildings at the edge of the main plaza may have been the quarter of *aklla*, the Inca women responsible for the manufacture of cloth and the native

153

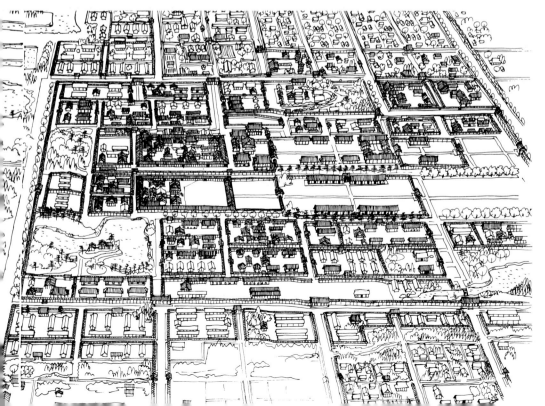

87 Heijo-kyo, now Nara (Japan), laid out on the Chinese model in the 8th century: imperial palace and northern blocks of the city, seen from the west. The palace area (centrally placed against the north wall as at Chang'an) consists of a series of walled compounds surrounding the inner palace. The city as a whole was divided into more than a thousand walled units. There were nine "zones" running east-west; each of these was divided into eight "quarters" by streets running north-south; each of those quarters was in turn subdivided into sixteen blocks; and each of those was divided into sub-units. (From Nishi and Hozumi)

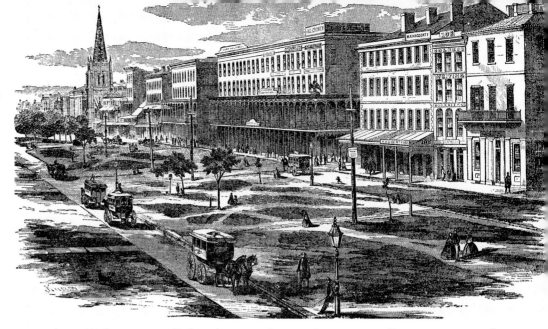

88 *Canal Street in New Orleans (Louisiana) was laid out after 1803 to separate French and American quarters, on ground formerly used as a common. A planned canal came to nothing, but left its name. The no-man's-land was beautified in the late 1850s, as this contemporary print shows, through the efforts of Judah Touro, a prosperous businessman, who paid for landscaping and for a fronting row of commercial buildings decorated with cast iron (center).*

maize beer.[66] The great walled enclosures of Incan Cuzco, according to accounts of the Spanish conquerors, should be associated with individual reigns: at the death of an emperor, his descendants and their families chose the seclusion of such a fortified tract for their communal existence.

The Chinese walled ward system is the strictest mechanism known to history for the regimentation and control of townsfolk. It had a life of several centuries, from the Han Dynasty (206 BC–AD 220) up to about 1000, and was exported to Japan. 87 The wards were called *li* at first, and there was considerable variation in size and occupancy. It was at Lo-yang, the capital of the Northern Wei Dynasty (495–534), that the city plan was first based on wards of uniform shape and size. "Each ward," a source tells us, "has four gates. At each gate there are two wardens, four sub-officials, and eight guards."[67] These gates were closed in the evening and opened in the morning, at fixed hours and to the beating of drums set up on the main avenues. Entrance was forbidden to non-inhabitants.

The disintegration of the walled ward in the period between the T'ang and Sung dynasties is attributed to the flourishing of trade. Commerce, once confined to two wards exclusively, burst its bounds. Shops, with their backs to the ward walls, appeared along main streets. An active street life undermined the internalized ward 189 system and the segregation of the commercial and residential spheres. The fixed schedule of movement in and out was abandoned. "For two decades," Sung Min-ch'iu wrote in 1071, "the sound of street drums has never been heard at all."[68]

When they do not rely on built barriers, urban divisions can assert themselves through less clearcut but equally effective devices. These include topographical features like rivers, ravines, and the modern penchant for the vertical segregation of hills and flatlands. "In most American cities," Grady Clay writes, "the richer you are, the less likely you are to confront the sinks."[69]

On level ground, the segregative power of transportation lines is acknowledged in the all-too-real fate of living "on the wrong side of the tracks." And literal isolation by means of empty spaces is as effective today as it was at the height of colonialism, when a verdant open belt was used to separate the European and native communities. A more urban format for the same idea is to have an exceptionally wide boulevard between neighborhoods that are meant to stay apart. A famous 19th-century example in the United States is Canal Street in New Orleans, 88 established as the boundary line between the established Creoles of the French

Quarter and the newly arrived Americans. The median of this gash-like, overscaled thoroughfare was called "the neutral ground," which, Peirce Lewis explains, was "a geographical recognition of the armed truce between Creoles and Americans."[70] (The phrase is now part of Orleanian patois meaning the median strip of any boulevard.) Modern city-planning came to rely on the radial avenue as a convenient divider in urban extensions. Wagner himself, in his *Grossstadt* proposal of 1911 for an open-ended expansion of Vienna, separated self-contained districts for about 100,000 people each by broad boulevards.

Pl.25 But it is in the intricate texture of Islamic *medinas* that we find, perhaps, the most inherently natural urban divisions. The dividers are the few through-streets of the *medina*. The residential units are ethnic neighborhoods, called *hara* in Cairo and Damascus, *hawma* in Algiers, *mohalla* or *pol* in India. They come about through the initial distribution of the townsfolk, or through subsequent migration. This migration can be by individuals and families over a period of time who seek their own kind according to the conventional urban behavior of Islam; or else by homogeneous migrant groups—military units, members of a ruling class, trans-ferred populations, or refugees—who arrive en masse.[71]

Except for Iraq, the form of these residential units in all Islamic cities is closed and inturned. Once within the neighborhood through a small entrance on the divider street, you are in a dim, private world of cul-de-sacs, and an architectural texture of
188 blind walls, arcades, overhangs and covered bridges. Here only one major street, by no means regular, forms a circulation spine. All or part of this unit might be sealed off at night with heavy gates at the points where the spine connects with the outside. In Ottoman Cairo and Aleppo nearly 50 per cent of the entire street network consists of dead ends. Open spaces are mostly to be found in the interior courtyards of the dwellings, and in the unplanned expansions at the junction of two or more alleys. In the *pols* of cities like Ahmedabad, the back walls of the houses either form the boundary of the neighborhood or else they are shared by the houses in the next *pol*. If there are shops at the edges of the *pol*, they face outward toward the spine at street level, with living areas facing inward above.

The population of the Islamic neighborhood was socially mixed, and in the absence of municipal government, self-reliant. The Indian *pol* is perhaps the most systematic in this respect. A *pol* council raised funds (entrance taxes from new members, annual membership fees, a percentage from the sale of a house), put issues to the vote, and oversaw the execution of public projects. Community approval was required for buying or renting property. Noncompliance with *pol* rules resulted in some form of ostracism: you were refused access to community facilities, excluded from community events, and received no assistance in time of family crisis.[72]

CULTURAL SEPARATION

Religious and ethnic isolation is based on the fundamental invariables of roots and beliefs. Since cities are rarely able to maintain a population that is pure in ethnic background and also unified in faith, and since patterns of intermingling are fragile at best, the incidence of fracture is a standard trait of urban behavior.

Now obviously ethnicity and slums are often related. But I am here emphasizing the segregation that comes about because of who we are, not primarily because of how much we make. Jewish ghettoes and Chinatowns were congested, rundown districts where some very rich people lived. They could not associate with their economic class, even if they wanted to: there were bars against it, not only privately drawn up covenants, but public laws as well.

The most fateful of these segregated quarters was the Jewish ghetto. The ghetto may have started as a preference of association, as with other "nations," but at some point it became coercive. By the 13th century, beginning in England and central-eastern Europe, Jews were subjected to geographic confinement. (There may be an even earlier chapter in the Byzantine Empire.) In other Western countries, France for example, segregation was never enforced by law, but had a voluntary basis. In the Muslim world, the Jewish ghetto, characteristic only of certain towns in North Africa (Fez came first) and Yemen, did not appear until the 15th century.[73] On rare occasions it would be walled in, and an uncharacteristically high density would then ensue, as it did in Rome where the walling of the ghetto came as late as the 16th century.

The main problems were the Jewish faith, and the issue of usury—both points of strong antipathy particularly in Christian states. The religious scruples were mutual. While Muslims feared that ritual uncleanliness might be visited on their mosques should Jews be allowed to commingle freely with the faithful, and were offended by Jewish refusal to segregate and seclude womenfolk, the Jews for their part feared the desecration of the Sabbath by Muslim or Christian.

The segregation was social, and obviously did not apply to business. On the contrary, Jews were invited in by rulers anxious to spur on trade, as the Este did in Ferrara in the 15th century. To afford them protection, they were sometimes settled next to the ruler's citadel. More commonly they were relegated to unpromising urban land. It was not rare for the Jewish ghetto to be moved or eradicated when its location proved desirable to the host city. This happened at Marrakesh and Constantine, for example, but also in the West. In Würzburg the Jewish community which had enjoyed the special protection of the bishop was expelled in 1348, the ghetto was burned down, and the burghers' city church, the Marienkirche, was built in this cleared area. The ghetto in Nuremberg lay between two independent parishes, in the lowlands of the Pegnitz River. It was obliterated in 1349 and made over as a marketplace.[74]

Total containment of the Jewish community was a Nazi obsession. Laws concerning interaction of Polish Gentiles and Jews were drafted in Berlin while the Eastern campaign was still in progress, and in October 1939 the first ghetto of the occupied zone was created in the city of Piotrków.[75] Over the next two years the process was repeated in urban centers throughout central Poland. Ghettoes were usually established in run-down districts, reenforcing the pretext that these were measures to quarantine a population likely to spread epidemic diseases. It was a self-fulfilling prophecy. As the entire Jewish population was packed into arbitrarily delimited slum quarters—in the case of Warsaw at a density more than fifteen times greater than that of the city at large—disease ran rampant.

Łódź's ghetto, created in February 1940, was in the district of Baluty. It was an area outside city jurisdiction until the inter-war period, and so had been built up without sanitary services or regard to public safety. "The only thing that distinguished the ghetto from the provinces," writes a contemporary observer, "was electric lighting."[76] Here, as elsewhere in Poland, isolation was cultural, hygienic, and economic. Nazi directives restricted free trade to that within the ghetto: purchases of food from the outside were paid for by Jewish labor organized by the local Council of Elders. The border crossing of the two worlds was at the fenced-in square on the Baluter Ring, which accommodated Jewish administrative offices and a disinfection station for those few outsiders—mostly police officials—who were permitted entry. To insure complete insulation from the rest of the city, three makeshift pedestrian bridges were constructed across the major arteries that cut 89

89 Łódź (Poland), *during the Nazi occupation. Jews enclosed in the ghetto cross a through-road by bridge, which prevents contact with Poles and Germans outside.*

through the ghetto. But not even this level of sequestration could satisfy the Nazi compulsion, and by 1942 the "resettlement" to concentration camps had begun.[77]

Exclusion can also start innocuously, through planning instruments such as building ordinances. So the herding of Chinese began in the 1880s in California, when laundries were banned from ordinary neighborhoods as a public nuisance. Since laundries were the main source of livelihood for the urban Chinese, as well as their social centers, the effect was to drive them into several blocks of the less desirable urban land, where they were forced to create those externally picturesque but internally appallingly overcrowded streets we call Chinatown.[78]

The Chinese episode illustrates one of the causes for the demographic pluralism of cities—immigration. America, as a country of immigrants, knows the vicissitudes of this procedure very well. It is the background of the Little Italys and Polish and Irish and more recently Vietnamese neighborhoods, of Cuban Miami and the vast, as yet unincorporated, expanse of Hispanic East Los Angeles.

The incidence of immigrant concentrations is universal. The North American pretense of "a melting pot" is exceptional. In Southeast Asia, the presence of Chinese and Indians since the 19th century in cities like Rangoon, Singapore and Bangkok was overpowering. In Rangoon by the early 20th century, native Burmans were in the minority, with the Indians accounting for over half of the population. These alien Asians were no less segregated than the ruling minority of whites. When Sir Stamford Raffles founded Singapore in 1819, he made provision for the influx of Indians and Chinese, and their separation, by designating areas for them south of the Singapore River, with the government area and the residential quarters of the Europeans on high ground from this riverbank to the Rochore River, and the Arabs to the northeast, close to the Malay Sultan's compound and the mosque.[79]

A principal motive for the arrival of alien groups is of course work, specifically small trade and unskilled labor; hence they have little claim to a choice segment of the urban frame. Long-distance commerce, as we saw, also created pockets of alien culture in the midst of cities. But those "nations" were by and large privileged pockets, allowed a considerable latitude of self-government.

90 Chinatown in San Francisco (California): the junction of "Dupont Gai," now Grant Avenue, and California Street, ca. 1908. The area was rebuilt after the 1906 earthquake by local architects, who combined standard modern techniques with Chinese allusions such as the pagodalike roofs.

The most dramatic mixture of peoples occurs through conquest. Overnight, a society of long-established patterns finds itself under the thumb of a foreign power, commonly of an entirely different cultural makeup, whose institutions and people have to be accommodated within the old fabric. There is a range of possible solutions, from the intimate cohabiting of the two cultures to total apartheid. It is not unusual for the conquering power to move from one of these extreme positions to the opposite as the occupation becomes permanent.

New Spain progressed from segregation to assimilation. In the early phase of the occupation, separate towns were laid out for the conquerors and the subject people. The *pueblos Indios* were placed at some distance from the *pueblos Españoles*, except in cases where the need for a large native labor force could be met by satellite towns or peripheral *barrios*. Indigenous quarters, by law, were denied any semblance of social stratification. Within the gridded Spanish settlement, in contrast, a strict gradation was maintained, with the elite classes of pure Spanish blood in the center, on or adjacent to the main plaza, and *mulatos* at the city edge or accommodated in subsequent extensions of the grid. But by the 18th century, the vast mixed population of *mestizos*, *mulatos* and others had invalidated the policy of monoracial towns. Thoroughbred Spaniards became so rare that proximity to the main plaza was now a privilege of wealth, not race.[80]

The case of South Africa demonstrates the reverse path. In the early towns of the Dutch and the British, the non-European population of slaves, servants and workers lived right alongside their masters. It was in the second half of the 19th century that perceived threats to the health and welfare of the Europeans lent force to a growing segregationist sentiment. Until the end of the century strict residential segregation was deemed impractical or unenforceable. Then Cape Town was the first city to designate a mandatory location for Africans, followed by Durban, Port Elizabeth and Johannesburg in the first decade of this century. Soweto was born in 1904.

The new native townships were first explained as way-stations, where Africans could learn Western ways before being allowed to mix residentially. The assumption here was that environment modifies behavior. But the draconian prescriptions of the Group Areas Act of 1950 systematically separated African, Indian and Colored people from one another and from the white minority. The divisions were made permanent through buffer strips and fences, and enforced through an elaborate construct of *apartheid* law.[81] To achieve this, massive demolitions in previously mixed residence zones were undertaken, and African areas too close to the center, which the whites reserved exclusively for their own use, were evacuated and razed. The most notorious instance of the latter policy was the 91 clearing of Johannesburg's "Western Areas"—Sophiatown, Martindale and Newclare.[82] The policies of apartheid were ruthlessly applied; they were extended to mining compounds and labor camps as well.

THE MODERN COLONIAL CITY

Johannesburg fits one model of the colonial urban experience: the European city, in this instance, came first, and the problem of locating the non-white population needed to be addressed in the initial stages of planning. To be sure, such cities were often laid out on the sites of existing settlements, but indigenous villages and rural clusters around religious shrines or palaces were judged insignificant by colonists for whom cultural value was synonymous with monumentality. Haiphong was built over a native citadel village and its surrounding market settlements, Rangoon on the site of the Shwe Dagon Pagoda and neighboring Buddhist monasteries.[83]

91 A scene in Sophiatown, outside Johannesburg (South Africa), after its destruction in Fall 1959.

92 The area of Delhi as it stood in 1857, before the "Mutiny"; drawing by A. Maclure. The walled city of Shahjahanabad is intact. The Red Fort stands beside the river; on axis beyond it is Chandni Chowk, a street lined with water channels and trees. The Jama Masjid rises on a height to the left. Outside to the north (right), on the ridge, is the British cantonment; a few villas are scattered nearby. This remained the civilian area until the creation of New Delhi, to the south, after 1912.

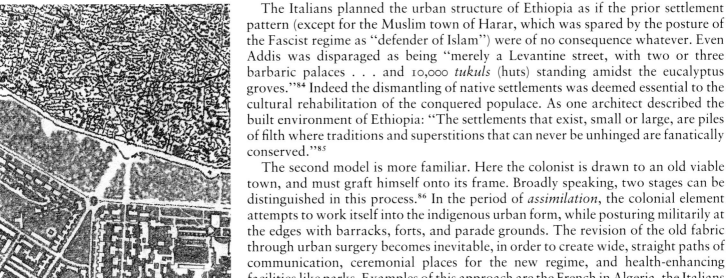

93 *The meeting of Shahjahanabad, or Old Delhi (north) and New Delhi (south). The two are separated by the walls of the Mughal city and a band of open space, the Ramlila ground, acting as a* cordon sanitaire. *This part of New Delhi, around Turkman Marg, was designed as a residential district for low rank government workers. The street pattern is radically different from that of the Islamic city.*

The Italians planned the urban structure of Ethiopia as if the prior settlement pattern (except for the Muslim town of Harar, which was spared by the posture of the Fascist regime as "defender of Islam") were of no consequence whatever. Even Addis was disparaged as being "merely a Levantine street, with two or three barbaric palaces . . . and 10,000 *tukuls* (huts) standing amidst the eucalyptus groves."[84] Indeed the dismantling of native settlements was deemed essential to the cultural rehabilitation of the conquered populace. As one architect described the built environment of Ethiopia: "The settlements that exist, small or large, are piles of filth where traditions and superstitions that can never be unhinged are fanatically conserved."[85]

The second model is more familiar. Here the colonist is drawn to an old viable town, and must graft himself onto its frame. Broadly speaking, two stages can be distinguished in this process.[86] In the period of *assimilation*, the colonial element attempts to work itself into the indigenous urban form, while posturing militarily at the edges with barracks, forts, and parade grounds. The revision of the old fabric through urban surgery becomes inevitable, in order to create wide, straight paths of communication, ceremonial places for the new regime, and health-enhancing facilities like parks. Examples of this approach are the French in Algeria, the Italians in Libya (e.g., Benghazi or Tripoli), and the British in their early days in India.

During the second stage—*association*—the European element is largely removed from the old city, isolating the indigenous population within its walls. A new city is built next to the old, the two separated by a green belt, or at the very least a broad avenue.[87] The English colonial city made a further distinction between civil and military institutions: the civil station and the cantonment. The civil station had its cricket ground and the chummery where single males lived. The cantonment was an extravagantly spacious enclosed area, separated from the rest of the city. In the French colonies, the planning of one of Madagascar's provincial capitals, Fianarantsoa, in 1900 marks the beginning of this "dual cities" approach.[88] European districts had a regular network of wide tree-lined boulevards, parks and playgrounds, country clubs and hospitals, and the ubiquitous villas or bungalows on their ample plots of land.

The unbuilt zone insulating foreign from native quarters is called in French the *cordon sanitaire*. As the name suggests, this form of segregation was rationalized as a hygienic measure, especially after 1899 when the relationship between malaria, mosquitoes, and their habitat of stagnant water was confirmed. British settlements in Asia and Africa established as the ideal a minimum separation between white and

94 *Meknès (Morocco), ca. 1925. The old walled town is on the left. Europeans at first lived on its eastern edge. To the right, on a ridge (as at Delhi,* opposite), *is the military camp, and beyond it the incipient "ville nouvelle," laid out but scarcely begun.*

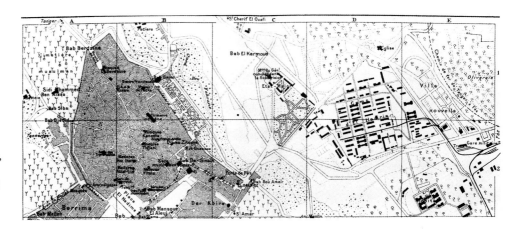

indigenous districts of 1¼ miles (2 km.)—the average flight distance of the *anopheles* mosquito.[89] Health precautions aside, this generous divider also served a critical military role, permitting the rapid mobilization of troops in case of native unrest.

94   The development plans for the Moroccan *villes nouvelles* of Fez, Meknès, Marrakesh, and Kenitra (later Port Lyautey) by French architect-planner Henri Prost in the 1910s and '20s wedded military camps to the *cordon sanitaire* to appease the tiny minority of colonials in these provincial towns, while in the thriving port cities of Casablanca and Rabat the isolation belt was abbreviated to the width of a boulevard.[90] The scheme evolved by Prost, under the Resident General Hubert Lyautey, also represents this second "associative" phase of colonialism's most articulate policy of conservation.[91] The isolation of the native town, Lyautey argued, safeguards a historic artifact, maintains traditional social structures, and, by encouraging tourism, produces economic benefits. He wrote:

> Large streets, boulevards, tall façades for stores and homes, installation of water and electricity are necessary [for Europeans, all of] which upset the indigenous city completely, making the customary way of life impossible. You know how jealous the Muslim is of the integrity of his private life; you are familiar with the streets, the façades without opening behind which hides the whole of life, the terraces upon which the life of the family spreads out and which must therefore remain sheltered from indiscreet looks. . . . All the habits and all the tastes [of these two ways of life] oppose one another.

URBAN DIVISIONS

Cities have traditionally set aside districts of specialized use, distinguished spatially and architecturally from their teeming surrounds. Earliest on the roaster are the lofty premises of palace and temple, sometimes occupying overlapping turfs, with fortified bounds reinforcing the assertion of god-given authority. The particularities of commerce and industry are evident in the geography of their urban appropriations. Manufacture has often found its home on the outskirts, where air, water and open land come cheap, and where city tariffs can be evaded. In contrast, market quarters have focused trade—and in the vertical extrusions of the central business district, its finance and management—downtown. Capital's claim to the heart of the city is countered by the American Civic Center as well as its Soviet Socialist counterpart, both paeans to the inflated administrative requirements of the 20th-century metropolis.

Pl. 10 Jerusalem from the southeast, a carpet of overlapping sanctities. First, Jewish: on the platform in the foreground stood the Temple. Then, under the Romans who destroyed the Temple, pagan. From the 4th century, Christian: the Holy Sepulcher Church, top left, stands on the presumed site of the tomb of Christ. From the 7th century, Muslim: Arab conquerors, for whom Solomon's Temple was a holy place, installed the octagonal Dome of the Rock and Al Aqsa congregational mosque on the Temple Mount, and next to the congregational mosque built their palace (its ruins are visible far left). And, since the Second World War, Jewish as well once more, as refugees streamed back to pray at the Western or Wailing Wall, a stretch of the substructure of the Temple platform (left, center).

The realm of trade

Pl. 11 · The Islamic bazaar: Kapali Carsi, the Covered or Grand Bazaar in Istanbul (Turkey), comprises some 60 streets, over 3,000 shops, 21 khans, 5 mosques, fountains, and a school, all in a zone that was locked up at night. The higher domed areas (far left) are bedestens, *for precious goods, the larger of them dating back to the mid-15th century; the "streets," or* suqs, *were rebuilt after a fire in 1546. The taller red-roofed building within the complex is a mosque.*

Pl. 12 · An occupational grouping: the tanners' quarter in Marrakesh (Morocco) occupies a traditional site, in the shadow of the city wall. Unlike wholly self-selected groups, tanners, with their smelly vats, tended to be pushed to the city edge or beyond.

Pl. 13 The American central business district: Lower Broadway, New York City, c. 1880. The street is already non-residential; buildings are getting higher, especially the headquarters of Western Union, whose web of telegraph wires gave an exhilarating sense of modern bustle to the scene. Local businesses paid to have their names participate in this graphic fortissimo of commerce.

Pl. 14 The market: Les Halles, Paris, 1885. The site had been a market since the Middle Ages. Growing concern for hygiene in the 19th century led to the construction from 1853 onwards of the finest of all iron-and-glass covered markets, by Haussmann's friend Baltard; each of the specialized pavilions (there were eventually twelve) had gas light and running water.

French officials went to great lengths to establish that their dual cities program was motivated by conservation and not racial segregation, an aspect of British colonial policy they disparaged. And in fact Lyautey never imposed ethnic or national restrictions on who was allowed to reside in the *villes nouvelles* or in the *medinas*. Natives simply had to "adapt to our customs," in the words of Prost, if they wanted to inhabit the European districts.[92] By the 1920s they had done so by the tens of thousands in Morocco. Colonial administrators could proudly take credit for the new residential mobility of North African Jews, who had up to this time been confined to a segregated quarter with gates that were typically locked at night.

Yet underneath the civilized intentions of this paternalist policy lurked a revised form of discrimination. The indigenous residents of Lyautey's European districts were wealthy elites able to afford the spacious detached villas stipulated by land-use regulations. Moreover, Prost's plans failed to account for the results of a surging migration of rural people drawn by the shift from a rural to an urban economy. Courtyards and rooftops were soon pressed into service to house newcomers to the *medinas*, where conservation-oriented building policies forbade highrise construction.[93]

French colonial administration in North Africa and Southeast Asia sidestepped outright apartheid and replaced it with class discrimination. The result was a *de facto* system of racial segregation, one made more insidious by its superficial appeal to progressive ideals of equal opportunity, public health, and cultural conservation. It was a formula that reflected social realities that were not unique to the colonies, as noted by the French planner of Hanoi and Saigon, Ernest Hébrard:

> Every European district needs a native district in order to survive; it will provide indispensable domestic servants, small businesses, and labor. . . . [These districts] correspond, in essence, to the business districts and working-class residential neighborhoods of our own modern cities which are, in truth, separated from the bourgeois neighborhoods without a definite line being drawn on a map.[94]

Pl. 15 The Civic Center of San Francisco, built at the instigation of the popular Mayor James Rolph, Jr., to proclaim the city's recovery from the catastrophic earthquake of 1906, is typically American in combining administrative and cultural buildings. Planned by Edward Bennet, a partner of Daniel Burnham, it reflects the formal, classical ideals of the City Beautiful movement. The domed City Hall was won in competition in 1912; around it in the group are the Public Library, State and Federal Office Buildings, Civic Auditorium, Opera House, and Veterans' Auditorium. Such an ensemble would, it was argued, form "a rallying point for the city's life. Here the best impulses may crystallize, inspired by the noble character of the edifice, into devoted action for the public good." (Watercolor by Jules Guérin, 1916)

ECONOMIC SEGREGATION

Divisions based on economic disparity are in some ways the newest. It is true that the general organization of the pre-industrial city did place the elite in the center of town, close to the administrative and religious institutions, while the lower classes—artisans and unskilled laborers—and the outcasts were pushed further out. But since, historically, the economic reality of many towns was for the poor, having few other options, to live off the rich—or to put it in more purely Marxist terms, for the rich to exploit the poor as servants, clients or renters—the two domains were interlaced.

That spatial order changed in the capitalist world of the last three or four hundred years. In the West the main challenge came from members of northern Europe's burgher class, who tended to seek one another's company in houses surrounding the town square. These leading citizens, many of them prosperous merchants, were sometimes referred to, in French documents, as *placiers*, from *place* or square. In time the rich, both titled and bourgeois, came to favor environments which would allow them more generous grounds. Heers points out a very early example, the Rue Neuve in Bordeaux, of the 1300s, built as an exclusively aristocratic street of *ostaus*, large noble houses with gardens.[95]

158

In Italy it took much longer to make socio-economic segregation acceptable. The alternatives were made explicit by Alberti, who took no sides. He wrote:

> There may perhaps be some who would like better to have the habitations of the gentry separate by themselves, quite clear and free from all mixture of the meaner sort of people. Others are for having every district of the city so laid out, that each part might be supplied at hand with every thing that it could have occasion for, and for this reason they are not against having the meanest trades in the neighborhood of the most honourable citizens.[96]

A setting similar to Bordeaux's Rue Neuve, based on wealth pure and simple, rather than the loose commonwealth of the clan, would not be seen in Italy for another *178* hundred years. The classic example is Genoa's Strada Nuova, which dates from the 1560s (see "The Street," below, pp. 192–93).

But these pioneering projects were the exception. Spatial sorting of the classes became the norm only through a slow and fitful process that started at the scale of the individual lot.

Where city centers were amended to accommodate higher densities by building over the cores of the blocks, residences on the exterior were by far the most desirable by virtue of their greater access to light and air. They commanded the highest rent, and were accorded by developers the most elegant rooms and spacious layouts. Such were the circumstances of the apartment buildings that proliferated in mid-19th-century Stockholm, Berlin, and Frankfurt. The German versions were known as *Mietskasernen*, "rental barracks." First developed by Frederick the Great to house soldiers' families, the dense complexes placed the well-to-do behind elegant façades and the poor around dim courts as narrow as 4.5 meters (15 ft.) wide—the minimum size for access by fire-fighting equipment.[97] Berlin police administrator and city planner James Hobrecht claimed these buildings fostered social integration; reformers condemned them as legalized slum housing.

Class segregation within buildings could be vertical as well. The pattern originating with the medieval mercantile house, and evident in Continental European apartment blocks built as late as the 1930s, put commercial uses on the *Pl.34* ground floor and elite households in the first story above the street level—the *piano nobile*, as it is called in Italian.[98] Amenities diminished with longer climbs up the stairway, so that the poorest lodgings and servants' rooms were found in the bleak garret with its incongruously pleasant rooftop view.

Broader patterns of segregation were also, until around the mid-19th century, patchy in complexion and intimate in scale. A localized geography of urban wealth based on streets of well-to-do houses was by far the most common. It was codified architecturally in the spare Neoclassical elegance of the Georgian terrace and the Parisian Restoration-era apartment building. Within the stylistic elements of the latter, a system of decoration can be discerned "whose function it was to express the social level of the city's various streets," according to François Loyer.[99]

The first full demonstration of the modern extremes of what geographers call "residential differentiation"—the conversion of social distance to physical distance—was seen during the 1830s in the recently industrialized northern English town of Manchester. There the explosive success of mechanized textile production triggered a flood of migrants looking for mill jobs that could triple what might be earned in agricultural work.[100] Subdivided and badly-maintained houses in the old town, along with jerry-built speculative rows tucked behind commercial buildings on the newer periphery, provided cheap accommodation. Warehouses and factories expanded to a scale nothing short of monumental. Industry debased the quality of

95 The "two nations" meet in Victorian London, as imagined by Punch in 1884. A clergyman and his ladies are investigating the conditions of the poor. One of the East End boys cries out, "'Ello! 'Ere's a Masher! Look at 'is Collar an' 'At!"

life in town while escalating land values. Affluent Mancunians needed little persuasion to sell off an urban residence at a profit in order to indulge the new craze for the suburban villa. Engels described the result: a city "peculiarly built, so that a person may live in it for years, and go in and out daily without coming into contact with a working people's quarter or even with workers."[101] Knowing his role as polemicist, we need to question the absolute accuracy of Engels's observation. The point that matters, nonetheless, is that the general perception existed in Victorian England of a divided city—a city of "two nations," as reformist debates would 95 phrase it.

Communities of exclusion

The spectacular transformation of the spatial and social blueprint of English industrial cities attracted widespread notice at a fateful moment. Cholera made its first deadly rounds of Europe in the 1830s, and newly invented techniques of medical cartography revealed a frightening affinity between pestilence and the patterns of crowding, poverty, and immigrant populations. Flight to the suburbs might remove privileged families from immediate threat to physical health. But what of the *social* afflictions of the poor? It was believed that without the civilizing presence of the better classes, an undifferentiated proletariat would succumb to the inclinations of the lowest in their ranks. The waxing of "infidelity and Socialism" in Manchester was explained as an inevitable consequence of the city's abandonment by the well-off.[102]

Reformist approaches to "the social question" were motivated by both altruism and the specter of contagion. The sanitary housing movement that swept Europe and America in the late 19th century was no exception. It addressed, and to its enduring credit helped relieve, the urban misery that was the Industrial Revolution's unanticipated product. On the other hand, the development of class-specific housing for the "worthy poor" served to refine the system of spatial segregation established by earlier bourgeois residential development. Solidly-framed neighborhoods of subsidized housing, like the London County Council's pioneering Millbank Estate of 1897–1902, furthered the ongoing compartmentalization of the various strata of the poor, a process that has been singled out as "the most dramatic change in the social geography of 19th-century cities."[103]

Of course the way working-class housing developments are deployed, and to what effect, has everything to do with the political context in which they are initiated. Municipal Socialism, with its dedication to the needs of a local working class, has one of the best track records. The Gratte-Ciel of Villeurbanne, France—a jazzy highrise ziggurat of low-cost flats, completed in 1934 and hailed as a populist triumph—was the product of such an administration. Vienna's monumental crop of inter-war housing estates was also the harvest of a Social Democratic city council. There the determination to wrest the provision of shelter away from the private sector and to treat it like a public utility, heavily subsidized by higher-income users, produced 60,000 new dwellings between 1920 and 1934. The policy also gave shape to one of the most remarkable working-class landscapes of the 20th century: the imposing sequence of housing blocks along the Gürtel, Vienna's outer ring. It was dubbed the "Ringstrasse of the Proletariat," and became a potent icon for "Red 96 Vienna."

Planned enclaves for the working class have also served less philanthropic ends. Rome's Fascist regime threw up a total of twelve *borgate rapidissime*, suburban enclaves of low-income housing, in the 1930s as part of a program of social control. All were situated on isolated peripheral sites, many near military or police barracks.

96 "The Ringstrasse of the Proletariat": a Viennese image contrasts a young working-class family in front of the Ernst Reumann Hof, one of the largest public housing developments along the Margaretengürtel, with members of the bourgeoisie promenading on the inner Ringstrasse.

The underlying logic was to prevent the urban poor from coming into prolonged contact with one another, thus reducing the risk of organized resistance by the Left.[104]

Rather than isolating a marginalized laboring class through relocation to distant suburbs, post-war public housing policy in the United States has confined the poor by making sure they stay put in the inner city. Chicago's Robert Taylor Homes of 1962, the largest public-housing project in the world, provides a compelling case study. Its location, stretching some 2 miles (3.2 km.) along the Dan Ryan Expressway in the heart of the city's so-called "black belt," was dictated by various strategies, all of them political, many of them shameful. As has been noted by Katharine Bristol, a recent student of American highrise public housing, the use of Federal funds to buy costly inner-city redevelopment sites rather than cheaper, unoccupied suburban land virtually dictated the construction of high-density residential slabs in order to keep the final cost-per-unit within reason.[105] From the politician's point of view, the required construction methods provided extra potential for patronage in the form of big building contracts. By using the structure of low-income housing to perpetuate segregation, both economic and racial, elected officials avoided the wrath of suburbanites, and kept a carefully composed mechanism of voting districts intact.[106]

The twenty-eight 16-story towers of the Robert Taylor Homes acknowledge the dead-end of planned residential differentiation. Today they contain America's poorest census tract, #3817, and are ruled by the economics of addiction and the doctrine of hopelessness. The conditions are not unique to American social housing. The violence and looting in 1985 at London's Broadwater Farm Estate, an award-winning complex of the 1970s, attests to a similar malaise in Britain. On the 97 Continent, the *grands ensembles* of the 1960s and '70s that ring Paris, Lyons, and Marseilles among others are home to growing concentrations of unemployed non-white French and immigrant laborers. Fear of what is there called the "Americanization" of the urban periphery—that is, its transformation into a highrise ghetto landscape—was bolstered in 1990 by four consecutive days of rioting in Lyons' Vaulx-en-Velin, which occurred one week after the completion of an expensive four-year program of renovation.

These acts of spontaneous demolition are in large part inspired both by the dulling monotony of the surroundings and by a general sense of exclusion from the mainstream. It is an ironic fact that exactly these qualities, uniformity and

the city

exclusiveness, which were pioneered in an earlier round of residential segregation for the elite, are now wholeheartedly embraced by the regulatory mechanisms that have divided our cities into internally homogeneous districts.

Zoning has been called "the practice of boundary management."[107] We have already touched on its role in sequestering American immigrant populations (see above, p. 108). This was one predictable consequence of zoning's primary goal: to protect investments in real estate and development. It does so by defining urban districts, confining these to specific functions, and spatially segregating incompatible users, like hospitals and wrecking yards. In late 19th-century Germany, zoning was first applied as a device for a broad organization of urban land by use; by 1920 American cities had refined legislation to the point where they could designate not just residential districts but, within these, areas reserved exclusively for single-family housing.

Suburban monotony is currently maintained in North America, as well as in parts of Europe, through an ever-increasing maze of exclusionary zoning laws. These can now specify large minimum lot sizes, minimal provision for multi-family dwellings, and restricted apartment sizes (a practice sometimes called "vasectomy zoning," as it insures that occupants will include few if any children).[108] Meanwhile, narrow definitions of exactly what constitutes a family are used to keep those living in non-standard household configurations—multi-generational or extended families, the elderly, the disabled, even religious orders—out of residential areas zoned for "single-family" use.[109] These practices expand the definition of residential differentiation to include the spatial segregation of people by household type, family status, and age. Or to put it in demographic terms, modern cities are places where "the different [age] cohorts take up separate quarters."[110]

The radical fragmentation of cosmopolitan populations and functions is being called into question by a chorus of challengers. On the American scene one of the first, and still perhaps the most articulate, was the late Jane Jacobs, who issued a virtual manifesto for the reintegration of the urban realm with her 1962 bestseller, *The Death and Life of Great American Cities*. In Europe, Léon Krier has pitted modern zoning, which he condemns as "the alienation and social division of intellectual production . . . solidified in the urban form," against his reverent notion *98* of the *quartier* or neighborhood. His projects for the renovation of Paris, London and Berlin advocate "de-zoning," and abandon single-use districts in favor of pedestrian-scale *quartiers*, with their vital mixture of residential, cultural, com- *Pl.30* mercial, and industrial uses. Both Krier and Jacobs make the claim that the great majority of urban industrial activity could be harmlessly reintegrated into residential districts, given today's strict pollution abatement standards.

These and other critics of recent patterns of fracture do not question the necessity of boundaries, but rather their application. The critical issue in the arrangement of modern cities, it seems, is whether urban divisions have brought about the demise of what they merely intended to systematize. The imperative of partition is to leave something whole in the process. In the past compartmentalization worked because there were strong centralizing forces that held cities together—the ruler, the religion, the primacy of trade. Nothing quite as powerful bonds urban populations today. Our conventions of delimiting urban problems through what amounts to regulatory quarantine have, in the final reckoning, denied us the experience of interdependence as a larger community. In a society riven by discrepancies in wealth, race and privilege, that experience may not be comfortable. It is, however, prerequisite to any hope for a lasting resolution of our differences. In the case of cities, to divide is not to conquer.

98 *Léon Krier's vision of the traditional city and the zoned city, 1984.*

the Anti-City.

3 · PUBLIC PLACES

THE NATURE OF PUBLIC PLACES

> Since piazzas are areas in villages or cities, empty of houses and other such things and of obstructions, arranged for the purpose of providing space or set up for meetings of men, it should be remarked that in general through piazzas the condition of man in this world can be discovered.

This remarkable observation by Petrus Berchorius, the 14th-century French mythographer, may be explained as a precocious humanist sentiment on the eve of the Renaissance. But it pays homage to a universal urban trait—the essentialness of public space. Without ringing declarations on the subject, cities of every age have seen fit to make provision for open places that would promote social encounters and serve the conduct of public affairs.

In the ways urban form is configured and inhabited, the bounds between public and private are far from discrete. Nor are Berchorius's "piazzas" the only urban territory for social and commercial intercourse. Streets are public places: so is the harbor waterfront. The subject of this chapter, therefore, is in a sense arbitrary. But street and quay are primarily places of transit, capturing public life in momentary pauses from a river of people in motion. the public place, on the other hand, is a destination; a purpose-built stage for ritual and interaction. Broadly, the reference is to places we all are free to use, as against the privately owned realm of houses and shops. They are themselves often defined, these public places, by the private architecture of house and shop. But the distinction of purpose holds—the fact that in public places we act in ways we cannot, or do not, in the private realm.

Part of this has to do with space: clearly, we cannot fit the evening *passeggiata* or a bullfight in the residential courtyard. But beyond this, there are two justifying aspects to the concept of the public place. One has to do with familiar and chance encounters. We go out to meet our friends and neighbors by the town well, at the park bench, in the square in front of the church. But since everyone is entitled to make use of public places, we will also see in the same park or square people we do not know or do not care to associate with. They might sit next to us, and they might do things that are unpredictable, things that we might find offensive or annoying. The charter of public places is freedom of action—and the right to stay inactive.

99 opposite The Piazza del Comune in Assisi (Italy) stands on the site of the forum of the Roman city. The portico on the right is that of the Temple of Minerva, built in the late 1st century BC; the lower part of its great flight of steps still exists, deep below the present street level. Next to it is the Torre Comunale, begun in 1212. Set into the ground story of the tower are the local standards of measurement, including sizes for bricks and roof-tiles.

The second aspect is a ritual one. Public places host structured or communal activities—festivals, riots, celebrations, public executions—and because of that, such places will bear the designed evidence of our shared record of accomplishment and our ritual behavior. They are where we would choose to commemorate a costly war, for example, and those who fell for us. They are where we would honor a ruler by setting up a monument to his name. And here one day we might converge to pull down the monument and damn his memory: so at the Revolution in the Place Louis XV (later Place de la Concorde) the statue of the king was replaced by a statue to Liberty and the guillotine.

The establishment of the main square itself often underscores this communal character. Homer contrasts the civility of Greeks with the anarchy and individualism of the Cyclopes who "have no assemblies to debate in."[1] The Spanish *Laws of the Indies*, promulgated in 1573, declare that "The main plaza is to be the starting point of the town" (Ordinance 112). In Brazil in the 18th century, "the Crown ordered a general gathering of all the local residents to determine together the most appropriate location of the plaza of the new community, in the middle of which the *pelourinho* (an ornamental column, the symbol of Portuguese authority) would be erected." Only then would a site for the church, and others for government buildings and the jail, be determined.[2]

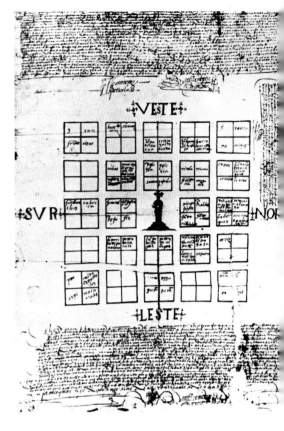

THE LIFE AND CONTROL OF THE PUBLIC

Indeed the fundamental aim of the public place is to ensconce community and to arbitrate social conflict. The program is a paradox. The square is where we exercise our franchise, our sense of belonging. We are meant to come and go as we please, without the consent of authorities and without any declaration of a justifying purpose. This is the "bestiaire fraternel," as Le Corbusier calls the Piazza S. Marco.[3] There are of course specialized functions—markets, militia drills, feast-day ceremonies—but even there the crowd has doers and watchers, the activity is understood at some level to be collective, and participation is both random and institutionalized. In some staged communal festivities, we have a chance to hold authority to public ridicule and reassert the popular source of all political power.

But these very prerogatives impelled ruling agencies early on to dominate the square. Physically, it was furnished with the symbols of government. Its space served as the setting for acts of legitimization, as well as for the public display of justice. The *pelourinho*, symbol of sovereignty, also served as whipping post. But even now, the public place is the canvas on which political and social change is painted. It is not enough to take over the reins of a city, to overwhelm an existing social order and supplant it with a new one; it is important to demonstrate this change in the design and uses of the public realm within the city.

The transformation of the Piazza della Signoria in Florence, from the forum of a free commune to the palace court of the Medici, has its parallels everywhere and in every period. We can, as Pierre Deyon has done, document similar adjustments in the fitting up of old medieval squares in the Low Countries to the reality of Spanish rule. Deyon's story recounts the fading of the power of small guilds and crafts in favor of big merchants, corporations and the *échevin* (deputy mayor), and the surrender of this authority in turn to princely patronage under the Spanish court. To make his case, he studies the evidence in the physical fabric of the squares, along with the iconographic evidence in popular festivals. These, a ritualized outlet for public displeasure against rulers and their policies expressed within a complex theater of processions, feasts and masquerades, were now revised with a view to

curbing signs of rebellion and insolence and redefining public life in terms of the urban elite and the prince.[4] Indeed, one of the central changes that characterize the rise of early modern Europe is "the gradual withdrawal of elites from participation in popular culture."[5]

The object of government in dominating the public place is to restrict access to it and regulate behavior within it. An orderly, orchestrated gathering in support of the State constitutes a proper official use of the central square. Unauthorized gatherings have to be guarded against. The formation of a crowd can be the first step to a popular challenge of authority. In Italy, popular movements are called *movimenti di piazza*, and "going down to the piazza" is a euphemism for insurrection.[6] When Cardinal Del Monte, governor of Gualdo Tadino in the mid-16th century, saw popular sentiment against the Papal State swell dangerously, he had a spine of houses built in haste down the middle of the main square, dividing it in two and thereby diminishing the space, and effectiveness, of a possible uprising.[7] More drastic still was the intervention of the tyrant Luchino Visconti at Parma. A few years after his conquest of the city in 1341, he threw up a defensive wall around the *Platea Communis*, complete with merlons and gates—a veritable fort which was named Sta in Pace ("stay peaceful")![8]

The recent upheavals in Socialist countries dramatized the power of the piazza. In Czechoslovakia, the Communist government tried force to keep the people from massing in Prague's Wenceslas Square—it failed and brought on its own demise. In China, the government was too late: Tienanmen Square, occupied by students and their sympathizers, had to be cleared after a few days with sufficient brutality to end the demonstrations and discourage their renewal. And the failure of the hard-line Communist coup was celebrated in Moscow's Manezh Square with a processional unfurling of a symbol of the new hearth of power: the banner of the Russian republic.

Pl.20

PRIVATIZED PUBLIC REALMS

A distinction needs to be made between this central public place and privatized public places used by small groups of citizens as a challenge, or substitute, or subsidiary, to the genuinely communal realm. For example, what the Germans call a *Wohnhof* is often no more than a pushing back of the house line to create a kind of open living space where children can play and the neighborhood fountain can find its home.

The clan piazza

Clan accommodation in medieval towns is an excellent case in point (see also p. 150). At its most clearcut, each clan neighborhood clustered around the small family square. The stronger the clans' grip on the city, the less likely it was that there would be a proper central piazza. Genoa, for example, where the feudal noble families were not held back by a strong guild structure or an authentic communal government, had no large public square until 1460. The communes, when they got to be assertive enough, constructed their public buildings and large municipal squares in open spaces (undeveloped land, gardens, vineyards, even woods) that often isolated these clan neighborhoods.[9]

102

Within the neighborhoods, the little square and a main street were twin centers of community life. Here were the *gentilizia* (the clan-sponsored church), and the *loggia* where menfolk met. The houses of the families that made up the clan clustered around the square.

102 Piazza S. Matteo, Genoa (Italy), the curia of the Doria family, centers on the church dedicated to the family's patron saint. We are looking at it from the portico of the house presented by the commune to Lamba Doria in 1298. Other family palaces are visible on the left.

The origin of this clan piazza in the feudal court or *curia* deserves additional emphasis. This was the castle precinct, walled and protected by a tall square tower, and occupied by the lord's mansion, the church, and several less lofty dwellings. The fortified seignorial court was a center of rural settlement, not yet subject to the law of the city. In some modified form, however, it was also present within cities—the Römerhof in Strasbourg and Torre delle Milizie in Rome are examples. The clan neighborhood is the fully urbanized variant of this rural enclave. The name of a public square sometimes preserves this affiliation for our own day. Such is the "Corte" dei Mecci, next to Orsanmichele, in Florence.

The best surviving specimen of the clan neighborhood is the Doria compound in Genoa, the Piazza S. Matteo, just to the north of the cathedral. At its heart is the church dedicated to St. Matthew, the patron saint of the Doria, which was founded in 1125 by Martino Doria. The steps are a 20th-century addition: originally this was a continuously sloped and paved area. On the church façade, we can still read the carved inscriptions commemorating major victories by Doria admirals of the Genoese fleet. The bounding family palaces, in the Lombard Gothic style of the church, had open porticoes on the ground floor. A Benedictine monastery to the north of the church housed the monks who attended to the spiritual needs of the Doria clan members. This piazza complex consistently employs for building material black and white marble in striped patterns—the use of marble being a privilege reserved for the cathedral, important churches, and the buildings of four Genoese noble families including the Doria.[10]

The English square

Parallels with this medieval pattern of privatized public spaces can be found in other periods. I would single out the English residential square, starting in the 17th century; once again, we have a random pattern of private development centered around squares, with no obligation to connect them into a coherent overall plan. These were estates laid out by ground landlords, and the houses were built on long-term leases by developers for a genteel clientele. Restrictive covenants ensured upper-class tenancy, and the enjoyment of the central garden, beginning with King (now Soho) Square of 1680–81, was the exclusive right of tenants. I shall return to the subject in the context of residential squares (below, pp. 163–64).

COURTYARD AND SQUARE

Historically, the enclosure of urban gathering-places was the prerogative of religious architecture. The atrium of the early Christian basilica and the *sahn* of the Muslim mosque were large urban courtyards entered through one or more gates and surrounded by covered porticoes. Earlier still come temples of ancient Near Eastern cultures. The courtyard of the Oval Temple at Khafajeh in Iraq, for example, was the largest open space in the city.   *255*

At times this courtyard would assume non-religious functions: in the main temples of the Hittite capital, Bogazköy, the courtyards served as marketplaces. In early Islam the communal treasury had its pavilion in the *sahn*. Official weights and measures were kept at the mosque; teachers held classes under its porticoes, judges heard cases, and the town crier read proclamations. In such instances, the true civic center of the town is the temple courtyard.

In Islam, by and large, public space is confined to residual, interstitial areas   *103* between cells—neighborhoods, bazaars, the mosque complex. The contrast with Western urbanism, which can be said to start out with the street system and the public places, is valid as far as it goes, but should not be overdrawn. There is a well-defined sense of public space in Islamic cities. Included in this concept, which has the backing of the law, are streets, *maidans* (translated inaccurately as "squares"), mosques, and cemeteries. Regardless of the private use of these resources, they could never be privately owned. Every member of society had equal claim to public places, be he Muslim or non-Muslim. "Whoever comes earliest to a public place has the right to make use of it through that day."[11] Except for women. In principle, a public space was considered unsafe for Muslim women, and to be avoided by them.

This discrimination, incidentally, also prevailed in ancient Rome. The forum was for men. If women were not specifically excluded, their reputation suffered by frequenting the forum too often or too long. Nonetheless, whatever the similarities, the *maidan* is not the equivalent of the Roman Forum or Siena's Campo. There was no distinct civic arena in an Islamic city, because there was no municipality as such with its own charter of privileges and responsibilities. The true collectivity, *umma*, was in the assembled crowds of the Friday noon prayer in the main mosque.

The *maidan*, then, was not politically charged. Small *maidans* were nothing more than urban vestibules to monumental public buildings. They "acted as a distributing node serving the masses moving in and out of the major buildings to and from the neighboring paths"; and they "accommodated the large monumental structures within the compact bulk of the old city." In cities like Cairo, it has been claimed, *maidans* had distinctive spatial patterns which changed under each dynasty, and informal conventions for shaping them are implicit.[12]

This concatenation of spaces survived in cities Islam lost to the West. It is what gave pre-modern Seville its special character. In the early 16th century Luis de Perzán reported that he had counted there "more than eighty plazas, great and small, where foods are sold."[13] The same Islamic predilection carried on in Valencia where several *placetas* did service in lieu of the conventional *plaza mayor*, and the market, the cathedral, and the town hall each had its own irregular scrap of open space.[14]

Material evidence for the assertion that the main congregational mosque—the Friday mosque—and its courtyard were the true forum of Islam comes from the

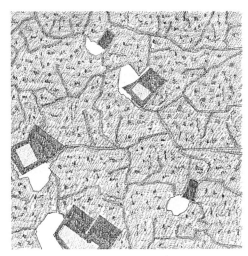

103 Public spaces in an Islamic city: mosque courtyards, and maidans associated with mosques and other public buildings.

treatment of Roman forums by the Muslim conquerors in cities that came under their dominion. The mosque was commonly placed over the forum, which ceased thereby to exist as an open space. This was the case in Aleppo, and in cities like Toledo and Valencia in Islamic Spain. Vital functions of the forum were moved elsewhere. When the mosque in Aleppo occupied the site of the Hellenistic/Roman agora, the foodstuffs market held there was moved to a *khan* outside the walls, near the market gardens that would ensure its supply. It is interesting that the name for the large court of the *khan*, "Dar Khoura," probably recalls the word *agora*.[15]

True enough, in the intervening centuries between Rome and Islam, the Byzantine or Visigothic basilica might have already appropriated the open space of the forum, so that in such cases the mosque would simply be asserting its symbolic presence by planting itself over the church. Even so, no extension of the open space was sought, and no square of comparable prominence was created elsewhere within the city. (Of the extramural *musalla*, I will soon give an account.)

The relation of temple courtyard to urban square can be an evolving one. To change the reference from Islam to Christianity, there is a certain ambiguity in monastic planning regarding the accommodation of a lay public on the premises. In Italy by the later 15th century the term "cloister" came to be applied to any quadrangular architectural space enclosed by arcades, whether it was part of a religious or a secular program. At Loreto, the space in front of the Sanctuary of the Holy House, an enclosed atrium-like area associated with the church, was reinterpreted by Bramante into a *piazza grande* emulating the ancient forum. This

104 Florence (Italy), Piazza of the Santissima Annunziata, from G. Zocchi, Scelta di XXIV vedute (1754). On the right is Brunelleschi's loggia of the Foundling Hospital, which at its completion in 1425 faced onto a shapeless space in front of an undecorated church (center). A century later, a formal piazza was created with the construction opposite of the loggia of the Confraternity of the Servites (by Antonio da Sangallo the Elder, 1516–25), echoing Brunelleschi's building. Finally, in 1601–8, the church itself was given a loggia, and an equestrian statue of Grand Duke Ferdinando I, by Giambologna and Pietro Tacca, was erected in the middle (cf. Pl. 27).

105 *A schematic image of the functions of the* atrio *in the New World, from the* Rhetorica *of Fray Diego de Valadés, 1579. In the center, symbolically, is the church supported by Franciscans; around the edge are illustrations of the sacraments and of missionary activities, including teaching by pictures (above left and right).*

fusion of atrium and urban square recurs in the Piazza of the Santissima Annunziata *104*, in Florence, with its uniform arcades that lock the church front to the sides of the *Pl.27* square.[16]

Like the better-known Mendicant Orders of the Franciscans and Dominicans, the Servites of the Santissima Annunziata practiced an outgoing spirituality based on an open relation with the lay public. Even before the Renaissance, these popular Orders, with their attachment to preaching, equipped their church grounds with ancillary spaces for open-air sermons. Often starting out at the city edge, the *20*, monasteries found themselves in time well within the city limits. The preaching *21* fields were transformed into ample squares which also served as markets and settings for popular festivals. The State contributed to their monumental decoration, treating them as it would civic squares.

The Mendicant squares in Spanish and Portuguese cities of the New World come in several variations. They might flank the main square or *plaza mayor*, but at some distance from it, as they do at Lima and Santo Domingo. Where there is a citadel, the Franciscan and Dominican establishments flank it and the *plaza mayor* is situated in front of it; Havana and Buenos Aires are examples. In settlements founded by one of the Orders themselves the Mendicant square is of course the main town square. Often, this quadrangular space in front of the monastery is located at the top of the urban grid, not in the center. The position may be explained by the fact that the Mendicants were transporting the medieval practice of their Orders to build at or near a city gate.[17]

The configuration of the *atrio* between monastic church and plaza, as well as *107* conforming to early Christian precedent—Old St. Peter's in Rome and S. Ambrogio in Milan come to mind—is probably not unbeholden to the courtyard of mosques. The friars of course would be familiar with famous specimens in the home country, some among them, the Great Mosque of Córdoba for one, converted to churches *106* after the Reconquista. The *atrio* was a walled rectangular space, with four domed *105* pavilions or *posas* at the corners connected by a paved way. Reached from the *plaza* by some stairs, this court could hold many more Indian converts than the church proper, and was the setting for open-air Mass, and religious shows hybridized with remnants of native ritual.

106, 107 *Mosque courtyards like that at Córdoba (right) offered a Spanish precedent for the* atrio *separating church façade from public square in Mexico (far right). There, it responded to the pre-Conquest Indian custom of celebrating religious rites in the open air.*

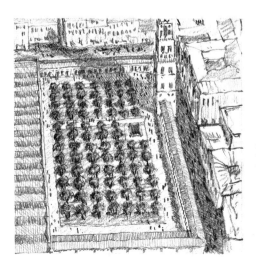

THE DISTRIBUTION OF PUBLIC PLACES

Where within the urban form public places are deployed is as often a matter of accident as it is of forethought.

The persistence of open space is one factor. A large public monument of one period with an open usable space may become a public square in another period, regardless of the shifts in the urban fabric during the interim. Piazza Navona in Rome was once the Stadium of Domitian, far from the residential core; the Hippodrome of the Great Palace of Byzantine Constantinople survived as the At Meydani or horse market of Ottoman Istanbul; and the elliptical Piazza del Anfiteatro in Lucca reveals its stock in its name. In the Western Middle Ages, cities of Roman origin sometimes trace their main town square to the ancient forum. Italian examples are the clearest: Piazza dei Cavalieri in Pisa; Piazza S. Michele in Lucca; in Umbria, the town squares of Assisi, Todi, Spoleto, Narni, and Orvieto. In northern Europe during the later Middle Ages, churchyards or cemeteries were sometimes converted to town squares with the church in the middle.

In cities planned anew, the choice for the emplacement of squares will be deliberate. Even so, the subsequent growth of the city may obscure the clarity of the original distribution, and some of the public places may be obliterated altogether. Of Penn's four supplementary squares for Philadelphia, arranged symmetrically around a main square, only two survived.

Centrality appears to be the norm for the principal meeting ground and representational space of a city, but all too often this primary site is fixed after the fact. In the course of synoecism, the government of the nascent municipality will try to create a centralized focus for the merging settlements, or simply accept an open space among them as the new civic forum and equip it accordingly. Siena's Campo is a graphic demonstration of the process. Boston Common, on the other hand, now in a commanding central position, had a marginal spot at the west edge of the city until the development of Beacon Hill and Back Bay.

124

Pl.16

99

108,
109

108, 109 Boston Common at the water's edge, and after the laying out on reclaimed land of Beacon Hill and the Back Bay area, when it found itself in the center.

AT THE CITY EDGE

In many Iranian and Iraqi cities, the *maidan* of the principal mosque was originally a horse-race course and polo field on the outskirts, which doubled as market. There is literary evidence for this from as far back as the 9th century. In Isfahan, the *maidan*

110 The Maidan-i-Shah, Isfahan (Iran), laid out in the early 17th century; from Cornelius de Bruin, Travels (1698/1731). A Ali Qapu, a belvedere/gate where the imperial palace meets the public space; B the Shah's Mosque; C mosque of Shaikh Lutfullah.

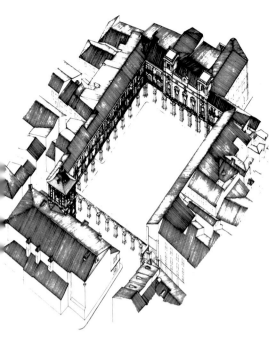

111 Ávila (Spain), the Plaza Mayor as it is today. The Casa Consistorial is at the north end (top), the church to the south. After constant challenges from the church for power and control over the open space, the council decided in 1770 to remodel the square. Construction went on slowly until the 1860s, when the present Casa Consistorial was built; a façade one room deep planned to conceal the church was left as a screen in 1912. (From Cervera Vera)

112 An extramural musalla *of the type found in Algeria. A long straight wall on the left, oriented to Mecca like the mosque within the city, allows it to serve as an open-air place of worship on special feast days.*

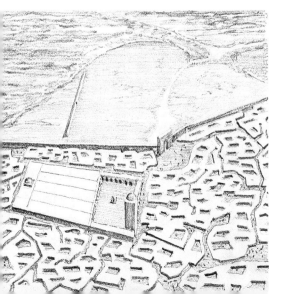

of the old city was originally located at the edge of the first settlement called Yahudiyya. When Kushinan joined Yahuddiya and the *maidan* found itself in the middle, it became a frame for the city's administrative and religious institutions.[18] In the new Isfahan laid out by Abbas I in the early 17th century, the large formal square *110* (Maidan-i Shah) recreated these mixed uses. It served as forecourt to the imperial palace and mosque, open-air market, and polo field.

There are Western parallels. Grounds for jousting tournaments, once in the mural zone of cities, were sometimes urbanized at a later period. In Haarlem, the tournament field outside the original fortified settlement of the counts of Holland, surrounded by knights' houses, became the marketplace of the developed city; the house on the west side belonging to the counts served as town hall, and the knights' houses were turned into shops.[19] Nancy's Place de la Carrière was transformed by Héré de Corny in the mid-18th century from a tournament ground at the edge of the old city to a parade for Nancy society bridging over to the new city.

The *plaza mayor* in many Spanish towns started out as an extramural market, and as the site for bullfights, local festivals and public gatherings. This is probably why, in its formalized later reincarnation as town square, it has no religious component; the main institutional landmark is the town hall. It is the one civic space not to feel the need of a fronting church, to resist such intrusion in fact.

The case of Ávila is instructive. The existence of the parish church of S. Juan on *111* the south side of the *plaza mayor* became a bone of contention in the long campaign of city authorities to give the area a formal plan. The church claimed proprietorship over half of the open space; the city council pointedly voted to furnish their Casa Consistorial (town hall) with a chapel "so that all people in the plaza might hear and see the Mass," and proposed an arcaded façade-building, just one room in depth, to screen off the church from view.[20]

The ambiguity about the role of religion in the secular institution of the *plaza mayor* with its extramural beginnings carried over into the *Laws of the Indies*. In Spanish towns of the New World, the church was to be a part of the city center "but at a distance" from the main plaza, the honor of frontage being reserved to "the *101,* royal council and *cabildo* (town council) and customs houses" (Ordinance 124). But *163* in Mexico City, the capital of New Spain, the cathedral and the viceregal palace *254* fronted the Zocalo, the central square.

The *musalla* in the Islamic world, also called *sari'a* in the western provinces, *112* deserves special mention.[21] Its history starts around AD 600 with the Prophet, who used to lead his entire early Muslim community to a field outside Madina for prayer, especially on feast days. Subsequently many cities chose an open space outside the walls, devoid of any buildings, large enough to contain the entire urban population—the men at any rate—in the Ramadan-related festivals of Ayd al-Fitr and Ayd al-Kabir. In Spain at least, the *musalla* often doubled as the *musara* or parade ground—and even as a battlefield. It was on this *musalla/musara* that the review of troops took place prior to military expeditions. In 1499, a manuscript of the time tells us, 30,000 Moors gathered in the *musalla* of Granada's Albaicín district and across the entire plain down to S. Lázaro to greet Their Catholic Majesties, "which was an admirable sight."[22]

The *musalla* also served for executions, since it had enough room for everyone to watch. The proximity of cemeteries transferred the term "musalla" to them as well. In smaller cities, the *musalla* probably held small markets. We also have accounts of prayers for rain conducted there in times of severe drought. This service had to be done in the extramural countryside because streets and plazas within the city were not permissible places of reverence, being noisy settings of ordinary life.

A feel for this barren piece of open land at the shadow of the city walls can be had today in Marrakesh's Jemaa el-Fna, at the edge of the medina, the original old town. The name means "Meeting of the Dead," because the heads of executed rebels were shown here. In the morning this was, and is still, the site of small tradespeople—sellers of fruits, sweetmeats and basketwork, barbers, and the like. Later in the day the performers would take over—storytellers, buffoons, wrestlers, snake-charmers, dancers, musicians.

In early Islam the vast field of the *musalla* had a wall in the direction of Mecca with a mihrab and an engaged *minbar* or pulpit, the essentials, that is, of an actual mosque. There is literary evidence that *musallas*, Valencia's for example, were sometimes fully enclosed by high walls. The one in Tunis, attributed to the early 13th-century Hafsid dynastic ruler Abu Zakariya, was built with towers along the periphery wall and decorated portals, a source says, "in the manner of a small city."[23]

TOWN SQUARES

In the distribution of public places, all things being equal, considerations of function and traffic prevailed.

Port towns, for example, often had their main square not in center-city but at the waterfront. The towns of New France in America, like New Orleans, are good modern instances. But we can go back—to the ancient Greek world. The earliest agora of post-Persian Miletus was built facing the bay. In Hellenistic Antioch, Glanville Downey writes, "the agora or marketplace, which is still the industrial and commercial quarter of the modern city, lay along the bank of the river."[24]

To the extent that the town square was both a civic center and a marketplace, as was initially the case with the Greek agora, port towns might well give preference to the waterfront location.[25] More likely, the two activities will have their own public places. In this way the city can exploit its waterfront commercial hub, and enjoy a separate center for its political life elsewhere in the fabric. At Livorno the completely enclosed and symmetrical cathedral square in the heart of town was a far cry from the rowdiness of the great open piazza on the harbor front, where the slave market was held. Palermo's medieval configuration is another example (see below).

In recognition of the main role of city gates as channelers of traffic and long-distance commerce, and the ceremonial nature of official entries like the Roman imperial *adventus*, the space on either side of main gates commonly developed into more or less orderly squares. The Piazza del Popolo in Rome and its many transformations are clearly creditable to its being for centuries the primary northern entrance into the city, from the construction of the Aurelian Walls in the 3rd century down to the pre-empting of this approach by the first railroad station. The fame of that great entrance is matched by the Puerta del Sol of Madrid, in front of the once fortified eastern gate whose bastions, demolished in 1570, gave the plaza its shape—an irregular opening in the form of two trapezoids joined at their narrow side. With its celebrated antique fountain popularly known as La Mariblanca, and free of any representational architecture, this converging point of Spanish highways was a more genuine center for the city than its grandiloquent neighbor, the Plaza Mayor. Since the 16th century, when the Calle Mayor which runs into it became the site of the daily *paseo* or promenade of town and court, the Puerta del Sol also served as a turnabout for the carriages.[26] Other European city-gate plazas of note are the Pariser Platz in Berlin, inside the Brandenburg Gate; the Königplatz in Munich; and the Place de France project for the Paris of Henri IV, of which more later.

113 *Madrid, Puerta del Sol, looking west toward the Calle Mayor leading into the center of town; from J. B. de Laborde,* Voyage pittoresque et historique de l'Espagne *(1806–20). At the right is the fountain crowned with a statue known as La Mariblanca.*

Looking back, we should take note that early Anatolian towns, Troy among them, traditionally had two plazas—one at the main entrance gate to the city and one in front of the palace. Inevitably a gate plaza, at least when it was outside the gate, sheltered market activities. In Sumerian cities too, the city-gate locale was a loitering and gathering place, "where legal matters might be adjudicated, where sales and contracting for services might be performed, or where *ad hoc* markets might appear and disappear in a relatively short period of time."[27]

The palace square has almost universal currency. Even in imperial China, where cities were not endowed with squares and great temple precincts had no formal open spaces, the palace compound was entered through an urban forecourt that terminated the ceremonial north-south axis. Palace squares distinguished the official residence of the ruler, provided a margin of defense between him and a potential mob, and by their nature functioned as *places d'armes* or parade grounds.

The extension of this privilege to nobility was tantamount to granting a private residence the dignity of a public building. Luis de Perzán noted the great number of small courts in Seville interspersed among the town squares, "too many to count—because there is no gentleman . . . who does not have a *placeta* in front of his home, nor is there a church without one."[28] The piazzas of Renaissance palaces in Rome, when singled out in this way, carried plaques with the name of the authorizing pontiff and the exact dimensions of the open space. Most often these were family residences of princes of the Church elevated to the papal throne, or those considered *papabili*. The Palazzo Farnese and its piazza were the handiwork of the Farnese Pope Paul III. By the same token, other buildings that might presume to public status would negotiate an allotment of open space. The usual transaction was for powerful individuals and corporate patrons to barter private for public land, and to be favored by the existing laws of expropriation in the annexation of small properties around them.

Lastly, squares will develop as a result of the traffic pressures of crossroads, or will be incorporated into a new town plan as crossroads features. These pressure points come at the juncture of two or more streets, or at intervals along a main avenue as in *114* the Mese of Byzantine Constantinople, where several forums were strung along between the Golden Gate in the land walls and the Great Palace at the tip of the peninsula. In "Baroque" city form, plazas will be inserted where radial avenues meet ring roads.

MULTIPLE SYSTEMS

The coordination of town squares into systems of urban design is a preoccupation of the Renaissance and Baroque periods. In the older towns, the systems are created through the accompaniment of existing public places with newly created squares. In new towns or town extensions laid out fresh, formal schemes are developed obedient to abstract rules of composition applied to the plan as a whole.

115 Palermo has a famous sequence of the first kind. This is the Cassaro, the main east-west (actually northeast-southwest) axis of the city, and the squares along its length, which together constituted the ceremonial center of the Baroque town, rather than a pre-eminent *plaza mayor* as would be expected in a city within the Spanish sphere.

The Cassaro (present-day Corso Vittorio Emanuele) stretched from the ducal palace to the sea. The terminal squares were of medieval origin. Neither had specific functions under Spanish rule, even though the Piano di Palazzo (now Piazza della Vittoria), being in front of the palace, was used for processions and military displays, and the Piazza Marina was the site of auto-da-fés largely because the Palazzo Chiaramonte on the square had become the seat of the Inquisition. Two

114 Constantinople, reconstruction of the city's appearance in the 9th–11th centuries, showing the string of forums along the Mese, the imperial way between the Great Palace (far right) and the Golden Gate (bottom left). The palace complex extends from the hippodrome to the imperial church of Hagia Sophia. The first of the four forums is that of Constantine, focused on his column; next come the Forum Tauri, Forum Bovi, and Forum of Arcadius. Halfway between that and the "rond-point" where the road changes direction is the line of Constantine's city walls, replaced in the 5th century by those of Theodosius II, farther out.

115 Palermo (Sicily), the sequence of spaces along the Cassaro, now Corso Vittorio Emanuele. Starting at the left, they are the Piano di Palazzo/Piazza della Vittoria (medieval); Piazza della Cattedrale (second half of the 15th century); Piazza Bologni (1567); Quattro Canti, at the intersection with Via Maqueda (early 17th century); Piazza Pretoria, just to the south (1460); the large and informally shaped Piazza Marina (medieval); and finally a seaside promenade running south from the Porta Felice (1580).

monumental gates at either end of the Cassaro formalized it as an entity. In front of the Porta Felice which marked the sea route to Messina, a marvellous promenade was inaugurated in 1580.

Besides these two principal squares, four others were created between the 15th and 18th centuries. Each had its raison d'être, and fitted within a general program of social and political cogency. The Church announced its presence in the second half of the 15th century with a design for a modern cathedral square. The large rectangle, enclosed by a marble balustrade, was the Palermitan announcement of the Renaissance and its formalism of urban space. The Piazza Pretoria of 1460, almost in the middle of town just off the Cassaro, functioned as a civic center. The Piazza Bologni, opened in 1567 on the Cassaro proper half way between the palace and the civic center, was the square of the nobility—an affirmation of the feudal rights of the Sicilian aristocracy. Finally, when a new avenue called Via Maqueda cut across the Cassaro at right angles in the early 17th century, the crossroads was treated architecturally as a florid octagonal square, known familiarly as the Quattro Canti, with corner fountains representing the Four Seasons.

The simplest multiple system in a new town plan is the double square. The scheme is the rule for 18th-century new towns in Brazil, where one square features the municipal standard or *pelourinho*, and the other holds the church, the town hall, and the butcher shop. But the scheme was first seen there in Salvador de Bahía, which was laid out as a Renaissance ideal city in 1549 under the first Portuguese Governor of Brazil, Tomé de Souza.[29]

In fact, it is in the context of ideal cities that multiple systems of squares were experimented with in the Renaissance, particularly in the influential Italian treatises of Pietro Cataneo (1554) and Vincenzo Scamozzi (1615). Their gridded urban schemes were punctuated with a central square supplemented or surrounded by secondary squares in a symmetrical arrangement. These ideal diagrams found their way into urban practice, for example, at Charleville in eastern France (built 1608–20), in Penn's plan for Philadelphia, and in the 18th century, in towns like Versoix and Carouge in France and the replacements of old Sicilian towns like Noto and Avola in the wake of the devastating earthquake of 1693. Even the town of Versailles, a zenith of Baroque design, had a series of mostly quadrangular squares within the residential grids on either side of the mighty trivium of the palace.

But as a rule, when the city-form is dogmatically Baroque in design, the constellations of squares assume a rich variety of geometric shapes and hold vista-fixing monuments, working in concert with the bold diagonals of the streetscape. These fanciful systems continue beyond the Baroque period proper, as part of the academic grand tradition of urban design. The lessons of L'Enfant in Washington, Joseph-Marie Saget in Toulouse, and Leblond and others in St. Petersburg were to guide the town-planning school of Haussmann and hundreds of colonial designers in this century, from Fez to New Delhi, in the placement and form of squares as in everything else.

MATTERS OF SIZE

The deliberate concern with the size of squares is a luxury afforded by new towns or town extensions. In towns with a long history, the open spaces are likely to have been inherited from a former urban chapter, or shaped improvisatorially.

If the square is central to the design of a new town, it will be scaled in relation to the town plan as a whole. In the *Laws of the Indies*, for example, its size proclaimed the ultimate size of the town. Ordinance 113 put it as follows: "The size of the *plaza* shall be proportioned to the number of inhabitants . . . thus the *plaza* should be decided upon taking into consideration the growth the town may experience." In the 18th-century new towns of Brazil, similarly, the town's *praça* was to be made large enough so that, as a document of 1747 puts it for the settlement called José de Faria, "it will not suffer from the defect of being stunted, when the town has the growth that is expected."[30]

One planned for the future, then, and hoped that the town's development justified the size of its square. The *Laws of the Indies* set a minimum size of 200 by 300 feet (61 by 91 m.), and a maximum of 532 by 800 (162 by 244 m.), for the main *plaza*. In all cases, a rectangular *plaza* at least one and a half times as long as it was wide was recommended, "inasmuch as this shape is best for fiestas in which horses are used and for any other fiestas that should be held" (Ordinance 112).

To size the square to the town's population means to have it be large enough for the uses people make of the square. In the words of Palladio: "[The] principal piazze ought to be made of such size, as the multitude of citizens requires, that they may not be too small for their convenience and use, or that, through the small number of people, they may not seem uninhabited."[31] For neighborhood needs, additional smaller squares would be provided.

But since the group uses of a main square will not be continuous, appropriate size is ultimately a matter of appearance. Single-purpose squares will inevitably seem "uninhabited" without their intended crowds, as do cattle markets or the Piazza of St. Peter's. If a multi-purpose main square is scaled to its most space-demanding activity, it is bound to appear overlarge. Parade grounds often require heroic dimensions, for example; so, when the main square must double as a *place d'armes*, it will have to be overdrawn. This is the principal reason for the vastness of St. Petersburg's central squares before the Admiralty and the Winter Palace, and *152* the immense dimensions of the royal plaza in Inca cities like the one at Huanuco *153* Pampa.

Matters of health and safety were increasingly brought up beginning in the 18th century in relation to the size of squares. After the Sicilian earthquake of 1693, the authorities of Catania proposed that the piazzas of the new city plan be large enough to serve as safe camping areas should disaster hit again, "offering a refuge for nearby property owners who could be close enough to their possessions to guard them."[32] In an unpublished treatise on civil architecture written in 1773, Paolo Labisi praises open spaces for providing ventilation and air, channeling rainwater away from houses, and giving "all of the inhabitants the ability to guard against earthshocks (from which God liberate us) by means of leaving their own houses and meeting in the open spaces to escape the perils of being hit by the ruins of buildings."[33]

The concern for "good proportions" in the *Laws of the Indies* attests to an esthetic preoccupation beyond matters of utility and functional size. Alberti for one, having categorized squares according to their various functions, discusses general rules of proportion that would apply to all of them. "I would have a square twice as long as broad," is the formula he settles upon. But he promptly moves to make clear that the size of the square and its architectural frame are interdependent. If the surrounding buildings are too low, the open space will appear too large; if they are too high, the space would be unduly restricted. "A proper height for the buildings about a square is one third of the breadth of the open area, or one sixth at the least," he writes (*De re aedificatoria*, viii.6).

Alberti does not warn that this relationship of the enclosure to its boundary walls, however it is calculated, has limits. We cannot indefinitely compensate for the dimensions of the surface by making the surrounding buildings higher. Beyond a certain size, the spatial experience will be weak, regardless of the building height in the periphery. The squares of Vienna's Ringstrasse, Palace Square in St. Petersburg, *116,* the Place de la Nation in Paris and the Civic Center in San Francisco are all cases *152,* considered to have exceeded effective dimensions. A strong pavement pattern might *Pl.15* assist in the illusion of a manageable scale, but is unlikely in itself to correct the spatial impression.

This criticism is made of modern squares. Urban historian Paul Zucker states the case categorically when he claims that modern squares are simply spaces marked as such on maps "which actually are no more than plain voids, empty areas within the web of streets."[34] The indictment is two-pronged, and the person to have presented it most forcefully was Camillo Sitte one hundred years ago. Modern squares are too open and amorphous to define a positive volume of public space; and this is so because the primary consideration in the design of the modern city is to ease the flow of traffic.

Sitte's target was the design of the Ringstrasse in his native Vienna. He deplored the vast open spaces he saw being shaped in the zone of the demolished inner fortifications, and the public buildings that floated within them, unanchored to circumscribed, appropriately scaled spaces, and largely unrelated to one another. The lesson of urban history was that public spaces must be viewed in three dimensions, as volumes carved out of the solid of the built fabric. For thousands of years squares and streets had been enclosed units, and served as legitimate urban stages of social interaction. That fundamental social value of public spaces was being sacrificed in the modern metropolis to the functionalist calculations of traffic engineers and the grandiloquent agoraphilia of planners. In the empty expanses of the Ringstrasse, people missed the traditional engagement of the public citizen with the buildings and monuments of his city, and developed the modern affliction of *Platzscheu*, the fear of open spaces.

DISENCUMBERING

Sitte also objected to the modern practice of liberating historically significant monuments from "parasitic" construction, and setting them out in open spaces. He railed against "the delusion that everything must be seen at once, that around a thing only empty space is in order." A liberated church with space all around it "will always appear like a cake on a serving platter."

The debate over "disencumbering" (*dégagement* or *isolement* in French; *Freilegung* in German) was at least as old as the preservation movement in Europe—a matter of decades at the time of the publication of Sitte's book in 1889. But it reached beyond the small circle of preservationists in the second half of the century when massive surgery in the inner city, epitomized by Baron Haussmann's *grands travaux* in Paris, threatened many historic monuments and raised issues of presentation for those which were spared.

The esthetic impetus for disencumbering is to be found in Neoclassicism. The notion of buildings as midspace objects has Renaissance precedent, of course, both in theory and practice. It is enough to mention the famous *View of an Ideal City* in the palace of Urbino from the 1490s, and the Renaissance exempla of S. Maria delle Carceri at Prato and Bramante's Tempietto in Rome. Ordinance 124 in the *Laws of*

116 Vienna, Schwarzenbergplatz, on the Ringstrasse, 1860s. This was the center of an aristocratic quarter composed of buildings which were part family palace, part rental apartment block.

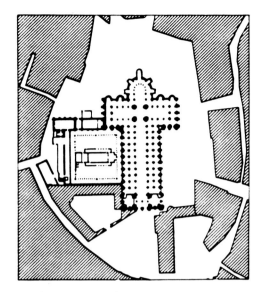

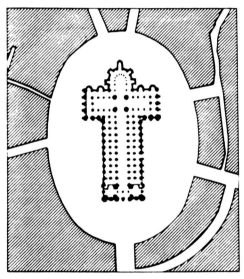

118, 119 Toulouse (France), the space surrounding St.-Sernin as it appeared ca. 1800 and as redesigned by J. P. Virebent in 1827. The place as actually built, beginning in the mid-19th century, is far less perfect in form. (After Mardaga)

117 opposite Brussels, cathedral of SS. Michel et Gudule, as it looked ca. 1900. A contemporary observer noted with satisfaction that it enjoyed "the advantage, so often denied to the noble edifices of great cities, of a magnificent position dominating its surroundings."

the Indies declares: "The temple [i.e., church] . . . shall be separated from any other building or from adjoining buildings; and ought to be seen from all sides so it can be decorated better, thus acquiring more authority . . ." Baroque design exploited the dramatic possibilities of isolation as well as the spatial continuities of engagement: Vienna's Karlskirche and Rome's S. Agnese in the Piazza Navona exemplify each 124 of these approaches. It was only in late 18th-/early 19th-century practice that the penchant for situating public buildings, often raised on a pedestal, alone in the middle of a square or on an island surrounded by streets, became an inviolable convention.[35] This was especially the case in Germany.

With this example of contemporary urban design at hand, it was easy to argue that medieval churches and certain other old buildings deserved the same treatment. Notre-Dame in Paris and Milan Cathedral were famous early cases, both disencumbered before 1870. Haussmann set a precedent of sorts with Notre-Dame, enlarging the parvis to several times its original size. The fresh attempts to complete unfinished medieval cathedrals, as at Cologne, encouraged these disencumbering tendencies.

The direct connection with Neoclassicism can be made in cases like the Place St.- 118, Sernin at Toulouse. The present form of this square around the great Romanesque 119 pilgrimage church is mostly the initiative of its restorer, Viollet-le-Duc, but the original project goes back to 1827. At the time of the Revolution, the church was engulfed by buildings; some were private houses, but the bulk of the accretion was property that belonged to the canons of St.-Sernin and could therefore be nationalized. The cloister was the first to be razed—in 1815. Expropriation of private property began in 1847, and the church was fully detached in 1852. In the absence of a master plan, the peripheral façades of the square vary in elevation. The space itself is roughly oval, a form which had already been used in the city at the Place de l'Ovale (now Place Wilson) of 1804–24, on the model of the proposed square for the Panthéon in Paris.[36]

Public buildings, it was presumed in this ideology, were to be treated as individual works of art. As the architect Herman Pflaume put it in 1893 with respect to Cologne Cathedral:

> It is an aesthetic rule that the viewer must not be disturbed when he is looking at a work of art. Just as a picture must not be displayed in an ugly or an inappropriate frame, something in the environs of the cathedral that distracts and disturbs the viewer must not be tolerated.[37]

How much free space around a monument was adequate for its proper viewing? On this critical issue, which entailed the very real cost of demolition, planners and traffic engineers on the one hand and preservationists on the other looked to architects for guidance. It was in fact a German architect, Hermann Maertens, who in the 1870s set out to determine scientific criteria for the practice of architecture and planning, based on Hermann Helmholtz's theories of physiological optics, in a book called *The Optical Scale in the Plastic Arts*.[38] The experience of architectural space, according to Maertens, is primarily dependent on the observer's angle of vision. A principal concern of his book, therefore, was to determine objectively the proper angles at which to view public buildings for best effect—and hence laws of 120 *Freilegung*.

A person's range of clear vision corresponded to an angle of 27 degrees, Maertens calculated; this translated into a ratio of 1:2 between the size of the object and the distance from the observer. So the normal standpoint for viewing a building clearly and easily was at a distance equal to twice its height. At a viewing angle of 18

degrees, with the viewing point moved back to a point three times as distant as the building was tall, the observer could get a sharper picture of the edifice framed by its surroundings. A point still further back, at an angle of 12 degrees and a ratio of 1:4, would allow the observer to appreciate the structure as part of its surroundings, as its silhouette locked into a picture of the city.

According to Maertens, since the observer changed his location continuously the width of the building was not very relevant in determining the distance of the viewpoint; the height was the only important dimension. He proposed to leave out the towers of churches in calculating this height, while domes counted because they constituted a larger part of the building's mass.

But the decisions for the architect could not all be reached through the simple application of optical formulas. Given a program of disencumbering, he was forced into an initial choice of degree. The range was from a straightforward enlargement of the space in front of the monument, to making it a free-standing, mid-space object. In the latter case, the exterior shell of the monument would have to be restored or rebuilt so as to offer elevations worthy of a public place.

The high point of the popularity of disencumbering was 1880 to 1910. Sitte was the principal voice for the opposition during this period; his book, also claiming to lay down objective principles for urban aesthetics, brought home if nothing else the arbitrariness of the whole debate. Sitte had some early help, notably a mayor of Brussels called Charles Buls who published his *L'Isolement des vieilles églises* in 1910. His was a compromise position. There could be no generally applicable rules. Disencumbering was right for Renaissance buildings, in line with the theoretical premises of its architecture, but wrong for Romanesque and Gothic buildings. There the picturesque element should be allowed to persist, the old surroundings preserved. Others combined this historical view with visual prescriptions of the Maertens school. *The American Architect* objected to the disencumbering of Gothic cathedrals partly on the grounds that the sculpture of the flanks, delicate and small, was made for close examination, while that of the front, comparatively bold, could tolerate a more distant view.[39]

This articulate resistance to wide spaces around monumental buildings had its effect. Sentiment changed sufficiently for cities to begin registering public regret for excesses, so that Ulm, for example, held competitions in 1906 and again in 1924 for plans to reduce the space of the cathedral square by enclosing or building up parts

120 *The effect on perception of a viewer's distance from the object—in this case, the portico of S. Andrea at Mantua—according to the theory expounded by Hermann Maertens in* Der optische Massstab in den bildenden Künsten *(1877). At a distance equal to four times the height of the object, the viewer sees it in the context of the city; at three times, it appears with its surroundings; a distance equal to twice the height gives the best view; anything closer makes an overall picture impossible.*

of it again. Another retraction came at Leuven (Louvain), Belgium. There a new straight artery connecting the city center with the railroad station had cut through the close-grained medieval texture in the 1860s and 1870s, boldly exposing the cathedral and the Gothic town hall on the originally small and sheltered Grand Place. Now in the heat of the Great War local architects developed projects for a screen block that would break the long unobstructed view and restore something of the intimacy of the original square.[40]

The cognate issue here was contextualism.[41] Proponents of disencumbering, indeed of radical urban surgery of any kind, held that ordinary buildings had no intrinsic value, and hence no claims to preservation, however old they might be. In his memoirs written after his fall, Haussmann challenged his critics to name "even a single monument worthy of interest, one building precious for its art, curious by its memories" that his administration destroyed—this despite a record of demolition that included some 4,300 old houses in central Paris alone.

To those appalled by such wanton wreckage, ordinary old buildings were worthy of respect for two good reasons. On an esthetic level they supplied picturesque settings for the grand monuments of history; our appreciation of this urban vernacular sprang from "delight in beautiful architectural contexts," as the Munich architect Carl Hocheder put it in 1908. And then there was a nationalist side to conservation, as the Heimatschütz (homeland defense) movement in Germany made clear. Building is history, and destruction of any building constitutes a loss of historical memory. Even a once ardent disencumberer like Joseph Stübben came around to talking of how humble buildings of the past "tell the suffering, struggles and triumphs of our forefathers. . . . They are the milestones with which our fathers opened the way of history."[42]

And that is exactly what the Fascists in Italy took exception to when they invested disencumbering with new life in the extensive urban renewal projects of the 1920s *272* and 1930s that changed the face of Italian cities. Not all buildings of the past had a right to survive, the Fascists argued, because not all communicable messages of a people's history were worth receiving. There were monuments, and they were sacred. Common buildings by contrast were profane documents "useless to the life of the spirit." The directive to eradicate this profanity came from the Duce himself in the very first months of his regime. "The millennial monuments of our history must loom gigantic in their necessary solitude," he decreed—and so they did, in spacious new piazzas which were the delight of traffic engineers.[43]

TOTALITARIAN SCALES

What these new, extravagantly scaled Fascist squares also provided were public spaces of appropriate size where mass rallies staged by the regime could be held. The Piazza Venezia in Rome, and its accessory spaces opened up by Fascist planners all the way down to the Colosseum, could accommodate the throngs the Duce required in front of his official residence for those scenographic opportunities he cherished.[44] In Milan, the sacred birthplace of Fascism, an enormous open space was carved out at Piazza S. Babila. Few towns, however small, escaped the void-making labor of the pick.

The Nazis chose to stage their extravaganzas in special environments designed outside the old towns, unhampered by the restrictions of urban spaces. The projects were extravagant, and mostly shelved when the war monopolized national energies. *121* But the built fragments of Speer's grand scheme for the Party at Nuremberg are adequate testimony.

The focus was the Zeppelin Field where middle and minor Party functionaries, the *Amtswalter*, held a yearly rally. To this limited program Speer added a vast field for military exercises, the Field of Mars, a stadium calculated to be the largest in history, a congress hall, for Hitler's cultural addresses, and a hall where performances of Wagner's *Die Meistersinger von Nürnberg* with which habitually the Party rallies began could be staged. An avenue $1\frac{1}{4}$ miles (2 km.) long, paved with heavy granite slabs strong enough for tanks, started at the Field of Mars, went by the stadium, crossed a reflecting lake, and terminated in the huge piazza of the Congress Hall. Beyond, at the extreme north where the old city came into view, was a parade ground for Party troops, the S.A. and S.S. "Why always the biggest?" Hitler asked in a 1939 speech to construction workers. "I do this to restore to each individual German his self-respect. In a hundred areas I want to say to the individual: We are not inferior; on the contrary, we are the complete equals of every other nation."[45]

In the opposite political camp, the Soviet Socialist city had needs of its own for mass demonstrations. Since the myth was sustained that Socialism was government *by* the masses, that sacred entity called the People, ritual gatherings of the citizens in the open, in the heart of the inner city, were considered essential. The square served as the point of convergence for the celebratory street processions from each of the various town districts. This meant an open space large enough to contain them all, or to appear as if it could.

Initially the call was for revolutionary re-enactments, and the extant squares made do. There is a contemporary description of a mass performance staged by N. Evreinov in 1920 within the immense semicircular square in front of the Winter Palace at Petrograd (St. Petersburg). Two stages, White and Red, were erected in front of the palace, connected by a high arched bridge. Upon them swarmed 1,500 "actors," including members of the Red Army and the Baltic Fleet. By the end of the improvised nocturnal spectacle, 100,000 people were taking part, joining the Red

121 *Nuremberg (Germany), a model of the buildings and parade grounds designed for the Nazi Party rallies by Albert Speer, 1937. In the foreground is the Field of Mars; beyond lie the stadium on the left and Zeppelin Field on the right, then a lake and a ceremonial entrance gate leading to the Luitpold Hall on the left and Congress Hall on the right. Only the Zeppelin Field and part of the Congress Hall were built. The latter was sentenced to destruction after the war, but its massive construction defeated dynamite.*

122 *Moscow, Red Square, during May Day celebrations in the late 1920s. The Kremlin is on the left, the late 18th-century Senate rising above the early defensive walls. Ahead is the 19th-century Historical Museum. The Iversky Gates and Chapel of the Iberian Virgin stood to the right of that building.*

123 *The vast scale of the Alexanderplatz of Socialist East Berlin is particularly apparent when its area is superimposed on an early 18th-century map of the old walled city (cp. Ill. 36).*

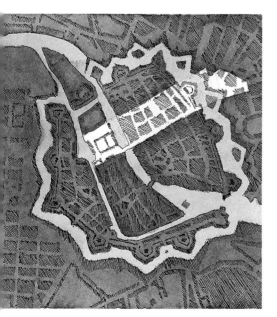

and White armies as they engaged in hand-to-hand combat on the bridge. "Kerensky" and his entourage once more fled the Winter Palace; the throng rushed the gates singing and shouting—until rockets announced the end of this "mystery play of the Revolution."[46] So the French Revolution had appropriated the public *182–* places of Paris for agitprop improvisations, and Soviet authors, aware of the *185* precedent, could boast twenty-five years after "The Storming of the Winter Palace" that there were days when in Soviet cities "Robespierre's dream of a public theatre in which the people act both the part of audience and stage cast comes true."[47]

In new cities the grand void of the center for "public merry-making and mass demonstrations" became a standard feature of planning. In old cities, a vast area of the center would be cleared of buildings, and turned into a composite public place to be used by the Party for its scripted rituals. This was a righteous purge of the capitalist city, this destruction of its cultural core, "where the central business district acts as hub around which other functions of the market economy arrange themselves."[48] The assault was pitiless and spared little. When Moscow architects tried to stand up for the Iversky Gates and Chapel of the Iberian Virgin at the edge of Red Square, they were overruled by Kaganovich, then head of the Moscow Party Organization, who declared, "My aesthetic conception demands columns of demonstrators from the six districts of Moscow pouring into the Red Square simultaneously."[49] The spatial dominance of the State and the Party was especially brutal in the Islamic cities of Central Asia where open squares were culturally alien to the tight mesh of the historic fabric.[50]

Moscow's Red Square was of course the prime model of the Socialist square. A *122* Bulgarian version was created after the Second World War in Sofia, where the old city center was replaced by Lenin Square, surrounded by massive government buildings in Stalinist style. East Germany could show Alexanderplatz in Berlin, and *123* the squares of Leipzig and Dresden. In China, the supreme Socialist setting is Tienanmen Square in Beijing, in front of the old Imperial City, where officials once received edicts at the Gate of Heavenly Peace. It was here that Mao proclaimed the establishment of the People's Republic of China. In 1958–59, the square was expanded from 27 to 98 acres (11 to 40 hectares). The Great Hall of the People occupied the west side, a building one quarter of a mile (400 m.) long; the Historical Museum occupied the east side. The Monument to the People's Heroes is now overshadowed by Mao's tomb.

TYPOLOGIES

Any attempt to classify squares will have to rely on form, or on use, but not on both. The reason is simple: squares that fulfill the same or similar functions through history do not by and large take on the same or similar forms. This being so, both formalist and functional approaches, embraced exclusively, cannot hope to do justice to this protean material.

On the side of use, the categories, which will vary from one classifier to the next, might in themselves be incontestable, but a main difficulty will hound them all, and that is the fact that squares have multiple uses and, further, that these uses change with time. Markets move, outdoor games are internalized, the *place d'armes* becomes obsolete. The forum of the Romans in its time was religious and political center, school and market, and a court of law—all in one.

THE FRAME AND THE PEOPLE

The central issue of public places is, in fact, versatility. And here the interrelation with form, in the broad sense of physical structure, becomes inescapable. In sum, the less specific the form of the square, the more possible it is to have a public place of mixed uses. With the market apparatus kept temporary and removable, for example, the market could become the area of the *passeggiata* in the evenings, or of a spectacle or a game of sports on some days of the year. By the same token, Baroque Naples could be contented with its medieval *larghi*, and show no interest in the formal squares of absolutism designed elsewhere: temporary installations in the Largo di Palazzo, those "gigantesques machines scénographiques" as Cesare De Seta calls them, were a much more flexible, not to say cheaper, way to deck up the irregular space for all sorts of occasions than the fixed architectonic program of a formal square would be, permanently committed at inception to a statement of power that must always remain provisional.[51]

So too in the conception of a new piazza, a certain amount of underdesigning, or a decision on the side of a generalized design, will pay off in terms of mixed use. The *154* *plaza mayor* of Spanish cities could double up as an arena for games while serving *160* for almost everything else as well because it forewent central monuments in the *162* manner of French royal *places*, or a central garden in the English manner. If you design elaborately for one purpose, you lock yourself into using the space for that one purpose. The Roman circus with its fixed *spina* and stone bleachers would have been pretty near impossible to use for much else. Only when the circus lost its functional identity and the specificity of its physical makeup in the post-Roman era, only when its structure, through dilapidation and destruction, was, as it were, *124* generalized, only then could it be pressed into service for a number of public open-air uses.

In the end, the main or steady uses of public places are very few; the improvised or occasional uses, quite diverse. Among the latter, I would count processions and festivals, public punishments (floggings, executions, auto-da-fés), annual fairs, civic events, publicly celebrated coronations, noble weddings and funerals, and socially *Pl.18* charged contests like the Sienese Palio or the thrice-yearly Calcio in Costume on the Piazza S. Croce in Florence.

It would be foolhardy to design squares for the convenience of such incidental *155* events. The Plaza Mayor in Madrid had a steady residential, as it did a commercial, purpose. It was designed with the ranges of apartments in mind, and the luxury

124 Rome's Piazza Navona occupies the site of the 1st-century Circus of Domitian. Its fashionable new life began in the 17th century, when the Pamphilj pope Innocent X rebuilt his family palace (left) and commissioned Borromini and Rainaldi's new church of S. Agnese and Bernini's Four Rivers fountain (center). It soon became the custom to block the fountain's drain in the summer, usually at weekends in August, to provide a cool setting for the carriage-rides of the rich. Pannini's painting of 1756 records the scene. The crowds eventually became more plebeian before the practice ceased in 1867 when the square's pavement was raised.

shops that lined the edges. Incidentally, it made for a dignified setting where the king could view auto-da-fés, or host bullfights and tournaments. The *maidan/takyah* in Bam (Iran), surrounded by two-story shops and resembling a caravanserai, once a year in the month of Muharram staged, as best it could, the Ta'ziya, the passion play of the Shiites.[52]

On such festive occasions, the architectural frame of the square, with its windows, balconies and galleries, made viewing room for the better class of *Pl.18* spectators. Public buildings fronting on it were decorated to suit the moment. Bleachers and demountable grandstands leaned against the palaces. The floor of the *Pl.17* square might be flooded with water, as the Piazza Navona was for the August *124* Festivals; or be covered with sand or earth for feats of riding, as the Campo in Siena still is during the Palio. For the rest, temporary installations transformed the daily space into a stage appropriate to the occasion, to be dismantled and removed when the spectacle was over. We have a rich visual record from the Baroque period of such stage sets in hundreds of commemorative prints and books. They range from ornament hung on the actual buildings of the square to total encasements and temporary structures erected independent of the buildings.

THE CLASSIFIERS

Attempts to look at squares in a comprehensive way have been few and far between, and they have come from the corner of the architect and the architectural historian. For this reason they have favored form over content.

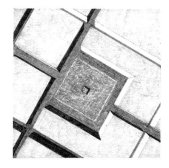

One of the earliest classifications of squares, in part according to function narrowly defined, is Joseph Stübben's in his magisterial *Der Städtebau*, now a century old.[53] A recent try, by Michael Trieb and others, basically repeats this pioneer work, adding to it the genres of the *place d'armes* and the *Wohnhof*, or neighborhood square.[54]

Stübben was a practicing professional, and he meant his book as a manual of city-planning. His concerns are therefore modern, although he is generous with historical precedent. Not surprisingly, the first category he identifies is that of traffic squares, more specifically, modern interchanges, circular or polygonal, best represented by the "star plazas" of Paris (Place de l'Etoile, Place d'Italie). His second main category, *Nutzplatz* or square of public use, comprises places for markets, parades, and public festivities. *Schmuckplatz* (or *Gartenplatz*), the third Stübben category, refers specifically to English garden squares, which Stübben much admired, and more broadly, to landscaped squares everywhere in Europe as the type came to be developed during the 19th century. The final category is "architectural squares," which include the forecourt (*Vorplatz*) serving a single monumental building; the built-on square (*bebaute Platz*), inhabited by a single building almost or fully free-standing; the square where the architectural frame, be it of uniform design like the Parisian royal *places* or the result of historical process, is, as it were, its own monument (*umbaute Platz*); and the "monument square" (*Denkmalplatz*) for those cases, like Trafalgar Square in London or Piazza dello Statuto in Turin, where the commemorative monument demands pre-eminent attention.

125 It is not unjust to say that Paul Zucker's taxonomy of squares in his book of 1959, *Town and Square: From the Agora to the Village Green*, is a refinement of Stübben's last category. "A history of the square," Zucker pronounces ominously, "actually means a history of space as the subject matter of artistic creation." This eliminates "haphazard" and "unsophisticated" public places, like the vast majority of medieval squares, and also justifies his stopping the narrative around 1800 because "the awareness of the third dimension vanishes almost completely during the flat nineteenth century"!

Zucker distinguishes: (1) *the closed square*, like the Place des Vosges, where the space is static and self-contained; (2) *the dominated square*, where the space is dynamic, that is, directed toward a terminal object which can be a church, a gate or an arch, a fountain (e.g., the Trevi in Rome), or a view (the sea in the case of the Piazzetta in Venice); (3) *the nuclear square*, where space is formed around a central statue, fountain, or other vertical accent—Zucker's concession to the small, medieval square, which "does not represent any aesthetic qualities or artistic possibilities"; (4) *grouped squares*, the combination of spatial units as in Nancy, Bologna, or St. Petersburg; and (5) *the amorphous square*—Times Square in New York, Trafalgar Square in London, and the Place de l'Opéra in Paris—whose spatial experience is too diffuse to be positive.

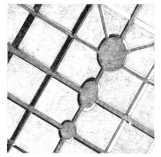

126–
131 Rob Krier's *Stadtraum* of 1975 (*Urban Space*, 1979) is an excellent analysis of urban spaces as systems, but it is also an abstract discussion, i.e., typology without history. Krier's examples come from everywhere, regardless of time: some are historical, some schematic summaries of his own, some proposed new designs. This is the practicing urban designer as against Zucker's architectural historian.

125 opposite *Public spaces as classified by Paul Zucker in* Town and Square *(1959): the closed square; the dominated square; the nuclear square; grouped squares; and the amorphous square.*

this page *Public spaces as classified by Rob Krier: a selection of drawings from his* Stadtraum in Theorie und Praxis *of 1975 (*Urban Space, *1979).*

126 *Rectangular squares with variations: [a] an imaginary square with modified corners; [b] Turin, Piazza di S. Lorenzo Nuovo (F. Navona, 1775); [c] Stuttgart, Rotebühlplatz (Rob Krier scheme, 1973); [d] Palmanova (Giulio Savorgnan, 1593).*

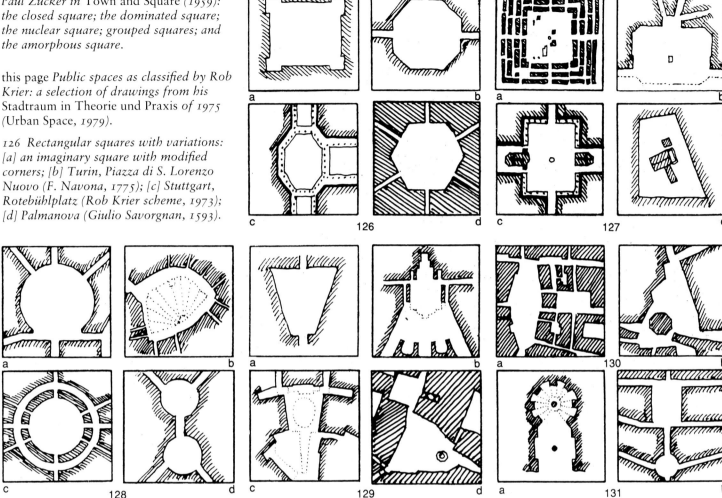

126

127

128

129

130

131

127 *Orthogonal plans for squares: [a] Freudenstadt (1599); [b] Bordeaux, Place Royale/de la Bourse (Jacques Gabriel, designed 1730); [c] Le Corbusier's "redents," 1922; [d] a variant with central buildings: Leptis Magna, Roman period.*

128 *Circuses and variations: [a] Paris, Place des Victoires (J. H. Mansart, 1705); [b] Siena, Campo; [c] a variant with an inset ring of buildings: Paris, Place de Louis XV (project by M. Polard, 1750); [d] combination of circuses (imaginary plan by Rob Krier).*

129 *Triangular squares and their derivatives: [a] Paris, Place Dauphine (begun 1608); [b] Versailles, Place d'Armes*

(J. H. Mansart and Le Vau, late 17th century); [c] Rome, Campidoglio (Michelangelo, 1537); [d] S. Gimignano, Piazza del Duomo and Piazza della Cisterna.

130 *Spaces which are angled, divided, added to and superimposed: [a] Verona,*

Piazza delle Erbe and Piazza dei Signori; [b] Volterra, Piazza del Battistero.

131 *Geometrically complex systems: [a] Ludwigsburg, on the ramparts (D. Frisoni, early 18th century); [b] Karlsruhe, Marktplatz and Rondellplatz (Weinbrenner, 1797).*

Krier formulates a typology of urban space which groups spatial forms and their derivatives into three main groups, "according to the geometrical pattern of their ground plan." The groups are ordered around the square, the circle, and the triangle. "Organic" and formalist squares are included in the same family, so that a highly irregular triangular space in a medieval town associates, classlessly as it were, with the Place Dauphine in Paris. The sympathetic attraction here is to Sitte, not Zucker. And when Krier worries about the modern period, it is not because it went flat, but because of what he calls "the erosion of urban space," of which erosion he gives a blow by blow account from 1900 to the Sixties.

132

133

134

135

136

137

138

139

140

141

142

143

144

145

146

147

SHAPES OF SQUARES

Fleshed out with historical context, the study of shapes is certainly a legitimate pursuit. We need to recognize, first of all, that the public places of geometrically ordered city plans and city extensions will be on a regular design, while "organic" cities will accommodate open space as they are able to in the improvised fabric of their history. This said, we can agree with Krier, no significant gain will be derived from treating the two classes of public place separately. The seemingly prodigious variety of irregular squares can, for the simple purpose of plan analysis, be seen to deviate within basic forms of geometry and their combinations; at the same time, the purest circle or square will possess visual rigor only to the degree that its building walls are uniform and its open space uncluttered.

A difference of another sort is also axiomatic. The shape of a medieval marketplace or civic square has a specificity contingent upon patterns of traffic that often predate the open space, and upon intricacies of process over time in the density and vigor of the confining structures. The popularity of triangular shapes, for example, can be explained through the incidence of traffic intersections of two or three country roads converging upon the town center.

A Baroque square, on the other hand, is an arbitrary product: or rather, it obeys the logic of some design theory which may consider shape a variable of formal beauty. So John Evelyn can comment on his post-Fire plan for London:

> [the streets are] not to pass through the city all in one tenor without varieties, useful breakings, and enlargements into Piazzas at competent distances which ought to be built exactly uniform, strong and with beautiful fronts. Nor should these be all of them square, but some of them oblong, circular, and oval figures, for their better grace and capacity.[55]

The triangle

The triangular public place of "organic" towns is almost always the inflated crossroads, the characteristic setting for open-air markets. The feature is a 132 commonplace of English medieval towns; it is likely to appear at the foot of the castle where three important roads come together. The shape is flexible: the sides tend to give, bulging or receding in gentle curves; the "points," where the converging roads open into the square, are loosely defined.

In geometricized form, the triangle is rare. The best-known instance, Place Dauphine in Paris, had a good enough excuse, its site being the prow-like western tip 133, of the Ile de la Cité. Otherwise, the straight-sided triangle usually turns out to be the 226 formalization of a prior, more irregular form, as with two key instances in Rome— Piazza Araceli at the foot of the Campidoglio (deflated by the Fascist landscaping of the Victor Emanuel Monument) and the double triangle of Piazza di Spagna. 134

The trapezoid

The principle here might be said to be the intrusion of a climactic façade on one of the points of a triangular plaza. The schematic reproduction of a perspective box so simulated might account for the identification of the type with the Italian Renaissance. The telltale sequence, which some scholars consider deliberate, consists of Bernardo Rossellino's square at Pienza (1459), Michelangelo's Campi- 135 doglio (1537), and the small unit in front of the basilica in Bernini's Piazza of St. 129c Peter's (1656).

The rectangle

As a perfect square, the form is relatively rare. Two famous examples are the Place
136 des Vosges in Paris and Queen Square at Bath. Because of the equality of the sides,
this type does not easily lend itself to architectural emphasis, directing attention
onto the open space. County and state capitals in the United States, which devote
one of the checkers of the urban grid to the town square, commemorate this fact by
137 placing the courthouse or capitol on a slight eminence in the middle of the space.

The common rectangle, on the other hand, is possibly the most frequently used
shape for the public place. One of its advantages is precisely that it allows a
138 directional axis toward a culminating monument. In the case of ancient Roman
forums, this is the main temple of the city, placed against one of the short ends (e.g.,
Pompeii).

The L-shaped square

Normally, this is a combination of two separate adjacent rectangular spaces, as with
the monumental case of the Piazza and Piazzetta S. Marco in Venice. Many of the
medieval specimens are certainly convergences of this kind. But, as Enrico Guidoni
has pointed out, the notion of a diagonal view of a public building, where two sides
can be visible at once, a notion which probably originated in Tuscany in the 13th
century as the product of an early interest in perspective, did influence the design of
139 integral L-squares, especially those of churches. The difference here is that the space
fixes a particular view of the public building in a premeditated way, rather than
being an accident of urban development.

The corner of the L-shaped square becomes a critical point of emphasis for the
visual cohesion of the space. In Venice this corner is stabilized with S. Marco's free-
standing campanile. The Renaissance prefers sculpture, like the Gattamelata of
Donatello in Padua at the northwest corner of S. Antonio, Giambologna's Neptune
Fountain in Bologna, and the statue of Cosimo I at the Piazza della Signoria in
Florence, also by Giambologna.

The circle and ellipse

In antiquity, these forms, though infrequent, were not unknown. The Roman forum
at Gerasa, and the forum at Antinoë (Antinoöpolis) in Egypt, founded in AD 132, are
both designed on the curve. The Forum of Constantine in Constantinople (Istanbul),
114 at the summit of the second hill, is known to have had rounded corners; the
emperor's triumphal column which fixed the center still stands.

Accidental medieval ellipses are survivals of Roman amphitheaters; I had already
Pl.16 occasion above to name Piazza del Anfiteatro in Lucca. The first stage in the
transformation of the amphitheater came with the conversion of the building into a
fortified clan stronghold. This was a common practice in the south of France where
each amphitheater was occupied by several groups of knights. The central space of
the arena was left open as the community piazza; the periphery was turned into a
circuit of defense, and houses were built on the seat tiers in concentric rows.[56] When
this arrangement could no longer be tolerated in the context of an independent city,
the defenses were dismantled and the open space converted to a public square.

The ellipsoidal or ovoid tendency of the *plaza mayor* in some Spanish towns,
154 Chinchón near Madrid and Pedraza for example, returns to the conception of the
public place as a setting for spectacle—in this case bullfights, open-air theater, and
the like.

The Renaissance revived these curvilinear types for its public places, as it did in its
18 architecture. To take the circle first, the first executed specimen is Place des Victoires

in Paris, 1684–87, designed as a residential square by Jules Hardouin Mansart. It had a monument to Louis XIV in the center and five streets emanating from it. Of these, two opposite ones in time formed an axis that counteracted the centralized layout, but determined the axis of the statue. When the original statue, destroyed at the time of the Revolution, was subsequently replaced with a much smaller version, and a street was added to the extant radials, the comparatively enclosed square degenerated into a traffic circle.[57]

The French name for these traffic circles, *rond-point*, derives from a term of landscape design which refers to a large circular clearing in parks or woods usually with a circle of grass in the middle. In the context of city-planning, the *rond-point* need not be bounded by a ring of buildings, but could be an open circular area, most likely extra-urban, on which avenues converge.

The perfect example of the urban *rond-point* is the Place de l'Etoile in Paris. In its *140* original form due to Napoleon I, the circumference was unbuilt. As reaffirmed under Haussmann, the *place* consists of twelve uniform blocks of houses, designed by Hittorf, narrower than the twelve incoming streets, with trees planted in concentric rings in front of the houses at the direction of Haussmann who disapproved of the *199* architect's work.

This urban *rond-point* is the French answer to the English "circus." The term is first used at Bath, a city whose Roman origins were known. The Circus there, of *141* 1754, was designed by John Wood the Elder in self-conscious emulation of a Roman amphitheater; it is, in fact, a kind of inside-out Colosseum, comprised of 33 houses. But "circus" is soon being used to describe a monumental form of crossing which consists of four curved splays on four corner blocks. George Dance provided examples of the type as early as 1768 in the London suburbs of Southwark and Lambeth, and John Nash followed suit with Oxford and Piccadilly Circus in the city *142* center.

Circular forms, as pure shapes, were a favorite of Neoclassicism. Napoleon's architects and engineers proposed huge circular plazas for a number of cities, conceived as full urban systems like Ledoux's celebrated proposal for the company town at Chaux. Milan's Foro Bonaparte around the hull of the Sforza Castle was to *143* be a great commemorative plaza and the new administrative center of the city. The circle itself, with a diameter of 1,860 feet (570 m.), was defined by porticoes and official buildings of stark Neoclassical design that included a theater, a customs house, an exchange, a bath and a pantheon. Of this grandiloquent scheme the only parts carried out were an arena modeled after the Roman circus, a triumphal arch (Arco della Pace), and a stretch of a curving street.

The hemicycle

The natural progenitor of this type is the concave recession in the building line across from an important public building like a church. The earliest examples seem to come in the first half of the 13th century, and the arrangement is widespread enough in Europe to suggest a northern rather than a Mediterranean origin. Never very deep, the concavity merely expands the street running along the public building and dignifies its façade without interrupting the spatial flow.

In the fully developed type, two variants might be distinguished, based on whether the plaza breaks the line of the curve to collect traffic or keeps this line intact.

(1) Open form   The half-circle in France may well tie in with landscape design once again. One of the definitions of *rond-point* in garden terminology referred, in fact, to the half-circle facing the main entrance of an estate. The unbuilt Place de

France, planned for Paris under Henri IV, is an urban translation of this same idea. The project involved an entrance—a new gate into the city, directly behind the Temple, in an area adjacent to the old city wall between the Porte St.-Antoine and Porte du Temple. The semicircular space that would open in front of this new gate was bounded by seven public buildings and streets radiated between them.[58] A late, *144* executed instance is the Place de l'Odéon in Paris of 1779–82. From then on the scheme becomes a standard feature of the academic school of planning.

145   *(2) Closed form*   By this I mean the architectural hemicycle, distinct from the preceding combination of semicircular space and radiating streets. When used as a forecourt to a specific building, it would come under Stübben's category of *Vorplätze*. The Baroque appreciated its molding of open space; Neoclassical architects appreciated the net sweep of its curve. Naples has three impressive urban exedrae, the earliest of them independent of a building. This Foro Carolino (by Luigi Vanvitelli, 1760), dedicated to the memory of Charles III Bourbon, civilized some of the huge Largo del Mercatello, which was a cattle and grain market. The grand niche in the middle was meant to hold the king's statue. The exedra at the Piazza del Mercato, of 1761, frames the existing church of S. Croce del Purgatorio. Piazza Plebiscito, across from the Palazzo Reale, is an extended parvis for the church of S. Francesco di Paola; it dates from 1817–36. In its original Revolutionary conception it was intended to have a "Temple of Justice" where the church now is.

One particular solution combines the virtues of the closed and open forms of the hemicycle. Here a cupping architectural half-curve splits in the middle to start a straight street directed away from the open space. The solution is especially effective on the inner side of a city gate, with the half-curve welcoming entering visitors and sending them on their way toward the center. In Rome's Piazza dell'Esedra, from the 1880s, the design acquires a historical dimension from the fact that the half-curve traces the exedra of the ancient Baths of Diocletian.

The British crescent is a residential version of the hemicycle, or rather a half ellipse, which first appears in Bath, at the Royal Crescent of 1767–75 by John Wood the Younger. This combines a grand architectural order with stretches of landscaping and natural views. The crescent becomes a standard device of British *148* planning from then on. By 1829 the New Town in Edinburgh, started in 1767, was sporting 13 crescents and 4 circuses. Dramatic natural views are framed by *146* Brighton's Kemp Town crescent and Bath's Lansdown crescent.

As adopted by Modernism the crescent had a mixed progeny. Mostly it is the built curve that is emulated, and not the masterful integration to an open landscape. The serpentine curves of post-war *grands ensembles* in France, La Grande Borne near Paris for example, or the crescents in Taby, the regional center of suburban Stockholm, are exhibitions of arbitrary form and not exemplars of public space. *147* Only the great horseshoe of Bruno Taut in Berlin of the 1920s, the Hufeisensiedlung, seems a worthy Modernist homage to the Woods.

A BOOK OF USES

The limits of this formal approach to open spaces are obvious. More recent scholarship, by contrast, focuses on the *uses* of public space. An account of squares from this viewpoint inevitably becomes a social history. This is not to say, of course, that the physical side can be ignored—every social activity must, after all, take place in a physical environment of some sort, more or less designed. It means rather, that while the uses are grouped and typified, the settings, historically specific, must be brought in by way of example as needed.

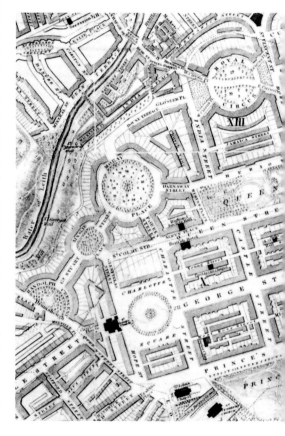

148 Edinburgh (Scotland), detail of the west end of the New Town; from James Knor's map, 1829. Starting at the bottom, the spaces are Charlotte Square, by Robert Adam (1791), part of the original layout; then, on the Moray Estate, designed by James Gillespie Graham after 1822, the generously planted Randolph Crescent, Ainslie Place, Moray Place, and Royal Circus.

149 *Athens, reconstruction of the Agora as it appeared in the 2nd century BC. The open space is crossed by the Panathenaic Way, the route for processions to the shrine of Athena on the Acropolis in the distance. Facing onto it are a number of stoas, long buildings with colonnades fronting lockable offices or shops: on the far side (south) is the Middle Stoa; then, reading counterclockwise, on the left the Stoa of Attalus; in the foreground the Stoa Poikile and Stoa of the Herms; on the right the Stoa of Zeus, followed by a temple to Apollo and a complex of buildings housing the Metroon (state archive) at the front and Bouleuterion (council house) behind, and finally the circular Tholos, in which the city's standard weights and measures were kept.*

The headings in a study of public places arranged according to use would include the following:

The civic center

Probably the two primary uses of public spaces have been as markets and as civic centers. Not uncommonly these institutions occupied the same space, but the desire to separate the two was likely to surface at some advanced stage of a city's existence. In either case, the transition from an open market to a tidier market hall can frequently be documented during the later Middle Ages, and by the 18th century covered markets are on their way to replacing the uninhibited bustle of the market square.

I have said enough about markets in the chapter on "Urban Divisions"; less on civic centers. If "civic center" signifies communal self-government, then its claim to universality in a history of squares would dwindle. Cities of most cultures were under the rule of local lords or an organized state. It is best to think of the civic center square, then, not as the expression of a particular form of government but as a place for public business and the display of the trappings of power. Even so, such a square may be absent from the urban fabric, as it is from the cities of imperial China, from market towns of the Middle Ages where business is conducted along the "high street," and even from a Classical city like Ephesus, where the colonnaded avenue running through town took the place of the missing forum.

The model of a democratic civic center remains the Greek *agora*.[59] In its origin it *149* was the open-air locus of citizens' meetings. When the Athenian Agora proved too small for this purpose, the general assembly moved to the nearby hill of the Pnyx. With the agora was created, for the first time in history, a public space as a necessary element of the urban landscape through which to express a community's collective political power. Here the laws were carved in stone and exposed to the public. In the laying out of new colonial cities, land for the agora and the temples was the first to be allotted. In Xenophon's *Anabasis*, the Ten Thousand, in their long trek from Persia to the Aegean, met many peoples who did not know the institution of the agora. To keep up his troops' morale and remind them of their Greekness, Xenophon invariably designated a provisional agora wherever they happened to stop. And Alexander, spreading Hellenic culture through new cities all the way into Central Asia, endowed them with an agora, a gymnasium and a theater, far more ambitious in scale for symbolic reasons than the city's actual importance. Pausanias later enunciates this truth when he says of a small rural settlement, "How can I give the name of city to a group of houses without a theater, an agora or a gymnasium?"[60]

As Jacob Burckhardt was the first to point out, *agora* derives from *agheirein*, to meet, and the word often refers to the assembly itself regardless of its site. From *agora* derives the verb *agorazein*, meaning to find oneself in the marketplace, to buy, to talk, to deal, to congregate. Roland Martin says the word means speech and the place of speech. The gods of the agora are protectors of the orator. So before the agora assumes a commercial role, its principal function is political and social.[61]

When the autonomy of the polis, its self-government, degenerates, so does the agora. When the Sicilian polis of Morgantina lost its independence, its great agora came apart: the east side with its grand stairs was planted, a Roman-type *macellum* (market) occupied the center; shops and workshops insinuated themselves in the open space. Martin sees the closing of the agora to traffic in the formal designs of late Greek and Hellenistic urbanism as a symbol of this weakening of the collective political power, which the old agora, open to all traffic, encapsulated. Fancy gates now enclosed the public space, porticoes surrounded it.

150 The forum of the Romans did its own gloss on the agora, but the idea was the same. Again, commercial activities took second seat to civic and religious ones—or rather the three were inseparable.[62] If commercial activities *per se* were not always central, the administration of commerce was. It was in the forum that the *mensa ponderaria*, the storeroom of the weights and measures of the city, was located. It was here that private instruction took place, where *magistri*, *grammatistae* and *rhetoris* (masters and instructors of language and rhetoric) set up shop. The administration of justice was such an important function of the forum that "going to the forum" (*ire in forum*) came to mean to go to court. For civil cases *in iure* (as opposed to cases *in iudicio*, which could be tried anywhere), the appropriate magistrate sitting in the forum was obligatory. The basilica, which, among other uses, served as a court of law, was an indispensable component of the forum complex. In the open stood speaking daises (the famous rostra in Rome) for public oratory of all kinds—from political speeches to eulogies of one's deceased family members if one were a citizen of substance. Here public announcements were exhibited—election posters, certain sale contracts, wills, adoptions. The coming of age of young boys with the donning of the *toga virilis* also might take place in the

150 Model of Rome at the time of Constantine, early 4th century AD, showing the area of the forums: the original Forum Romanum (A), the Forum of Caesar (B), and the imperial forums built successively by Augustus (C), Vespasian (D), Nerva (E), and Trajan (F). The Forum Romanum lies at the foot of the Tabularium or state archive on the Capitoline Hill (1); near its western end stand the Arch of Septimius Severus (2) and the Temple of Saturn/Treasury (cp. Pl. 33). It is edged on the south by the Basilica Julia (3) and Temple of Castor and Pollux (4), and on the north by the Curia (5) and Basilica Aemilia (6); its eastern end is closed by the Temple of Divus Julius (7). The Sacra Via leads on past the Basilica of Maxentius/Constantine (8) to the Temple of Venus and Roma (9) and skirts the Colosseum (10).

151 Vigevano (Italy). The Piazza Ducale was created by Bramante in the 1490s for the Sforza Duke Lodovico il Moro. Originally the ducal presence was more obviously dominant: the arcaded buildings stopped short of the towered castello, which surveyed the public square from the top of a monumental staircase. It was pushed into the background in the late 17th century, when the region had come under Austrian rule.

forum. It was the setting for games during the Republic, but eventually only the *pompae*—processions that preceded the games—passed through.

What the emperors did was to appropriate this civic center of Republican Rome. The process was a natural result of one of its functions—to be an open-air museum of the city's memories, the locus of celebration of its triumphs and traditions. Strewn with commemorative monuments which both celebrated and admonished, it was now recast as an exaltation of one-man rule. Where the dominion of Rome had been represented by statues of Aeneas and Romulus, the emperor was awarded pride of place. Collective memories of community in time became narrowly identified with dynastic propaganda.[63] In the capital itself a splendid series of forums dedicated to the glory of reigning emperors siphoned away much of the authority of the old forum of the Republic.

Much the same recurred in the late Middle Ages. The hard-won independence of city-states from feudal bonds had revived the civic square by the 12th century. A major difference now was the place of religion, never seen as a competitor in Greco-Roman antiquity but rather as a bulwark of the State. The long grasp of temporal power by the bishops in the earlier Middle Ages would pit Church against commune, and force a split between religious center and civic center. In many cities the cathedral square with the bishop's palace stood apart from the *piazza pubblica* with the town hall and its dependencies. Although the two public forums could be some distance away, they were usually neighbors interlinked in a variety of ways— through fountains, stairs, or porticoes. Even in new towns like the French *bastides*, the church was normally offset in its own space.

But from the 14th century onward the contest was a new one—between commune and *signori*. Everywhere the city states were made subject to autocratic sway. And the dynastic ambitions of the Medici, the Este, or the Sforza, or higher still, the royal houses of Europe, were asserted through the physical remaking of the civic center or through the substitution for its centrality of another piazza more unequivocally associated with the lord's dominion. At Vigevano, the Sforza obliterated the civic center of the commune under a vast formal square designed by Bramante in the spirit of a Roman forum. At Mantua, the Gonzaga developed their own palace square a

short distance away from the derelict civic center. And in the great capitals of Europe
160 over the next two hundred years squares were set out as magnificent frames for the
princely statue, rid of all the clutter of a citizenry governing itself.

When constitutional monarchies and the instruments of the Liberal State
succeeded the Age of Absolutism during the course of the 19th century, the civic
center dispersed its concentrated energies into multiple squares, some showcasing
branches of the prodigious new bureaucracy, and others framing new cultural
39 institutions. In Vienna's Ringstrasse, where the panoply of the Liberal State was
disposed in one broad urban swath, the ill-defined oversized squares that so
discomfited Sitte highlighted the Parliament and the Town Hall, the Palace of
Justice and the University, the Burgtheater, two major national museums, the
Opera, a concert hall, and a number of academies and art buildings.

The *place d'armes*

Putting armed forces on display has served two purposes in the history of cities: to
reassure the citizenry that its defenses were on the ready, and to discourage it from
challenging authority. The space for this display was therefore linked with the
architecture of power—the ruler's palace or a representative civic center. In small
more or less self-governing towns, the town square was often the place where the
militia exercised in public. This was one function of the New England common.

The parade ground within the city could also be a vast affair. When Carlo
Giovanni Rossi was charged in 1819 with the reconstruction of Palace Square in
152 St. Petersburg, between the Winter Palace and the General Staff building, his
instructions were to make "the space of the square its dominant element," and
provide a "proper architectural setting" as "a stage for huge military parades."[64]
This is a fair statement of the component features of a parade ground: an assembly
area for of processing troops, which might be a building on the square or a
subsidiary open space linked up to it; a point of emergence, like the triumphal arch in
the middle of the great curved façade of the General Staff building; a grand
architectural backdrop which would ensconce the reviewing stand; and the parade
space itself.

Inca towns were laid out around a large plaza which served for state ceremonies
153 involving troops. The one at Huanuco Pampa had enormous proportions, 1,800 by
1,150 feet (550 by 350 m.). It communicated through formal gateways with two
smaller subsidiary plazas. Near the center was a large platform of dressed-stone

*152 St. Petersburg, Palace Square, from
Ricard de Montferrand's publication
celebrating the erection of his column in
memory of Alexander I, 1836. The space
lies between Rastrelli's mid-18th-century
Winter Palace (right) and Rossi's early
19th-century General Staff Building (left);
beyond, it extends past the towered
Admiralty and links up with squares by
St. Isaac's and the Senate.*

masonry where the Inca himself or his representative sat presiding over astronomical observations and parades. We know as much from Cristobal de Molina, who wrote:

> in each town there was a large royal plaza, and in the middle of it was a square high platform with a very high staircase; the Inca and three of his lords ascended it to speak to the people and see the army when they made their reviews and assemblages.[65]

With an ever larger military presence, centrally located parade grounds became distinct from a much larger extramural area for regular maneuvers. Paris's was on the left bank, laid out about 1770 in front of the huge Ecole Militaire complex by Jacques Ange Gabriel. In this century training areas migrated even farther away from cities, because of the pressure on urban land and changes in military technology. In Europe the only profit to cities from the ostentatious militarism of the past is that the old parade grounds have survived as central open spaces. Familiar examples are Vienna's Heldenplatz and the Horse Guards Parade in London.[66]

Modern colonial powers, during the period of assimilation, inflicted summary destruction upon subject cities to procure their military stage. The French razed the city center of Algiers to create a vast parade ground at the meeting point of three major arteries that focused on the Friday mosque. The British did the same in several Indian cities, notably Delhi (see below, pp. 254–55).

Games

The public nature of games, and the passions aroused by their long-enduring rivalries, are a familiar aspect of modern life. In the past, games acquired an added importance because they were sometimes ritual enactments of the contest among social classes, vehicles of political unrest, and an expression of interstate belligerence.

The Nika revolt of 532, which nearly toppled the Emperor Justinian from the throne of Byzantium, was sparked by the rivalry of two groups of supporters in the hippodrome, the Blues and the Greens, the equivalent in effect of political parties. The ferocious competition between London and Westminster over wrestling in the late Middle Ages went beyond the ardor of the game. Kings regularly figured as participants in jousting tournaments, and there was a clear sense in the Renaissance that this participation was proof of the prince's health and virility, that is to say, a political matter. The rivalry of Siena's *contrade* or wards is ritually fought out each summer in the Piazza del Campo through the Palio, an urban horse race with *Pl.18* medieval origins.

The relation of games to public places is an intimate one. At its most innocent, public places like the civic square, because of their size and centrality, were the only suitable setting for some games in the absence of a specialized architecture for them. "It is a custom handed down from our ancestors," Vitruvius writes, "that gladiatorial games should be given in the forum" (*De architectura*, v.1). The specialized environment, the amphitheater, comes after the accommodation of the public spectacle in the all-purpose central plaza.

This is also true of bullfights. The game began as an aristocratic entertainment, with common people participating only as spectators. The subjection of the bulls was done by groups of knights, in a show of horsemanship. A crude form of bullfighting began as early as the 12th century, as part of royal functions, and the first location was the jousting field outside the walls. When the game had grown more refined and spectacular, it was transported to public squares, with the streets

153 opposite Huanuco Pampa (Peru). At the center is the vast plaza. Around it were houses and walled compounds: to the east (right), rectangular open spaces, for feasting, lay between the central square and the Inca's compound. A compound close to the center of the north side seems to have been the quarter for women who wove cloth and brewed maize beer.

154 *Chinchón (Spain). The Plaza Mayor is elliptical, like an arena. For the August bullfights its balconies are supplemented by wooden seating and barriers.*

leading to them temporarily closed off by barriers and fences, and appropriate constructions put up as the fiesta required. In their design the new squares of the 17th century acknowledged the needs of the game. The shape was regular; there were few exits; and the framing buildings had balconies.

155   The Plaza Mayor in Madrid, designed by Juan Gomes de Mora on the model of the *plazas mayores* at Lerma and Valladolid and built between 1617 and 1619, is representative. A rectangle of 434 by 334 feet (151 by 117 m.) framed by four-storey houses on porticoes of granite harboring shops, the space could hold 50,000 spectators crowded on the square itself and the balconies and windows of the houses which were rented out for the occasion. In a special type of *plaza mayor*, one or more sides of the square featured continuous wooden galleries over a ground story that was almost exclusively geared to the comings and goings of the bullfight. Examples
154 include Tembleque, Almagro, Chinchón and S. Carlos del Valle. They were owned by the Church or the nobility, and were rented out to individuals for religious feasts and bullfights.[67] We are close here to the authentic bullring of later times.

In the first half of the 18th century, the nobility lost interest in the game. It was probably the great bullfight in the Plaza Mayor of Madrid in June 1725, in the presence of Philip V, that marked the end. Philip did not care for these spectacles, and so the nobility saw no reason to patronize them either. At any rate, the bullfight changed into something popular, played by commoners, and the bull was henceforth killed in single combat. Then, special enclosed spaces began to be designed specifically as bullrings, so the entry of the public could be controlled (i.e., so one could sell tickets). The first purpose-built bullring, a temporary one of wood, was erected in Seville. Soon thereafter others appeared in stone, beginning with Madrid's in 1745.[68]

Jousting itself had begun in extramural open spaces before it was moved to elaborately designed plazas like the Cortile del Belvedere at the Vatican. By then the violent, martial nature of the original tournament had metamorphosed into stylized play, with little chance of serious hurt or death.[69] From that period, we have records of tournaments being held in places like the Piazza Navona in Rome, Piazza S. Croce

155 *Madrid, Plaza Mayor: reconstruction of a bullfight by noblemen on horseback. Note the balconies full of people, and the royal loggia in the center on the left.*

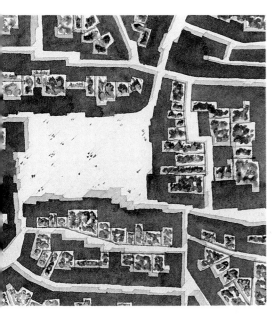

156 A "turbine plaza." Streets enter at the corners, but thanks to their angling there is no sense that the square is a mere interlude for through traffic.

in Florence, el Borne in Barcelona, and in Paris at the Place Royale (des Vosges) and *Pl.17* the Place du Carrousel between the Louvre and the Tuileries, a small square in a tangled pattern of narrow streets first used for this purpose by Louis XIV in 1662.

"Carrousel" is the formal term for an elaborate set of games that includes all the various displays of jousting. By and large, what was needed was an ample but bounded space, generous access routes for the processing participants to enter the arena, an official "box" for king and high dignitaries, and a "box" for judges. As an aspect of the scene's chivalric element, women played an important role as spectators.[70]

Traffic

The convergence and distribution of traffic has always been a raison d'être for the urban square. It is obvious that the needs of traffic would be at odds with the nature of the square as a gathering place. A debate over priorities can be sensed throughout history, even when the issue is not specifically engaged.

The forum in Roman towns was closed to traffic; a crossroads feature, it was nonetheless placed just off the crossing of the two main axes, or to one side of the main artery that was the stretch of the interurban high road running the length of the city. In the medieval new towns of southern France, the street system was often independent of the open space of the main square, in that the streets were directed through arcaded passages which framed the ground floor of boundary buildings. A common type of square in the medieval towns shaped not by survey but by accretive growth is the so-called "turbine plaza." Here streets enter at the corners or close to *156* them, but are not continued in a straight line across the space. The arrangement was held up by Sitte as an object lesson to modern planners for putting the needs of traffic second to the essential nature of the square as social container.

The English square of the 17th and 18th centuries was exclusive on principle. In contrast, the contemporary royal *places* in France were nearly always projected with complementary avenues, even if the chief purpose of these was to create vistas for the royal statue. The author of a pamphlet published in 1771, probably the architect "Athenian" Stuart, ridicules the squares of London for trying to be "mock-parks in the middle of the town," and defines an urban square as "a large opening, free and unencumbered, where not only carriages have room to turn and pass, but even where the people are able to assemble occasionally without confusion."[71] Earlier in the century, Germain Brice had a similar reaction to the attempt to convert the Place des Vosges in Paris into an English square, with a fenced-in garden planted at the expense and for the sole enjoyment of the immediate occupants. "Their outlay was completely superfluous," Brice wrote in 1725, "because a square should never be obstructed or circumscribed, on the contrary access to it should be free and easy."[72]

In Italy, the medieval preference for secured squares continued into the Renaissance. In both periods squares were often isolated from their surroundings by means of chains, and even gates, that blocked streets of access. Alberti's stance was ambivalent. A square to him was more like a building than it was space surrounded by buildings. His stress was on assembly rather than passage. At the same time he could write that "cross-ways and squares differ only in their bigness, the cross-way being indeed nothing else but a small square."[73] That a street junction brings together people as well as traffic may be self-evident, but so is the fact that social intercourse must be confined to the edges and traffic allowed to flow unimpeded through the open space. But as a modern student of Alberti's urban thought, W. A. Eden, points out, "If one may call a street-junction a small square, one may just as

well call a square a large street junction: and that, in fact, is what most city squares have tended to become in the interval between Alberti's day and our own."[74] This was Sitte's lament, and his grim assessment was that this confusion of priorities had brought about, in Eden's words, "the disintegration of the city as a society of men and of buildings."

Stübben sorts out the conflict technocratically by giving traffic its own unquestioned public concourses, in exchange for keeping it off other kinds of squares. With the advent of the motorcar, as later editions of his book acknowledge, these modern interchanges acquired a specialized design. New features included pedestrian underpasses, a raised central platform, and *éperons*, wedge-shaped obstacles at the entrances to the interchange meant to prevent direct collisions. Much of this invention was associated with Eugène Hénard, city architect of Paris, 157 whose proposal for a *carrefour à giration*, a roundabout for the automotive age, was given its first trial at the Place de l'Etoile in 1907.

The residential square

Housing and town squares have been compatible at least since the Middle Ages. The shopkeeper and the merchant lived above his business premises, which had to be on or near the town center, i.e., the market square. In new towns, the plots around this open space were allotted to the most important merchants and their families who

157 Eugène Hénard's "carrefour à giration," proposed in 1906 for the junction of the Avenue de Richelieu and Boulevard Montmartre, Paris from his Etudes sur les transformations de Paris, 1903–9. Its combination of pedestrian underpasses, a raised central platform, and "éperons"—wedge-shaped obstacles meant to prevent collisions—was tried out at the Etoile in 1907. With a hole in the middle as here, rather than the Arc de Triomphe, the scheme reappeared in a number of cities in the 1960s.

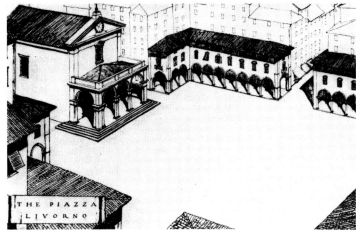

THE PIAZZA LIVORNO

158 above *Metz (France), the "Champ à Seille"; engraving after Claude Chastillon, early 17th century. Surrounded by merchants' houses, this square belongs to a large international family of medieval arcaded marketplaces. Henri IV's links with Lorraine, and his visit to Metz in 1602, make it a possible French inspiration for the Place des Vosges.*

159 above right *Livorno (Italy), Piazza Grande, laid out ca. 1600. Grand Duke Ferdinando I of Tuscany applied the formula of symmetrical arcades around a square focused on a church that had grown up gradually in the Piazza of the Santissima Annunziata in Florence (Ill. 104). Here the arcades continue around the side facing the church. The piazza influenced Inigo Jones's design for Covent Garden (Ill. 161). (After Peets)*

built their own houses. In New Spain, the most socially prominent of the immigrating Spanish population lived around the *plaza*. But of course in all these cases the space itself was the public gathering place of the whole town.

The "residential square" so-called is at once more unified and more exclusive. The term is used for a range of houses of more-or-less uniform and continuous frontage grouped around an open space, the whole design planned and executed by a single agency and not the inhabitants themselves. In many cases public use of this space is limited, and commercial activity, when present, is not the dominant concern. Until the 19th century, the sponsors are princes or members of the upper class; thereafter, private developers take over.

The type originates with the Renaissance, and matures in the 17th century. The leading examples are in Italy, starting with imperfect specimens like the Sforza square of the 1490s at Vigevano, and the square at Livorno (Leghorn) a hundred *151* years later. The first formally designed or redesigned Spanish *plazas mayores* are not *159* much later—Valladolid's in fact dates from late in the reign of Philip II (1556–98), and Madrid's is building between 1617 and 1619. In Paris the trend of royal *places* *155* begins with Henri IV: the Place Royale (des Vosges), begun in 1605 as a center for *Pl.17* silk manufacture, was converted to strictly non-commercial uses in 1607.[75] In London Covent Garden was first, in 1631. The only other early claimant may be the *161* Piazza Reale in Turin from 1621.

It is also just possible that the startling appearance of planned squares in the Islamic world during the 17th century might be related, however indirectly, to the example of Baroque residential squares. The two outstanding cases are the Registan in Samarkand, in which three important monuments from the 15th to the 17th century were coordinated around a sand-floored market square, and the huge Maidan-i Shah at Isfahan with its uniform portico-screen of two stories. *110*

The passage from Vigevano to the Place des Vosges or Covent Garden is neither direct nor clean. The Italian model most likely to have played a part is said to be Livorno: the human intermediaries, the Medici and Inigo Jones. It was Ferdinando *159* de' Medici who built the primarily residential piazza of uniform design in the center of Livorno, the port of the Dukedom of Tuscany to which he succeeded in 1587. This was possibly the first fully symmetrical square to be built in Europe. Jones visited it, and remembered it at Covent Garden. He could as well have derived his scheme via Paris, where the same Medici influence may have been present at the Place des Vosges through Henri's queen, Marie de Médicis.[76]

But there was also more immediate French precedent from the late Middle Ages available to Henri IV. The vast triangular *place* at Pont-à-Mousson bounded by houses on arcaded porticoes, and the two squares at Metz, one an elongated 158 triangle, the other a perfect square called "le Champ à Seille" (today Place Coslin), come to mind.[77]

Whatever their pedigree, the Parisian royal *places* were a distinctive group. They were sponsored directly by the French kings, or developed in their name by nobility 160 (Place de Louis le Grand, later Place Vendôme, initiated by Louis XIV; Place des 18 Victoires by the Duc de la Feuillade). In either case they celebrated royal power, while at the same time launching a speculative venture of housing. The obvious royal symbol was the statue of the king in the middle of the open space, which was scaled so that it would tower over the square, the head rising above the cornice line. The originals, destroyed during the Revolution and variously replaced, were huge— the statue of Louis XIV in the Place des Victoires was 33 feet (10.6 m.) high including the base; his statue in the Place Vendôme, showing him in the guise of a Roman emperor, was 22 feet (6.7 m.) high.

It would seem that the formula of the royal statue as the center of the residential square we owe to Cardinal Richelieu. Henri's *places* left the center free. Place 226 Dauphine had the royal statue outside the square, at the western tip of the island; it was set up after Henri's death, in 1614.[78] Only when Richelieu had installed an equestrian statue of Louis XIII in the Place des Vosges in 1639 was the iconography of the royal *place* complete, and the model ready for export to the rest of France, and also abroad. A treatise by Francois Lemée of 1688 codified the guidelines for situating statues, with specific application to the *places royales*. By then Parisians had begun to question the wisdom of this commemorative practice. If one continues to provide a statue-square for each reigning prince, one has to choose between two alternatives, the Abbé Laugier proclaimed: "either depopulate Paris or enlarge it every time a statue is set up."[79]

Although the royal *places* are often represented as residential enclaves having no public functions at all—no market, no daily bustle, no church-related events—this is not necessarily how they were conceived. Place Dauphine was intended to accommodate ground-story shops; Place des Vosges, as we have seen, a nascent silk industry. Louis XIV envisaged the Place Vendôme as a monumental square, the intellectual and administrative center of the capital. It was to be surrounded by the royal library, the mint, the academies and the chancellery, but the intention ran afoul of the economic reality. Nor were later royal squares strictly residential. Nancy's Place Royale (Place Stanislas), with Louis XV in the center, was focused on the new town hall. The splendid Bordeaux squares, built from the 1730s onward, *Pl.4,* also allowed public buildings, like the Bourse and the hall for tax authorities, into *127b* their residential frame.

In England, where overt exaltation of the sovereign was not the issue and where entire estates were in the hands of single owners, the residential square had a less complicated history. The earliest example, Covent Garden (1631), where an active *161* market was installed by the century's end, is *sui generis*: after Covent Garden, shops were never allowed on the square proper, and the market was always tucked away in an inconspicuous spot of the estate. The series more properly begins in the 1660s with St. James's and Bloomsbury Squares, the latter, whose patron was the Earl of Southampton, being the first in London to be formally called a "square." In the middle there might be a statue of the king (e.g., in Soho Square, London, and Queen

161 London, Covent Garden; engraving by T. Bowles, 1751. The square was begun by Inigo Jones in 1631 for the 4th Earl of Bedford. Its pattern, combining arcaded buildings and a church, recalls the Piazza Grande at Livorno (Ill. 159)—though it was initially open to the south, the side from which this view is taken. The initial mix was of houses and shops; the market was introduced in 1661, as a further source of revenue for the Bedford Estate.

Square, Bristol), but its scale was modest, not grandiloquent; and there was of course no *pavillon du roi*, or other special emphasis in the residential frame. Indeed, in contrast to the French residential square, there was no fanaticism about uniform façades; even the style was not always consistent. The building of a square, like a street, was often put in the hands of several developers, who were not necessarily bound to the same overall design. Eventually the uniformity of the residential development became more common. Queen Square in Bath (1729–36) has four grand but disparate sides; Bedford Square in London (begun ca. 1775) is not only uniform but given architectural emphasis by the use of stuccoed, pedimented centerpieces on each of its sides. Unified designs remained characteristic of its successors in the remarkable "squaring" of the Bedford Estate which had begun with Covent Garden and continued for over two hundred years.

162

161,
179

PUBLIC PARKS

The central areas of English squares, associated today with immense plane trees and greenery, were originally austere. A change of attitude is marked by the passage of Acts of Parliament in 1766 and 1774 empowering first Berkeley, then Grosvenor, Squares to raise a tax to pay for the maintenance of grass and trees. The 1771 pamphleteer poured scorn on what he saw as an unseemly development:

> Almost every other square in London seems formed on a quite different plan; they are gardens, they are parks, they are sheep-walks [the reference here is to Cavendish Square which cooped up "a few frightened sheep within a wooden paling"], in short they are everything but what they should be. The *rus in urbe* is a preposterous idea at best.[80]

That he was not alone in his view is suggested by the fact that many squares remained unplanted until after 1800.

162 *London, Bedford Square, ca. 1775–84. Behind the houses, instead of gardens there were mews—narrow private alleys giving access to accommodation for horses, carriages, and servants. That on the north (left) survives; those on the west and south were later transformed into public streets, a common process. The enclosed center of the square received its now-immense plane trees in the 19th century.*

163 *Santa Fe (New Mexico). The* plaza
mayor *was planted as a public garden on
the American model starting in 1866,
shortly before this photograph was taken.
(New Mexico had become a U.S. territory
in 1850; it did not become a state until
1912.)*

The porticoes of the plaza *and the
streets running out of it were prescribed in
the* Laws of the Indies *as "of considerable
convenience to the merchants who
generally gather there." San Francisco
Street on the right leads to the cathedral.*

But by the mid-19th century, the fashion was established. A London guidebook of
1851 rationalized the design of the city's residential squares—including their
fencing—in terms of the salubrious qualities of urban greenery: "open railing . . .
though occupying some of the space, hardly impedes the circulation of air, but,
according to modern chemists, actually helps to renew its vital principle."[81]

Old town squares now sprouted trees and patches of vegetation. Jackson Square
in New Orleans, the *place* of the old French town, got the treatment, along with an
equestrian statue of Andrew Jackson. The once barren Spanish *plaza* of Santa Fe
blossomed, at the time when its old public rituals no longer mattered to the 163
American occupiers. And many garden squares were created anew, enough of them
to justify Stübben's designation of a distinct category. If most are nothing other than
picturesque capsule parks confined within the city block, there are also exceptional
designs like the Plaça Reial in Barcelona with its dignified Neoclassical frame and
the stately palms on the paved floor; or the Piazza Vittorio Emanuele in Rome whose
landscaping incorporates the Roman ruins called the Trophies of Marius.

The inspiration for the *Gartenplatz* was unmistakably English. The French even
used the word *square* for the type. But Spanish scholars are right to emphasize the
salón as an early phase of the 19th-century garden square. The *salón* was a flagstone-
paved area sealed off by a high border of planting, and elevated above street level
from which it was entered by a flight of steps. Filled with elegant furniture, fountains
and exotic plants, it fostered exclusiveness—an attempt "to rationalize the
consumption of urban space through the segregation of a few sites for use by the
dominant class."[82] Seville had two at the city edge, installed in the 1820s at the time
of the demolition of the walls. The Jardín de Delicias was both urban social space
and advanced botanical garden which used steam power to irrigate its specimens. If
the irrepressible social mix of public spaces endemic to Spain thwarted the
pretensions of these *salones*, their influence was felt in *plaza* design later in the
century—and in the development of urban parks.

The public park proper, that is, an open space belonging to the public as of right
and provided with a variety of facilities for the enjoyment of leisure, is a story linked
to the industrial era. The precedent is compromised.

A BACKWARD LOOK

Open land within the city limits was not at all exceptional in antiquity and the Middle Ages. Since the activities of the countryside did not stop at the city gates, fruit and vegetable gardens at the backs of houses spread patches of green through the urban form. Commons where town cattle could graze were often not much beyond the built-up area, and doubled as recreational grounds. Nineveh is said to have had large open spaces within the walls "in which cattle may have been kept and into which herds were probably driven in time of war."[83] "Within the town," the *Laws of the Indies* specify, "a commons shall be delimited, large enough that although the population may experience a rapid expansion, there will always be sufficient space where the people may go for recreation and take their cattle to pasture without them making any damage" (Ordinance 129). The New England common, far too small and barren for actual grazing, was a gathering place for the cattle of the townsfolk, first in the morning, whence a herdsman would lead them out to pasture, and again in the evening so that each owner could claim them and lead them back home.

The widespread tradition of sacred woods predated urbanization almost everywhere. In Rome these *luci* inspired the names of entire regions—e.g. Mons Esquilinus means "hill of the oaks" (*aesculi*), and Collis Viminalis means "hill of the willows." When Rome became a city, the spirits were anthropomorphized and housed in temples, but the groves remained, tended and protected by religious sanctions. Then they too began to shrink. The Luci Vestae originally covered an area between the residence of the priestesses of Vesta, in the Forum, and the lower slopes of the Palatine.[84] By the Augustan age only a few trees remained.

Also venerable is the practice of making the gardens of public buildings and the private gardens of the very rich accessible to all, under certain conditions and schedules. In China, especially under the Sung, urban gardens were open to the public on festivals and holidays. The custom continued into the 19th century, as a source writing in 1865 makes clear: "In Spring they open their gardens and people wander in to admire, staying till the moon is full."[85]

Ancient Rome had a wealth of special gardens open to everyone. Public buildings famous for their grounds included the Portico of Livia on the Esquiline, the portico at the Theater of Pompey, and the wooded grounds of the Mausoleum of Augustus. Of private gardens which were in effect public parks, we can cite the gardens of Caesar in Trastevere, deeded to the Roman people in the dictator's will; and the gardens of Agrippa in the Campus Martius, which included an artificial lake, a canal, and grassy open areas.[86] The idea of the large private pleasure park, or *horti* (gardens), was first introduced to Rome in the 2nd century BC. The inspiration was Hellenistic. Alexandria, for example, was known for its lush parklands which covered over one-fourth of its entire area. The best known *horti* of imperial Rome were those of Maecenas, of Sallust, and of Lucullus on the Pincian Hill.

Naturally, much of the open space for general use lay beyond the city limits. The chief practical designations were pasture lands and agricultural fields, drill grounds and cemeteries. Public claims to air and recreation clashed with these special interests and with invasions of private ownership. The areas closest to the edge of town, because of their accessibility to commoners without carriages, were the most bitterly contested.

In England the story had to do with the public's use of open fields and Crown parks through the means of establishing customary rights or privileges.[87] According to a maxim of common law, enjoyment of property over a long period of time

164 London, detail of an engraved map, ca. 1557–59, showing the area of Moorgate and Bishopsgate. Within the wall lies the City, its dense fabric relieved only by the cloisters and gardens of monastic establishments—here those of the Augustinians (Austin Friars), whose buildings at the Dissolution had become Crown property and then the house of Henry VIII's Lord High Treasurer.

Beyond the wall in Moorfields, just outside Moorgate (left), people and dogs are taking the air, and laundresses are at work (cp. Turin, Pl. 2). Farther out lies Finsbury Field, with its windmills and archery butts. A path edged by wooden posts links the two. To the east, a linear suburb has developed along the road north from Bishopsgate, backed by hedged gardens and fields.

conferred a right to its continued enjoyment. In the early 15th century, the City of London had easy access to Moorfields through Moorgate, "for ease of the citizens, *164* that way to pass upon causeys into the field for their recreation."[88] The leaseholders of the property resisted steadily, fencing off their fields, but the citizens would fill in the ditches and take down the hedges, and the law would side with them. An Act of Parliament in 1592 had the following provision:

> That it shall not be lawfull to any person or persons to inclose or take in any part of the Commons or Waste Groundes scituate lienge or beinge within thre Myles of any of the Gates of the saide Cittie of London, nor to sever or to devide by any Hedge Ditche Pale or otherwise, any of the saide Fieldes . . . to the let or Hindraunce of the traynyng or musteringe of Souldiors or of walkinge for recreacion comforte and healthe of her Maj. People, or of the laudable exercise of shotinge.[89]

Acts of this sort and royal decrees furthered this fierce struggle to establish "customary access." A critical episode for London was the confirmation by Henry VIII of the right of the people of the City to practice archery in Finsbury Fields. Later James I confirmed the rights of citizens to Lincoln's Inn Fields, adjacent to the quarter of law students between London and Westminster. Property owners there too put up a long fight, but the students, by their constant vigilance and appeals to the law, managed to keep a large open square free of construction, and there it is to this day. So with Gray's Inn to the north.

By the 17th century, customary access began to prevail in Crown property. Charles I opened the gardens of Whitehall Palace, and the bowling green there was soon being treated, in spirit at least, as a public meeting place. Hyde Park was also Pl.21 opened to the public some time between 1630 and 1640, and we have accounts of both horse-racing and foot-racing there; in fact, there was soon a regular racecourse called "the Ring." Later still, Londoners fought hard to keep Hampstead Heath and other open spaces and commons free of enclosure and development.

The princely, or aristocratic, tradition of providing limited public access to gardens has a long history. To open royal parks, or the gardens of a noble villa like the Villa Borghese in Rome, periodically was an established custom by 1700, as was 165 the provision of public promenades. For the former, the example of the Tiergarten—the royal hunting grounds—in Berlin is cited; it was opened to the public in 1649 for "pleasure strolling." After the French Revolution, parks formerly belonging to the aristocracy or the Church, for example the Parc de la Colombière in Dijon and the Jardin Thabor at Rennes, became permanently incorporated into the public realm.

165 Berlin, the Tiergarten; engraving by Daniel Chodowiecki, 1772. In the right background is a refreshment area under canvas.

Of public promenades intentionally so created, early examples are Le Peyrou at Montpellier, 1688–93; La Papinière in Nancy, completed in 1766; the Jardin de la Fontaine at Nîmes, on a Roman site, 1745–60. The practice of turning town fortifications into promenades I have discussed in "The City Edge" (pp. 32–33).

The cemetery should also be mentioned as a public park of sorts. Especially with the disfavor of churchyard burial grounds during the Enlightenment for reasons of health and decorum, and the establishment of planned extramural cemeteries, some of the churchyards became public gardens. These were controlled by private "burial boards." In the City of London by the end of the 19th century, there were 362 burial grounds, of which 41 were still in use; of the rest, mostly closed down in the 1850s, some 90 were public recreation grounds. In 1884 an act called the Disused Burial-Grounds Act was passed to prevent building on these open spaces.[90] Of the planned cemeteries, the so-called rural cemeteries in America, beginning in 1835 with Mount Auburn in Cambridge, Massachusetts, were designed as semi-public picturesque gardens; they are generally considered a major inspiration for Olmsted's urban parks in the second half of the century.

THE MODERN PARK

For the modern public park, properly so called, where the story starts is mostly a matter of definition. One candidate is the Englischer Garten in Munich, begun in 1804 to a design by Friedrich Ludwig Sckell and an American named Benjamin Thompson. In defense of the claim, we can adduce the urban site, and the fact that the new landscape in the English manner is not related to any official building like a castle or a palace but is its own excuse. But the patronage puts the park in the princely tradition; it was commissioned by the Elector Karl Theodor when his seat of government had been moved from Mannheim to Munich. *166*

The Englischer Garten is interesting for another reason. It was an early attempt, not very well realized, at a *Volksgarten*—a German concept of the late 18th century that stressed the park as a medium for public education and the mingling of social classes. The Munich park was meant to have buildings with pictures of national history, statues of heroes, and monuments to important events.

The social mix is important, because the opened up royal park and the public promenade often had a genteel bias. This was shown in the preference for carriage and equestrian traffic. Period pictures usually show elegant people in fancy coaches or on horseback; in London's Regent's Park, thrown open in 1838, it was necessary to "be a man of fortune, and take exercise on horseback or in a carriage," and no provisions of any kind were made for pedestrians. Earlier, under George II, when Kensington Gardens were opened to public visits on Sundays, sailors, soldiers and servants in livery were explicitly excluded. St. James's Park was for a long time open only to those who had received royal permission to use it, and the issuance of a key.[91] And in Denmark, when the royal garden of Frederiksborg was opened to the public in the early 18th century, small enclosures were reserved "into which ordinary people could be driven, when it pleased the Royal family to take the air in the garden."[92]

The person who is most commonly credited with proposing the idea of a public park as we think of it today is J. C. Loudon, in the 1820s. Loudon thought it a means to "raise the intellectual character of the lowest classes of society." He considered this ideal fulfilled in his Derby Arboretum, on a then peripheral site given to the town by a philanthropist. The park was meant to excite common interest in trees and shrubs.

But the first genuine park, as against an arboretum or botanical garden, was probably Birkenhead Park, across the Mersey from Liverpool, designed by Joseph Paxton in 1843. It is distinguished by its separation of different types of traffic, a feature that influenced Olmsted at Central Park a few years later. Of Birkenhead he wrote:

> in democratic America, there was nothing to be thought of as comparable with this People's Garden. . . . And all this magnificent pleasure-ground is entirely, unreservedly, and for ever the people's own. The poorest British peasant is as free to enjoy it in all its parts as the British Queen.[93]

Another candidate, this one debatable because the site was a royal grant, is Victoria Park in East London, intended especially for the working classes and enacted by Parliament in 1842. It was created in a congested urban situation, and meant to make amends for the fact that all of London's parks at the time—Hyde, St. James's, Kensington, Regent's, Crown properties even when open to the public—were at the fashionable West End of town. That was the extent of a public park tradition until mid-century, even though "after 1837, largely due to the exertions of Joseph Hume in the House of Commons, all parliamentary enclosure acts were required to contain provisions for some public open space."[94]

By the 1860s most areas of London and the northern industrial towns had public parks, though none of the distinction of Birkenhead. In the meantime the park had become an integral part of a city plan in Haussmann's Paris, where Alphand and others redesigned the Bois de Boulogne and created the Parc Monceau, Parc Montsouris and Buttes-Chaumont as well as 24 smaller public gardens or *squares*. Olmsted and Vaux's Central Park and Prospect Park (Brooklyn) brought the public park to American cities. And the idea spread further afield. A Cabinet Proclamation in 1873 required each prefecture of Japan to designate sites suitable for parks.[95]

Olmsted's importance was to see that towns can be planned around parks, and to create parkway systems like those at Buffalo and Boston. His influences were Andrew Jackson Downing, the transatlantic counterpart of Loudon and the first American, along with William Cullen Bryant, to campaign for public parks; the American rural cemetery; and Birkenhead, which Olmsted visited in 1850.

The Olmstedian park was also to be for all classes, and the aspiration was that the habits of the worker would be improved as he came into contact with his social superiors in these contemplative surroundings. In America "the worker" was a positive term for the despised immigrant. Through the uplifting experience of park attendance, Olmsted hoped to crush the separate ethnic identities of immigrant groups, the street culture of Italian and Irish neighborhoods, and create the homogenized American. He would deny the worker the rough pleasures of sport; he would insist on an unadulterated rural experience, and bring him face to face with what he called "a specimen of God's handiwork."

Sports were a contentious issue since the early history of the public park. Birkenhead did think of play, and had a simple open space devoted to sports. In Manchester, Joshua Major argued for the provision of such areas as early as 1844. But the perception that sports were incompatible with the peaceful enjoyment of nature was strong. Only after the rise of organized sports in the 1870s did the tide turn in favor of opening up the parks to a variety of physical and cultural activities.

This early generation of public parks and their successors have seen periods of decline and neglect, and called up repeated campaigns of reform. And despite the intentions of designers like Loudon and Olmsted, these leafy urban enclaves often seem to be the setting of the conflict between classes more than their reconciliation.

166 *Munich, the Englischer Garten.*
Conceived in 1789 by the American
Benjamin Thompson (Count Rumford),
the Bavarian Minister for War, it was
designed by F. L. Sckell in the picturesque
English mode and completed in 1808. The
circular Monopteros was added by Leo
von Klenze in 1838.

167 right *Plan of Birkenhead Park, near*
Liverpool, laid out by Joseph Paxton in
1843. The scheme was a sort of early
garden suburb: rows of houses, in terraces
and crescents, surround a central park
enlivened by serpentine lakes and crossed
by winding carriage roads and intimate
paths for pedestrians. This illustration was
published by Alphand, Haussmann's
landscape architect, in his great volume
Les Promenades de Paris (1867–73).

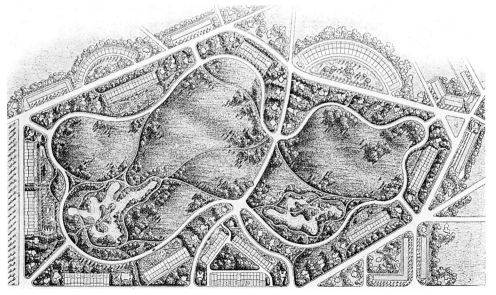

In this, parks remain true to the long tradition of public places we have outlined here, that "common ground where public culture is expressed and community life developed."[96] The safer and more well-behaved these places are, the likelier it is that this mission has been inhibited. Today many parks post long lists of disallowed activities at their entrances; at dusk they are likely to be locked up. Here and there, to be the safest of all, the park is off limits permanently. The lovely central park of the little town of Sausalito on the San Francisco Bay is roped off and has posted a sign with this sad message upon it:

THIS PARK IS FOR YOUR VIEWING PLEASURE. DO NOT ENTER.

A public place could have no terser epitaph.

THE PUBLIC PLACES OF TODAY

But the story of the public place is far from over. The old squares of historic cities continue to be used, of course. A number have been radically altered to inject them with a vitality more attuned to modern sensibilities. At the same time, an impressive array of new squares has seen the light of day on all continents.

One of the most ambitious programs was undertaken by the post-Franco Socialist city government of Barcelona in 1980. New squares and parks were seen as an opportunity to revitalize shabbier districts, as well as to exorcize forty years of dictatorship which had seen the city's public places as potentially threatening arenas of Catalan insurrection.[97] Barcelona's new urban open spaces are striking in their uncompromising modernity. Hard surfaces and steely constructivist pavilions *Pl.23* characterize the Plaça dels Països Catalans, next to the Sants railroad station. A towering mosaic-encrusted figure by Miró lords over the Parc de l'Escorxador on a site previously occupied by abandoned slaughterhouses. At the Parc del Clot, rambling greenery, an open plaza used for ball games, and fragments of 19th-century industrial architecture are knit together masterfully.

PUBLIC PLACES

Within the dense press of the built fabric the greatest luxury of all is empty space. Whether it is used for the spectacle of pomp or for play, the open frame is politically charged; the activities encompassed, freighted with consequence. Only here can a representative portion of the populace mass to make its mood known at a glance. Public space as it is successively reshaped is an artifact of the collective passions that bind society: from civic protest or regimented ceremonies of consensus, to leisure pursued in an arcadian idyll, or through the ritualized consumption of products and aestheticized environments. Even at its most trivial, the mere presence of a public realm is testimony to the insistence of our need periodically to rediscover the physical fact of community.

Pl. 16 Lucca, in Tuscany, provides a particularly vivid example of the persistence of public space. The Piazza del Anfiteatro (center) was built on the remains of a Roman amphitheater, houses standing where there were once tiers of seats and the arena serving as a marketplace. The triangular space in the foreground opens in front of the Romanesque church of S. Pietro Somaldi. The line of trees in the distance marks the extensive ramparts built in the 16th and 17th centuries.

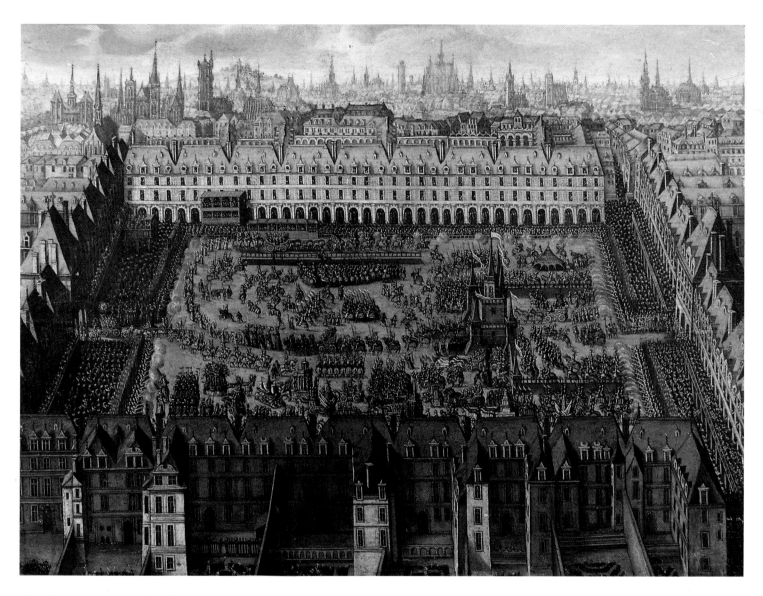

Royal games, popular rivalries

Pl. 17 The Place des Vosges, originally Place Royale, built in 1605–12 as part of a deliberate scheme by Henri IV to provide Paris with monumental open spaces, was the setting for elaborate public spectacles. On its completion a carrousel was held to proclaim the forthcoming marriage of Louis XIII and Anne of Austria. It had all the requisites for such an event—efficient access routes, circulation space under the arcades, and windows for the spectators. In design the square is uniform, except for the higher Pavillon du Roi to the south (left) and Pavillon de la Reine opposite, but behind the facades the houses are irregular.

Pl. 18 The Campo in Siena (Italy) acquired its ceremonial function by accident. As the main open space in the city, in front of the Palazzo Pubblico, it became the natural venue for the Palio, a horse-race contested each year on 2 July and 16 August between the various contrade or districts. Medieval in origin, it is an affair of colorful costumes, banners, excitement, and passionate rivalries. In this photograph the competition is over; the crowd has overflowed onto the course and clusters around the banners.

Where the crowd gathers, history is made

Pl. 19 *Piazza del Popolo, February 1849. The Roman Republic is proclaimed in front of the twin Baroque churches designed as a "façade" for the city inside the important northern gate. The Pope had fled, to the evident discomfort of the priest on the right. Roman freedom, however, was only temporary: it was another twenty years before the city could join an independent Italy.*

Pl. 20 *Prague's Wenceslas Square has over the centuries witnessed Bohemia's and Czechoslovakia's agonies and triumphs. In 1989 its crowds felt that victory was near. Built as part of the 14th-century New Town, Wenceslas Square was the largest open area in the city. The ground slopes downward from what was formerly a gate and walls, now the site of the National Museum, floodlit in the background.*

Public parks

Pl. 21 Hyde Park in London was a royal preserve, opened to the public in the 1630s and only gradually democratized. John Ritchie's painting of 1858 shows users ranging from the very rich to grubby barefoot children, but chiefly "respectable." Visible in the background are Marble Arch and the houses of Park Lane.

Pl. 22 New York's Central Park, by contrast, was intended from the start in 1857 to be a place of relaxation and uplift for the working class as well. Its designer and apologist, Frederick Law Olmsted, provided a naturalistic lake and meandering paths, some for pedestrians only, and a formal area around the Bethesda Fountain.

Public places of today

Pl. 23 *The Plaça dels Països Catalans, or Plaça de Sants, in Barcelona (by Helio Piñón and Albert Viaplana, 1983) was created by the Socialist city council after Franco's death as a symbol of Catalan nationalism and a statement against Fascist bourgeois traditionalism.*

Pl. 24 *"Town Square" in Runcorn New Town (England) is the heart of the shopping mall, opened in 1971. It was described as serving all "the traditional purposes"—sitting around, public meetings, Christmas carols—"in all-weather, air-conditioned comfort." The space is private, though, not public; and the choice of name suggests a feeling that something had been lost.*

Cities with sites lacking a genuine landscape of time have been happy to invent one. Squares planted in new towns or on the blank slate of sweeping urban redevelopments often set out to recreate some of the layered wealth and authenticity of historic Old World squares, and do so by adopting one of two strategies. They might seek to distill and translate esthetic "essences": this is the "townscape" confraternity of Gordon Cullen and the Krier brothers, concerned with Sitte-esque volumetrics and the visual incident. The alternate strategy resides in recalling more or less directly specific frames of history. In New Orleans, Charles Moore's Piazza d'Italia (1978), where lurks the spirit of Rome's Piazza di Trevi, does it with humor and in a refracted way, as historical collage. At Tsukuba Center (1983), north of *168* Tokyo, Arata Isozaki embeds a recognizable facsimile of Michelangelo's Campidoglio—but less as plaza than "a garden in the Zen tradition, into which the visitor looks rather than walks."[98]

Other newly created squares, paradoxically, set out to recapture what their designers seem to consider a lost cause. At its most rudimentary, the old names are called forth as if they might instigate a round of imitative magic. The French new town of Evry calls its public place the Agora. Columbus, Indiana, has designated its retail mall The Commons. The "Town Square" of the English new town of Runcorn *Pl.24* is the atrium hub of its shopping center, recently described, without any sense of irony, as serving all "the traditional purposes—for meeting people, chatting, sitting around shrubs, and trees and sculpture, for public meetings, exhibitions, the Christmas carols and so on—but with everything in all-weather, air-conditioned comfort."[99] Even Paris has given itself a Forum: the sunken plaza bracketed by three descending tiers of luxury boutiques at Les Halles.

Harmless and witty as all this public banter may be, it delays the moment of our reckoning. We must be willing to accept the fact that the social world of cities that played itself out in the old town square is dying; we will not bring it back by designing imitations of the Piazza S. Marco or the Hauptmarkt of Nuremberg.

The slow demise started more than a century ago. Sitte was only the most articulate of its early witnesses. As progress spread, the piazza died. Newspapers first, and then radio and television, preempted the role of the piazza as the disseminator, and maker, of news. Modern water systems killed the socializing power of the public fountain. A revolution in mass marketing and consumption drained the piazza of its pivotal role in economic life. Crime, which once had been a desecration of *communitas* and so required a ritual public cleansing, now spirited its consequences to the seclusion of the jail. With the neutralizing or outright dismissal of kings, and the laicization of culture, power and faith muted their public manifestations. The royal monument made way for monumentalized abstractions: Louis le Grand turned into Liberty, and then a holed hulk by Henry Moore.

Efforts to reinvest the urban plaza with purpose emphasize the use of public space as an artist's canvas. We are shown signature designs by artists, architects or landscape architects—each a unique and idiosyncratic creative vision—and given a chance to consume an esthetic experience in lieu of the kind of social experience that was the town square's *métier*: the free interaction of strangers. In contrast, the "grand manner" tradition as a whole believed in standard, almost interchangeable designs that followed rules and shared common features. Today's "designer squares" reject the role of a neutral space for the artful display of architecture, civic monuments and people: now the space itself demands to be interpreted, admired, enjoyed as a theme park might be enjoyed.

An influential and premonitory project was Robert Venturi's unrealized design of 1966 for Boston's Copley Square. He set out to make a "non-piazza," filling up the

space with a grid of trees, tall lampposts and stepped mounds. Instead of "an open space to accommodate a non-existing crowd," he proposed a private experience for those who strolled through the maze or sat in a sheltered corner. American plazas devoted to esthetic introspection are mostly private initiatives, focal accents for speculative office complexes (a topic I will return to). Examples include the psychedelic melange of paving patterns and reflective glass at Harlequin Plaza (1982) in Greenwood, Colorado, and the more sedate Williams Square (1985) at Las Colinas, Texas.

The trend is expressed in European projects as well. The projected Ludgate Square in London, floating over railroad tracks, features a huge tilted slab of lawn leaning up against a wall, a two-ton rock atop a horizontal window looking down onto the rails, and a fountain that holds no water. The 1985 renovation of the *cour d'honneur* of Cardinal Richelieu's baroque Palais Royal in Paris added a cryptic grid of boldly striped columns truncated at varying heights: the low ones perfect, we are told, "for sporty joggers who can gallop over them," others just right "for a picnic table or for mimicking a stylite."[100] These proposed uses are clearly after-the-fact rationalizations: gone is the solicitude that would consider real public utility as the generator of form. When popular opinion rose against the lack of amenities in *Pl.23* Barcelona's hard-edged "Plaça de Sants," the city's architect-in-chief characterized the outcry as "regressive" and "ignorant." "This discussion about 'hard' or 'soft' squares," he countered, "shows a strange lack of culture in our country. The 'Plaça de Sants' is the most important urbanistic event of our day."[101]

The self-importance of the "designer square" as a status-laden art environment traces its immediate ancestry to the image-making function of the corporate highrise plaza. The notion of enhancing a building economically and esthetically by providing a margin of greenery and air around it was recognized early in the 20th century by one of the chief spokesmen for the American City Beautiful movement, Charles Mulford Robinson. He argued that although the recent crop of grand urban plazas failed to realize their social potential, they still had esthetic and economic benefits; adding variety, beauty and stateliness to cities, and increasing the value of adjacent buildings by assuring light and conspicuousness of vantage point.

The first plaza-equipped highrise project of major consequence, and handily the most popular solution of all, is New York's Rockefeller Center (1931–49). The *169* tightly scaled sequence of spaces begins on Fifth Avenue with the channel of gardens

168 The square as work of art: Arata Isozaki's plaza in the new town of Tsukuba City, 1983. The sunken central area combines the famous patterned paving of the Campidoglio in Rome with elements from Japanese gardens; gridded paving around it marks out an area reserved for pedestrians and cyclists. The ensemble has an experimental character, as there is no tradition of communally used public spaces in Japan.

169 New York City, Channel Gardens in Rockefeller Center, laid out in 1932–35, looking toward the RCA Building. In winter the sunken plaza at the end, below the statue, is transformed from a café into a skating rink, and special Christmas lights attract great crowds.

that lead down to a sunken plaza used as a café or skating rink. The architecture respects the defining wall of the avenue, trapping its public open space within the mass of the buildings and behind the legitimate line of the sidewalk.

Post-war developments of comparable scale seriously changed the ground rules. Skyscrapers usually occupied only between one-fourth and one-third of the total site, leaving generous offerings of open space in response to the newly popular Modernist urban esthetic, but compromising the continuity of the streetscape in the process. The practice of elevating the plaza on a podium as much as a story above street level, popularized by Gateway Center (1950–53) in Pittsburgh, and the Seagram Building (1954–58) and Chase Manhattan Bank (1961) in New York, reinforced the private control of these open spaces by divorcing them from the street edge.

The prevalent economic theory, promoted by architects, was that the amenity value of open space would justify charging higher rents, which would bring in more revenue than the owner stood to lose from the unoccupied space. When the first returns did not bear out this prediction, many American cities, anxious to increase their public realm at private expense, began in the late 1950s and early 1960s to extend zoning exemptions allowing a premium of extra stories to towers which left open space on their site. This the developer did by pulling the skyscraper back from the street line on one or more sides. But since the law did not set down design criteria for this bonus public space, the plazas were mostly inhospitable stretches of hard paving or unnegotiable pools of water, perhaps adorned by a sculptural piece of renown, but otherwise barren of amenities for inhabiting and enjoying the corporation's gift to the city.

New York arrested and reversed this disintegrative trend in 1976; other North American cities soon followed its lead. The nature of the public space to be provided by the developer favored with a code variance was now spelled out. Options ranged from a simple sidewalk widening that would befriend café crowds to midblock pedestrian concourses and public "outdoor rooms," be they plazas integrated with the street environment or intimate "vest pocket parks." In all cases it would be the responsibility of the developer to furnish the public space with trees, kiosks, movable seating, and other amenities that would encourage daily use, and to guarantee the maintenance of this apparatus.[102]

Also a 1970s phenomenon was the atrium, a covered public place within the building block that had the benefit of safety and climate control. Of the early examples, the most impressive was the Crystal Court, the enormous plaza of the IDS Center in Minneapolis (1968–73), covered with a clear plastic and steel-truss grid and encircled by a walkway providing access to upper level shops. The architects maintained that given the Court's central location, it would conjure "a genuine old-world public square on which the entire town converges."[103]

In fact, the analogy is specious. As long as the public space has been provided through the courtesy of a private concern in line with its own interests, that space cannot stand in for a genuine town square. This is so, first, because the consignment of urban memory to a corporate atrium would be tantamount to debauching the principles of community; and also, because the extent to which a private gift can be considered authentically public is always conditional. When the IDS Center was acquired by a new management company several years ago, one of their first moves was to remove all public seating from the Crystal Court. Loitering for more than a few minutes there will now rouse the private security personnel. And the former users of the space, mostly older folk whiling away a few hours in conversation, have no recourse: the matter is entirely out of the city's hands.

170 opposite, top *American zoning trade-offs: more open space means greater permitted height.*

171, 172 opposite, center and bottom *Stark public spaces resulting from the 1961 New York City zoning code, and user-friendly spaces encouraged by the 1976 revision of that code.*

173 above *Minneapolis (Minnesota), Crystal Court in the IDS Center, by Johnson/Burgee Architects, 1968–73.*

Most radically, perhaps, our own peculiar rituals of social interaction have eased into a set of privatized public places unique to our time, including the atrium, theme parks, shopping malls, and those "festival marketplaces" made popular in the United States by developer James Rouse. They are flourishing as the social accouterments of a suburban settlement pattern that dominates most of North America, and which is making rapid headway in much of Europe as well. Its spatially discontinuous landscape of detached houses and office parks is woven into a seamless succession of private realms by the automobile's cocoon of seclusion. Encounters with traditional public places—and with the traditional city center itself—are increasingly superfluous to the daily rounds of suburbanites. Only the call to consume forces them back into something akin to a public realm, and of the most antiseptic and regulated sort at that. I am referring, of course, to the shopping mall.

Pioneered in 1956 by Victor Gruen's Southdale Shopping Center in the suburbs of Minneapolis, Minnesota, the enclosed mall is a speculator's rendition of a downtown built to serve a motorized clientele. On the outside are acres of parking and bland, windowless walls enclosing retail space; inside, a sequence of courts, air-conditioned and lit by skylights or clerestory windows, connect rows of shops to one or more large department stores. Gruen recognized that this indoor circulation space could prove a major attraction in its own right, and at Southdale loaded it with eating areas and a children's zoo.

Replicated hundreds of times over throughout the United States and Canada, the shopping mall is now a fact of life. It is extremely important to whole classes of people, especially teenagers and the elderly. And it presents us with some interesting social and political issues. Shopping malls are run by private holding companies, not by the city or the merchants. These owners control the "mix" of businesses, and they prefer chains. There is also the issue of free speech. In 1968 the U.S. Supreme Court voted that no distinction could be made between public places like streets and the privately-owned mall, in so far as exercise of First Amendment rights like picketing and leaflet distribution were concerned. The decision was reversed in 1971. But then again in 1980 the Court said that freedom of speech on private property can be protected under doctrines derived from State constitutions. California and several other States have since then identified shopping malls as new public places in the American social landscape.

Eccentric behavior, however it might be defined by mall management companies, is still grounds for ejection, though. Toronto's Eaton Center forcibly removed about 30,000 people in 1985 alone; police there regularly issue trespass tickets to undesirables. Taking photographs on the premises of a mall, even in the parking lot, is often enough to bring out security guards. Urban sociologist William Whyte reports that some elderly mall visitors have learned to evade accusations of loitering by carrying a single shopping bag to mimic active consumption.[104]

Questions regarding one's civil freedoms within this tenuous shadow zone between public and private domains will soon be posed world-wide. The American mall formula, which stresses location at strategic junctions of major highways, arrived in France in the late 1960s. One of the first, Parly 2 near Versailles, was patterned closely on Southdale by French developer Jean-Louis Solal, who went on to build more than thirty other malls in France, Spain and Belgium.[105]

England experimented with malls in its second generation of New Towns in the
Pl.24 early 1970s. I have already mentioned Runcorn's; Milton Keynes, the last of the New Towns, encloses its retail services in a shopping center as well. By the mid 1970s London had gotten its first true suburban mall: Brent Cross, at the junction of the M1 and the North Circular. Since then, regional megamalls have risen close to Gateshead (Metrocentre), Dudley (Merry Hill), and Sheffield (Meadowhall).

Today, Hong Kong and São Paulo both have malls by the dozen. Guatemala City boasts the Peri Roosevelt Mall; Uruguay, the Montevideo Shopping Center; Reykjavik, Iceland, the Kringland Mall. The arrival of the Christmas shopping season at The Mall in Kuala Lumpur is heralded by indoor styrofoam snow flurries, Malaysia's bow to the latest North American trend which mixes retailing and theme park entertainment. The exemplar being studied by developers around the world is
174 the megamall outside Edmonton, Canada. Few can hope to match its carnival cornucopia, a partial inventory of which includes reproductions of New Orleans's Bourbon Street and of a Parisian street, a golf course, an indoor ocean pool with rubber beach and water slides, and a reproduction of a gallion floating in a tropical lagoon with live fish and four submarines. But to entice a public for whom retail entertainment and socializing is just one of a host of possible leisure activities, even small operators have followed suit. California's Santa Monica Place hired an artist to build a 200-ton sandcastle. The Potteries Shopping Centre in Britain's historic ceramics-producing town of Stoke-on-Trent lures the souvenir-hungry in for a look at the world's largest teapot—made of Fiberglas, of course.

174 *Edmonton (Canada), shopping mall, begun 1981. The galleon is a reduced-scale replica of Christopher Columbus's* Santa Maria.

Our public places were proud repositories of a common history. We have largely abandoned that sense of a shared destiny, and our public places show it. What is left may not be much, but it is crucial. We still want to be with other people, if not engaging them directly at least watching them stroll by. The public places unique to our time may be thoroughly privatized. Their motive may be no more noble than to lure us to buy. But having been drawn to the mall or boutiqued-up old town square for "recreational shopping" and the obligatory stop for food, we discover each other and might remember the place when we want to stage a public event, or celebrate a private event in public. And, who knows, we may yet learn to do better. After all, was not the messy crossroads prelude to forum and *Münsterplatz*, and the shapeless market outside the city walls sire to the straitlaced *plaza mayor*?

4 · THE STREET

INTRODUCTION

The history of the street has yet to be written, either as urban form or as institution. It should, of course, be both. For on the one hand, the street clearly belongs to the history of architecture and urban design in the strict sense of physical fact. The street is an entity made up of a roadway, usually a pedestrian way, and flanking buildings. How each one of these is articulated, how they interact, in what ways the design of the street walls is controlled and guided—these are questions of form pure and simple. There is the matter of sidewalks; of street furniture; of paving; of trees and greenery—each with its own, as yet very incompletely known, story.

Categories that remain within the esthetic realm include the hoary distinction between curved and straight streets, which so preoccupied the post-Sitte planning debate in modern Europe.[1] Also partly in terms of form, one can specify *types* of streets, as one might distinguish building types. We have, to name a few: colonnaded avenues, boulevards, alleys, covered streets, the *Ringstrasse*, the ceremonial or processional axis, the riverside walk, and so forth.

But the street as an institution is an equally critical subject. Beyond its architectural identity, every street has an economic function and social significance. The purposes of the street traditionally have been traffic, the exchange of goods, and social exchange and communication. All three are inseparably related to the form of the street—the material ways in which these activities are housed and helped along. There are intricate levels of social engagement encouraged and hosted by the street structure. The street, in Joseph Rykwert's phrase, is human movement institutionalized[2]— and human intercourse institutionalized. In this way, therefore, the history of the street is about both container and content. If the correspondence of the two cannot be perfectly synchronic, it is because the frame of the street is more permanent than the uses made of it.

We are of course concerned with the *urban* street—with roads when they are *in* a settlement, defined by buildings. The connection between roads in the country and streets in town is nevertheless an intimate one. To cite two instances:

(1) At some point in the history of human settlement, and in all parts of the world, natural paths of passage became highways, and these linked up with towns. The Via Lata of ancient Rome was nothing more than the urban stretch of the Via Flaminia, the consular highway that traversed the peninsula from north to south.

175 opposite Warsaw, Krakowskie Przedmieście, ca. 1770. Bellotto records the architectural events on this prosperous suburban street leading to the edge of the Old Town—the palaces of the nobility, the large church of St. Anne on the right, the column in honor of King Sigismund in the Castle Square—and he also shows the life within it: traveling entertainers and beggars, aristocrats, soldiers, priests and foreigners, luxurious coaches and lumbering wagons.

This is the logic of the Hellenistic/Roman colonnaded avenue that formed the
212 spine of cities like Palmyra, Antioch and Djemila, but also of the "high street" of
medieval towns, indeed of so-called linear towns in general from prehistoric
Khirokitia in Cyprus to Soria y Mata's *Ciudad Lineal* and Miliutin's Magnitogorsk.

(2) In the process of urbanization, country patterns of paths, lanes, and trails
leave their impress on the urban street network. Synoecism absorbs the lines of
communication of the constituent villages; urban developments are bounded by the
45 roads that once divided agricultural and pastoral land.[3]

HISTORICAL NOTES

The beginnings of a street history have to be conditional. Pre-urban villages had
buildings, but their paths were not always streets. Let me insist on two, by no means
obvious, facts.

There was a time before streets, even in the proto-urban environment of Western
Asia. Take Çatal Hüyük in Asia Minor (7th–6th millennium BC): it was really one
intricately assembled complex without streets. All pedestrian movement was made
on the roofs of buildings, and social interaction might have taken place in the
courtyards.

A little later at Hacilar, also in Asia Minor, narrow lanes appear for pedestrians.
Perhaps the fact that the town was now fortified made it possible to have open areas
among housing groups. The principle of the prevalence of house groups over public
spaces persisted in the pre-industrial world. It applied to Eskimo igloos and other
American Indian settlements, the compounds of African villages, and traditional
villages in the Middle East and Asia.

The street is an invention. At present it may be possible to locate the first
176 conscious street in history at Khirokitia, dating from the 6th millennium BC. This
spine of communication, running uphill from the riverbank and down on the
opposite side of the hill, was built of limestone and raised considerably above
ground level, with stone ramps leading down at regular intervals among the houses
huddled on either side. The primacy of Khirokitia may be challenged in future
scholarship. But that the institution of the street developed somewhere, wholesale
or in part, is not to be doubted. It is surely wrong to take the street for granted.

We can cite small pieces of early evidence from a number of locations in modern
Turkey. In Beycesultan (about 1900–1750 BC), remains were unearthed of a
graveled, that is, paved, street. Paving is important. Our very word "street" derives
from the Latin *sternere*, which means "to pave." The implication of a delimited
surface, an artificially marked off open space, already recognized in Khirokitia,
becomes central to the early development of the street and the conception of street
hierarchies.

Indeed here at Beycesultan, unlike at Hacilar where all courtyards and lanes were
of the same character, there is *a differentiation of streets*. The street separating the
two mounds is a major artery, the streets within residential areas are local ones.
Similarly at the considerably earlier Mohenjo Daro, the Harappan city of the Indus
Valley, the broad thoroughfares that formed the loose grid were distinguished from
the alleys, parallel or at right angles to them, on which the houses fronted. These
streets were unpaved, yet they were equipped with brick drains and brick manholes.
At the Minoan hill-town of Gournia in Crete, an upper ring-road hugged the summit
where the palace was situated, while a second ring-road ran along the east quarter of
the lower town on the plain; cross streets, sometimes cut into by steps, linked these
two prime arteries.

*176 Khirokitia (Cyprus), the raised
limestone-paved street of the Neolithic
settlement, lined with the remains of
circular huts.*

At the *karum* of Kültepe (about 2000–1900 BC) we have a very early instance of two crossing "main streets"; the north-south one is wider, and has *sidewalks* or pavements for pedestrians on both sides, a possible first for this feature of street design.

A number of themes remain relevant throughout the history of the street, whatever the period. One of these has to do with a variety of private challenges to the public control of the street space and the corresponding public effort to preserve the integrity of the street channel, and keep it free of encroachments.

The key reality here is that the street remains the stage of a constant struggle between private and public interests. And the moral is that when public control falters, private abuse becomes endemic. The public good requires that the street space be kept open, accessible to all, and equipped for its functions. By explicitly defining an outdoor space for general use, the community makes a commitment to this principle. The private urge is to appropriate this space for one's own purposes. This is done in one of two ways: through encroachments, and through blockage or privatization. The great antiquity of both practices is a matter of record. Henri Frankfort, the premier student of ancient Mesopotamia, tells us that there

Tradition regarded it very inauspicious to usurp public space for private use. An omen text reads: "If a house blocks the main street in its building, the owner of the house will die; if a house overshadows [overhangs] or obstructs the side of the main street, the heart of the dweller in that house will not be glad."[4]

And a saying of the Prophet Muhammad, "La dharar wa la dhirar," was sometimes interpreted to mean "No infringement, whether profitable or not."[5]

Encroachments are incremental over time. In this instance, abutters consider the street as unoccupied groundspace into which they might extend their built premises.

177 Street blockage in 15th-century Cambridge (England): King's College, founded by Henry VI, occupies a site crossed by several existing lanes. This plan shows the original proposal for the buildings (shaded), of which only the famous chapel, on the north side of the main court, was built in this form. (From Willis and Clark)

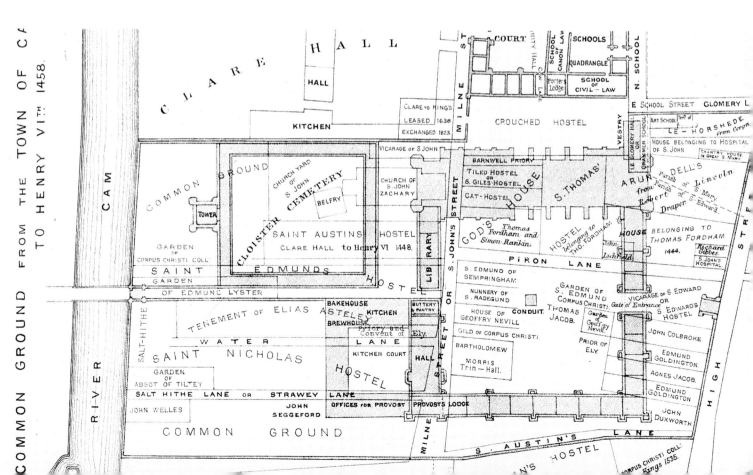

I will have more to say on the subject further along. In the second instance, the street space is eliminated outright by building over it; or else control over street movement is established for factional gain. An example of the latter strategy is the creation of jurisdictional pockets in medieval cities by powerful clans. I have commented on this phenomenon before.[6] The struggle of medieval communes like Florence or Siena to unstop their balkanized thoroughfares, I pointed out, symbolized the need of a government to be in full control of its network of public spaces.

Blockage can also be occasioned by institutions unable, or unwilling, to fit within a given pattern of urban streets. In medieval England, for example, the creation of monastic and ecclesiastical precincts caused the truncating or complete closing off of streets and lanes. The same holds for the college precincts of Oxford and *177* Cambridge.[7]

278– Demapping streets for the sake of overlarge buildings has been negotiated between private interests and city authorities at least since the Renaissance. The Strozzi struck a deal of this sort with the Florentine state in the late 15th century to create a sufficiently ample plot for their family palazzo: the foursquare structure stretched over an existing small piazza and an alley, which were suppressed, while *278–* another street was shifted. In modern urban renewal projects where vast areas of the *280* old city are cleared, demapping is a common planning procedure. In San Francisco in the late 1960s, the private developer who built the Transamerica tower, frustrated by the area's small parcels, assembled two blocks on either side of Merchant Street and successfully petitioned the city to close the street, arguing that its function as a "service alley" was no longer urgent. Public response was hostile, and "street vacation," to use the legal phrase, has since been made much more difficult in order, in the city's words, "to protect against the accumulation of overly large parcels of property under single ownership on which massive buildings could be constructed."

178 Genoa (Italy), Strada Nuova, a mid-16th-century private street of palaces. The original paving was to be of brick, with flagstones at the sides.

PRIVATE STREETS

The process of creating legitimate, which is to say independently owned, private streets is obviously one way to be exclusive without resorting to physical force or seeking adjustments within an extant streetscape. In the broadest sense, a private street is one for which public authorities assume no responsibility. This is because the open space serves only the property owners directly involved, or is exclusively intended for such humble, private uses as the temporary storage of refuse or the parking of vehicles. The classic locus is the back alley or the English mews. When these service corridors are gentrified and turned into residential strips, they usually enter the public domain.

But this ad hoc, typically low-life privacy of alleys and cul-de-sacs should be distinguished from the self-conscious creation of private streets for the privileged few. The aim here is exclusive: to live without city interference in a setting that allows for a concentrated display of superior taste. This aim is fundamentally anti-street. Those who choose to live in such secluded oases within the urban structure are willing to forego the public benefits of street life, not least, from their point of view, the mixed admiring crowds of public streets, for the sake of avoiding accompanying nuisances.

178 The exemplary Strada Nuova (now Via Garibaldi) of Genoa was a State initiative built to serve a private clientele. It was the Doge who created this street by decree in 1550 for the merchant aristocracy, and high members of the republic's administration supervised its execution. Situated on the hillside between the castle and the town, the Strada Nuova was intended as a civic monument. The straight street with a uniform width of 30 palms (25 feet/7.5 m.), and the palaces, together made up an ideal urban fragment in the new Renaissance style. The purchasers of the building sites were obligated to put up palaces of predetermined size holding to a straight line. The main entrances had to face each other across the street space. The street was inaccessible to vehicles, being blocked at one end by a garden and at the other by stairs.

Obstructions to traffic in the form of gates and bars were introduced to London's *179* West End estates in the 18th century. The goal was to prevent the privately-owned streets lined with elegant Georgian townhouses from being used as cross-town thoroughfares, especially by traffic originating in the less reputable districts to the north. One of the first of these gates, built in the 1750s, served to bar undesirables from the Bedford estate. Residents who paid a deposit for a "silver ticket" were granted access; servants could pass through the gate only "in their attendance on the master, lady, or children of the family." Later, gates generally opened for all upper-class vehicles from 7 a.m. to 11 p.m., but remained closed to omnibuses, empty cabs, and all forms of commercial through traffic.[8] The century-long proliferation of these barriers created havoc for cross-town travelers and blocked traffic generated by the new railway terminals at Euston, St. Pancras and King's Cross. Despite a groundswell of public criticism, the gates were not outlawed until the 1890s, when two Acts of Parliament succeeded in removing the last fifty-five barriers.

The private streets of St. Louis, Missouri, conform to the precedents established by English residential estate planning. These "places," as they were called, were

179 Private London: gates on the Bedford Estate, at the Taviton Street entrance to Gordon Square, photographed with a gatekeeper shortly before their demolition by the London County Council in November 1893.

born in part because of the lack of municipal zoning and other legally binding protections of private property. First in line was Lucas Place from 1851; the last, Beverly Place and Parkview from 1905. Most of these private streets conformed to the city's grid plan, but since the public space was owned by the occupants, the street's design and use could be controlled through detailed deed restrictions, ensuring that the places were free of the depredations of heavy commercial traffic and "the encroachment of street cars, switch tracks and objectionable buildings."⁹ The contemporary version of St. Louis's places can be seen across America in exclusive residential enclaves with names like "Blackhawk" and "Whispering Woods," where security kiosks and electronically activated gates bar public access to roadways that wind through manicured suburban landscapes.

THE STREET AS PUBLIC SPACE

These private creations are exceptional. The only legitimacy of the street is as public space. Without it, there is no city. Practical needs—access to adjacent property, passage of through traffic—come to mind first because they are obvious. But the fundamental reality of streets, as with all public space, is political. If the street was an invention, it set out to designate a public domain that would take precedence over individual rights, including the right to build what one wants where one wants and the right to treat the open space as one's front yard. The street, furthermore, structures community. It puts on display the workings of the city, and supplies a backdrop for its common rituals. Because this is so, the private buildings that enclose the street channel are perforce endowed with a public presence.

This political and communal aspect of streets is best attested to by popular street celebrations which after the Renaissance, in the era of princes, were gradually banished or interiorized. Two examples should suffice.

In Coventry, streets were processional settings all through the year. During Midsummer and St. Peter's nights (24 and 29 June), bonfires blazed on the streets

180 Rome: Pius VI in procession on the Via Papale, during the ceremony of the possesso, *approaches the end of his journey, the stairs and ramp leading to S. Maria in Aracoeli and the Campidoglio. All the other buildings shown in this painting of 1775 were destroyed a little over a century later, when the Victor Emanuel Monument was erected.*

181 *Washington, D.C.: Lyndon B. Johnson's motorcade drives down Pennsylvania Avenue from the Capitol toward the White House in 1965.*

and informal gatherings took place. "These occasions," the historian Pythian-Adams notes, "were widely acknowledged celebrations of neighbourliness." Other rites involved the carrying through the streets of the Corpus Christi host or the Midsummer fire. Such activities "periodically added a mystical dimension to [the] utilitarian valuation of the immediate topographical context. While doing so, they underlined further the physical inescapability of communal involvement." Then, between 1450 and 1550, almost all of these popular ceremonies went indoors. The only open-air ceremony to survive was Rogationtide. Rites associated with May Day, Hock Tuesday or Midsummer were banished from the streets.[10]

In Renaissance Rome, Richard Ingersoll has shown, progressive physical changes along the main processional route of the Middle Ages called the Via Papale, a scraggly path stretching from the Vatican to the Lateran, made manifest the very real power adjustments between the Church, the noble houses and the commune. From the Castel S. Angelo on the river marking the start of the independent papal quarter of the Borgo, to the commune's center on the Campidoglio at the other end, the route provided staged opportunities during the Middle Ages for the assertion of the power of the people against the claims of the bishop of Rome. Politically the most significant occasion was the *possesso*, when a newly elected pope traversed the city 180 heading for the official papal residence at the Lateran. Along the way he was ritually harassed, knocked out of the saddle, and otherwise subjected to the crude will of the Roman people. He in turn pacified the mob at five points along the route with the traditional throwing of coins. By the time of Leo X (1513–21), the *possesso* had been transformed into a demonstration of the pope's right to be in the city, with the orderly, disciplined participation of all classes of society, so that the ceremony came to resemble a magnificent entry of the lord, the Classical *adventus*.[11]

THE THEATER OF POWER

An American civil ritual made its debut in January 1805 when Thomas Jefferson, after a brief oath-taking ceremony at the construction site of the U.S. Capitol, rode with a few congressmen and well-wishers down the muddy morass of Washington's Pennsylvania Avenue. Such was the modest birth of the secular procession that 181 consecrates each new American presidency. The inaugural parade binds the poles of national and federal power, traversing the mile-long stretch between the White House and the Capitol. From Jefferson's austere addition of four rows of Lombardy poplars to the ostentation of thirty-nine wooden "Grand Arches" constructed for Garfield's triumphal ride in 1881, the changing physical form of "the Avenue" has reflected political mood. It is a stage for exhibitions of public power as well. Here women's suffragists demanded the vote in 1913; 15,000 war veterans sought benefit payments and were rewarded with tear gas in 1932; eleven mule-drawn wagons launched Martin Luther King's 1966 protest march against poverty.

It is precisely at moments of political transformation that the street renews its currency as a medium for ceremonial assertions of power. In modern times this has been particularly true of societies forged through revolution. Here the secular procession is deliberately cultivated as a mass affirmation of changed social roles and values. British sociologist Christel Lane has identified two phases in the development of these public observances. The initial period of enthusiastic participation tends to be short-lived. It is followed by a decline in spontaneity characterized by wooden re-enactments of a fully articulated body of rituals.[12] Good examples of the process are to be found in the revolutionary culture of late 18th-century France and early 20th-century Russia.

. LA PLACE DE LA BASTILLE .

. LA PLACE DES INVALIDES .

. LA PLACE DE LA REVOLUTION .

. LE CHAMP DE LA FEDERATION .

The idea of harnessing the vitality of street theater to the goal of revolutionary re-education was Robespierre's. "Man is nature's greatest phenomenon," he proclaimed in 1794, "and the most magnificent of all spectacles is that of a large popular festival." For the new republican holidays sumptuously mounted mass processions were organized that wound their way through Paris to sites charged with political meaning, such as the Champ de Mars. Neoclassical pomp was 182– provided by triumphal arches, secular altars, and other set-pieces designed by 185 Jacques-Louis David, who staged these productions with the authority of "a virtual Minister of the Arts."[13] The popularity of these collective celebrations declined sharply after the fall of the Jacobin regime as the effects of State control came to outweigh participatory zeal. Under Napoleon Bonaparte the parades were reduced to military displays with citizens there merely as spectators.

182–185 "Stations" on the processional sequence through Paris devised by Jacques-Louis David for 10 August 1793: the fountain of Regeneration in the Place de la Bastille, from which deputies drank on behalf of all citizens; a colossal figure of the French People, next to the Invalides; burning the emblems of royalty in front of a figure of Liberty, Place de la Revolution (de la Concorde); and a re-enactment of the oath of Federation at the Champ de Mars.

Initial Soviet experiments with ritual procession fused elements of contradictory Russian precedents – the pre-revolutionary traditions of carnival-like coronation jubilees and of protest demonstrations. For May Day 1918, red flags, banners, and posters adorned Nevsky Prospekt in Petrograd (St. Petersburg). Much of the temporary street decor was radical in style as well as political content, thanks to a highly placed patron of the avant-garde, A. V. Lunacharsky, who served as Commisssar of Public Education. Later parades acquired more of a carnival atmosphere as costumed buffoons and comic floats ridiculed Communism's enemies—among them the bourgeoisie, black market speculators, priests, and drunkards.

Under Stalin political manifestations were standardized and drained of revolutionary *élan*. In 1930 a Central Staff for the Conducting of Holidays was founded in Moscow. Amateur and avant-garde initiative was abolished; the new protocol downplayed the individual's celebratory movement through the streets of the city, emphasizing instead the critical moment when the participant filed past the Party viewing stand. The change was reflected in the shift toward "a more miserly disposal of decorative emphases" after 1933, with monumental portraits of Marx, Engels, Lenin, and Stalin reserved for central squares.[14]

In established totalitarian states, the temporary nature of processional street decoration clashes with the pursuit of immutable rule, carnival playfulness with the need for sober conformity. Mass observances of political fealty are designed to strike a military chord, and power is reified permanently in monumental architecture. The transformation of Moscow's Gorky Street/Tverskaya into "the celebratory highway of the capital" in 1937–39 is one response to this program; Hitler's grandiose plan for Berlin's great north-south axis, with a remodeled Unter den Linden as a cross-axial boulevard, is another.[15] As in the Soviet case, Nazi Germany placed public ritual under the jurisdiction of Party institutions, in this case the *Hauptkulturamt* and the *Volkskulturwerk*.[16] Light, the color red, the flag, and the swastika were invested with symbolic significance: how they could be combined to create a highly regimented ceremonial streetscape was tested on Unter den Linden in 186 1939, before bombing raids made street lighting a pre-war memory.

186 Berlin, experimental lighting in Unter den Linden, 1939.

CULTURE AND CLASS

In the normal, everyday state of the street, the relative balance between the abutter's freedom of action and the identity of the public domain, independent of any regulating influence of laws, is ultimately a cultural matter. It depends on the traditional needs and attitudes of society, which of course change over time.

The private element, in the tug-of-war between the public and private nature of streets, is represented by houses and shops. At certain times in history this private element is paramount. This is so in Mesopotamia, in ancient Greece, in the cities of Islam. The common denominator here is a prevalence of inturned courtyard residences. These do not contribute much to the street except to act as boundary wall. They do, of course, have doors, through which people enter into and exit from the street channel and negotiate with passing vendors; and they have high windows in which plants bloom and heads appear. When the houses are combined with ground-floor shops, the dual function of the street is perfectly expressed in the nature of the street walls: they are at once the streetfront and the "back" of the houses.

How much beyond this concession to the commercial value of the street the abutting houses choose to go in communicating with the public space will depend, practically, on the demands of the housing structure. A main factor in this respect is the degree to which houses are dependent on the street's light and air. This in turn is a function of density. To the extent that urban lots are fully built up, their ability to enclose an open courtyard space will be limited. In ancient Rome, in contrast to the inturned single-family *domus*, apartment houses like the ones of Ostia opened up their façades with big windows and balconies, in order to get light into the individual units and extend their constricted space.

But these practical considerations are only one side of the story. The determining factor is culture. Some societies are demonstratively outgoing, others are not. In Islam, the seclusion of women from the public eye, and the sanctity of family privacy, are sufficient grounds to seal the lower ranges of the façades or obstruct the view of the passerby. Even so the function of the street as theater for housebound women and children is essential. A balcony or a window is a viewing stand, and so the Islamic house perforates the upper range but, by means of finely detailed lattice-work, screens the occupant who uses these openings to look out.

Class comes into it also. The *hôtels*, or townhouses, of the upper classes in Paris intentionally withdrew from the street to the back of a courtyard, and so did the mansions of the rich in London. A 1771 pamphlet on London, probably by the architect James Stuart, noted that, to men of rank and fortune, "a gateway with a spacious court within is both stately and commodious; but the front to the street should still present something that intimates a relation to the society in which you live; a dead wall of twenty or thirty feet [6–9 m.] high, run up in the face of your neighbours, can only inspire horror and dislike."[17]

In dense, multi-story street walls, status was established through height. The concept of the *piano nobile*, the floor above street level which could provide privacy and a degree of relief from the pressures of street activity, was alike familiar to ancient Roman *insulae*, Renaissance palazzi, and the Parisian housing block of the 19th century. In the Western medieval house, with the place of business at ground level in touch with passing traffic, the residential component was relegated to the upper stories.

For the Chinese of all classes, dependence of the house on the public space of the street was never important. The design of the residential street was affected

187 Reconstruction of insulae *at Ostia, near Rome, with shops and cookhouse on the ground floor and the best apartments on the floor above.*

188 An inward-turned Islamic street in Isfahan (Iran).

189 opposite A scene in Pien-ching (modern K'ai-feng), capital of the northern Sung; from Life along the River on the Eve of the Ch'ing Ming Festival, *by Chang Tse-Huan, 12th century. The houses are set back from the bustle of the street, screened by shops and by their own blank walls. A courtyard can be glimpsed top left. the shop in front advertises itself by scrolls sticking out into the street space; to the right is a public well.*

accordingly. The traditional Chinese house was structured on the principle of courtyards one behind the other. What defined the street might well be nothing more than the outer courtyard walls. Upper-class mansions usually had one large gate on the street, flanked by two low buildings occupied by servants and tradesmen and workmen. In the case of the smaller house of artisan and shopkeeper, the work premises were up front, the house proper behind. The common street scene in later imperial China, when the strict segregation of markets was eased and the tightly sealed residential wards were opened up toward the street space, featured uninterrupted strings of booths and shops concealing the low houses behind. Tall poles, often decorated with cloth streamers, held up the signs for the shops.[18]

THE REGULATED STREET

As a rule, however, the spatial standards of the public domain are established neither through benign laissez-fairism nor through cultural force of habit. The common course is a process dictated by law and constantly negotiated. Public control is exercised in the name of safety and circulation, but also in order to give esthetic distinction and unity to the streetscape. Haussmann's Paris is the tail end of a long story, whose beginning goes back much further than the celebrated building codes of city states in medieval Tuscany.[19]

270

The climax of esthetic street regulation is the pride of Baroque urban design. Prescriptive façade design gave the new districts of 17th-century Dresden and Berlin a visual uniformity that belied the private and speculative nature of development.[20] A century later German cities were still drafting regulations mandating the minimum height of new construction in order to acquire a "big city" look. Düsseldorf ordinances of 1835 and 1855 required all houses to have at least two stories. Ulm imposed its two-story rule in 1866. Such restrictions minimized the view of bare flanks of tall buildings standing out above low buildings.[21] Often accompanying these minimum height regulations were others for minimum façade widths. The Ringstrasse in Cologne, planned by Joseph Stübben in 1880, is a late example.

51

At their most basic, building codes and street ordinances seek to guard against fires and other disasters, to ensure public health and safety, and to improve the flow of traffic.

Public safety

Throughout history, decrees against wood construction are as frequent as major urban fires. Roman laws opposed wooden balconies. The Neronian measures for a modern, fire-resistant city after the disastrous fire in AD 64 included a proscription against timber beams, and the prescription of porticoes in front of houses and apartment blocks "from the flat roofs of which," Suetonius explained, "fires could be fought." For the most part, such decrees prove ineffectual—or are diluted from the start because of organized opposition.[22]

The success of anti-fire legislation after the Great Fire of London in 1666 is exceptional. After blithely ignoring repeated injunctions against timber construction, the City that was so spectacularly burned to the ground was one of lath and plaster houses, their timbers coated with pitch. The laws now set down that the rebuilding was to be in brick and stone, and every aspect of house construction was spelled out in detail. Furthermore, four house types were specified, each related to a particular street width. Two-story houses were only allowed on "by-lanes," four-story houses limited to the "high and principal streets." The unruly ways of London were finally stemmed (see below, p. 247).

191

192

190 *Possible hazards of a medieval street: projecting shop counters and shutters, stairs leading down to cellars, posts, temporary ladders, jettied structures, and hanging signs.*

But the most vexing and persistent abuses of street space came in the guise of ad hoc building protrusions that impeded transit and endangered pedestrians. In the Middle Ages, these included the counters that projected from shops and the *190* awnings that protected these counters from the weather, external stairs, and various means of expanding one's property without actually encroaching on the street, such as bridges between buildings, balconies, and cantilevered upper stories or jetties.

A covered landing at the top of the exterior staircase was probably the origin of the North European oriel, which is essentially a projecting window recess or covered *1* balcony. The feature was especially popular with the late Gothic houses of Switzerland and Austria, where lavishly decorated oriels sometimes ran through all the stories like a tower, or extended across the full width of one story. Linz on the Danube has a number of surviving examples. In Germany, the oriel window and external pulpit, sometimes serving as private chapel, were relics of the upper gallery that surrounded the South German farmhouse. The bay window was first cousin to the oriel. It provided more light and a wider field of vision. Bay windows often carried up through several stories were characteristic of the English middle-class urban house at the end of the 16th century. They lost their popularity in the next century as the trend toward classical façades spread through the building industry, but were revived in the Regency period, and remain a symbol of domesticity to *198* this day.

There were laws in many cities about all of these projections. In Florence, jetties or *sporti* were tolerated in lesser streets, more strictly controlled on main streets. In *305* Faenza, early 15th-century statutes established a system of jetty zoning for the whole town. The system specified on which streets they could go, and how wide or high they could be.[23] In Nuremberg, strict building ordinances set limits to ornamentation, ensured an undeviating building line for the rows of houses, and determined the number of oriel windows that would be permitted.

The English parallel should be evoked. Encroachments on the "high street" were strictly controlled, and one can show in places like Winchester that house frontages moved little if at all from the 11th to the 20th century. On side streets, control was more lax. In those extending from the city wall to the High Street, we can see the walls closing in more and more as they approach the commercially attractive intersection, where incentives were greatest for encroachments on the public space.[24]

In the remaking of London after the Fire of 1666, John Evelyn pleaded "that no Bay windows and uncomely jettings, nor even Balconies (unless made of iron) be for the future permitted.[25] A century later, the clean, flat street wall was being legislated for. An act of 1771 singles out streets in the county of Middlesex which are ill-paved, "and the passage through the same greatly obstructed by posts, projections, and other nuisances, and annoyed by spouts, signs, and gutters." The act prescribes "that all houses and buildings hereafter to be built or new fronted shall, for the effectual and absolute prevention of all manner of projections, annoyances, and inconveniences thereby, rise perpendicularly from the foundation." Any offending new house would be pulled down and removed.[26]

Signs deserve a special mention. Painted emblems identifying shops, either attached to or jutting out from the façades, were a common street fixture. The 1771 "James Stuart" pamphlet on London colorfully, and contemptuously, describes them as "monuments of national taste" and ridicules those who regretted their pulling down: "the cat and the fiddle, goose and gridiron, and the like, being regarded as the greatest efforts of inventive genius; and Cheapside often compared *192*

to the Medicean gallery, for its choice collection of paintings; blue boars, green dragons, and kings heads."[27] Another nuisance was the bow-windows of shops that more aggressively encroached upon the footways.

The Paving Act of 1762 had already prohibited the use of hanging signs in Westminster. Though this ordinance was ignored by inns, the shops did shift to the use of fascias above their windows. By the 19th century, protruding or swinging street signs were being actively condemned. An act of 1834 concerning the South London district of Bermondsey makes liable to removal all "signs, sign-irons, sign-posts, barbers' poles, dyers' poles, stalls, blocks, bulks, showboards, butchers' hooks, spouts, water-pipes."[28]

By the end of the century, with the signs gone, the new menace was street advertising. G. L. Gomme, in his book on Victorian London of 1898, bemoans the street litter of his time: "the sky-signs, without one single element of artistic construction, lime-light and electric-light letterings, posters covering hoardings sometimes for considerable distances . . ."[29] In the United States, the land of privatism, "the billboard nuisance" was if anything more acute. Many billboards rested on the ground, and the spaces behind them were used as dumping ground.

The evolution of a street: Cheapside, London, 1638–1831

191 above Before the Fire of 1666, Cheapside was a grand late medieval commercial street, with timber-framed houses on an irregular building line and all the features later legislation was to condemn: jettied upper stories, water spouts shooting rain off the roof onto the passerby below, and projecting shop counters, awnings, and signs. (The shops themselves are concealed here in honor of a royal procession.) Note the market cross in the middle.

192 opposite, above Post-Fire, ca. 1750: houses of fireproof brick or stone—four-storied, since Cheapside was a "high or

principal street"—form a continuous line,
enhanced by balconies above the shops,
and their roofs are drained through lead
downpipes. Wren's new St. Mary-le-Bow
stands at the far right. By this time the
17th-century shops had been transformed
with glazed, often bowed, frontages, and
hanging signs, at first banned, had
reappeared. The roadway is paved, the
sidewalk sheltered by posts.

193 right A closer view of the junction of
Cheapside, Poultry, and Bucklersbury in
1831 reveals further changes: the shops no
longer project, and they have fascias
bearing names rather than an image.
Underfoot, pedestrians have a raised
sidewalk with a kerb.

194 *Billboards in Atlanta (Georgia), photographed by Walker Evans in 1936. With the automobile age, outdoor advertising became larger and more aggressive, as it now had only seconds to arrest the speeding traveler's attention.*

They obstructed light, sunshine and air. But these considerations were secondary to the concern with the unwholesome nature of the messages advertising liquor, tobacco and lurid-sounding plays with titles like "Why Girls Go Wrong" or "A Rose of the Tenderloin." The cardinal issue, as always, was that struggle between the public and private uses of the street. As a prominent New York lawyer put it in 1910, "The landscape in the country and the open spaces in the city do not belong to the man who chooses to pay a few dollars for them."[30]

Public health

Ordinances related to public health were usually spurred on by the outbreak of epidemics. An early instance is the ban against outbuildings (*gaisi* in Neapolitan) included in the urban regulations of 1553 in Naples, a ban which was prompted by the serious plagues of 1529 and 1530. Until the 19th century, the law set housing standards only in so far as the public realm, and not the health of the inhabitants within the houses, was affected. In terms of the street space itself, the main concerns were congestion and exposed sewage.

Drains for the siphoning off of surface wastewater and sewers for its disposal were not unfamiliar in the pre-industrial world. Dora Crouch has documented the subject in detail for ancient Greece.[31] To take an early example from another cultural sphere, Etruscan Marzabotto had streets that (in the words of Ward-Perkins)

> incorporated a very carefully planned and executed system of drainage, with a uniform flow from north to south and from east to west. Along the broader streets there were two drains, and one along each of the secondary streets, and at frequent intervals smaller drains led into them from the individual houses.[32]

In the Middle Ages, from the 13th century onward, these matters gained attention anew. Several late medieval towns in England—London, Leicester, Hull, etc.—had public latrines. In addition, fresh water brought by pipe or open conduit was to be found in London, Exeter and Bristol by the 14th century.[33]

195 *Cheapside conduit, London, 1585. Large leather water-jugs stand around the public fountain.*

195

196, 197 Paris streets old and new. Above, *with the traditional central gutter, uneven surface, and overhanging houses—though by then these had drainpipes (from A.L. Joanne,* Paris illustré, *1863).* Below, *with a neat pavement of granite blocks over a labyrinth of pipes for sewers, water, street hydrants, and gas; note the public pump at the far left (from E. Texier,* Tableau de Paris, *1853). Virtually the only feature the two scenes have in common is the wall-mounted gas lamp.*

By and large, however, drainage in the pre-industrial city was a simple affair: cities made do with a depression in the middle of the street. Projecting roofs or long spouts poured rainwater into this central gutter. Evelyn deplores this arrangement. He writes that

> for the universal benefit (especially of those, who are not born to ride in coaches) that intolerable nuisance of spouts and gutters might be strictly reformed, and the waters so conveyed by close and perpendicular pipes (where they cannot be *192*
> avoided) or to drop only from above the Modillions, as from Italian roofs[34] *Pl.27*

—presumably sufficiently clear of the houses to leave a sheltered passage for pedestrians.

For pre-Haussmann Paris, Sir Francis Head describes the streets with their "rude *196*
ill-constructed pavement of round stones for carriages, horses, and foot-passengers" and down the center "a dirty gutter, which, in heavy rain, looked like a little trout stream."[35] The few underground sewers into which the gutters might drain were leaky and clogged easily. Wastewater found its way into rivers, moats and canals. Excrement was dumped into these same places, or hauled away in carts. In Germany, Hamburg was the first to install a sewer system with flush toilets in houses, taking advantage of a major fire in 1842. Other German cities slowly followed suit, substituting sewers for cartage. Hobrecht designed the system for Berlin, deviating wastewater to agricultural land outside the city.[36]

The model was England, which was far in advance of the Continent on street-incorporated services. England introduced and popularized storm drains, sewers and piped water some time around 1800. Then Paris took the lead. The hygienist *197,*
Parent-Duchâtelet studied sewer systems in great detail in his *Essai sur les cloaques* *227*
ou égouts de Paris (1824), and the prefect Rambuteau set about to apply some of the findings shortly thereafter. The provision of pipes under the roadway to carry off rainwater and waste was not enough: a stream of water had to be continually available to flush away street debris. So a system of mains was installed which carried water from the River Seine to a network of hydrants which flowed on demand to clean the cobblestone streets. This went along with the proliferation of sidewalks, and the installation of roof gutters and drainpipes to collect rain water and channel it directly to the curb. We have it on the testimony of Rambuteau that in 1832 there were 39 kilometers (24 mi.) of water mains and 217 hydrants, while by 1850 there were 358 kilometers (218 mi.) of mains and 1,837 hydrants.[37]

Congestion was perceived in terms of street width and the overall height of flanking buildings. Narrow, canyon-like streets kept sunlight from reaching ground level. The general remedies were to set height limits, and to widen streets correspondingly. The first were hard to enforce; the second had prohibitive costs when attempted in the older quarters. In the newly built areas of town, the demand for wide streets became habitual after the 17th century. This had as much to do with the increasing use of coaches as it did with health matters. But by the late 19th century the perception that narrow, crowded streets encouraged the incubation and spread of disease, especially cholera, was firmly established. The connection is transparent in the fact that legislated street widths in England were promulgated in national Public Health Acts, like the ones of 1848, 1858 and 1866, which led to the ubiquitous suburban "bye-law street" as the substitute for the outlawed back-to- *198*
back housing.[38] This new street type consisted of long stretches of terraces cut through by infrequent cross-streets. At the back ran correspondingly long, narrow alleys between walled-in yards intended for toilets and the removal of ashes and rubbish. This arrangement of back alleys aped the mews system of affluent rows *162*

developed in the previous two centuries for the stowing of private coaches. The width of the bye-law street was set at as much as 40 feet (12 m.), far in excess of practical need and disproportionate to the modest height of the two-story houses; yet there were no proper front gardens and no trees.[39]

In Germany, in the mid-19th century, the cult of the wide street was dominant. The *Fluchtliniengesetz* (Law of Building Lines) of 1875 was designed to encourage broad thoroughfares; it allowed municipalities to lay out streets up to 26 meters (85.3 ft.) wide without compensating property owners along their line. But this ostensible concern for light and air stopped at the building line. Behind it came the private space of the deep blocks, where developers filled every inch of the property with huge buildings; here many of the inhabitants had no benefit whatever of the light and air of the ample streets, as they breathed through narrow courtyards and less.

The situation was made worse by regulations regarding the height of abutting buildings. Codes normally set building height in proportion to street width. This meant that the wide streets of Germany condoned uniformly tall buildings—indeed encouraged them. Wide streets were more expensive to construct, and since this cost was assessed to the owners of adjacent property, it had to be recovered by building as dense and tall as you could get away with.

After 1880 Germany became disillusioned with the cult of the wide street. By the end of the century narrow streets were being recommended for residential areas. "Bigness yielded to intimacy, the imposition of schematic forms to the apotheosis of irregularity and individuality."[40] Wide streets were now seen as unhealthy because they fostered wind and dust.

198 Whitehall Road, Small Heath, Birmingham, a typical late Victorian wide bye-law street. Between the front doors of the houses, a round-headed opening gives access to yards behind. This photograph was taken during the war, in 1941, when the terraces had suffered damage.

Traffic

The correlation of street width to traffic created hierarchies of another sort. The amount of anticipated traffic is the most straightforward objective in deciding street widths. There are major traffic arteries and quieter, residential eddies. At the bottom of the hierarchy stand the alleys providing access to the rear of properties. But the logic of circulation has not always guided city-making. Residential streets of status could elect a grand scale incommensurate with their modest traffic flow. And paths *Pl.27* of main commercial activity were often near-impassable bottlenecks, willingly tolerated on the premise that crowds in tight quarters were the key to contagious shopping. Street-widening in the heavily congested city center of the early automobile years was not always welcomed by the store owners who were considered its primary beneficiaries. "The appearance of business *being done* is good," an American merchant wrote in 1915, "and wide streets, unless well occupied, give an opposite impression."[41] The consensus of the time was that main traffic streets offered the best opportunities for shops provided they were not wider than about 50 to 70 feet (15–20 m.).

In the origin of linear towns, the traffic artery *is* the street, which widens for the 75 market and runs into the highroad at the other end. Streets parallel to the "high street" come about as the town's size increases; cross lanes are kept to a minimum. But even in more balanced urban configurations, the concept of the "main street" is pretty standard.

So, often, is the distinction between parallel streets in one direction and cross streets in another. In Scottish towns like St. Andrews, this distinction had linguistic affirmation in the Middle Ages. The wide east-west streets were called "vicus" in Latin and "gait" in Scots, as in Northgait, Mercatgait, etc. The narrow north-south lanes were called "venella" in Latin and "wynd" in Scots, as in Fisherwynd.[42]

A slightly different categorization pertains in the *bastides* or planted towns of southwest France and Wales, the colonial towns of eastern Germany, and many other medieval towns of older origin. The major traffic streets, with the greatest width, are there of course—these are called *Verkehrstrassen* in Germany, or *carrières* in French. They commonly connected the points of entry into the walled town. Residential streets, built without provision for shops and trade activities, carried traffic along adjoining household plots. The third category, the narrowest, are called in German *Wirtschaftsstrassen*, or occupational streets. City officials of medieval Florence used a slightly different method to categorize the three classes of streets they recognized: there were *viae publicae*, the major thoroughfares; *viae vicinales*, neighborhood streets, often blind alleys; and *viae privatae*, or private streets. The city gradually purchased the latter, opening and widening them as needed.

The common perception of the congested medieval city where land is at a premium is probably more appropriate for the post-medieval period. Medieval streets in the West were not especially narrow. Bristol had several streets that were a full 50 feet (15 m.) wide, and many more of 35 feet (10 m.). Stratford-on-Avon, at its founding by the Bishop of Worcester, was laid out with new streets 50 feet wide and the main market street was made 90 feet (27 m.) across.[43] Even in 10/11th-century Novgorod, some streets were 16 to 24 feet (4.9–7.3 m.) wide. At the same time, we have to stress the presence of extensive areas of yards, gardens and orchards behind the houses, which contributed to an air of openness. Ampleness had its dangers. Encroachments were more tempting. The main market street at places like Stratford-on-Avon, Chipping Campden, and Ludlow sprouted a permanent row of 75 shops down the middle.

The case of Islam is, as always, unique. The main distinction that holds in Islamic cities is between through-streets and residential cul-de-sacs. The through-street is a public right-of-way, traditionally wide enough for two packed camels to pass. The cul-de-sac is the private property of people living around it.[44] In general, the street pattern in these cities is not designed to enhance mobility and exchange. Freedom of movement through the urban form was not in itself valued. On the contrary, the insularity of neighborhoods was a self-conscious system of collective privacy, as the courtyard house was of family privacy. And even in the streets that were meant to carry traffic, the very limited width was "a built-in system of traffic control."[45]

In the modern period, street widths based on functional categories began to be codified. In Paris just after the Revolution, e.g., the following functional categories were established: "short routes", 6 meters (20 ft.) wide; "intermediate routes", 10 meters (33 ft.) wide; "inner arteries," 12 meters (39 ft.) wide; "big thoroughfares leading from one end of Paris to the other," 14 meters (46 ft.) wide.[46]

This is still at a time when sidewalks were non-existent, and mass transportation had not reached the modern city. Those two phenomena would make widths of this sort unworkable. By the time the boulevard as a generic street type was adopted, the main roadway might still be 12 meters wide, but, separated from it by rows of trees, there were now two *contre-allées* each 6–8 meters (20–26 ft.) wide. In the older streets a more reasonable width had to be forged by widening the original channel—at first just one side of it, for the sake of expediency and cost, and by Haussmann's time, in extravagant *éventrements* that not only demolished both banks of the channel but a considerably broader swath of buildings as well (see below, pp. 266ff.).

Pl.25 (margin left)
199, (margin left)
227 (margin left)
269 (margin left)

199 *The Avenue des Champs-Elysées is the archetypal Parisian boulevard-type street, laid out under the prefect Rambuteau from 1828 on the* contre-allée *system: the central roadway is flanked by gravel strips, in which trees are planted; beyond them are the asphalted* contre-allées, *and then sidewalks.*

The street occupies the line of a 17th-century planted avenue leading through parkland from the Tuileries Palace. Rambuteau began its urbanization and provided gas lighting, but there were few houses until after 1840. The Place de l'Etoile around the Arc de Triomphe (from which this view was taken) was built up in 1858 by Hittorf.

SIDEWALKS AND PAVING

Two perennial concerns with respect to the flow of traffic were the quality of the street surface and the separation of vehicles from pedestrians.

The sidewalk, the commonsensical response to the second concern, remained exceptional until relatively recent times. The ancient world, Rome at any rate, was certainly aware of raised pedestrian strips along the edge of streets. Etruscan *200* Marzabotto had a grid of broad, paved streets, as much as 50 feet (15 m.) wide (the secondary streets averaged 16 feet/4.9 m.), equally divided between the carriageway and a pair of raised pavements. The Roman word for sidewalk was *semita*, and references to this feature go back to the 3rd century BC.[47]

In the post-Roman period, as part of the general deterioration of streetscapes, sidewalks went out of use almost entirely, until their re-emergence in the modern period. Here the primary credit is given to England. The earliest reference to the provision of sidewalks, or at least raised footpaths, seems to be in Evelyn's post-Fire plan of London, where he proposes to use left-over bricks "found amongst the rubbish" for "the elevations destined for the foot causeys before the fronts of houses," or—if you were prepared to spend more—"Purbeck [a hard British limestone] and flat stones."[48] Indeed, sidewalks were provided on most reconstructed streets.

In times when there were no sidewalks, distinctions were commonly made between the carriageway and the pedestrian strips. The "Stuart" pamphlet on London says that for the "ease of horses" the midway was "paved with huge shapeless rocks, and the footpath with sharp pebbles for the benefit of the feet."[49] In Turkish Sofia, the streets were unpaved, except on the sides where there was a pebble pavement for pedestrians.[50]

Beginning in the late 18th century a series of improvements in street design were introduced and popularized in England. These included macadam (crushed rock) paving, storm drains and sewers, piped water, house numbering—and sidewalks. *193* Rambuteau's regime in Paris adopted some of these improvements in the 1830s and *199* '40s, including sidewalks, but here unlike England the form was associated with rows of trees. The sidewalk often provided a site with improved drainage and protection from soil compaction and injury for street trees which until then had had to struggle for survival at the edge of the roadway. In 1822 only 267 meters (876 ft.) of sidewalks existed in all of Paris; by 1848 the total had risen to 260 kilometers (161 miles).[51] Haussmann claimed in his memoirs that "they were nearly unknown before 1845,"[52] but this is not quite accurate. Since the mid-18th century there were private initiatives to construct foot pavements (*trottoirs*) for some exclusive streets like the Rue de l'Odéon (1781), but these consisted of uneven and unconnected limestone slabs. Nonetheless by 1835 Mrs. Trollope felt inclined to "bless with an humble and grateful spirit the dear little pavement which . . . borders most of the principal streets of Paris now." They were narrower than the "enormous esplanades on each side" of Regent and Oxford Streets, but she was confident that "in a few years . . . it will be almost as easy to walk in Paris as in London."[53] Furthermore, in the early boulevards, a walkway (*chaussée*) was provided in the middle, flanked by ditches which were later filled in and replaced by wooden barriers and then, in 1811, by round border stones.[54] But Haussmann was technically correct in that it was only with a law of 1845 that the installation of proper sidewalks was made mandatory, the cost being split 50–50 between the city and abutters.[55]

The history of street paving is also fitful. Khirokitia's main street was paved. So *176* were all streets in Priene of the 4th century BC. Main thoroughfares in Roman cities

200 were paved with large stone blocks, and the polygonal tufa paving of the highways, familiar from the hyperbolic evocations of Piranesi, was also carried through into urban stretches like the Sacra Via that crossed the Roman Forum. Preoccupation with giving the earthen roadway a hard surface returns in the later Middle Ages. In 1286, four citizens of Lincoln, in England, were commissioned to "arrange for the paving of the high road running through the said town, taking care that the better sort who have tenements on or abutting upon the said road contribute thereto in proportion to their tenements." Nottingham's municipal pavior was appointed in 1501; he was supposed to "make and mend all the defaults in all places of the said town in the pavements."[56]

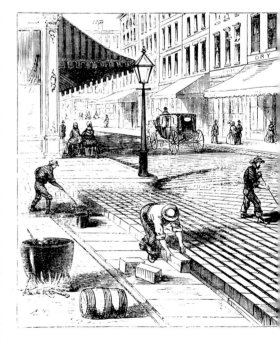

The tradition of compelling property owners to bear the cost of street paving is persistent. An odd case of financing street paving is contained in the 1533 urban improvement law in Naples: an unprecedented tax levied for the purpose on monasteries, who were the largest landowners in the city.

In Paris, the story dates back to an order of Philip Augustus in 1184. Having seen from the palace windows the horse-drawn wagons stir up the mud on the streets, and smelled the fetid smell that that produced, he called in the city leaders and the provost, and "gave the order to pave the main streets with big stones."[57] "Paveurs"
225 begin to appear in documents of the 14th century.

The Westminster Paving Act of 1762 took any remaining responsibility for paving streets away from individuals and assigned it to commissioners empowered to tax abutters for the cost. A consequence of expecting individuals to do the job had been that the pedestrian walk directly in front of the houses was much smoother than the roadway, which was paved with round pebbles. An observer in 1726 noted that "the pavement is so bad and rough that when you drive in a coach you are most cruelly shaken, whereas if you go on foot you have a nice smooth path paved with wide flat

201 Log-paved streets were found throughout the Slavic world; this reconstruction shows an example at Meissen, in eastern Germany, ca. 11th century. (After Herrmann)

202 Chicago (Illinois): laying a Nicolson pavement, 1859. Pine blocks dipped in tar are fixed to a plank base, then covered with pitch and gravel. The technique was invented locally in 1857.

stones, and elevated above the road." This pedestrian path was separated from the roadway by timber posts which defended the pedestrian from wayward carriages. *192* The Act now specified that good Purbeck stone replace the pebbles in the better streets, and that stone curbs and raised sidewalks be universal. It also replaced the drainage kennel in the middle of the street with curbside gutters.[58] These provisions eliminated the need for timber posts, although the new gas lamps with their fixed bases also formed an effective line of bollards.

Stone-paved streets in England existed in pre-Conquest times, as excavations in Church Street, Oxford, have shown. Thereafter, the common Oxford paving material was gravel. In Winchester, it was "a spread of small flints over chalk."[59] Rubbish accumulated very fast over this cover, and rains caused havoc. Cobblestone pavements proved long-lived despite the fact that they were uncomfortable to walk on—"Pavements fang'd with murderous stones," as Coleridge called them[60]—and exceedingly difficult to clean. Macadam, named after its Scottish inventor, became widespread with the arrival in the 1860s of the steam roller and the mechanical stone crusher. This type of roadway used crushed stone on a surface graded for proper drainage. Granite blocks were the ideal heavy-duty stone, durable and easy to *197* maintain, but they were also more expensive.

Brick found favor intermittently. In medieval Siena, the Campo and the main axes of the *terzi* or separate town districts were brick-paved. The Strada Nuova in Genoa was to be paved with bricks in the center and smooth flagstones on the sides. Brick pavements had been used in Holland since the 13th century. But the modern *Pl.28* popularity of this surfacing material came in the late 19th century with the perfection of vitrified brick and the use of concrete for foundation.

Wood has also a venerable history as a paving material. The log pavement goes *201* back to the Bronze Age. In Old Russia, when most streets were narrow, crooked and unpaved, the few cases of pavement "consisted of round, unhewn poles inserted into side logs," according to Gutkind.[61] In Novgorod log-paved streets may well go back to the 10th–11th century. At the end of the 17th century, a traveler speaks of the "bumpy pavement of tree trunks" in reference to the streets of Moscow.[62] In Gutkind's words, the system consisted of a pavement surface

> of thin poles, about 4 to 8 inches [10–20 cm.] in diameter, laid along the longitudinal axis of the street and covered transversely by split half-logs of 16 to 20 inches [40–50 cm.] in diameter notched on their convex side to fit onto the longitudinal poles. The flat upper side of the transverse logs formed the road surface, providing a good base for the runners of sledges that were probably used in winter and summer alike.[63]

Sledges, because excavations have failed to reveal traces of wheels or wheeled vehicles. These wooden streets were renewed repeatedly, with the old pavement forming the foundation for the new. So far in Novgorod twenty-eight street levels have been discovered. One reason for the rising level was that the yards flanking the streets, separated from them by stake fences, were piled with dung to be used as manure and with other waste products, and in time found themselves at a higher level. Sir Leonard Woolley describes the obverse case in ancient Ur. Since refuse was dumped into the public space outside the front door and trodden under foot, the street level rose steadily, and the occupants kept up by raising the threshold and by adding inner steps as required to reach the original floor.[64]

Wood was also widely used in America since Colonial times. Besides log or "corduroy" roads, plank paving became commonplace from the 1850s, and just before the Civil War an improvement called the Nicolson pavement came into use. *202*

This consisted of treated square wood blocks, coated with tar against decay and nailed to a plank base. The Upper Midwest preferred round cedar blocks grouted with gravel and tar.

Paving was protected as much as possible; late medieval municipalities in England regularly prescribed against carters with over-heavy loads or with iron-shod cart wheels. The kinds of paving were directly relevant to street cleaning. Beyond flushing drains and open gutters, the street surface had to be cleaned periodically. Many cities had regulations about this quite early in their history. Often abutters had the responsibility of cleaning the front of their property, up to the middle of the street. In Germany, Düsseldorf was famous for the cleanliness of its streets. The task was presented as an aspect of good citizenship. "The streets," New York City's civil engineer Edward Very wrote as late as 1912, "are but the hallways of the great municipal house, and municipal householders should find pleasure in keeping them [clean] as does the competent housewife."[65]

But by the later 19th century, in Europe ahead of America, private companies hired by the city began to do the job, or the cities themselves undertook the service. Municipal cleaning was confined to main streets; alleys did not receive this service, and often incorporated suburbs too had to fend for themselves.[66]

203   The great turning point in street paving came with the perfection of asphalt. Made of two basic components—bitumen and an aggregate like sand or stone dust—it was flexible enough to withstand shocks, impervious to water, and able to expand in warm weather. From about 1885 on it became the all-purpose, modern street cover in both Europe and the United States. Its smooth surface would prove a happy match to automobile tires.[67] Philip Gilbert Hamilton wrote in 1900: "True lovers of Paris . . . tell me that the mere sensation of the Parisian asphalt under the feet is an excitement itself."[68]

203 *Street-cleaning trucks on the smooth, waterproof asphalt of Pennsylvania Avenue in Washington, D.C., 1905. The Capitol is in the background.*

THE DESIGN OF STREETS

To suggest that practical matters like safety, health and traffic were the only consideration in the long history of regulating the streetscape would be tantamount to mechanizing that history. Municipal authorities at all times were as likely to be preoccupied with seemliness (that is, visual appeal and decorum)—often explicitly so. In Viterbo, for example, mid-13th-century statutes prohibited the construction of external stairs because they "prejudiced the appearance of the street."[69]

The esthetic urge expressed itself most purely in ornamental additions to the street space, among them fountains, monuments of various sorts, and the marking of crossroads by special architectural features like the Roman tetrapylon or special trees like the banyan or pipal tree, representing the heaven-tree of Indian mythology, which stood at the crossroads of Indian towns laid out on the basis of mandalas. In China, in towns where the street pattern was structured about a cross formed by two main streets connecting the four gates, there was a drum tower at the intersection. The tradition of erecting special gateways to commemorate important events or virtuous deeds starts in the T'ang dynasty. The gates, of timber or stone, might be inscribed with the name of the street, and also sometimes a poetical allusion or evocative inscription.[70]

The process of laying out streets left monuments of its own. Roman street corners were often marked with *cippi* (stone street markers), as in Ostia. This Roman practice survived and can be documented in several North Italian cities since at least the 13th century. In Sabbioneta in the 16th century, stumps of cutstone marked all corners to designate the city blocks for the construction of houses. Another example is Mantua. The phrase "piantare . . . i capi di strada" (setting out the street-ends) is used by a late source about the final laying out of Guastalla in 1564.[71]

In periods of self-conscious urbanism, the integrity and beauty of street design was in the hands of special officials. In the Hellenistic kingdoms the care and embellishment of streets were entrusted to a body of controllers: a law defining the duties of the office survives. In post-antique Rome the office of the Maestri delle Strada dates back at least as far as the 13th century. A statute of 1363 charged the Maestri with "the clearing and repair and oversight of buildings, streets and roads," and during the next century their authority to demolish obstructions of any sort was made explicit. This came to include the expropriation and demolition of buildings for the public good. The Maestri were also responsible for paving streets, and seeing that they were kept clean.

In Florence, elected officials called the Ufficiali della Torre were charged, since 1349, with keeping streets clear, ordering demolitions when necessary, and enforcing design criteria. In 1389, e.g., when Via Calzaiuoli was renovated between Piazza della Signoria and Orsanmichele, the new façades were required to have the same standardized arch forms at their base. Standardization gained in popularity in 15th-century Florence as the increase in the demand for buildings began to favor specialized workers producing standard details (like cornices or mullions) that would be ready for assembly.[72]

In late medieval Tuscany, streets came to be seen, for the first time since Classical antiquity, as the basic unit of urbanism. Properly formed, streets reflected honorably on the city and facilitated its work. The primary requirement of a beautiful street was regularity—a smooth paved surface, a consistent slope, and linear clarity.

Straightness was a virtue. Officials were instructed to build streets that were *Pl.27* "pulchrae, amplae et rectae"—beautiful, wide, and straight. Via Larga (now

Cavour), built in the early 14th century to facilitate the transportation of grain to the market at Orsanmichele, was to run from the gate in the old wall to one in the new circuit along a course measured "ad cordam et recta linea" (i.e. a straight line measured by a cord).

In older streets, straightness was achieved piecemeal. Corners of important houses or monuments served as markers or survey points. Meantime new construction was required by the *podestà* or chief magistrate to conform to the building line of adjacent properties and to present a straight façade to the street (the first regulation on this dates from 1258). Abuses were forcibly corrected. A law of 1294 singled out a whole area as defective, and prescribed that all the houses for a certain street length be cut back and the street "be straightened and the deformity eliminated."[73] Materials were also regulated in Florence; stone and brick were required up to a certain height, as much as 16 *braccia* (9.3 m./36 ft.), from the street level.

Full uniformity in street frontage was a main preoccupation of urbanism in the Grand Manner. I discussed the ramifications of this earlier in these volumes.[74] There we saw that the beginnings came much before the Baroque. One device that ensured patches of uniformity was the result of speculative row housing, known in Italy since the 13th century and in England not much later.

THE BUILDING LINE

This concern for a decorous street entailed a long-term program of defining the street space within firm, continuous street walls and, to the extent possible, controlling the overall design of these walls.

At the crux of the matter is the relation of the street line to the building line. When the two are congruent, the structure of the public space is unequivocal. As abutting buildings arbitrarily push back from the street line or protrude beyond it, an ambivalent spatial zone is created along the street channel which blurs this structure.

In purely architectural terms, the ideal expression of a building as a three-dimensional artifact presumes the coordinated treatment of the four elevations. But in the making of streets the identity of each building must submit to the overall structure beyond its limits. Generally speaking, the dignity of a free-standing object is accorded to public monuments, while the ordinary fabric takes form out of more or less contiguous buildings, as if the streets were carved out of what was once solid mass.

In cultures where there is a strong sense of the homestead as an individual, detached unit, there will be a corresponding indifference to the formation of enclosed street spaces, that is, of streets as well defined volumes of exterior space and corridors of movement.

Take Russia. In the early 18th century, the standard urban unit was still the
204 individual homestead of rural derivation. The houses of boyars and wealthy merchants were situated in a courtyard off the street, while picket or wattle fences and outhouses and gardens interrupted by whitewashed huts lined the roads.[75] It was Peter the Great who in 1714 ordered his noblemen, under threat of punishment by the rod, to erect their mansions in his new capital city of St. Petersburg "like the
205 buildings of other European states . . . on the line . . . and not in the middle of the courts."[76] There were similar attempts earlier on to ensure a continuous building
206 line. In Philadelphia, laid out in 1683, William Penn pleaded that "the houses built be in a line, or upon a line, as much as may be," and the regulations for Williamsburg,

Building lines:

204, 205 In Russia, before and after Peter the Great, early 18th century

206 In Penn's Philadelphia, after 1683

207 In Williamsburg (Virginia), late 17th/ early 18th century

208 *In the Herculean Addition, Ferrara (Italy), ca. 1490*

209 *Continuous façades in the Grand Manner*

210 *In Ledoux's Chaux, late 18th century*

211 *In Garnier's* Cité Industrielle, *1904*

in Virginia, specified that on the main avenue, Duke of Gloucester Street, the houses *207* would "come within six foot of the street, and not nearer," that they would "front alike," and the lot be enclosed "with a wall, pails, or post and rails."

The Renaissance struggled with this conflict between the continuity of the street wall and the integrity of the single building mass. It conceived of the street, in its ideal state, as the orderly array of heterogeneous buildings, each preserving and expressing its own three-dimensional mass while assisting in the volumetric definition of coherent public space.

At the Herculean Addition of Ferrara, created around 1500, the streets are a *208* compromise between the shadow-filled, tunnel-like effect of continuous walls and the visual distinction of individual buildings and blocks. The designer, Biagio Rossetti, kept the perspective strong, but eschewed bilaterally symmetrical palace fronts. At the same time he broke up the vertical planes of brick with green spaces and through-views into courtyards and gardens, so that the streets were patched with light, and the pedestrian had a feeling for crossings and the integrity of the blocks. The special highlighting of block corners with pilasters of white marble aided in this perception of a corridor defined by individually articulated units.

This solicitude for the single building block, exceptional even in the Renaissance, faded away entirely in the Baroque period, in favor of a continuous and uniform street wall. The trend indicates a move away from an interest in the design of the solid to an interest in the design of the void. The street perspective composed of heterogeneous buildings, and even styles, graduated to a perspective of unified building types and styles. Laws commonly required the walling off of unbuilt lots, in *209* order to maintain the visual coherence of the public spaces.

But the conflict did not disappear. The primacy of the single building returned, first, with the monument-fixation of Neoclassical planners. This reversal was anticipated by Fischer von Erlach and Piranesi, and fully celebrated in the work of Ledoux. In such Neoclassical schemes as Ledoux's Chaux, the town disintegrates *210* into a series of isolated buildings, in an arrangement reminiscent of Modernist predilections in this century when the city would be seen as open land into which buildings are introduced as objects. In between Ledoux and the Modernists, we can single out one more application of this open form. In Vienna's Ringstrasse and the blocks beyond, empty space flows around monumental structures—this against the *270* contemporary boulevards of Haussmann's Paris which adhered instead to the *199* Baroque precedent of uniformly bounded street volumes.

In most urban theories of the Modern Movement, the dissipation of the street walls is a given. In Garden City practice, the building line is definitely separated from the street line, setting the precedent for later Modernist dogma. In Soria y Mata's *Ciudad Lineal* of the 1880s, the streets were laid out on the old grid system, but the houses were placed in isolation from each other. This is true as well of the influential *Cité Industrielle* designs by Tony Garnier, displayed in Paris in 1904. As Rob Krier *211* puts it, "Their proposals dissolved the traditional urban form and created in its place a villa landscape.[77]

PORTICOES AND PORCHES

Even allowing for the strictest correspondence of the building line with the edge of the public space, the street wall cannot definitively separate the public from the private realm. As shopping activity spills out into the street and restaurants and cafés take up the sidewalks, so the public space infiltrates courtyards where there are workshops we need to do business with or garage space for our motorcars. Street design has worked out a variety of conventions to negotiate this transitional zone.

One recurrent device in the West is the ground-story arcade, often sheltering shops. Roman Ostia had arcades, and Axel Boethius long ago demonstrated the Mediterranean continuity of that formula in the Middle Ages and later.[78] The beginnings go back to Republican times. Nero's *nova urbs* made porticoes obligatory, as has been mentioned. The word used in Suetonius and Tacitus, *porticus*, which can simply be rendered as "covered colonnade" or "porch," here probably refers to vaulted arcades.[79]

Street arcades were aggrandized in the Empire's colonial settlements to an extent impossible in Rome itself, given the narrow, alley-like quality of most of the city's arteries. The long, twinned rows of scarred columns preserved at Ephesus, Timgad, and Palmyra suggest the splendor rather than the function of these urban corridors. Monumental colonnades, surmounted by a continuous entablature and a roof spanning from road curb to building frontage, provided the armature for covered passageways that lined primary thoroughfares. Colonnades often distinguished the major axis of town grids in Rome's territories.[80]

This architectural treatment was not unique to the eastern provinces. The fashion of arcaded streets had spread across the Empire by the end of the 1st century AD, with modest porticoes prevailing in the west and the more elaborate colonnades in the east. Absolute consistency of these street borders was more the exception than the rule. It was found in showcase settlements like Timgad, or acquired through extravagant reconstruction programs, as in Palmyra.[81] More common was an

212 left *Palmyra (Syria), the grand colonnade, looking toward the monumental arch, late 2nd–early 3rd century* AD. *Most of the columns on the left side of the street have fallen, but the right side is virtually complete. Behind the porticoes were individual shops.*

213–216 opposite *Porticoes and porches: in Roman North Africa; in Paris's Rue de Rivoli (Percier and Fontaine, begun 1800); in Bern (Switzerland); and in middle America.*

217 below *Arcade types in Bologna (Italy); print by Antonio Basoli, 1832 (note that the figures are far too small in proportion). We are standing in the Strada Maggiore (the urban stretch of the ancient Roman Via Aemilia), under the earliest surviving arcade. The Casa Isolani was built in the 13th century as a flat-fronted house opening directly off the street; its owners soon enlarged it by adding a jettied upper story, supported on oak posts pushing out into the roadway. Opposite is the* palazzo *built for the composer Rossini in 1824–27 by F. Santini.*

intermittent screen of supporting piers and columns, sometimes carrying balconies or other superstructures. What mattered was not uniformity, as William MacDonald points out, but the rhythmic continuity that invested these backdrops for public business with a suggestion of "the existence of an ordered world against which the chaotic untidiness of life might be measured."[82]

The currency of these open ground stories suffered in the troubled times after the collapse of the Roman Empire, and closed façades came to prevail. But porticoes did not disappear altogether: they survived in some degenerate form until the full re-emergence of the open street with its rows of shops in the later Middle Ages. If porticoes developed a bad reputation in the Renaissance and became targets of urban renewal, it was because shop and house owners were prone to clutter them with refuse and night vice thrived in their dark recesses. In the late 15th century Ferrante of Aragon, King of Naples, counseled Pope Sixtus IV to follow his example by tearing down porticoes and widening the streets.[83] But rehabilitated and made an integral part of total street elevations, the portico stayed in use—the standard convention for street uniformity and continuity in Baroque Turin, in Padua, Bern and Bologna, and in the great arcaded streets of the 19th century like Paris's Rue de Rivoli and the Quadrant in London by John Nash (1813). The *Laws of the Indies* prescribed arcades for the *plaza* and the four principal streets emanating therefrom, pronouncing them "of considerable convenience to the merchants who generally gather there." Indeed, street vendors still trade in the arcade of the Governor's Palace in the main square of Santa Fe, New Mexico.

Alberti, looking back, advocates the portico for its environmental and social values. He cites Diodorus to the effect that porticoes were made for the convenience of servants, but he says they are not the only beneficiaries: porticoes are "rather for the common use of the citizens" (*De re aedificatoria*, v.2). Further he writes:

> I would have the portico be not only a convenient covering for men, but for beasts also to shelter from sun or rain. Just before the vestibule nothing can be nobler than a handsome portico, where the youth, waiting till their old gentlemen return from transacting business with the prince, may employ themselves in all manner of exercise, leaping, tennis, throwing of stones, or wrestling. [v.8]

At Bern, the arcades in front of all the houses along main streets were prescribed by building codes, from the 13th to the 19th centuries. The codes allowed the façades to change in style in accordance with the popular taste of the day, so long as the proportions stayed the same. These arcades remained the property of the municipality. The covered way was independent of the street level, and was reached by stairways, while cellars were directly accessible from the street.

Bologna's porticoes are celebrated. Alberti's fondness for porticoes may well have come from his days in Bologna. The city's streets have an aggregate of 21 miles (34 km.) of porticoes, continuous along private residences and the grand loggias of public buildings. The tradition is long. It starts in the early medieval period with rather improvised wooden porticoes; in time construction was regularized with brick and occasionally stone piers or columns, and the porticoes more soundly integrated with their buildings, the arches becoming load-bearing elements for the upper stories.

These porticoes were both part of the private dwelling to which they were attached and, in so far as they incorporated the sidewalk pavement, clearly for the use of all. Property owners as early as the 13th century were obliged to provide for the upkeep of their segment of pavement and to guarantee its public accessibility. A 1249 statute decreed that "all the porticoes of the city and the suburbs would be maintained to a height of . . . 2.66 m. [8 ft. 8¾ in.] from the ground so that anyone could ride on horse beneath them, and no one could excavate; if the prescribed height was exceeded, a fine would be imposed."[84]

In Florence the portico was more selectively used. Its presence was a sign of privilege. The Florentine loggia in late medieval and Renaissance palaces served as the site of family ceremonies like marriages and funerals, and the signing of important documents. In 1470 there were still 17 of these aristocratic loggias in existence, among them that of the Rucellai, which is described by a member of the family as being "per honore della nostra famiglia, per aoperarla per le letitie e per le tristitie" (for the honor of our family, to use on joyful and sad occasions). The loggias were eventually walled up, and interior courtyards of Renaissance palazzi absorbed their functions. At the Palazzo Medici-Riccardi the walling up is evident; it was done in 1517, and the heavy windows that replaced the open arches are attributed to Michelangelo. This concealment of the house at street level has been interpreted as a symbol of the dissolution of the extended family of the Middle Ages, every unit of which now looked only after its own.[85]

A modern equivalent to this open area of family display is the American wooden front porch. Its origin is rural, but by the end of the 19th century it was at home in urban residential neighborhoods and suburbs alike. The front porch came to be viewed as a symbol of an authentically American way of life. As late as 1952 a popular magazine could rhapsodize: "The front porch is an American institution of high civic and moral value. It is a sign that the people who sit on it are ready and willing to share the community life of their block with their neighbors."[86] By then, the automobile had extended the family's social circle, television had interiorized family leisure, and in new suburban developments recreation had already shifted to the privacy-minded backyard.

218 *An urbanized front porch in Oakland (California), photographed with its owners, the Rix family, in 1855.*

SOME STREET TYPES

Classical antiquity recognized a wide variety of street types, as we can judge from the terms used. Latin sources mention the *via* and the smaller *vicus*, the *clivus* or steep rise, the *semita* or zigzag path (the same word was used for sidewalk), the *fundula* or cul-de-sac, *scalae* (a *clivus* with steps), and *platea* or avenue. *Angiportus* meant a narrow passage, often curved, between rows of houses.[87]

These are primarily physical distinctions having to do with width and relation to urban topography. The intention in what follows is rather to focus on some persistent themes of the urban streetscape and their regional variations. The list is not exhaustive, nor is the discussion of each theme complete. I want merely to indicate what it is possible to do in a book of streets, and to underline the difficulty of settling on a system of types for a public place that embraces both conventions of form and a range of uses, the two as much at odds with as they are responsive to one another.

WATERWAYS

The subject here is rivers and canals as streets. These could be analyzed, at the very least, on the basis of four design criteria: the watercourse itself and its management (embankments, piers and the like); the walkways on one or two sides; the nature of the flanking buildings, especially in relation to the width of the waterway; the bridges that constitute the crosswalks. The classic exemplars of the West are Venice,

219–222 opposite Waterway-streets: flanking a canal in Amsterdam; the Victoria Embankment in London; interlocking systems of canals and roadways in Suzhou (China); and the 17th-century Chahar Bagh in Isfahan (Iran).

223 right *London's Victoria Embankment, under construction near its eastern end at Blackfriars Station in 1867. Behind an outer facing of granite blocks lie a tunnel for gas and water mains (1) and the great sewer (2), then earth fill, and finally the tunnel of the underground railway (3).*

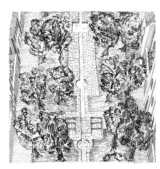

and Dutch cities, whose canal streets are surely one of the most distinctive, and gracious, inventions of urban design.

In the case of Venice, there is a fully efficient dual circulation: boats on the canals, *Pl.26* pedestrians on flanking walkways and cross-bridges. The constituent elements of the main canal streets of Amsterdam and other principal Dutch towns are the quays *219* for loading and unloading, the tree-lined roadways behind these for pedestrian and carriage traffic, and the banks of houses, each different from its neighbors and yet related to them in the making of the street wall through height, materials and design details. This is the familiar scene of Dutch canals flanked by rows of buildings. The width of the waterway is critical to the success of such a street. If it is too wide to be crossed by a simple bridge, the buildings on one side become isolated and the urban effect is lost. And if the buildings stretch on beyond a certain length, the result is tedious ribbon development. So highlights on the skyline—the tower of a church, a windmill, the mass of the town hall—become critical for the success of this urban picture.

The Renaissance was much taken with the idea of the canal town.[88] Filarete's Sforzinda was to have every other street be a canal for easy cargo transport, and much of the open space was assigned to water. Leonardo, like Filarete, was preoccupied with water streets: a canal grid is a feature of his project of the 1490s for *239* Milan.

Lining the urban stretch of river banks with trees is coeval with the similar landscaping of ramparts. When Louis XIV captured Tournai (1667), he had the quays and the city walls planted with trees. The projects for the beautification of cities in Napoleon's empire, Rome for example, invariably included riverwalks lined with rows of uniform trees. But it was when these esthetic pleasures came to be viewed as the finishing touch of basic engineering works related to the prevention of floods and modern sewerage systems that the riverwalk assumed the monumental form of the Paris *quais* and the Lungotevere in Rome. This was a 19th-century phenomenon.

London's Victoria Embankment from Westminster to Blackfriars, begun in 1864, *220*, typifies these riverine improvements. The main structure consists of spare granite *223* walls, impressive in themselves, with little architectural ornament. Behind the walls are tunnels for gas and water mains and a main intercepting sewer, and finally the tunnel of the District Railway. Furthermore, the embankment supported a new street up to 100 feet (30 m.) wide that was meant to relieve east–west traffic congestion in the metropolis. It came with handsome cast-iron lamps in the form of entwined dolphins, rows of trees, and "Cleopatra's Needle," a gift of Egypt's Mehmet Ali set up in 1877. All this replaced "The offensive mud-banks and the mean and unsightly buildings which disfigured the shores of the river."[89]

In Rome, the Lungotevere ("along the Tiber") system was spurred on by the disastrous flood of December 1870; the whole monumental complex of embankments, conduits, tree-lined boulevards, and a series of new bridges was not complete until the early years of this century. The width of the boulevard on each side, the Lungotevere proper, was set at 14 meters (46 ft.) and then enlarged to 20 (66 ft.), of which 6 (18 ft.) were to be taken up by continuous porticoes on the city side. A small segment of this treatment can be seen on either side of Ponte Sisto, but the idea was soon abandoned. Both here and in London, land values dramatically appreciated along the embankments and redevelopment flourished on a grand scale.

Away from Europe, the region that most favored waterways is China. At Ningpo, at the confluence of the Yu-yao and Feng-hua rivers, the network of canals reached almost every section of town. Shanghai is another classic water town, where the maze of canals gave direct access to nearly every house and place of business—especially before the city was walled in the 16th century. The frequency of Chinese cities laid out with a water-course structure was due to the fact that, before the railroads, water transport was the most efficient way of transporting bulk materials like salt and grain. The shipment of tax grain to the capital was essential for maintaining unified state power. This and the complementary need for irrigation urged the building of main-line canals as a priority, certainly by the time of the Sung dynasty in the 10th century, and this in turn influenced the planning of cities.[90]

THE STREET

More than a mere traffic channel ensconced within the city's solid mesh, the street is a complex civic institution, culture-specific and capable of dazzling formal variation and calculated nuance. Islam cultivated the recondite twists and intimate scale of the neighborhood cul-de-sac. Venice and its Dutch counterparts elaborated footpath and waterway as interdependent systems of communication. Of Italian and French parentage, the Grand Manner vocabulary of broad avenues and arrow-straight vistas gained international currency as the sine qua non *of elegant urbanity.*

Used as public thoroughfare and residential meeting ground, linear market and vehicular track, streets demand delicate compromises between contradictory functions—a balancing act complicated by the advent of the automobile, and subsequently rejected by Modernist planners insistent on the separation of functions. Most recently a new generation of designers have attempted to rescue the street from the extremes of segregation by recalling earlier forms, while weighing the scales in favor of pedestrians.

Pl. 25 Shushtar (Iran) displays the traditional Islamic pattern of residential cul-de-sacs and rare sinuous through-streets, bordered by the walls of courtyard-centered houses. Juxtaposed to this delicate net are wide straight streets and traffic roundabouts typical of the Haussmannizing activities of Reza Shah in the 1930s.

Types and designs

Pl. 26 opposite In Venice, canals are the roadways, quays and bridges the sidewalks and crossings. This is the Grand Canal at the old, wooden, Rialto Bridge. By 1494, when Carpaccio depicted the scene, walkways supported on wooden pilings (visible in the distance beyond the bridge) were being replaced by stone-and-brick quays. A hanging inn-sign on the left invites passing trade, as in a conventional street on dry land.

Pl. 27 right, above Florence was famous for its "beautiful, wide, and straight" paved streets, whose design had been regulated since the 14th century. The Via de' Servi, seen here, leads directly from the Duomo to the Piazza of the Santissima Annunziata; its effect was made more theatrical at the beginning of the 17th century, not long before this view was painted, by the erection of a colonnade in front of the church and an equestrian statue of the Medici Grand Duke. Along the street itself, the basic unit is the large palazzo, sheltering more than one family and class below broad projecting eaves.

Pl. 28 right, below A street in Haarlem, recorded by Gerrit Berckheyde in 1680. In contrast to Florence, the Dutch town displays the single-household residences once characteristic throughout the North Sea area, their individuality emphasized by a variety of steep gables, with a few level cornices in the new classical style. Projecting signs advertise the wares of the ground-floor shops. (Further booths cluster around the Groote Kerk in the distance.) The roadway is carefully paved with two colors of stone; the sidewalks are of brick, used for paving in Holland since the 13th century.

Pl. 29 Elevating the pedestrian: the "high street" of the Alexandra Road housing estate in London, designed by Neave Brown for Camden Council (1968–79), is a raised pedestrian concourse above a linear car park, stretching for 1,000 feet between an existing street and railway line. The set-back dwellings frame not gardens but lightwells to the parking below: this is terraced housing reinterpreted for the age of the automobile. Probably the last and most ambitious of the large comprehensive redevelopments of the inner city originating in the mid-1950s, it was praised as a low-rise, high-density enclave in opposition to the pattern of apartment towers set in open space.

Pl. 30 The return of the street: an impression by Carl Laubin of the center of Poundbury, the new town near Dorchester (England), as planned in 1991 by Léon Krier for the Prince of Wales. In reaction against the Modernist separation of traffic and of functions, the scheme envisages a return to a mix of houses and shops, and aims to reduce car traffic and encourage walking and cycling. The traditionalist form of the buildings, itself a reaction against the uniformity, large scale, and "inhuman" feel of much post-war development, has aroused intense controversy.

Suzhou in southern Jiangsu province, although it lies inland, is called the Venice 221 of China.[91] The canals there had some 300 bridges crossing them, eventually built mostly of stone. The bridges had high arches and broad pavements. The city gates were "twinned," to accommodate both road and waterborne traffic. Indeed a double system of water and road transportation prevailed throughout, the street system paralleling the canals. Each property was serviced from both street and canal. The main entrance to the house was from the street; the canal gave access to the rear or service entrance.

One final variant of the waterway, from another cultural sphere, is the type found in Safavid Iran and Mughal India. Here the canal runs down the center of a tree-lined avenue. In Isfahan the garden-avenue known as the Chahar Bagh ran through the 222 palace grounds for nearly a mile to the Zayandeh River, across the Allahavardi Khan Bridge, and then up rising ground to a vast royal estate called the Hazar Jerib (Thousand Acres). The avenue was 60 yards (55 m.) wide and lined with palatial suites and kiosks. Eight rows of plane trees and poplars were spaced across its width. Besides the canal down the center, there were tanks of various sizes and shapes, and many fountains.

The Chandni Chowk in Shahjahanabad, the Emperor Shah Jahan's new city at 92 Delhi (1639ff.), was a more public promenade. It extended from the Red Fort westward in a straight line until the walls, was lined with trees, and carried a deep, marble-lined canal down the center. The model was clearly Isfahan's Chahar Bagh. But the intention was urban. Fancy shops of uniform design under long arcades lined the sides, selling sweets and jewels and waterpipes; and scattered among them were coffeehouses—a fashion that was learned from Safavid Isfahan. The shops were small one-room units, behind which were corresponding small warehouses where goods were stored, and above the warehouses, living quarters for the shopkeeper's family. Here, and in the main south avenue of Faiz Bazar, ran segments of the impressive Nahr-i Bihisht (Canal of Paradise) that collected water from the Yamuna River at a point 75 miles (120 km.) upstream and entered the city at the Kabul Gate. The paradisiac symbolism of running water in Islamic thought is clearly pertinent in this context.

The marble-lined canals of both Chandni Chowk and Faiz Bazar were filled in by the British after 1860, the shade trees were cut down, and the streets repaved from curb to curb. The Chahar Bagh at Isfahan was also regularized and is now a public thoroughfare. The terminal phase of all waterways—from the California beach-front town of Venice to Bangkok—involves their being filled up and turned into regular streets for the sake of the mighty automobile.

THE BRIDGE-STREET

The medieval practice of lining bridges with houses and shops began as an ad hoc development. By 1400 the taste for regularizing these, by building bridges as streets designed and executed in a single phase, had emerged. Florence, always precocious, rebuilt the Ponte Vecchio in the 1340s. It was a completely controlled environment. 224 The roadbed was 9.8 meters (32 ft.) wide and 101.5 meters (333 ft.) long; it was flanked by 48 shops and opened out at its center into a piazza overlooking the river.

The redesign of the Rialto in Venice dates from the 16th century. This bridge across the Grand Canal was intended for pedestrians only. As built in 1588–92 by Antonio da Ponte, after a competition that drew illustrious names like Palladio, Sansovino and Vignola, it was flanked by rows of shops opened up in the middle by two arches affording views of the waterway.

On London Bridge, abutting buildings grew haphazardly since its redoing in stone in 1176. Only by the early 18th century were regular three-story structures introduced. Curiously, transverse buildings divided the street space of the bridge into sections which could be entered through gateways.

Medieval Paris had several bridges linking the Ile de la Cité to the banks of the river: the Petit Pont, on the Notre-Dame side, going south to the left bank; and the Grand Pont and Pont Notre-Dame, going north. The bridges were paved, at least from about 1200 on, and had towered gates at both ends, toward the island and on the mainland. Life on them is illustrated in an early 14th-century manuscript of the *Life of St. Denis*.[92]

The outfitting of the new stone Pont Notre-Dame with terraced houses in 1508–12, attributed to Fra Giocondo, was the first ensemble planning that Paris had known. The roadway was flanked on each side by thirty-four identical arcaded houses, gable-roofed with narrow brick- and stone-trimmed street fronts, and timber-framed backs. This hybrid construction technique was superficially elegant, quick and economical, and avoided overloading the structure. A triumphal arch closed the bridge off at one end and two small towers framed it at the other. The absolute regularity of the composition attracted the admiration of contemporaries and was protected by city council regulations forbidding alterations by tenants.[93] One reason that a designed street could be created so effectively here was that Parisian bridges were traditionally a property of the king, so he could do with them as he pleased. But even the previous Pont Notre-Dame had buildings on it, including 60 uniform houses built in 1421.[94] So did the Petit Pont, rebuilt in stone by Louis VII in the 12th century, with mills and rows of houses along the roadway parted in the middle to give a clear view of the river. The Grand Pont had 68 goldsmiths' shops and workshops on one side and 72 money-changing stalls on the other in the 14th century—hence it became known as the Pont au Change.

In the context of all this, it is not surprising that the Pont Neuf of Henri IV (begun by Henri III), which joined the left and right banks across the tip of the Ile de la Cité, was hailed as the bridge without houses, confined to traffic, promenading, and to

224 The Ponte Vecchio, Florence, was rebuilt in its present form in the 1340s, with an open central belvedere. Early tenants of its shops were tanners (who used the river water below), pursemakers, and butchers. In the 1550s Vasari used it as the base for an elevated corridor linking the Palazzo Vecchio and Uffizi on the north bank (right) to the Pitti Palace on the south. In 1593 Grand Duke Ferdinando I expelled the smelly butchers in favor of goldsmiths and jewelers, trades still there today.

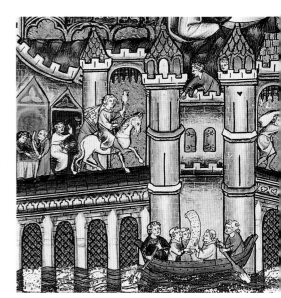

225 opposite, below *The Grand Pont in Paris, depicted in the* Life of St. Denis, *1317. Note the fortified tower, the paved surface, and, to the left of the knight on horseback, a goldsmith in his shop.*

226 right *Paris, detail of a map of 1653 showing the bridges linking the Ile de la Cité to the banks. Leading to the left bank (right), from top to bottom they are the Pont de l'Hôtel-Dieu, Petit Pont, and Pont St.-Michel; to the right bank, the Pont Notre-Dame and the Pont au Change (the former Grand Pont; cf. Ill. 225). All these are lined with houses, those on the Pont Notre-Dame dating from 1508–12. At the bottom is the Pont Neuf (1578–1607), a broad and elegant novelty without houses, punctuated by a statue of Henri IV.*

The convention of this map, depicting only major buildings, brings out the division of the Ile de la Cité between the religious district around Notre-Dame, to the east (top), and the sovereign district of the royal palace—later the Palais de Justice—further west. Near the palace, at the western tip of the island, is the Place Dauphine, begun by Henri IV in 1608; its arcades were to serve as a merchants' exchange, to relieve pressure on the Pont au Change.

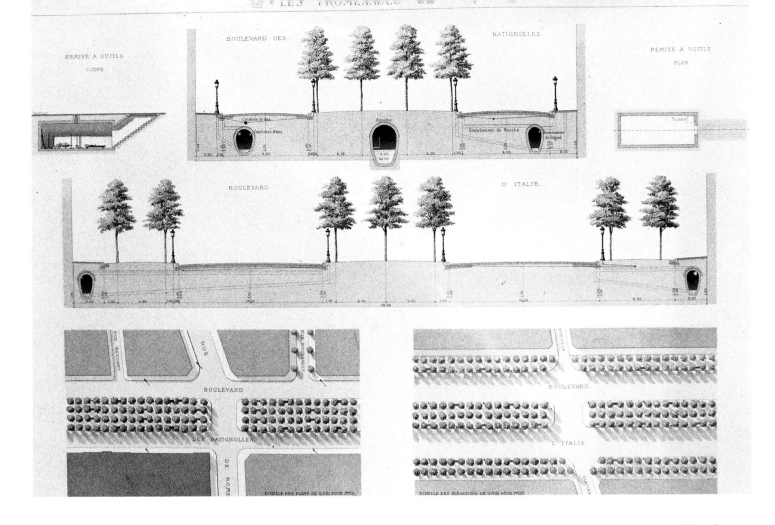

boatmen.[95] It was the longest bridge of Paris until fairly recently (270 m./886 ft.), with generous sidewalks augmented by semicircular platforms over the piers, and an incomparable view. It has been called "un belvedere pour le peuple." In addition to the famous statue of Henri IV by Giambologna and Pietro Tacca (cf. Florence, Ill. 104), the bridge had a pumphouse called La Samaritaine which lifted the Seine water to feed the fountains of the Louvre and some other palaces.

With the growth of coach traffic, constricted bridge-streets became obsolete. The houses on the medieval bridges of Paris were demolished just before the Revolution. John Evelyn a century earlier had advocated the same treatment for London Bridge, and proposed to replace its houses with an ornamented "foot way elevated on each side . . . Or if they will needs have shops, let them be built of solid stone, made narrow and very low, like to those upon the Rialto at Venice; but it were far better without them."[96]

THE BOULEVARD

18 The extra-urban origins and subsequent history of the French boulevard and avenue, and their American interpretation, have been reviewed fully in *The City Shaped*.[97] In Paris during the 19th century, as we saw, the tree-lined avenue was brought up to date with those new features first popularized in Great Britain: macadam paving, storm drains and sewers, sidewalks, etc. These improvements 199 were used to rebuild the Avenue des Champs-Elysées and the Grands Boulevards

227 A plate from Adolphe Alphand's Les Promenades de Paris (1867–73), showing the Boulevard des Batignolles and Boulevard d'Italie in section and aerial view. The streets are gas-lit. Underground there is provision for gas and water mains, drains, and sewers.

in the 1830s under Rambuteau. It was Rambuteau who also created tree-lined esplanades along the banks of the Seine, to which the city's booksellers gravitated, deserting the arcades of the Odéon and the Palais-Royal. Together with the Rue Rambuteau, cut through the old blocks in the center of Paris, these esplanades *269* served as the model for Haussmann's *grands travaux*.

Under Adolphe Alphand, Haussmann's chief landscape architect, classic solutions of planting were developed for the new urban boulevards depending on their width and use. A graphic convention for street sections became common, showing the relation of the trees to the pedestrian and vehicular zones, and to underground service systems and streetcar tracks. Alphand produced an influential catalogue of these urban landscape solutions, *Les Promenades de Paris*, a beautiful *227* book with engraved illustrations representing both urban parks and boulevards. The city ran nurseries to have fully grown trees available at all times. There were some 80,000 street trees in Paris in the 1870s, twice as many as in 1852, Haussmann boasted in his memoirs.

On streets less than 15 meters (49 ft.) wide, or streets of any width with sidewalks less than 3 meters (10 ft.) wide, Paris planted no trees. In the wider streets, the best-known arrangement was the *contre-allée* system; here there was a wide asphalt or paved footway (the *contre-allée*) separated from the roadway by a wide gravel strip in which trees were planted. Two examples are the Champs-Elysées and the Avenue de Wagram. The Boulevard d'Italie had three rows down the middle and two each down the sides. The Boulevard des Batignolles banked four magnificent rows in a formal green median taking up much of the roadway, and no trees on the sides.

A strictly Spanish rendition of the urban boulevard is the *paseo*, meaning promenade, also called *alameda*, from the Spanish word *alamo* which refers to certain kinds of poplar and elm trees. The walk and the shade—these are the invariables; the actual design varies considerably from city to city. The two great series of *paseos* in Madrid and Barcelona are distinctive both in their physical makeup and in their pattern of insertion within the urban fabric. In Madrid several connecting stretches 2¼ miles (3½ km.) long, called collectively the Paseo del Prado, link the old town with the newer residential quarters. The section called Paseo de Recoletos represents the type at its most elaborate. Traffic lanes for tramways and commercial vehicles are at the edges; between them are promenades along one of which runs a strip of gardens, and an ample roadway. The Ramblas of Barcelona are *228* also the backbone of the city. The main stretch, from the Plaza de Cataluña to the harbor and the Columbus monument, has a broad walkway in the middle lined with plane trees and bracketed by proper street spaces on the outside with sidewalks and shops.

In the United States, George Kessler became a strong advocate of this Hispanic promenade, and proposed to install specimens in Kansas City and Cincinnati. Kansas City's Paseo was the downtown segment of the extensive park and boulevard system designed by Kessler in the early 1890s. A seedy nine-block run was converted to a landscaped promenade adorned with fountains, a pergola in three flights, an architectural terrace, a sunken garden, a small lake, and stretches of lawn—something between a *paseo* and a park. As late as 1933 Webster Avenue in Boston was widened and redesigned as a *paseo* called Prado (now Paul Revere Mall), on the model of the Prado of Havana. The two irregular sides were isolated from the abutting buildings by continuous high brick walls equipped with attached seats; a pavement of brick with patterns of bluestone provided a festive surface to walk on; and the rows of linden trees led the eye to historic churches at either end.[98]

228 Sitting and strolling in the median strip of the Ramblas in Barcelona.

COVERED STREETS

The standard image is of 19th-century arcades: glass-roofed, exclusively pedestrian, adorned with bilaterally symmetrical interior façades. J. F. Geist, in his definitive survey of this type, cites all witting and unwitting precedents.[99] The covered linear bazaars of Islamic towns are an obvious instance.

In the standard *suq* or bazaar there is no residential component. At night it is eerily empty. The most familiar type consists of a series of covered streets topped by vaults or domes, dimly lit from high small windows, or lit artificially; the crossing is raised higher than the rest of the bays and is sometimes opened to the sky. This linear strip is seen as connecting tissue, between mosques and city gates, or mosques and public paths. At Herat the bazaar took up the four axial streets that led from the main city gates to the center. There the arms of the cross met at a domed structure which was called the *chahar-su*, the "four directions." In cities like Isfahan the bazaar is a cool, dim, seemingly endless sequence of vaulted spaces, with tremendous directional force, yet plenty of encouragement to linger. The tunnel effect, scored by shafts of sunlight from clerestory and roof, is softened in the lower zones by the merchandise displayed—an effervescence of color, texture, and smell.

The arcade was a private speculative venture, usually cut through large blocks by the acquisition of "soft," inexpensive property deprived of street access. Its roof was, whenever possible, raised above those surrounding it and given a glass vault that pulled natural light into the interior. This insinuation of paths into built-up blocks was already a Parisian tradition when the arcades started at the time of the Revolution. (Many of these mid-block pedestrian shortcuts can still be seen in the Faubourg St.-Antoine, the Faubourg St.-Denis and Charonne.[100]) That tradition was then combined with the new technology of metal-and-glass roofing.

Pl.11, 229

80

229 above left *In the bazaar at Kerman (Iran).*

230 above *In the Galleria Umberto I, Naples (Italy), 1887–91.*

There are now some 280 19th-century arcades in the world.[101] Famous ones are the Burlington Arcade, London; the vast *gallerias* in Milan and Naples; and the equally vast Galeries St.-Hubert in Brussels. The first in Paris was the Passage Feydeau, which opened in 1791 (and was demolished in 1824). It was prefigured, though, by the wooden galleries of the Palais Royal which in 1786, just before the Revolution, were fitted with shops and gaming parlors as a profit-making enterprise. Then came the Passage du Caire in 1799, and a year later the Passage des Panoramas.

The arcades in Paris have been explained as a consequence of the development of outlying districts: they were built through the big older blocks as shortcuts to the center. Loyer thinks the arcade is the forerunner of the department store, as well as the modern enclosed shopping mall.[102] The popularity of the *passages* can also be seen as a sign of the sad state of the normal Parisian streets. In Vienna, where shopping streets were pleasant and clean, the arcade did not establish itself.[103] There was only one, within the Austro-Hungarian National Bank building, now known as the Ferstel Passage (1856–60). And indeed in Paris, once Haussmann's boulevards provided the proper open-air ambience for the middle classes, the *passages* went into decline.

THE ADVENT OF THE MODERNIST STREET

In October 1910, the Royal Institute of British Architects sponsored a major conference in London on city planning. At least three schools of thought were represented among the many prominent names in attendance, schools which summarize de facto the range of modern attitudes about street design. Technocrats led by German planners like Joseph Stübben and the city architect of Paris, Eugène Hénard, stressed the technicalities of modern urban traffic and the engineering of street construction, while they stayed within the esthetic formulas of the Grand Manner. Chicago's Daniel Burnham brought along spectacular exhibits of City Beautiful designs, the latest interpretation of the Grand Manner which sought to recast familiar urban prospects in terms of the newborn American skyscraper. The British contingent, led by Raymond Unwin, emphasized garden cities, and arranged trips to Hampstead Garden Suburb and Letchworth, both inaugurated a few years earlier.

UNWIN AND LE CORBUSIER

Unwin proved the great conciliator. His *Town Planning in Practice*, which appeared the year before the conference, is the authoritative testament of modern urban design as distilled from the long history of Western city-making. His conception of the street was modern, but not Modernist. Neither the skyscraper nor the motorcar is seized on as a portent of a revolution in street function. And throughout Unwin insists that street design is an art. The technical demands of the civil engineer are, for Unwin, simply the foundation for good street design. Beauty, he tells us, is an urban "amenity" that needs to be addressed as decisively as the 19th-century "bye-law street" dealt with urban sanitation. This is the assignment for the 20th-century planner: to "infuse the spirit of the artist into our work."

This said, Unwin takes a positivist approach, and sets out to reconcile the apparent contradictions between the informal and formal schools of urban design.

231 *Hampstead Garden Suburb*, London:
Linnell Drive, 1923.

While validating both schools of thought, Unwin considers it normal that a designer would favor one approach over the other. *His* preference, his treatise makes clear, is for the cozy picturesque effects of the Germanic neo-medievalists inspired by the writings of Camillo Sitte. But what is essential is not the streetscape's style, but that it conform to the overarching qualities required to produce "satisfactory street pictures," namely visual variety and spatial closure. The design of a succession of urban tableaux which are revealed as a viewer moves along the street is, by Unwin's reckoning, the basis of the planner's art.

Town Planning in Practice establishes the observable and the empirical—specifically the mechanics of spatial perception and the requirements of traffic and sanitation—as the driving forces behind the design of streets. It represents a masterful summing up of the rich variety of urban form assembled through the eclectic experiments of the 19th century. Unwin's charter is to refine the palette of street types available to the "artist" (as he repeatedly calls the urban designer).

The premiated plan for Letchworth Garden City (1904) submitted by Unwin and his partner, Barry Parker, explored the possibility of a marriage between formal and informal planning, but with clumsy results. At Hampstead Garden Suburb, under the counsel of Sir Edwin Lutyens (who was appointed consulting architect in 1906), the formal elements proposed by Unwin—stately squares, radial streets, straight avenues and rond points—retain their integrity and become an organizing framework for the weave of roads that constitutes the residential fabric. This play of formal streets—"of such a size as adequately to introduce a sense of scale and of the due proportioning and relation of the parts"—against a finer infill becomes the standard device with which Unwin establishes a legible spatial hierarchy. The suburban scale and tone of residential lanes is reinforced by their narrowness (the Hampstead Garden Suburb Act of 1906 exempted them from bye-law legislation); and by Unwin's signature breakthrough, the independence of the building line from the street line.

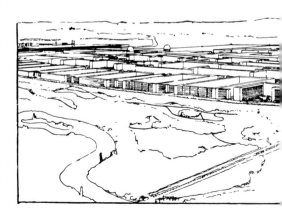

Le Corbusier's withering scorn for such painstakingly knit compositions is legendary. His project of "A Contemporary City for Three Million People," 232 presented at the 1922 Paris Salon d'Automne in a vast diorama, is the polar opposite of Unwin's ideal town. According to the designer himself, the display shocked its audience into "a sort of stupor." The closed vistas so cherished by Unwin are blown wide open; in fact, all traditional formulas of streets are indiscriminately rejected, chief among them the *rue-corridor*, "streets in narrow trenches walled in by seven-storied buildings set perpendicular on the pavement and enclosing unhealthy courtyards, airless and sunless wells. . . ." Instead, Le Corbusier proposes "great blocks . . . of flats opening up on every side to air and light, and looking, not on the puny trees of our boulevards today, but upon greensward, sports grounds, and abundant plantations of trees."[104] The blocks will be lifted up on *pilotis* (stilts), and linked by a gridded network of elevated highways and ground-level service roads. The modern street is "a new type of organism, a sort of stretched-out workshop. . . . The various stories of this stretched-out workshop will each have their own particular functions."[105] The four functions aligned about the axis of the street—housing, work, recreation and traffic—must now be strictly separated. This will not allow for the enclosure of space in the conventional manner of city-making. The street, in a sense, will be separated from the buildings.

Nowadays, when so much of what he said has become commonplace, we tend to forget what an absolutely revelatory proposal Le Corbusier's was. It came at a time when automobiles, by our standards, crawled through towns: in Germany, for example, the maximum legal speed in built-up areas was set until 1923 at 15 kilometers per hour (9 m.p.h.).[106] For Le Corbusier the traditional city's hindrance of fast traffic was an obscenity. "A city made for speed is made for success,"[107] he claimed, and it took automotive velocities to bring his street pictures (to use Unwin's term) to life. To follow Corbusier as he moves through his creation is to witness an epiphany:

Suppose we are entering the city by way of the Great Park. Our fast car takes the special elevated motor track between the majestic skyscrapers . . . to our left and right on the outskirts of each particular area are the municipal and administrative buildings; and enclosing the space are the museums and university buildings. Then suddenly we find ourselves at the feet of the first skyscrapers. But here we have, not the meagre shaft of sunlight which so faintly illumines the dismal streets of New York, but an immensity of space. . . .

Our car has left the elevated track and has dropped its speed of sixty miles an hour [97 k.p.h.] to run gently through the residential quarters. The "set-backs" permit vast architectural perspectives. . . . And sky everywhere . . . Their outlines softened by distance, the sky-scrapers raise their geometrical façades all of glass . . . an overwhelming sensation. Immense but radiant prisms.

As twilight falls the glass sky-scrapers seem to flame.[108]

232 *"A Contemporary City for Three Million People," by Le Corbusier: drawing of the diorama exhibited in 1922. In the center is the* cité *(the business district), with office towers surrounded by lower commercial and entertainment buildings. Clustering around it on a diamond plan are apartment blocks on the angled linear* redent *principle; at the corners are further apartment blocks enclosing courtyards. The city is bisected by elevated highways for fast traffic 40 meters (130 ft.) wide; other main roads cut across the grid. Between them, the ground is reserved for pedestrians.*

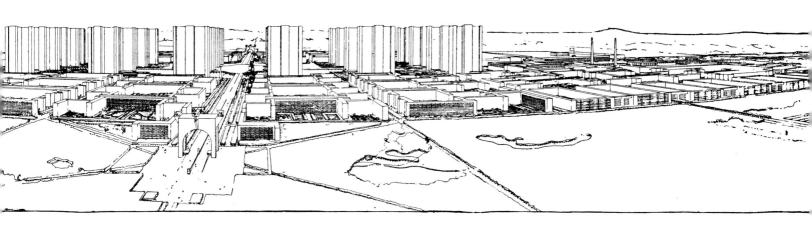

There was something irrevocable about Corbusier's lightning presentation of the future of the street. A British planning expert far outside the Modernist camp, S. D. Adshead, was moved to conclude in 1930 that "though M. Le Corbusier's city is never likely to be built, we are convinced that the "Pack Donkey" methods of the medieval builders, even when led by Camillo Sitte, the prophet of historicist planning, will have to give way to the measured motor tracks of Le Corbusier, if populations of millions instead of populations of thousands are to be accommodated in the city of to-morrow which certainly are a misfit in the city of today."[109]

Adshead had of course no way of knowing that these apparently inimical essays of urbanism I have been contrasting—one an appreciative omnium of the long history of European street design; the other a calculatedly shocking rejection of this legacy—would nevertheless be in the end the two constituents of much of our recent streetscape. Improbable as a fusion of these antithetical points of view may have seemed at the time, it is exactly that marriage of Unwin and Le Corbusier, in the guise of picturesque suburban streets and multi-lane superhighways, that characterizes the most rapidly expanding settlement pattern in late 20th-century United States: the "sub-suburbs" that make up the farthest city edge, and the privately-driven new towns program.

233 *An American sub-suburb: curving streets on the bank of a superhighway.*

PRECEDENTS TECHNOLOGICAL AND SOCIAL

In fairness, Le Corbusier's radical proposals for a new streetless urbanity were not products of parthenogenesis. Seen historically, they summed up and transcended a variety of reformist ideals that were already in circulation. The multi-level arrangement of city services and traffic paths had found earlier expression in the installation of underground gas, electric, water, and sewage lines hidden beneath Haussmann's wide, hygienic boulevards and the Embankment in London, as well as in the elaborate underground passages of, say, New York's Grand Central Railroad and the London Underground.

But more than just the culmination of a series of technological precedents, Le Corbusier's dissection of the street is also a final step in a longstanding and widespread reformist agenda to eliminate the street as a social environment. For many champions of social reform, Victorian London's poverty, overcrowding, and defective sanitation became fused into a monolithic indictment of the spatially confined neighborhood street. As early as 1838 the Select Committee considering plans for the improvement of the metropolis voiced their condemnation of "districts in London through which no great thoroughfares passed" fostering disease and "a state of moral degradation deeply to be deplored." The committee recommendation supported the liberal use of demolition in such districts not only to facilitate the circulation of air through these warrens, but to force traffic of a more "respectable inhabitancy" through laborers' quarters. The social habits of this population, "being entirely secluded from the observation and influence of better educated neighbors," would surely improve through emulation and enforcement of the social norms of the better classes.[110] The role of narrow, airless, or deteriorating streets as a primary culprit for social and physical ills was reaffirmed in the 1890 Housing of the Working Classes Act.[111] In America as well, social reformers like Jacob Riis and philanthropist Alfred T. White mounted a concerted attack on the use of the street as a social space by the lower classes. They spoke of breaking the "street habit" as a critical aspect of rehabilitating the poor, and proposed the enclosed central courts of model tenements as alternatives to the animated sidewalks and front stoops where children played and their parents gossiped, laughed and fought.[112]

234 below *Mullen's Alley, New York City, ca. 1888–89, photographed by Jacob A. Riis as part of his survey of slum housing conditions.*

235 *A sketch by Le Corbusier from* La Maison des Hommes, *1942 captioned: "100 per cent of the ground is given over to pedestrians. Cars roll along their motor roads sixteen feet [5 m.] above the ground. The impossible has become possible: separation of the pedestrian from the automobile has been accomplished."*

236 below *Paris, Rue Mallet-Stevens, by Rob Mallet-Stevens, built 1926–27.*

Le Corbusier's "Contemporary City" of 1922 proposes a similar redistribution of 232 social life within the immense "courtyards" of *immeubles-villas* (villa-blocks, i.e., apartment buildings composed of two-story maisonettes). Residences in these "closed cellular developments" back onto a verdant interior park studded with athletic facilities and tree-lined promenades. These proletarian housing blocks, framed by a grid of streets devoted solely to vehicles, are complemented by upper-class luxury residences configured as a continuous linear block which he names *à redent* or "indented unit" housing. The *Ville Radieuse* (Radiant City) design of 1930, a second iteration of this ideal city scheme, expunges all architectural references to class distinctions and advances the *à redent* arrangement as a universal urban housing formula. It is with this fateful construct of a settlement pattern devoid of streets that Le Corbusier, through his position at the helm of the Congrès Internationaux d'Architecture Moderne (CIAM), branded into Modernist urban design the mandate for a streetless city. In article 16 of its Athens Charter of 1933 the organization declares:

> the house will never again be fused to the street by a sidewalk. It will rise in its own 235 surroundings, in which it will enjoy sunshine, clear air, and silence. Traffic will be separated by means of a network of foot-paths for the slow-moving pedestrian and a network of fast roads for automobiles. Together these networks will fulfill their function, coming close to housing only as occasion demands.[113]

COMPROMISING MODERNISM: EARLY EXPERIMENTS

With the publication of *La Ville Radieuse* in 1933, Le Corbusier could presume to speak for all of Modernism in stating: "Streets are an obsolete notion. There ought not to be such things as streets; we have to create something that will replace them."[114] Such pronouncements were ultimately successful in portraying Modernism as a united front in pursuit of a common set of goals.

In fact, a review of the formative years of Modernist urbanism reveals quite a different story. The 1920s saw the emergence of a number of designers who were committed to the new architectural idioms, but who saw the possibility of compromise at the urban scale. The effect of Modernism, as far as they were concerned, would register only by the insertion of exemplary accents into the old cities. This is the strategy that had announced the arrival of the Renaissance to tangled cities of the Middle Ages. Others, inspired by the dazzling speed of modern city traffic, proposed an expressionistic street scenography based on horizontal movement. Let me take a moment to review a few of the experiments in Modernist street design that were struck from the record by Modernism's biographers.

The Rue Mallet-Stevens in Paris, commissioned by the banker Daniel Dreyfus in 236 1925, is one attempt at an insinuative Modernist urbanism. Its architect, Rob Mallet-Stevens, held that "Streets bordered by houses, public buildings, and especially monuments . . . must become the educators of the population."[115] Along the one-block length of his street the monuments are a sequence of single houses which reject the representational language of historic styles for a new architectural idiom of non-frontal composition. What Mallet-Stevens achieves here is to put the Modernist villa—canonically presented as a pavilion standing in the open space of exposition grounds or on a secluded suburban site—on an urban street. For that reason, and because this street remained unique, it was dismissed by Modernism's apologist Sigfried Giedion as an inconsequential set-piece, the product of an intellect preoccupied with the trivia of fashion.

In Germany, architects of the Gläserne Kette (Glass Chain) group—whose members included Hans and Wassily Luckhardt, Erich Mendelsohn, and Hans Poelzig—explored an alternate vision of the Modernist streetscape. "Modern man," Mendelsohn claimed, "amidst the excited flurry of his fast-moving life, can find equilibrium only in the tension-free horizontal."[116] In fact, the spatial perception of Berlin's streets had changed in a tangible way after 1923, when the city speed limit jumped to 35 kilometers per hour (22 m.p.h). Mendelsohn's oracular call found expression in projects like his celebrated Universum complex of 1927, and in the Luckhardt brothers' 1929 Alexanderplatz scheme for a streamlined circular traffic hub banded in slick ribbon windows, where the vertical ordering traditions of traditional façades are abandoned for the sense of movement suggested by streets walled by slippery horizontal glazing.

But recognition as the most prolific investigator of Modernist streetscapes should go to another urbanist of Germany's Weimar period, Ernst May. May had apprenticed with Unwin, and after working on Hampstead Garden Suburb continued a long relationship with his master by post. In 1925 he found himself at the head of Frankfurt's housing authority with a broad range of powers for zoning, planning, and design development. His team of architects and planners acquired land outside the city to build a series of twenty garden-suburb satellite communities. The conceptual model is Unwin's; but credit for the imagery and variety of non-traditional "street-pictures" in the early *Siedlungen* goes to May. The communities built in 1926–29 are laboratory experiments that bend, break, and serrate the street wall to invent new, often asymmetrical compositions. In Römerstadt a straight street is sent through a series of jogged displacements to create a Modernist version of Unwin's enclosed street volumes. Elsewhere in the development, a continuous curving façade is juxtaposed with the staccato rhythm established across the street by the blank ends of housing rows separated by allotment gardens; at an intersection the elements of the composition are switched to the opposite sides of the street. The Niederrad estate's saw-toothed street is perhaps the boldest of May's experiments, and its contrast with the conventional block across the way spells out both the promise and the inherent problems in his path toward a Modernist streetscape. Despite the volumetric fireworks, May's street is deadened by its wall of inward-turning residences oriented toward back gardens rather than the sidewalk—as

237 *Berlin, project for rebuilding the Alexanderplatz, by Hans and Wassily Luckhardt and Alfons Anker. This busy central area was the subject in 1929 of a new* Fluchtlinienplan *to provide for a bigger traffic intersection, wider streets, and extensive subway works. The land was compulsorily purchased; a massing model was drawn up by Berlin's planner, Martin Wagner. Building height was doubled, to compensate for lost space and to increase the value of the plots for resale to private developers. This scheme won the ensuing competition, but the job went to the runner-up, Peter Behrens.*

238 left *Frankfurt-am-Main (Germany), Bruchfeldtrasse, with the outer edge of Ernst May's Niederrad housing estate of 1925 on the left.*

239 *Leonardo da Vinci, scheme for a multilevel circulation system for Milan, ca. 1490. The roadway, left, drains into a subterranean canal. Also subterranean, to the right, is a service street. The arcade level above is reserved for people of gentle birth.*

240 below *Le Corbusier's vision of a region "irrigated" by the "7 Vs," ca. 1947. V 1 is a regional through-road; V 2, a major urban road; V 3 a road for motor traffic only, without sidewalks; V 4, the traditional "main street" of shops and daily life, often following a pre-existing organic road; V 5, a minor street branching off toward housing; V 6, either a path leading to the house door or the "interior street" of an apartment block; V 7, circulation through linear parks containing schools, sports grounds, etc.*

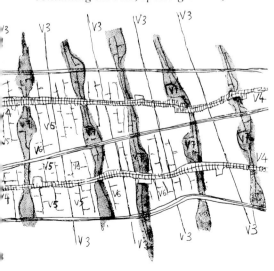

much Modernist anti-street sentiment as the legacy of his exposure to Unwin's Garden City ideals. May abandoned his flirtation with Modernist street design in 1929, the year Frankfurt hosted the second CIAM conference. At Westhausen, a satellite suburb begun that year, a simple grid of *Zeilenbau* (line construction) housing supersedes the complex spatial inventions of May's earlier experiments. Streets are disengaged from housing frontages and serve only as access lanes; a parallel set of greenswards now constitutes a separate pedestrian environment.

ELEVATING THE PEDESTRIAN

The Modernist vision of a streetless urbanity ultimately foundered on CIAM's inability to deliver on its promise of a separate system of pedestrian movement that would supplement high-speed traffic networks.

Again, these ideas had gone through a long period of germination. In the Renaissance, elevated passageways were built as a secret means of communication between princely buildings. The Corridoio Vasariano in Florence was created in the 1550s for Cosimo de' Medici, first Grand Duke of Tuscany, to link the Palazzo Vecchio and the Palazzo Pitti. Beginning at the Palazzo Vecchio, it forms the upper level of an arcade along the river at the end of the Uffizi block, crosses the Ponte 224 Vecchio, goes across the façade of S. Felicita and through a number of houses, and so reaches the Pitti which was itself linked to the Belvedere fortress. Leonardo's project of around 1490 for Milan is another eminent precedent. His proposed reconstruc- 239 tion of the city is served by a grid of porticoed pedestrian streets over a service level of alleys and waterways. Social stratification is designed into the system as well: the street level was reserved for *gentiluomini*, while the *poveraglia* was consigned to the depths below.

Prototypes of the vertically segregated paths for people and vehicles that Le Corbusier described crop up in turn-of-the-century projects as well: in France, Eugène Hénard's multi-level "Street of the Future" (1910), and in America, Edgar Chambless's linear "Roadtown" of the same year come to mind. Rotterdam's Spangen housing estate of 1919, with its stacked townhouses served by an aerial street system of wide corridor-balconies, is striking in its prescience of the design notions which would gain currency with the rise of International Modernism.

All of these examples fall short of the CIAM criterion of complete segregation of pedestrian and traffic routes, however, because their walkways and streets, although vertically segregated, run as parallel systems. What was called for in Modernist theory was a continuous network of paths and streets that, rather than duplicating each other at different levels, diverged entirely to create two distinct realms: one for people and one for cars. Le Corbusier's endeavors toward these ends became more specific but less successfully realized as time wore on. His 1947 *unité d'habitation* (large residential unit) at Marseilles, invoked by Françoise Choay as "the summation and symbol of all the [Corbusian] theories of town planning and dwellings,"[117] was widely celebrated for the provision of communal space in the form of interior streets. Two of these accommodated urban services (post office, food and clothing stores, pharmacy, hairdresser, laundry, even an eighteen-room hotel), others provided access to apartments. These two types of the *rue intérieure* were categorized as V 5 and V 6 in a seven-part street hierarchy Le Corbusier invented at this time. The universally applicable "7 Vs," as he called them, ranged 240 from high-speed regional roads (V 1) to pedestrian paths routed through a park-like urban setting (V 7). But despite his vehement proselytizing the system was nowhere fully adopted; and in subsequent commissions it lost much of its credibility as the

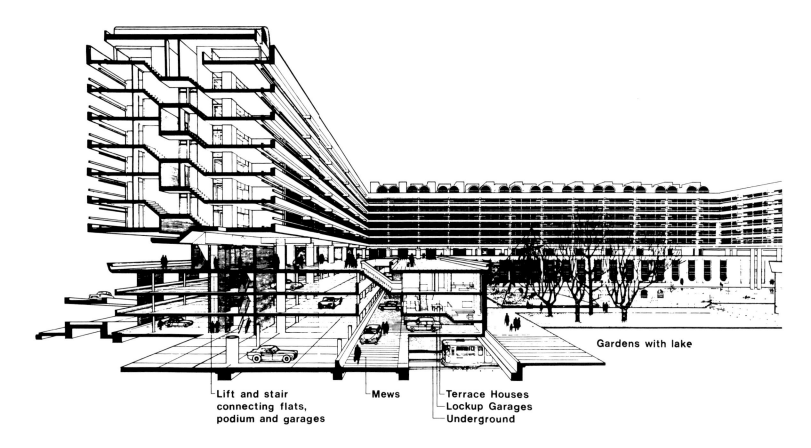

Lift and stair   Mews   Terrace Houses   Gardens with lake
connecting flats,   Lockup Garages
podium and garages   Underground

vaunted "interior streets" came to look like what architects of a less theoretical inclination call "double-loaded corridors."

The assignment of correcting the "*rue intérieure* mistake" was taken on in the Fifties by members of a circle of British architects who called themselves Team X (Ten). Alison and Peter Smithson's unbuilt Golden Lane housing project for London (1952) featured wide, open-sided decks that "would be places, not corridors or balconies: thoroughfares where there are shops, post boxes, telephone kiosks. . . . The refuse chute takes the place of the village pump."[118] Although the Smithsons were never able to realize this concept in large-scale built work, others did. The massive Park Hill and Hyde Park housing estates (1957) by Sheffield city architects Ivor Smith and Jack Lynn have streets-in-the-air threaded through blocks at every third level, as do the serpentine slabs by founding Team X members Georges Candilis and Shadrack Woods at Toulouse–Le Mirail (1962). The use of low-rise roof platforms as an elevated pedestrian precinct is probably best illustrated in *241* London's Barbican Estate by Chamberlin, Powell and Bon, a redevelopment project sited in a precinct of London which was largely destroyed during World War II. *Pl.29* Another version is presented by the Alexandra Road estate, also in London.

North America's street substitutes came about through commercial rather than state initiative, taking the form of networks of subsurface passages, like those of Houston, Toronto, and Montreal, and skyway systems—"elevated pedestrian circulation systems" in the jargon of planners. Like suburban shopping malls, these examples of the continued privatization of public space work against the street as the primary place for social interaction. They try to replicate its experience in a controlled environment which drains its energies but cannot quite match its vitality.

241 London, Barbican development, by Chamberlin, Powell and Bon, designed 1959, built with modifications through the 1960s and '70s: section through terrace block, podium, and underground railroad.

American skyways have been criticized for promoting class and ethnic segregation: Minneapolis's system is particularly controversial in this regard.[119] The system is private: it closes down after business hours. Owners of the buildings to be connected negotiate the financing and design of each new section—the city gets involved only when a bridge directly abuts a public building. The walkways are primarily used to connect offices, hotels, and department stores along a corridor dotted with fancy boutiques. It is a program that caters to the well-heeled, and can be seen as inhibiting its use by the poor. Since these pedestrian routes are not genuinely public, they can hardly be considered a true alternative to the street network.

The bankruptcy of these revisionist interpretations of Modernism's doctrine of an urban street substitute could no longer be ignored by the late 1970s. By turning whole blocks into isolated citadels, these schemes render the street corridor little more than a glorified service alley. Most damning of all is the ingratitude of the obdurate pedestrian, the supposed beneficiary of aerial passageways and rooftop plazas, who from London to Toulouse can be seen shunning these carefully engineered environments and seeking the ground level when given the opportunity.

THE RETURN OF THE STREET

If, in the biography of the modern street, the Twenties and Thirties are the decades that condemned it to death, the Sixties and Seventies will be remembered as the decades of its attempted resurrection. For Western Europe the motivating force was a younger generation's anger at being cheated of their built patrimony, first by the insane vindictiveness of the war, and then by the equally vindictive zeal of a heavy-handed Modernist reconstruction intent on suppressing the comfort and familiarity of the traditional streetscape (see below, pp. 261–64). In America the revival of the street was announced by the concurrence of the public outcry against the urban freeway program and the passage of the Historic Preservation Act of 1966, which allowed "landmark" status to be conferred not just on single structures but on entire streets of buildings. Perhaps most important were the convulsions of public protest on both continents that brought crowds of people out-of-doors to occupy city streets and plazas, investing these once again with political life and civic purpose.

The point that had to be reached officially in order to address the muzzling of the automobile was the general admission that the benefits of a society of car owners were countered by the adverse impact of this mobility on the environment and the quality of life. A document for this awakening was England's Buchanan Report of 1963, *Traffic in Towns*. The report recognized the motor vehicle as a beneficial invention, and predicted an astronomical rise in its numbers. But accommodating these numbers in already strained settings would frustrate door-to-door accessibility and damage the urban environment—danger to pedestrians, anxiety, noise, air pollution, and visual intrusion were likely outcomes. The solution? Create areas within towns and cities where considerations of the pedestrian environment took precedence over the movement and parking of automobiles.

Europe came to embrace this idea whole-heartedly. Here I am talking about the segregation of vehicles and pedestrians at ground level—not the vertical separation espoused in various forms by the designers of the functionalist street, be they CIAM Modernists, Team X revisionists, or traffic engineers. In the immediate post-war years city planners had experimented with the transformation of certain business streets into pedestrian thoroughfares; these projects proved successful and were duplicated across Europe. In Germany alone there were 63 pedestrianized areas by 1966, 182 by 1972, 370 by 1977. One of the most extensive of these systems is in Nuremberg, where the pedestrian streets are supplemented by a dense network of shopping arcades and public parks. Another well-known and successful example is the Strøget in Copenhagen, where five existing streets running from the Town Hall to the city's central square have been linked and kept free of motorized traffic.

These car-free shopping streets in the old urban cores inspired the design of new streets that had the same qualities. Two of the best known are Rotterdam's Lijnbaan (1951–53) by J. H. van den Broek and J. B. Bakema, and Queensway (1956–59) in Stevenage New Town. Both were deemed immediate successes by planners. Lijnbaan combines a row of lowrise shops backed by highrise housing slabs. Queensway invokes the memory of a mixed-use street with one or two floors of housing running above many of the storefronts. Today both are tawdry and depressing places, with gray the predominant feel, if not the actual color. The construction is partly to blame. On these "high streets" resurrected in a minimalist mock-Miesian idiom, even materials like masonry end up looking like cheap panel construction. Where the old town center has the variety that comes of use and the patina that comes of being there a long, long time, here the diversity is programmed in, and the life of a generation or two reads as neglect.

The suburban shopping mall (see pp. 185–86) takes much of the credit for launching, and nearly sinking, the campaign to pedestrianize shopping streets in the United States. By the 1960s the middle-class flight to the suburbs virtually guaranteed that suburban shopping centers would be the successors to "Main Street." Downtown business leaders and city officials fought the flood of shopping malls with elaborate pedestrian street schemes, and the malling of Main Street began in earnest. The earliest examples come from Kalamazoo, Michigan (which called itself "Mall City, U.S.A."); Miami Beach, with Lincoln Road Mall (1962); and Pomona, California (1962). In these and dozens of other towns, asphalt was replaced by concrete or tile pavements punctuated by shade trees and planter boxes, fountains, benches, and kiosks. It is an artificial and sanitized design vocabulary, part regional shopping center, part Disneyland. These pedestrian malls were usually launched with much fanfare, but without a coherent long-range program of urban improvement—one reason for the financial failure of many of them. By the 1980s the fad had lost steam. Eugene, Oregon, tentatively reopened a single block of its mall to traffic in 1987 and saw an increase in business reinvestment and fewer shop vacancies there. Other cities, such as Oak Park, Illinois, dispensed with their pedestrian mall and have become models that are likely to be emulated elsewhere.

In the end, the more important aspect of standing up for the pedestrian may come not from shopping districts, but from the design of residential neighborhoods. The lead on this front is Dutch, specifically in the form of a new prototype for the residential street called the *woonerf*, literally "living yard." The name was coined in 1963 by Professor Niek De Boer of the Technical University of Twente to describe a street in which the primary function would not be driving and parking, but walking and playing. By the mid-1970s, after trials in a number of Dutch towns, the *woonerf* was adopted nationally and given its own distinctive traffic signage. The request to reconfigure a street comes from its residents, and the city must then conform to it. Pedestrian use is encouraged through design elements such as a clearly marked threshold distinguishing the *woonerf* from the network of thoroughfares, intentional ambiguity of paving materials to disrupt the perception of the roadway as a linear traffic channel, speed bumps to slow cars, and the insertion of planting and staggered parking to block continuous sight lines. The concept spread to Germany

242 Copenhagen, the pedestrianized Strøget. In the background is the tower of the Holmens-Kirke.

243 opposite Rotterdam, the Lijnbaan area, by Van den Broek and Bakema, 1951–53. At the heart is a pedestrian street lined with low shops; behind are housing slabs. Cars are relegated to high-speed through routes (bottom; cf. Ill. 266) and to parking lots behind the shops.

244 *A Viennese* Wohnstrasse. *The roadway is constricted by a widened, planted sidewalk area; pedestrians have priority.*

244 and Austria as the "livable street" or *Wohnstrasse*, and by the mid-1970s variants had sprung up as far away as Berkeley, California.

Perhaps the most ambitious attempt to loosen the automobile's stranglehold on the city street is being made by the architecture and planning team of Andres Duany and Elizabeth Plater-Zyberk. At Seaside, Florida, their initial plunge into citybuilding, streets range in character from formal to informal, volumes are carefully defined, vistas closed.[120] Like Unwin's, theirs is a streetscape shared with traffic but designed around pedestrian needs and pleasures. And like their British predecessor, whose intimately scaled residential streets at Hampstead Garden Suburb required an Act of Parliament to circumvent legislated standards, Duany and Plater-Zyberk have discovered that the traditional streetscape they are attempting to revive is in most places illegal.

"Car traffic has become the central, unavoidable experience of the public realm," according to the planning team, because the automobile's claim on the city has been frozen into legislation across the United States. Municipal ordinances emphasize above all else provisions for high-speed traffic and an abundant number of parking spots. Such ordinances are, in the words of Duany and Plater-Zyberk, "virtual recipes for urban disintegration."[121]

The team's weapon of choice against further encroachment of the automobile on pedestrian territory is a regulatory tool: the Traditional Neighborhood Development ordinance, or T.N.D. It is a genetic code for urbanity, consolidating the vernacular wisdom of towns like Charleston and New Orleans with exacting new standards and dimensions for streets. The street-animating rowhouse is revived by the T.N.D. as a standard housing type. Walking is encouraged by locating shops within strolling distance from homes. Sidewalks are a minimum of 12 feet (3.7 m.) wide where there are shops, and street trees are mandatory. The new formula has found favor with developers gambling that a generation born and raised in the suburbs will pay for the privilege of walking rather than driving. T.N.D. communities are rising at Kentlands, near Washington, D.C., Nance Canyon in California, and Wellington, Florida. And Duany's collaboration with Léon Krier in England under the patronage of Prince Charles promises to make Poundbury, their *Pl.30* urban extension plan for the city of Dorchester, a foreign showcase for the T.N.D.

These are, admittedly, rarefied experiments. They cannot, nor do they pretend to, address the erosion of the urban environment wherever parking lots and elevated expressways have proliferated at the expense of a streetscape that afforded pleasure and refuge. There the task of taming the automobile is compounded by both the scale of the problem and the lack of a mandate. For despite our fascination with the charm of pedestrian shopping streets and refurbished historical districts, most of us still conform to Sir Colin Buchanan's pessimistic assessment that "people are prepared to trade off their environment in return for motorized accessibility." The fundamental loss we must address is the loss of street culture.

In the past, the street was the place where social classes and social uses mixed. It was the stage of solemn ceremony and improvised spectacle, of people-watching, of commerce and recreation. In its changing architecture, its slow shifts and adjustments, in its sometimes wholesale reincarnation, the street was also our communal register—the safeguard of those continuities of culture and place that made us as street users vastly and substantively older than our age and infinitely wiser than our natural gifts. This street of the past was an untidy place, physically and morally, but it was also both school and stage of urbanity, which in the end means nothing less than the belief that people, as Gerald Allen put it, "can live together in proximity and interdependence."

In all this the container mattered, of course, but it was not what mattered most. If street design took certain turns, it is because that is how we wanted to live. "A street is a street," wrote Maurice Culot and Léon Krier, "and one lives there in a certain way not because architects have imagined streets in certain ways."[122]

That is why I cannot see the point in reviving the container without a solemn commitment to reinvest it with true urban vigor, with urbanity. As long as we would rather keep our own counsel, avoid social tension by escaping, *schedule* encounters with our friends, and happily travel alone in climate-controlled and music-injected glossy metal boxes, the resurrected street will be a place we like to visit every so often but not inhabit—a fun place, a museum. But it will also stand as the burial place of our hopes to exorcise poverty and prejudice by confronting them daily; the burial place of our chances to learn from one another, child from bagwoman and street vendor from jock; the burial place of unrehearsed excitement, of the cumulative knowledge of human ways, and the residual benefits of a public life.

5 · URBAN PROCESS

THE FALL AND RISE OF CITIES

LONDON AND LISBON

The transformation of London from a medieval half-timbered warren into a Renaissance city of paved streets and brick buildings began in a baker's house on Pudding Lane at around 1 a.m. Sunday, 2 September 1666. The Great Fire started routinely enough—one of many such mishaps the City endured every year.[1] This time the unforeseen outcome was an urban cataclysm. The fire spread fanned by a 246 strong east wind, first into Thames Street, and then on to the open wharves nearby with their stacks of hay, lumber and coal. For several days the flames raged out of control through the narrow streets and lanes with their timbered houses, and along the warehouses and docks of the riverfront. To create fire lanes many buildings were pulled down before they were consumed, on the King's express orders to "spare no houses, but to pull down before the fire every way." In the eleventh hour, panic-stricken by the inferno that seemed unstoppable, the authorities brought in gunpowder, and laid flat entire streets. More than 13,000 houses in all were destroyed, along with St. Paul's Cathedral and 87 parish churches, the Royal Exchange, the Custom House, and the Guildhall.

Reconstruction efforts began before the worst was over. Temporary housing for the refugees was authorized in the open spaces outside the city walls; new markets were established; prisons were moved; London Bridge and its approaches were cleared of rubbish. But most streets were impassable because of piles of debris, port facilities were in ruins, the wharves were blocked, their landing stages destroyed, the water pipes cut. And the City was deprived of all major revenue. Customs and Excise were bankrupt, chimney tax revenues dried up, and with the City's property in ruins, rents were hard to collect.

Rebuilding fast, or at least conveying the urgency of prompt reconstruction, was critical. The threat that the merchants would abandon the City for the safe and legally less restrictive suburbs was real enough. There was no question, it was soon recognized, of an entirely new ground plan along the lines of Wren's or Evelyn's. But duplicating the old model, given the sad performance of the City fabric during the Fire, was also intolerable.

245 opposite *The Theater of Marcellus in Rome, built in the 1st century BC, as it appeared ca. 1865. In the Middle Ages it became the fortress of the Pierleoni family; in the 16th century Peruzzi converted part of it for the Savelli into a palace, of which the infilling walls and altered windows can be seen here. The lowest floor held shops and workshops. Gradually the ground level rose by some 12 feet (4 m.), burying almost half the Doric order.*

The Commissioners appointed by the Privy Council and the City, having discussed "whether streets shall be laied out in the places where they formerly were, or in such other as shall be demonstrated to be more for the beauty and convenience of the citty," settled for a middle course whereby main streets would be widened through the equitable redistribution of property. For that, an exact survey of every plot and a record of ownership, rents, specifics of inheritance and other such legal matters was indispensable. But the survey seems never to have been completed. The debris of the Fire had raised the ground level by at least two feet (60 cm.), and the occupants who were ordered to clear and survey their plots did not comply. The streets were not fully opened up until December, and a severe winter forced the suspension of building for several months thereafter. By then the moment for any radical replanning of the burnt area had passed. "Something might be done by isolated exchanges," T. F. Reddaway concludes in his classic account of the Fire, "but, apart from that, compensation would have to be paid in actual cash to those expropriated for the public benefit. From this time forward the extent of the improvement possible was clearly defined by the funds available to pay for it."

Three separate authorities were involved. The King and his Privy Council, and Parliament, were active on the broad issues of rebuilding. An Act of 1667 was largely in the nature of a building ordinance: it regulated things like paving, spouting

246 London, showing the area burned in the Great Fire of 1666 and the City in flames; engraving by Wenceslas Hollar, 1667. On the west side, the fire spread beyond the line of the old walls, left exposed, to the boundary at the Temple. In rebuilding, the web of streets shown here was largely retained. Note, incidentally, how the area of Moorfields to the north had been urbanized since the 1550s (cp. Ill. 164).

gutters, bows and jetties. Its most far-reaching provision was to establish four standard house types for streets of different width and to prescribe the details of design and construction—heights, number of stories, thickness of walls and depth of cellars. A second Act created the Fire Court, with broad competence "for Determination of Differences touching Houses Burned or Demolished by reason of the late Fire." It settled more than fifteen hundred cases amicably, dealing with the intertwined occupancy pattern of London that involved the interests of ground landlords, proprietors, tenants, and lessees.

But it was finally the City and its organs that had the unpleasant task of enforcing building codes, negotiating for even the minutest strips of private land needed in modifying street lines, and struggling to keep a balance between the need to move ahead by expediting the erection of buildings over the sad landscape of ruins and the need for vigilance against abusive construction. The commonest infringement was for property owners to move the official stakes that marked street lines, and to build fast enough so that, if detected, the City would have the thankless choice of destroying new houses or altering the street lines. In the reigning situation where private enterprise was left to rebuild London, unsubsidized and subject to stringent regulations, the prudent path was one of compromise. Public funds accounted only for projects like the Fleet Canal and Thames Quay, and the replacing of public buildings.

Progress was slow: after three years, the City was still only modestly recovered. More than a third of the foundations had as yet to be staked, and temporary structures were everywhere in use. Labor was scarce and so were materials. The Companies were slow to rebuild their headquarters. There was no set timetable, no specified order of progress in the completion of streets, and house building was entirely random. Only after a full decade had gone by did London look habitable. It was a better-built city: the houses were all of brick or stone, and construction standards were high. A certain degree of uniformity was evident. The streets conformed roughly to their previous pattern, but were now straighter, wider, and *191,* held a steady line of frontage. Gradients had been reduced. Wren's spires for the new *192* parish churches began to accent this tidy cityscape, and St. Paul's eventually added to it a measure of cosmopolitan splendor.

Medieval London was let go of. But not London's medieval ways. An inflexible, parochial self-interest lost residents to the suburbs. Many who had fled the flames never returned, prospering in new centers of trade. The City made concessions to fill the empty houses. It was too late. Close to bankruptcy, it had no option but to surrender its franchises into the King's hands. "The Fire which had modernized its buildings," Reddaway concludes, "had not been able to modernize its policy. Morally bankrupt, . . . its position was revealed by the downfall of its finances." If the story of reconstruction ended in success, it was because of the enterprise of private individuals. The City as an administrative structure survived the Great Fire. "But from henceforward the private wealth which had carried London in triumph through its ordeal by fire was to become more and more the source and expression of its greatness."

Lisbon's holocaust lasted ten minutes.[2] On 1 November 1755, All Saints' Day, a Saturday, at about 9:40 in the morning, the ground shook violently. There were two further shocks about a minute apart, and the capital lay in ruins. An hour later the waters of the Tagus River swelled in three towering waves spilling over the city between the Alcantara docks and Terreiro do Paço (Royal Square). The fires that were inevitably triggered by the collapse of buildings burnt for six days. At the end little was left of this city of 250,000 inhabitants, which had boasted of being the richest in the West. In the name of the King, an appeal was sent to the colonies of the Portuguese Empire by the man who found himself in charge, the Minister of State Sebastião José de Carvalho e Mello, future Marquis of Pombal. The merchants of the city made a generous offer to the Crown—a surcharge of 4 per cent on customs duties for every imported item. England sent food; Hamburg, four ships loaded with construction materials. Pombal ordered that a survey of every destroyed quarter of the city be prepared, and prohibited any new construction until official plans were published. The homeless squatted in the public squares and the vast grounds of the monasteries. Noblemen and well-off merchants built wooden temporary structures, some of them quite fancy; in six months 9,000 of these "shanties" went up, the majority imported from Holland.

In a first professional response on the issue of reconstruction, the renowned military engineer close to the Court, eighty-year-old Manuel da Maia, spelled out four options: rebuild the city as it was, this being the speediest form of recovery; keep the old building height but widen the streets; reduce the height to two stories while increasing street width; or pull down all of the destroyed Baixa, the lower city, and lay down a new orderly street plan. A final option would be to abandon the city altogether and start clean on another site.

The decision to go with a new street plan was made promptly, and at the highest level. Pombal and his circle were firmly in charge, and they were able to suppress whatever resistance there might have been to a clean slate. The old order was represented by the aristocracy and the Jesuits. Pombal found his allies instead in the new moneyed class, the powerful merchants and bankers who had grown rich through the Portuguese Empire overseas. Traces of this shift are embedded in the reconstructed city. The square on the water, the Terreiro do Paço, the official public square before the earthquake flanked by the Royal Palace and government buildings, was now enlarged, given continuous porticoes, and renamed Praça do Comercio. The Palace was moved.

247 Lisbon. The gridded Baixa or lower town rebuilt after the earthquake of 1755 stands out clearly. It extends from the riverside Praça do Comercio inland as far as the Rossio. (Non-gridded developments beyond that are later.) The area on high ground to the west was also rebuilt in a rationalized way: see Ill. 248. The hilly Albaicín district, to the east, retains the labyrinthine character of the pre-earthquake city.

248 Lisbon. Post-earthquake design for the Rua Nova de S. Francisco de Paula, climbing a hill to the west of the Baixa.

The new Baixa extended from here to a northern square (Rossio) at the opposite, land edge of the city. The ground level was raised by four feet (1.2 m.), covering the ruins. The plan had a principal author, Eugenio dos Santos. It was a basic grid with identical blocks. This uniformity extended to the buildings themselves—three- or four-story houses, painted ocher, with standard features and almost no decoration. The flat façades followed the street line, and climbed slopes in a mechanically direct 248 path: only the roofline was staggered to maintain the same number of floors throughout. The lateral walls of the houses were raised above the roof level, a preventive measure against the spread of fires. To minimize the damage of a future earthquake, an ingenious invention called the *gaiola* was incorporated in the construction. This consisted of a wooden skeleton, independent of the load-bearing walls, which would be able to hold up the floors and roof if the walls collapsed.

In putting up the houses, the traditional on-site involvement of craftsmen and materials became overnight obsolete. All the elements could be prefabricated on a large scale, brought to the staked streets, and assembled. The iron balconies, drastically simplified in relation to the ornamental bravura of the first half of the century, came in sections that could be assembled in any desirable length. Historiated decoration was abandoned, in favor of simple friezes made up of two motifs—a starred blue flower and a yellow cross of St. Andrew.

This summary of the rebuilding of London and Lisbon illustrates the varying processes through which cities respond to major disasters that devastate their frame. The primary issue is the street plan: the pure options are strict reconstruction on the same lines, or a radical redrawing of those lines. London's was an inevitable compromise. To follow the latter course, in the way of Lisbon, the city must be able to wield the kind of public authority that can take possession of all private land, and redistribute it equitably within the matrix of the new street plan. The alternative, public purchase of the property needed to redraw the streets, is too costly and slow to be practicable except for selective corrections.

The opportunity to rationalize the buildings themselves, or at least their street front, is also present. The same centralized authority which drew the street lines can provide models for the new buildings and enforce adherence to them. In the case of Lisbon, this process amounted to a rigid system of standardization which revolutionized building practices. London was able to create a relatively homogeneous streetscape, instead, through the commoner assertion of public authority—building codes—which justifies itself on grounds of public safety and health.

A reconstruction on this scale cannot fail to have social and political consequences. Municipal control is likely to shift to those elements which were most active, and effective, in the process of reconstruction. The new Lisbon was created at the expense of the once powerful Jesuits and contributed to the enfeebling of the Crown. The new London tilted the balance of power away from the Corporation.

Disasters, natural or manmade, and the rebuilding that follows are one aspect of my subject in this chapter. Cities also are subjected to forceful change through programs of urban renewal. Both of these are violent interventions of short duration. Far less dramatic is the incremental transformation of city form through the thousands of daily adjustments to its fabric due to the owners and users of private property. I propose to discuss each one of these three categories of urban change, with the purpose of clarifying the physical processes they entail and their social consequences. The aim throughout is to scrutinize specific transmutations of what was, or is, there. I leave out of the discussion the beginnings of new towns, wholesale additions to an extant core, the serial growth of towns like Cairo or Cracow, and acts of incorporation or annexation. These broad-stroked urban changes I have taken up in other, more appropriate contexts.

URBAN LONGEVITY

We need to stress the premier fact that cities are long-lived artifacts. Their tendency is to continue. Unattended, the artifact decays and disintegrates. But as long as there are people in residence, the city will renew itself without letup in unrehearsed *ad hoc* procedures or more methodically. The usual pattern is a combination of the two.

There are of course terminal episodes, when a civilization ceases to exist and the cities it supported die. Nothing replaced Mohenjo Daro and Harappa after that mysterious Indus Valley culture came to an end. Nothing replaced Mycenae and Tiryns. Teotihuacán's abandonment seems to have been absolute as well. And there are incidences of ephemeral settlement plantings, like unsuccessful *bastides*, or mining towns that became ghosts when the riches of the soil were exhausted. But the governing principle of urban history is to go on living as long as there is a sustaining power and a population that can make use of the urban artifact.

In classic instances of longevity—Rome; Damascus; Jericho; Jerusalem; Benares—the time span of continuous occupation is about 2,500 to 3,000 years. Damascus started its existence in the second millennium BC. The first town on the site of Delhi was Indrapath (Indraprastha) on the banks of the Yamuna River; that was in the 6th century BC. Today it is the neighborhood of Purana Qila in greater New Delhi.

The proof of continuity is often plain to see in the interlocking of history within 63 the same urban context. In Moscow's Kremlin, the Cathedral of the Assumption and the Trinity Tower, both of the later 15th century, rub shoulders with the 18th-century Senate and the 20th-century Presidium of the Supreme Soviet. It is at the very least noteworthy, not to say astounding, that physical remains of Rome's founding years, eight centuries before Christ, are still there to be seen in the Forum. If these are embedded in the soil as mere palimpsests, a few hundred years forward and actual standing forms can be visited in the midst of the modern town—the temples at the Largo Argentina, for example.

These historic accents are what stands out through the commoner process of layering. In the past, when a city was leveled by cataclysmic events—earthquakes 249 or sacks—a new layer rose over it after a short or long spell. There are nine superimposed Troys before we get to the Middle Ages. At Gordion, the archaeologist today is able to distinguish, starting at the very bottom of the site, a Hittite layer, then Phrygian, Cimmerian, Lydian, Persian, Greek, Galatian and

249 Herculaneum (Italy), the Palaestra. The Roman city lies beneath a thick layer of tufa that rolled down over it in the form of boiling mud from Vesuvius in AD 79. Above, a new town eventually grew up. Thorough excavation of the dead city means destruction of the living, and much of it still lies under bustling streets.

Roman layers, while he can get his provisions at the modern village of Yassihüyük which is still claiming the site.

In this process of layering, nothing much of the beginning may survive in the end, but the city is still there where it started (site), and its present form is the last phase of many major and minor readjustments, each one of which had to work with what was there at the time, even if what was there was only building foundations. The survival is often in fragments of spatial structure—a modern avenue that runs over an ancient path, or the central plaza that goes back to the forum of the Roman period. Not building over a spot through many centuries may prove as significant as superimposed layers of construction.

DISASTERS AND THEIR AFTERMATHS

STAYING PUT

The most normal practice by far, after a major disaster, is for the city to rebuild where it stood. Post-fire London and post-earthquake Lisbon are not exceptional in this respect. One of the earliest recorded cases was Rome. After the terrible sack by the Gauls in 387 BC, some insisted on re-establishing the city at nearby Veii where the people had taken refuge. The Senate was debating the issue, we are told, when some troops marched by through the Forum and their centurion gave them the order to halt: "Hic manebimus optime" (Here is a good place for us to stop). The senators, taking this as a divine oracle, decided to do the same.

Of all the dozens of cities devastated by the Second World War, almost all chose to rebuild. There was talk of abandoning badly bombed cities. It was rumored that Polish leaders considered relocating Warsaw, and the Soviets debated moving Stalingrad. St.-Malo gave some thought to leaving its rubble as a war memorial, and rebuilding farther south on the mainland. But practical reasons and local and national symbolism won out in the end. The replacement of Berlin with a new city on a new site was considered and rejected, in part because of the traffic network that centered on the city, amounting to about 3,800 miles (over 6,000 km.) of streets, and the vast subterranean services, railways and local transport.[3] Depending on how thorough the destruction has been, the pertinacity of landownership patterns can make it difficult to abandon old boundaries. If foundations and walls of gutted buildings and utility lines underground can be fixed, you are not likely to give that up and begin at the beginning. A year after the end of the Second World War 900,000 people were back living in the ruins of Hamburg, even though it had been 80 per cent gutted. Beyond any practical arguments, there is also the fact that this is after all your home and you want to come back to it. It is where you raised your children and buried your parents and celebrated new births.

War can also relocate entire towns. Cassino in Italy is one of them: after 1945 it was moved from its precarious mountainside location to a level site not more than 2,000 feet (600 m.) away. The ruins of the old town—hardly visible in fact, so thoroughly was it leveled by the bombs—were declared a national monument where no construction was permitted.

Earlier examples of towns that moved are Noto and Avola in Sicily after the earthquake of 1693; Antigua in Guatemala after the 1773 earthquake; and San Miguel de Tucumán in Argentina, founded in 1565 and relocated in 1685 to a site 60 miles (100 km.) north for reasons that are unclear, but probably to avoid regular flooding and attacks by Indians. After the earthquake of 1783 in Calabria and Sicily the Bourbons of Naples who ruled the area moved more than thirty-five medieval cities from their hill strongholds to flat accessible plains and gave them modern grid plans. There are also cases in Sicily where some townspeople refused to abandon their hillside, while the new town grew on more suitable terrain. So Ragusa Ibla continued to be inhabited even as the gridded new town endorsed by the Spanish administration developed its own identity.

URBAN CONFLAGRATION

250 Fires were the commonest agent of urban destruction until recent times. History records only the most famous, which means those that did the most extensive or *246* spectacular damage—Rome, in AD 64; London, 1666; Moscow, 1812; Chicago, 1871—but no city was immune to the terror of flames.

Take Russia and Finland. The towns, being built of wood until this century, burnt down repeatedly. It is estimated that on the average one Finnish town every thirty to forty years was destroyed by fire. In the 19th century, particularly severe instances *Pl.31* were the fires of Pori in 1801 and 1852, Oulu in 1822, and Turku in 1827 (which the Finnish historian Lilius calls "the greatest Scandinavian fire").[4]

In the Finnish case, the most effective way to stop the burning of towns would have been to abandon wood construction for something less combustible; but this was not countenanced even for public buildings. Short of that, preventive measures had to do with the rearrangement of the urban fabric. In the 17th and 18th centuries one such measure was to rid the waterfront of burghers' warehouses which hindered access to the water during fires.

The most thoroughgoing legislation was promulgated for Turku after the fire of 1827; it provided the standard set of responses throughout Finland. The streets were to be widened to a minimum of 30 ells. The town was to be divided into fire districts by 40-ell-wide cross streets. House lots were to be larger; only three sides of any lot

250 *Aftermath of a fire in the Old Town of Edinburgh (Scotland). Irreparably damaged stone tenements (of the spectacularly tall type characteristic of the city) are demolished with a system of chains. From* Eight Engravings of the Ruins occasioned by the Great Fire in Edinburgh on the 15th, 16th and 17th November 1824, *by William Home Lizars, "published for the benefit of the sufferers."*

could be built, the fourth side being left open for a fire lane planted with trees. The height limit for wooden houses was reduced to one story. Craftsmen working with open fires were to be located at the edge of town in small lots, with every other lot being an open garden. There were to be a number of public squares in order to disperse the city.

The result of all this was a fundamental change in the makeup of the traditional gridded wooden city in Finland. High-walled closed streets were gone; the street wall was opened with spaces between buildings, the streets themselves were wider, *306* the density reduced, and the city profile low. Around the squares the public buildings stood alone, continuous frontages being discouraged.

EARTHQUAKES, FLOODS, AND HURRICANES

Because of the vividness of photographs, major earthquakes of the last one hundred years are more immediate to us than historic cases which were no less devastating. When these tremors are incident to the eruption of a volcano, reconstruction is impossible. But paradoxically the city may stay petrified under the ashes waiting to *200,* be unearthed. The saga of discovering Pompeii, which perished in AD 79 along with *249,* Herculaneum and Stabiae, began in the 18th century. The site still attracts tens of *251* thousands every year, not all of them students of ancient architecture. Visitors also come for the kitchens in mid-meal, the election posters, the corpses of dogs and their masters, the desperate scenes of last-minute flight, and the salvagers and looters who died retrieving a strongbox or a precious object—everything trapped under a blanket of ash.[5]

The history of earthquake-resistant technologies is both brief and ill-studied. I mentioned Lisbon's remarkable invention, the *gaiola*. In Calabria two years after the tremor of 1783 the Bourbons made mandatory a house type called the *casa barracata*, which stipulated a continuous foundation and an x-braced wooden framework embedded in the interior walls, with vertical and horizontal members running through all exterior walls. The type lasted in Calabria for quite a while, and then fell into disuse perhaps because of its association with the unpopular Bourbon government.[6]

251 A street-corner bar in Pompeii (Italy).

San Francisco, 1906; Messina, 1908; Tokyo, 1923; Skopje, 1963; Managua, 1972—here the evidence of the disaster has effectively been concealed by the post-earthquake city. San Franciscans focused on fire damage. The citizens endorsed a special earthquake-resistant water system, which still serves the city today. The Great Kanto Earthquake of September 1923 devastated much of Tokyo and neighboring Yokohama. The reconstruction was based on a comprehensive plan that included the increase of the area of the street network, zoning, and the redistribution of urban land in accordance with the new streets. To achieve this last goal, nearly 60,000 buildings, almost all timber-framed houses, were dismantled and moved to new sites.[7]

Flooding has a distinct set of consequences for city form. In certain urban situations, heavy rainfall by itself could wreak havoc. The Sudan provides an interesting example. Up and down the Nile there was a farflung network of fairly large settlements connected by caravan routes. Probably Khartoum alone will be familiar to a Western audience. About 1900 the cities of the Sudan were taken over by the British, and some of the older ones—Sinnar, Barbar, al-Damir—were relocated on new sites. As the abandoned towns were built of impermanent materials, just a few decades of normal rainfall were all that was required to erase their remains.[8]

252 Floods are most damaging to waterfront property and bridges. The fury subsides as the water spreads to the adjacent flat areas, and there is little to do but wait for it to withdraw. Though the loss is obviously not negligible, the city form is basically unaffected. Old photographs of rowboats afloat in boulevards and plazas are deceptively placid, with no sense of imminent danger. But even at its most benign, a flood will rupture utility lines and leave deposits of mud along the streets and within the buildings which are extremely difficult to remove. And of course it is a matter of degree. The great flood of 838 in northern Holland wiped out the town of Medemblik.[9]

Hurricanes have their own pattern of destruction. Buildings are blown away and their debris piled some distance from where they had been, sometimes around others that remain standing. Whole blocks are wiped clean down to the ground. In the great
253 Galveston, Texas, hurricane of 1900, nearly half the houses in the city were swept away. To prevent the recurrence of such devastation, most structures, surviving and new, were raised several feet on new foundations to a level above the storm tide. "Every building, tree, pipe, and fire hydrant . . . was raised as 14 million cubic yards of sand were pumped into the city."[10] At the same time a massive seawall 3.3 miles (5.3 km.) long and 17 feet (5 m.) above mean low tide was put up along the waterfront, as a barricade against the ocean.

252 *The Lungarno in Florence, near the National Library, during the flood of November 1966.*

THE DESTRUCTION OF WAR

DAMNATIO MEMORIAE

Short of war, which is indiscriminate and anonymous, there are hostile practices that involve the destruction of property of specific state enemies or resurgents. Several examples chosen at random will suffice.

The destruction of monuments associated with a hated and overturned regime, an architectural *damnatio memoriae*, was common in the high circles of the Roman Empire. Upon the murder of Nero, his extravagant Golden House (*Domus Aurea*), a sprawling villa in the center of town, was built over by the Flavian dynasty which succeeded him; the Colosseum and the Baths of Titus were intentional replacements that catered to the people. The sweeping destruction of Church and royal property during the French Revolution was punishment meted out against the representational landscape of the Ancien Régime. To this day Israel routinely demolishes houses of Arabs suspected of having acted against its interests; so the Emperor Titus had destroyed the Temple in AD 70 to punish the Jews for their own *intifada*.
74 The first congregational mosque in India, the Quwwat ul-Islam in Delhi, was built ca. 1200 of re-used materials from as many as twenty-seven demolished Hindu and Jain temples. "It was the custom," says a contemporary source, "after the conquest of every fort and stronghold [by the Muslim armies], to grind its foundations and pillars to powder under the feet of fierce and gigantic elephants."
92 The British in turn devastated Mughal Delhi after the uprising of 1857. About 80 per cent of the interior of the imperial palace was destroyed, an area which had contained royal pavilions, gardens, barracks and living quarters for artisans, and the building converted into a garrison called Delhi Fort. A field of artillery fire was then created by clearing an area 300–400 yards (275–350 m.) broad along the west and south perimeter of the fort, which meant the annihilation of many prestigious

253 *Aftermath of the Galveston hurricane of 9 September 1900. Destruction was wrought not just by wind but by water, as the wood-built city on a sandy island off the Texas coast was submerged by the wind-blown sea.*

neighborhoods set close to the royal compound, and the displacement of thousands of people. (Sixty years later it was a grim no-man's-land in an overcrowded native quarter, made pointless by the British move to the splendid frame of New Delhi.)

Property seizure and destruction (raze or burn) was the normal way medieval Italian communes dealt with disgraced families. Guelph property was systematically destroyed in Florence between 1260 and 1266 after the Guelphs were exiled. Such judicial destruction became so common that in 1348 Orvieto, sick of living with ruins, passed a resolution in the city council that "forbade, thenceforth, any magistrate or officer to destroy any house, for whatever reason, whether condemnation, or banishment, or misdemeanour, or any other."[11] Not Florence; she was still pulling them down in 1382 when the Giraldi houses were partly destroyed and the ruins burned because a young Giraldi had murdered Francesco di Giandonato of the opposite camp.

Recent examples of this form of premeditated demolition are provided by the Persian Gulf conflict, as well as the urban guerrilla warfare that has devastated cities in Yugoslavia. The Gulf War is often said to have transformed the technology of destruction into a surgically conducted operation guided by lasers and computers. But the calculated devastation inflicted upon Basra's Shiite shrines, as well as the more recent violation of Croatian cultural sites like Vukovar Castle and the Baroque buildings of Varazdin, are tragic reminders of the continued viability of war strategies that transform monuments into enemies.

There are two common ways of dealing with the targets of a *damnatio memoriae*. One of them is to build something over the condemned property which symbolically shows the defeat of the subject and the ascent of the new power. That is what the Flavians did; that is what Constantine the Great did when he built St. John Lateran in Rome over the barracks of the Equites Singulares who had opposed him in his contest with Maxentius; bazaars and residential areas went over the destroyed palaces of the Fatimids in Cairo under Saladin and his followers; the center of Mexico City buried the monumental heart of Aztec Tenochtitlán; Mehmed II's 254

254 Mexico City. In the center is the main plaza, the Zocalo; to the east (left) lies the cathedral; to the south, the viceregal palace. The Great Temple of Tenochtitlán stood on a site between the two, beyond the cathedral. Further remains of the Aztec ceremonial complex have been found throughout the area: during work in 1790 to install waterpipes and paving in the Zocalo, the famous Aztec Calendar Stone and statue of the mother-goddess Coatlicue were discovered.

255 Córdoba (Spain). The great mosque, with open courtyard, minaret, and covered prayer-hall, became the Christian cathedral after the city's conquest in 1236. It remained substantially unaltered until the 1520s, when the center was destroyed and replaced by a high chancel and choir. The mosque itself (begun in 785) replaced an earlier Christian church on the site, and that church had appropriated a Roman temple of Janus.

Christian for nearly eight centuries, Córdoba remains Islamic in its urban fabric: the courtyard of the former mosque is still the only significant open space in town, and the streets are labyrinthine.

mosque was raised over the church of the Holy Apostles in Constantinople which was pulled down for that purpose. And so on.

255 The other option is to convert the condemned monument to another use. The Córdoba mosque became the Christian cathedral at about the time that Hagia Sophia was being converted into a mosque at the other end of the Mediterranean. St. Petersburg's august Kazan Cathedral weathered the Communist era serving a sixty-year sentence as a museum of atheism. These single acts are usually part and parcel of massive environmental conversions, in cases where a drastic cultural revolution has occurred. The confiscation of Church property by Henry VIII in England, by the Revolutionary government in France, and to a lesser degree by the Italian government after Unity, are well-known instances. Concerning the example of Revolutionary France, Loyer notes that beginning in 1793 some 1,000 acres/400 ha. in Paris (the city then contained 8,330 acres/3,370 ha.) were confiscated from the clergy and turned over to real-estate developers.[12]

This sort of punitive reassignment is to be distinguished, I think, from what one might call emulative repossession. Here a subsequent user chooses to identify with the aura or power of the building he is re-using, as was certainly the case with feudal nobility fortifying ancient Roman monuments as family strongholds. Common targets were the gates of the ancient walls, as at Turin and Aix-en-Provence, tombs along the consular highways, theaters, and especially amphitheaters, which were 245 sometimes turned into a community fortress by groups of knights. In houses ensconced within the porticoes or in the arena itself lived the families and dependents of the nobles. That was the case in Nîmes: when the Albigensian crusade was launched in the early 13th century under Louis VIII, the arena was seized and the nobles dispersed.[13]

This may be the proper place to raise the issue of *spolia*. The phenomenon involves recycling bits of one city in the building of another, often with symbolic intent. The case of taking *spolia* from conquered cities and incorporating them into significant structures in the conqueror's city has many examples throughout history. When the Jin destroyed the Northern Sung city of Bianjing in 1126, for example, they carried north screens, doors and walls to use in the palaces of their capital 256 Zhongdu.[14] And in Cairo the door of an-Nasr's medrese and mausoleum complex was taken as trophy from the Crusaders' church of St. John at Acre.

256 Cairo. The medrese and mausoleum of Muhammad an-Nasr incorporates a Gothic door taken from the church at Acre after the defeat of the Crusaders in 1291.

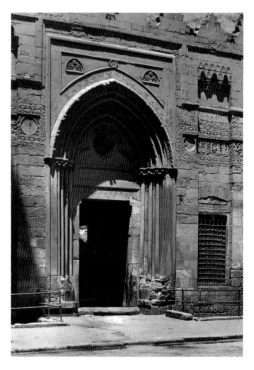

257 *Lidice (Czechoslovakia), looking from the site of the church.*

SACKS, LIGHT AND THOROUGH

Demolition is hard work. In the ancient and pre-modern world, troops sacking a city were more likely to be interested in loot than the systematic dismantling of the fabric. The damage was mostly caused by fires set during the attack. Some cities were simply too well built to bring down. The tremendously solid Inca masonry of Cuzco thwarted the efforts of the Conquistadors to raze the city to the ground, as they had done at Tenochtitlán. The new city rose on the foundations and walls of the ancient center.

The famous sacks of Rome by Alaric's Goths, the Vandals, and others in the early Middle Ages, psychologically devastating though they were for the inhabitants and the reputation of the Eternal City, were much less destructive than their legend suggests. The path of the Sack of Alaric in AD 410, for example, is revealing. His troops entered the city through the Porta Salaria in the northeast, and immediately attacked the palace and gardens of Sallust just within. The imperial residence on the Palatine also suffered, as did aristocratic mansions on the Caelian and Aventine. Public baths, with their precious building materials and rich collections of art, were targeted next. In the Forum the Senate building and the Basilica Aemilia were set on fire. But the sanctity of St. Peter's and St. Paul's was respected. In other words, Alaric's men in their three-day rampage went after centers of luxury and government authority.

There have of course been more thorough sacks. After the successful siege of Carthage in 146 BC, the Romans "undid" the city: they plundered and burned it, ploughed its ruins, and sowed them with salt. They dedicated the site to the "infernal gods." (The story is in Polybius.) In retaliation for the assassination of the Nazi governor Heydrich in 1942, the Czech village of Lidice was erased from the map. Its population was murdered, or sent to concentration camps and orphanages. "All signs of its layout were disguised. Even the river was rerouted and the site 'landscaped' to blend with surrounding fields and grazing lands."[15]

Historical figures famous for their savage takeover of cities include Genghis Khan and Timur. The accounts are harrowing. Between 1205 and 1215 the Mongols conquered China and captured Beijing. They took Bukhara in 1220, and initiated a series of brutal sacks where resisting cities would be burned to the ground, and every living creature put to death. The Mongol sack of Baghdad in 1258 led by Hulagu, grandson of Genghis, is said to have lasted forty days; a fire swept most of the city, including the main mosque and the tombs of the Caliphs. The Mongol Miran Shah had, it is said, the perverse idea of destroying all his predecessors' famous buildings, so that if he could not be remembered as a builder of great buildings he would at least be remembered as the destroyer of them.

And then there is record of strange cases when a ruler destroys his own city so as not to deliver it to the enemy. That was the case of the destruction of Old Cairo (Fustat) by the last Fatimid, because he could not see himself defending it against the Crusaders. The contemporary historian Maqrizi describes the event: the Caliph "sent 20,000 jars of naphtha to Fustat and 10,000 torches, the whole of which was distributed over the town. The flame of the fire and the smoke of conflagration rose to heaven: it was a terrible sight. The fire continued consuming the houses for 54 days from the 29th Safar. . . . From that time Fustat fell into the state of ruin in which are today the mounds of Misr."

Sometimes an adversary will force a city to participate in its own destruction. This is commonly the case when the conqueror demands that the city walls be razed, as did Napoleon of several cities he crushed.

259　　The Nazi sack of Warsaw will always have its own indelible place in the history of war. The city had known punitive demolition before, for example when the Russians demolished the housing district to the north after the insurrection of 1830–31 to make room for a fortified citadel. But this was different. The destruction of Warsaw was deliberate Nazi policy. Bombing began in September 1939. In October Hitler approved the governor-general's proposal to destroy Warsaw Castle, after removing all valuable works of art. Later plans called for the demolition of the existing city in its entirety. In 1940 a plan for a colonial new town, entitled "Warschau—die neue deutsche Stadt," was drawn up by the Nazis for a cleared site. This new city was to be for 100,000 Germans; the Polish population, reduced to serfdom, was to be interned in a vast camp on the opposite bank of the River Vistula. The plan was never realized.

In August 1944, Nazi-occupied Warsaw rebelled. For sixty-three days ground artillery and bombing pounded the city, killing 250,000 people. When it was over the German command evacuated the main area on the west bank, which at the time of the war was home to over 1,250,000 people. Hitler's memorandum of 11 October 1944 declared: "Warsaw has to be pacified, that is, razed to the ground." The *Vernichtungskommando* (Destruction Detachments) were formed and for three months they went at it, demolishing house after house, street after street, felling trees, dynamiting underground installations. "The city was divided into areas for destruction. Corner houses were numbered. On selected buildings and statues special inscriptions were made indicating the proposed date of demolition."[16] By the time the city was liberated, in December 1944, 800,000 people were dead, and of the 25,000 or so buildings that had existed in western Warsaw only about 1,200 were left standing.

THE SECOND WORLD WAR

This round of destruction was obviously unprecedented. The traditional tank and artillery attack by an enemy army demolished cities in a matter of weeks: aerial bombing produced similar results in hours. With the development of the long-range bomber, cities became principal targets and the destruction of civilian settlements a military objective. The explicit intent of aerial raids on built-up areas was to disrupt economic production through indiscriminate destruction of the urban infrastructure and through civilian terror. This is categorically different from bombing strategic settlements like ports and industrial sites in order to slow down the war effort.[17]

Area bombing was employed experimentally in the 1930s in the Sino-Japanese War, the Italian conquest of Ethiopia, and the German-assisted Spanish Civil War by nations that a decade later would themselves become its victims. Momentum for the use of urban bombing was provided by two disastrous cases of military bungling, both by the Nazis. On the afternoon of 10 May 1940, three Luftwaffe bombers heading toward strategic targets in France became disoriented and dropped their payloads on the German town of Freiburg-im-Breisgau, blowing up an airfield, a barracks, and a childrens' playground. Within hours Germany's Propaganda Ministry, assigning blame to the allies, promised to exact a five-fold revenge on a French or English town.

In fact, the next casualty was a Dutch city. Thwarted in their attempts to conquer Holland with ground forces, the German command fell upon a hostage strategy: surrender by 14 May or lose Rotterdam. Through a lapse in communications, bombers couldn't be recalled despite progress in negotiations. In just over seven

258 opposite London during the Blitz: the area of the docks, in the East End, on fire after a German air raid in September 1940. On the left is the Tower of London, on the right Tower Bridge.

259 below Central Warsaw, around the Old Town Square, as it stood at the end of 1944.

minutes a square mile (2.8 sq. km.) of the historic city core was in flames. About 265 1,000 people died, mostly civilians: allied sources inflated the figure by a factor of thirty. The vicious circle of escalating propaganda, weapons innovation, and destruction had begun.

For the night raid on Coventry later that year, Nazi forces fire-bombed the city center to help subsequent waves of bombers find their target: the term "Coventration" entered Nazi propaganda language. The Allies copied and perfected the German strategy of combining explosive and incendiary devices. Lübeck was chosen to test the new Allied approach; it was lightly defended, compact, and relatively easy to find. This fine Hanseatic town "did not attract the attention of the bombers because it was important, but became important because it could be bombed."[18] Hitler's "Baedeker raids" of 1942, named after the line of tourist guide-books, targeted English cultural centers like Exeter, Bath, York, and Canterbury in reprisal for the loss of historic German cities.

But the decisive advances in long-distance aircraft and the technology of urban devastation were now being made by the Allies. During the battle of Hamburg, in the summer of 1943, nearly 1,000 tons of napalm cascaded out of the night sky onto the city's medieval core. Within forty minutes, individual blazes merged into a single conflagration generating hurricane-force winds as air rushed in to feed the flames. Here the firestorm consumed 8 square miles (22 sq. km.); the American raid on Tokyo of March 1945 razed 16 square miles (41 sq. km.) northeast of the Imperial Palace. By comparison, the atomic raids at Hiroshima and Nagasaki together leveled just under 6.5 square miles (17 sq. km.).[19]

These unparalleled methods of urban destruction had their own characteristic geography. Old downtown districts of flammable timber construction were favored bombing targets. So were low-income residential areas with their concentration of industrial workers, as the fate of London's East End during the Blitz and the pattern 258 of ruin in Exeter attest to. Suburban areas were theoretically the least vulnerable because damage caused there was least likely to affect the warring party. But suburbs on the opposite side of the city from the direction of the bombers' approach were sometimes targeted to take advantage of the behavior of nervous flight crews who dropped bombs as soon as possible to escape enemy ground defences. If bombers were instructed to overshoot the city center, bombs dropped prematurely would still hit it. The swath of destruction below the flight path, called "creep back," could be as long as 30 miles (50 km.).[20] In masonry cities like Munich its pattern can still be discerned in the sudden interjection of monotonous blocks of 1950s apartments in an otherwise early 20th-century suburb. No such vestiges of this geography of urban annihilation remain visible in Japan. "The combustible nature of most buildings meant there were not even the ruined skeletons and rubble of a built-up area as in Europe; all that remained were great expanses of scorched, flattened wasteland scored by the trace of street patterns and a moonlike scatter of bomb craters."[21]

RECONSTRUCTION

To speak exclusively of "post-war" reconstruction is misleading on two counts. Firstly, the business of rebuilding could not wait for the end of hostilities. As soon as the bombs fell, streets had to be cleared of rubble, utility and water lines repaired, lightly damaged housing made habitable. Secondly, while the war was still on comprehensive planning for the period of peace was actively under way. On the German side many of these planners, people like Bernhardt Reichow and Konstanty Gutschow, made the passage to post-war practice without much trouble.

The first chapter of reconstruction, in Germany at least, was the period of the "politics of ruins."[22] Since there was no money to build, and no banks to extend loans, the main negotiable commodity for several years was rubble. "Rubble re-use organizations" were formed, and every city developed its own policies about the handling of rubble. At the same time thousands of "rubble ladies" swarmed over the ruins everywhere, providing free labor to property owners: they were the first heroic brigade of post-war reconstruction. The mayors were ultimately responsible for managing this gargantuan task; Adenauer was removed as mayor of Cologne in October 1945 for allegedly mismanaging rubble removal. The rubble was first piled into mountains; they survive, often hidden by lush park landscaping, as reminders of rubble politics—the popularly nicknamed Monte Klamott (Mount Trash) in Berlin, or Monte Sherblino (Mount Shards) at Birkenhof in Stuttgart. In Kassel, with the help of every citizen between the ages of sixteen and sixty, over 2 million cubic meters (2.6 million cu. yds.) of rubble was gathered and used to extend a cliff called Schöne Aussicht (Beautiful View). Mounds of debris deposited in a northern suburb of Munich are now much admired as the rolling, green site of the 1972 Olympics.

But the real purpose of rubble handling was salvage and re-use. The State often paid for the removal costs, but allowed no sale on the open market and no profitmaking. Nails, boards, bricks—everything possible to use as is would be singled out; the rest would be transformed into something usable. Enormous quantities of tile splinters, for example, were made into concrete additives. In this effort the line between rubble and ruins was a very fine one. Thousands of reparable buildings ended up in rubble heaps. "In Germany, more that was worth saving was destroyed after the war," President Scheel remarked in the European Year of Preservation, "than during the war."[23]

But true reconstruction began remarkably soon—as early as 1949. On both sides, there was some optimism that bombing would allow for the rational re-planning of the devastated cities. This is of course a common sentiment after disasters. Henry

260 "Rubble ladies" (Trümmerfrauen) cleaning the graffiti-ridden portico of the Reichstag in Berlin in August 1948, when the building was allocated to the city government.

Ward Beecher, preaching on the Sunday following the Chicago Fire of 1871, declared that Chicagoans had needed it "for their physical and moral regeneration."[24] And one remembers the Dutch architect and planner H. P. Berlage in 1919 writing of "Happy Belgium ... which is now the first country that will be able to put into practice the clear notion of building the modern town."[25] In fact, since Berlage's day we have become so obsessed by planning, and the functionalist approach of Modernist theory, that we have created what Hewitt calls "a geography of reconstruction."

From the Modernist point of view, the accretive cities of the industrial era were already hopelessly obsolete. The bombs were simply helping the process of converting Europe to a new urban order. Once again, this line of thinking was non-partisan. Both East and West believed in the necessity for decentralization, and in the creation of new infrastructures, including comprehensive systems of fast traffic arteries. For Germans especially, the official Nazi view of a dispersed settlement pattern, with the population tied to the soil, made the bombing of cities like Hamburg a prelude to the future metropolitan order. Indeed after the final devastation of that city in July 1943 the authorities planned to disperse the refugees in a huge area around Hamburg by way of a test case. The Modernist émigré Walter Gropius saw it that way when he returned to Germany from Harvard in 1947 as an American advisor on reconstruction. The high degree of destruction suffered by Germany made it, he said, "the best place to start breaking up cities into home towns and to establish the small-scale communities, in which the essential importance of the individual can be realized."[26] And Gropius was articulating not simply a German solution, but an international charter for the urban salvation of the West.

The replacement of destroyed old quarters with the Modernist canon is consistent and easy to read. The old spatial structure of streets and squares is ignored. In a loose planted space bounded by traffic arteries, housing slabs are arranged in a non-symmetrical pattern that often favors the diagonal. Strictly zoned as a residential sector, the plan does not admit of mixed uses except for a grudgingly inserted row of shops at pains not to appear integrated with the housing blocks. There is no compromise with history. Hansaviertel in West Berlin (1954ff.) at the edge of the Tiergarten typifies the new thinking. It was intended as the Modernist manifesto of the Fifties, in response to the traditionalist reconstruction of the war-ravaged cities adopted in Eastern Europe. *261– 263* *Pl.36*

The basis of the East German policy was a document called "Sixteen Principles of Urbanism," hammered out at the highest level, in consultation with the U.S.S.R., shortly after the division of Berlin in 1948–49. All the major premises of Modernist planning were systematically refuted. The notion of city form as a response to high-speed traffic was rejected, as was the strict separation of functions: residences, workplaces and cultural facilities must be integrated. Spatial enclosure of streets by a traditional block formation would be reasserted. In terms of style, historicism was declared the guiding principle—new building had to reflect, however superficially, its region's golden age: Gothic for Rostock, Baroque for Dresden, Classicism for Berlin. *Pl.35*

In reality this ideological confrontation between East and West obscured the similarities in reconstruction practice common to both sides of the Iron Curtain. The main spatial change was that the post-war arrangements allowed for much more open space, even when pre-war population densities remained unchanged. The answer of course was the general acceptance of monolithic apartment buildings as the norm for residential construction. Surviving fragments were often allowed their place, and helped to dramatize the change of urban scale.

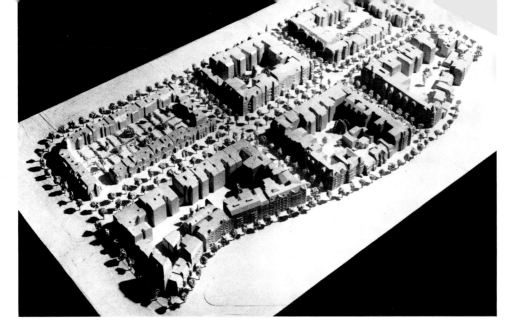

261–263 Reconstruction in Hamburg (Germany): an area of six city blocks in Grindelberg, a wealthy neighborhood near the center, as covered with apartment buildings before the war; as left in ruins after 1943; and as rebuilt for the occupying British forces to house their families. (The curved street in the foreground of the models lies on the far side in the aerial view.) The slabs were erected in 1946–56 by a large consortium of architects, including R. Lodders and F. Streb. The number of dwelling units was reduced by some 15 per cent.

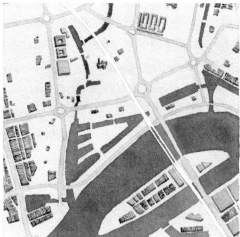
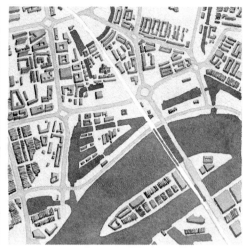

264–266 *The center of Rotterdam (Holland) before its destruction in 1940, in 1945, and ca. 1965. In the late 1930s the fabric was dense, crossed by a few through-streets, the railroad (shown in white), and canals, notably the Coolsingel (far left). The three large buildings near the top of the Coolsingel—the Town Hall, Stock Exchange and Post Office—will remain a constant through the ensuing transformations.*

By 1945 most of the buildings had been destroyed by bombing, and reconstruction had begun. The canals have been reduced in number and reconfigured (the Coolsingel has disappeared); there are new docks; a new overhead railroad; and new streets on a larger scale linked by roundabouts.

By ca. 1965 about 60 per cent of the area had been filled out. The new Lijnbaan development appears upper left, parallel to the road replacing the Coolsingel (cp. Ill. 243, where we are looking south from the major road at the top).

Modernist urban design orthodoxy, as codified in the Charter of Athens, did assert itself on rare occasions in totally destroyed city centers, but was most at home in the open city edge. The best example of a city reconstructed according to the Charter is Rotterdam. Even so, contradictions and compromises abound—and make for a more interesting cityscape. Coolsingel, the main pre-war shopping street, was retained along with the surviving Town Hall, Stock Exchange and Post Office. But it was turned into one of the main post-war traffic arteries, being denied a chance to create a symbolic core between the old periphery and the new Modernist center. Hoogstraat, also kept as a traditional shopping street, was flanked by a rather confused mix of building types.

In the center, bombed clean in a day, no equivocation was possible. A decision on how to reconstruct it had to be taken. The forbidding obstacles of property ownership were not an issue here. All of the area was acquired by compulsory purchase: it was a true *tabula rasa*, both physically and economically. Compensation was not paid immediately, but the sums were inscribed in the so-called Great Book of Reconstruction. Every landlord was to receive, after all the planning was complete, a new site of equivalent value but not necessarily in the same place. Preferences could be expressed, so that by 1945 the entire destroyed area had been assigned "building land reservations." Compensation for the bombed building would be made only after the landlord had invested an equal sum in the new construction.

The bombed area was eerily clean and framed by the familiar landmark strokes of the old townscape. A broad triangle which inscribed the old fortifications was bounded by the river Maas (Meuse) along the south. The railway coming from that direction traversed the center raised on a viaduct, and the main railway station was at the top of the triangle. One of the sides of the triangle included Coolsingel. The first impulse right after the blitz was to make sure that the principal elements of the old city were to be recognizable. The planner, Willem Gerrit Witteveen, claimed that "the original, totally naturally formed character of the old central city behind the dike with all its vital elements will be retained. It will merely be put into a framework which befits our time."

For all the plans and working drawings, there was no new construction until the end of the War. By then the conservative sentiment was pushed aside, and a new plan directed by C. van Traa dismissed the old street structure, laid down a broad supergrid, and prescribed a new scale for development within it. "The scale of the open space is based on the scale of the Maas," von Traa wrote. "The horizontal development of the center of Rotterdam has seen its end. The architectonic structure of Rotterdam will be vertical."

At first the "Free Space Atmosphere" managed to frighten small businesses enough so that they hesitated to build at all. The new scale called for large buildings, which meant substantial investment. Not surprisingly the banks took their place in the void, as did the Vroom en Dreesman department store. By 1950 a main shopping area began to take shape anchored on the old Lijnbaan, now given a Modernist veneer. Then, quite at random it would seem, construction spread out slowly over the vast open spaces—highrise housing slabs; a wholesalers' building near the station and a huge warehousing and distribution complex; and after 1960, a concert hall.

It is hard to know if Rotterdam center should be judged a success for the Modernists' program of reordering the post-war cities of Europe. We have little to compare it with. But it does point up the fact that Modernism is only at home on clean slate sites, and is unable to make common cause with the remnants of previous urban orders. Its organizing schemes are sweeping abstractions that set a crushing urban scale unworkable except for very large cities. None of this was helpful for the historic towns of Europe which needed a gentler and more intimate touch. So a pragmatic formula developed without much theorizing. In Germany the old city plans were saved, with some exceptional alterations for the sake of modern transportation. There was a clear difference between this *Altstadt* (old precinct), framed by a new ringroad, and the *Vorstadt* (suburbs) where scale and style were largely on their own.

On the issue of historicism, too, common sense prevailed. It was never a question of precise recreation of buildings that had vanished. What was prescribed for the *Altstadt* was rebuilding on a scale similar to that of the historic city. Details, proportions, bay systems, and materials were to harmonize. Most insistently, the old pitched roofscape and its characteristic cover of tiles were to be retained. Even Warsaw and Dresden, promoted as showcases of a more resolute attitude to bring back the historic landscape, were evocations rather than strict reconstructions of the historic urban landscape. There, as elsewhere, the scope was limited to single buildings or city fragments.

These historicist attitudes toward reconstruction began during the First World War. Belgian reconstruction was ordained by King Albert a year after the outbreak of hostilities. The nation committed itself to undertake the restoration of all war-damaged property. But actually there was no nationwide planning, and the upholding of pre-war ownership patterns made it practically impossible. State intervention remained limited to the public domain. And there the past was to be the model. It was not a question of literal recreation. This past was idealized, and became the acceptable taste. As the historian M. Smets put it, "The proposed images remained abstractions, which turned history into a model."[27]

It was the urban downtowns and the village centers, then too, that were so recreated as the most representative part of the historic environment. As one of the planners, J. Coomans, explained in relation to his plan of Ypres: "It is sufficient to determine the exterior view of the façade, without indicating the interior disposition of the buildings."[28] In these centers, matching private façades were strongly encouraged. It all represented, Smets concludes, the last phase of a long historical span when

267 Post-war rebuilding in the Altstadt *of Frankfurt-am-Main (Germany). The ground floors of the ancient "Salzhäuser" in the historic Römerberg survived; the new structures above have gabled roofs and surface decoration as a concession to their location. In the background is the Paulskirche, which as a monument was carefully restored. This view is taken from the street seen in Ill. 1: the modern sign "Zum Engel" marks the replacement of the famous late medieval house.*

society was depicted as a huge corporation driven by similar ideals. The reference to a medieval town is not fortuitous. It clearly reflects a social value. Workers and employers are supposed to be brought together by the homogeneity in style of their houses, while the conception of public space made the ideal of middle-class beauty accessible to everybody.[29]

These same beliefs motivated the historicist wave after the Second World War. In the reconstruction of the historic center of Warsaw, the new master plan intended to *268* resurrect the street pattern and the massing, or skyline, of the old city. Key reference documents included Bellotto's views of Warsaw painted for King Stanislas August *175* Poniatowski in 1767–80; inventory plans of historic monuments prepared before the war by the Polish architectural establishment; and old photographs. In addition, rubble was sifted to recover authentic fragments of historic buildings, which were used in the reconstruction. During the works, the medieval walls were discovered; green colors characteristic of the old town reappeared. The demands of modern traffic were met by moving some older buildings and by creating a tunnel near Castle Square to divert vehicles onto a new east-west artery.[30]

The Polish Communist government was conscious of the strong emotional ties of the inhabitants with their city when it vowed to reinstate Warsaw as capital and reconstruct it. As a prominent sociologist put it, "individual attachment to old forms is a factor of social unity."[31] But a policy of fastidious recreation of the old center—which was, after all, an artifact of the triumph of mercantile capitalism—presented certain ideological ambiguities. The solution (as in Gdańsk, where the *Pl.37* historic center was similarly recreated) was to reproduce historical façades while incorporating modern improvements credited to Socialist Realist planning. The

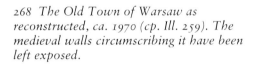

268 *The Old Town of Warsaw as reconstructed, ca. 1970 (cp. Ill. 259). The medieval walls circumscribing it have been left exposed.*

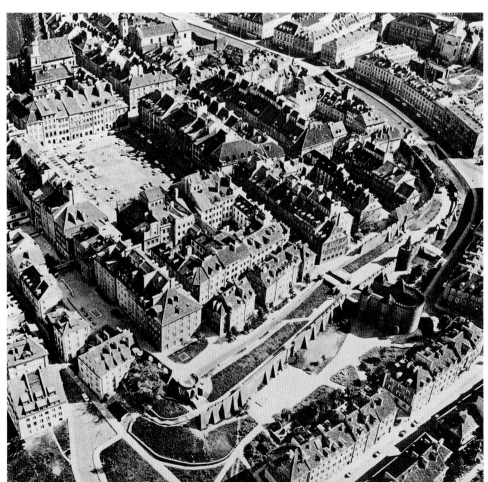

dense, built-out city fabric demolished during the war was replaced with a pattern of courtyard blocks. Public access to the mid-block parks was provided by leaving arbitrary gaps along the new street frontage. Historic buildings that survived or were resurrected were adapted to modern purposes. Noble palaces became ministries, public offices, and seats of social and cultural organizations; patrician rowhouses accommodated restaurants, shops and apartments. The cost of reconstruction was borne by the State, but also supplemented by voluntary contributions from all over Poland.

HAUSSMANNIZATION

Pl.34 Our theme shifts here from reconstruction as a response to wartime devastation to planned demolition for the purposes of urban renewal. The most famous exponent of massive urban surgery is Baron Haussmann, whose *grands travaux* redrew the plan of Paris between 1850 and 1870, providing a model for old cities everywhere anxious to meet the needs of modern traffic. These incisions were referred to, neutrally, as *percées* or cuts; the word *éventrement*, on the other hand, literally "disembowelling" or "eviscerating," suggested a surgical metaphor in line with seeing the city as subject to pathological disorders. This term precedes Haussmann; it belongs in the discourse of the Enlightenment. The Italian version is *sventramento*.

I am distinguishing this particular form of destruction from the punitive actions of war—although there is much that is punitive about demolition as a device of city-making. The Fascists openly used urban renewal to get even with their enemies in cities like Parma (where the populist quarter of Oltretorrente had stood up against them) and Socialist Bologna. In any case, expropriation is rarely welcomed by those who inhabit the condemned property, and it is always an arbitrary intervention performed coercively. Haussmannization is often synonymous with social engineering in that it relieves the cities of their populist ferment and isolates the possessing classes from the pressure of the poor and the unempowered.

Eminent domain—the power of condemnation and compulsory purchase—is legalized force. Its exercise justifies expropriation, and the central fact of expropriation, however scrupulous the procedure or fair the recompense, is coercion. Private property is commandeered against the wishes of its owner for some presumed public good. After the surgery, the redesigned urban land might be turned over or sold to a third party, and it is that developer, enterpreneur, or perhaps the city itself, who enjoys the benefits of the new arrangement, not the original property holder.

The overall benefits of Haussmannization, as the state repeatedly advertises, are supposed to be public health (tied to slum clearance and access to light and air), the smooth flow of traffic, the creation of modern housing and business premises, and social order. The French concern in this last regard was the thwarting of street barricades, whose origins are credited to 15th-century Paris.[32] Haussmann's success in dealing with this threat is obvious in that in the 1871 Commune uprising, revolutionary strongholds were in areas where there had been no *éventrements*—Montmartre, Belleville, Buttes-aux-Calles.[33] But note that Haussmann's interven-
38 tions and their consequent displacements "may have instigated as much social unrest as the plan was designed to suppress."[34]

Haussmann's Paris, with its broad, elegant boulevards and vistas artfully focused on monuments, also became a model for something else—for urban life as a work of

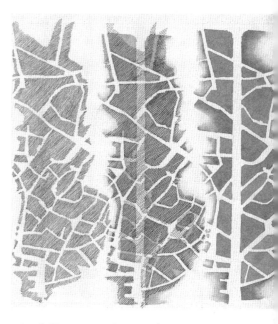

269 A *Haussmannian* percée *in Montpellier (France). Left,* the zone through which the Rue Foch was cut, after expropriations in 1862–63; right, the proposed new layout; center, the two superimposed, to show their relationship. One side of an existing open space, the square in front of the Palais de Justice (bottom), was used for the new connector.

270 *Paris, Place de l'Opéra, looking down the Boulevard des Capucines, ca. 1890. Here Haussmann's planning met the line of planted promenades laid out in the 17th century over obsolete fortifications (see p. 33). Until 1858, when work on the area of the new Opéra began, the north (right-hand) side of the boulevard was open. Houses lay in a parallel street further north, at a lower level, on the line of the old moat. All that disappeared under architecture of a special type designed for this newly created* place, *which cut the old boulevard in two. On the right is the Grand Hôtel of 1860, with the famous Café de la Paix on its ground floor.*

art, as esthetic experience, a public spectacle *sans pareil*. It is in fact evident that many of his emulators were less interested in the functional aspects of his program than in the urbanity and worldliness it conferred on their cities. What I am chiefly concerned with here is the legal and physical problems entailed by the simple notion of selective demolition in the name of progress.

PUBLIC UTILITY AND THE LAW

The legal presumption that running new streets or opening squares against the grain of the old streetscape is for the public good has a relatively short history. The violation of private property rights for the welfare of the community was always more clearly argued for public works like aqueducts and sewer lines than matters of planning in the abstract or concepts like circulation—or worse, "urban embellishment." In France's "Declaration of the Rights of Man" issued in 1789, Article 17 specified that "Property is an inviolable and sacred right; no one can be deprived of it unless a public necessity, legally established, requires it, and upon just previous compensation." The Law of 1841 which Haussmann inherited spoke of "grands travaux" (public works), and said that they were decreed by the legislature; "public necessity having been declared by the administrative power, the courts, after having ensured that the regulatory formalities were followed, order the expropriation of private property; the indemnity is fixed by a special jury." The law makes specific reference under *grands travaux* only to royal roads, canals, railroads,

271 *Philadelphia (Pennsylvania): Fairmount Parkway under construction in 1918, as seen from the City Hall tower. In the distance lies Fairmount Park, site of the new Art Museum. The Medico-Chirurgical Hospital is still standing in the way, but would soon be gone.*

reservoirs, and docks. Even when interpreted to include urban development, the enabling agency could only demolish property that fell within the lines of the proposed new street. Further legislation in 1850 relative to the clearing of insanitary housing paved the way for Haussmann's claim that the rehabilitation of entire blocks could be seen as a matter of public utility. A decree of March 1852 concerning the streets of Paris went further: it asserted for the first time that "In all expropriation projects for the widening, straightening or the formation of the streets of Paris, the administration will have the option to include the totality of the affected real estate, if it determines that the remaining fragments are not of an area that would permit the putting up of salubrious constructions."[35]

This legal sanction of the concept of excess condemnation went hand in hand with new associations of landowners, encouraged by Haussmann, which had the power to reconstruct a block or a section and impose a majority decision on members who held back. The French example led to similar expropriation laws in Belgium (1858, 1867); Italy's "Expropriation for Works in the Public Interest" (1865), which is mostly about legally binding master plans for the city form; and England's Housing of the Working Class Act of 1890 which permitted the expropriation of slum property in the interest of building healthy housing. But none enjoyed the generous provisions of excess condemnation which Haussmann secured for himself, and no city quite matched the scope and comprehensiveness of his *grands travaux*.

Haussmannization in this sense applies more to single projects, three or four incisions at most, than to anything approaching the rational citywide system of its namesake. His only match, in the scale of the undertakings and the logic of circulation that supported it, is New York's Robert Moses, the Haussmann of urban expressways (see below, p. 275), who was given to utterances like this to describe his work: "When you operate in an overbuilt metropolis, you have to hack your way with a meat axe."

Moses is of course the spectacular exception. His immense power, pieced together through the consolidation of a number of "authorities" he headed, was beyond review. In the United States as a rule the exercise of eminent domain for public works was strictly restrained by the courts, and expropriation for urban changes was almost never sanctioned. This lack of legal authority is what rendered the City Beautiful movement impotent.

Most of the great projects remained on paper, even when they scrupulously stayed clear of the private realm. A 1917 report notes that the previous decade's efforts to widen Chestnut Street in Philadelphia from 50 to 60 feet (15–18 m.) could take effect "only as rapidly as buildings abutting upon the street are rebuilt."[36] Another attempt at Haussmannization on the part of Philadelphia, this one having to do with the proposed new avenue that would link Fairmount Park with City Hall, was nearly *271* thwarted. This is what was extraordinary about the urban renewal program of the Fifties: the Federal Government itself was willing for the first time, as we shall see, to test its powers of eminent domain in city centers all over the country in the name of slum clearance.

THE TAKING OF PROPERTY

Before cities could install the laws in the modern period to let them exercise forced condemnation, they had ways of "persuading." Princely power, for one thing, often carried the day. We are told that when Henri IV set out to open a number of new streets in Paris ca. 1600, he was impatient with recalcitrant parties. The new Rue du Ponceau was going to go over an old drain; three property owners thought this would depreciate their property and terrified the neighborhood by chasing and killing the workers. The Prévôt (provost-marshal) arrived and strung up the miscreants—and was praised by the King. In another instance, when the Augustinians objected to the opening of the Rue Dauphine because it would go through their property, Henri gave them until the next day to comply. "If your wall is not down by then, I will myself arrive with a cannon to open the Rue Dauphine."[37] There is also a description of the opening of a new bazaar-street ordered by Timur in Samarkand, and entrusted to three of his architects who were told to speed things up. They began to pull down the houses in a great hurry, "and as the houses came down, their masters fled with their clothes and all they had: then, as the houses came down in front, the work went on behind."[38]

The opposite attitude is to go to great lengths to prove that private property is unassailable, and can be taken only with the free concurrence of its owner. Augustus, whose wishes on the matter would have gone unchallenged, put on a great show as the law-abiding magistrate of the old Republic in assembling the site for his Forum. He chose to reduce the size of the project and deform the plan, Suetonius *150* states (*Aug.* 56), because he did not wish to eject the owners of houses. And Cicero, who was the manager of land acquisition for Caesar's Forum, stressed the amount paid to owners, including some form of indemnity. Pliny notes that "Julius Caesar spent 100,000,000 sesterces simply for the site on which his forum was built."

The first Muslim rulers were very scrupulous. Saleh Ali Al-Hathloul cites the case of the second caliph, Umar, who wished to enlarge the Prophet's mosque at Medina, and bought the houses which were in the direction of the extension. One person refused to sell. Umar gave him three "options": sell for whatever price he wanted to name; have a new house built for him by the public treasury wherever he wished in Medina; donate the house to the community as charity for the extension of the mosque. The man would not budge. The two sides agreed to arbitration, which favored the man's position; Umar gave up the attempt to seize the man's house, and only then the man gave it to the community as a gift.[39]

On the issue of slum clearance, where derelict property was involved, Muslim jurists allowed municipal authorities to tear down the property if the owner would not or could not, and sell the rubble to provide the cost of labor. If the property was reparable, the proprietor might be forced to do so, or others would be allowed to rebuild and collect rent in the amount of the cost, after which the property reverted to its original owner.[40]

The most delicate transaction, even for uninhibited regimes, was the taking of devotional buildings and places. This seemed to test the limits of imperial power in ancient Rome. Caesar had an early brush with the issue of desecration. "Caesar took the blame," Dio Cassius writes, "for tearing down the houses and the temples [in the area of the Theater of Marcellus] and also for burning the images." His defense could only be that he held at the time the office of *pontifex maximus*, or high priest, who alone could authorize changes in religious property. Temples and cemeteries could not in any case be demolished outright, but had to undergo ritual burial (*congestio terrarum*). The disturbance of the dead was considered especially heinous, and the desecration of tombs or cemeteries was no light matter. Constantine the Great was accused of *violatio sepulchri*, a serious offense which amounted to sacrilege, in building Old St. Peter's over the Vatican cemetery. In fact, most of the Roman tomb buildings had their upper portions demolished and then filled with earth without being disturbed, as the laws of ritual burial specified.

In Roman cities cemeteries could only be located outside the city limits, but of course they were in the way of future development. When burial was distributed throughout the city, conflicts were frequent. In the modern period urban renewal often entailed building over burial grounds or relocating them, both alternatives vehemently resisted by the religious authorities and the families of the deceased. In Muslim countries projects of this sort were likely to earn their authors, however high in rank, the stigma of being an enemy of the faith. When Grand Vizier Fuat Pasha condoned a plan for a section of Istanbul that included burials in the gardens of mosques, he was accused of being "Frenkperes"—"Westernized," or, more broadly, an offender of Muslim values. His response was feeble: the new work when finished, he said lamely, was bound to please the souls of the dead.[41]

Once property was legally condemned, it had to be demolished and disposed of, clearing the space for the new street. A word about methods of demolition. Until fairly recently, the work was done with long picks, shovels, and small carts. It is 273 curious to see in photographs and prints of demolition sites at the time of Haussmann this intensive and time-consuming hand labor, and a caricature of him as "artist démolisseur" shows him wielding a pick and a trowel. Fascist oratory and literature is full of references to the "piccone risanatore" (the healing pick), the reference of course being to slum clearance as a program of public health; and once, in a speech delivered in March 1932, Mussolini spoke lovingly of "his majesty the pick." The Duce liked to show up in condemned neighborhoods, climb up to a 272 rooftop, and give a speech to inaugurate the work of demolition ending with a

272 Mussolini with his "piccone" helps in the work of widening the Via dei Sediari in Rome, 1936. Photographers are on hand to record the event. Such images (often photomontages) were widely published to show the Duce's enthusiasm for reinvigorating the city.

273 *Demolition and clearing by hand in Paris, ca. 1857. Old theatres in the Boulevard du Temple make way for Haussmann's new strategic Boulevard du Prince Eugène (now Boulevard Voltaire).*

rousing "ed ora la parola al piccone" (and now let the pick have its say). A company in Bay City, Michigan, is credited with having built the wrecking crane in 1883. Then in the late 1950s dynamite became increasingly acceptable. An early experiment *97* showed that it took only seventeen seconds to demolish two apartment buildings, "at about two-thirds the cost of conventional demolition."[42] By then of course steam shovels, earth removers and other such inventions had vastly speeded up the task of clearing rubble.

The traditional hand labor of demolition sites, conjuring a penal, almost Sisyphian aura, was perfectly appropriate to the aims of Haussmannization. These urban interventions were always justified as public works programs providing employment to thousands. To aspire to go faster would have been counterproductive. And then there was the matter of salvage. Building materials from the condemned property were meant to be re-used. The slower and more primitive the methods of demolition, the more likely that these materials would be preserved intact. Once again in the pictures one notices the care with which roof tiles are stacked, large boards are carried away to piles at the edges of the site, and bricks and stone are cleaned of mortar and carried away on wheelbarrows. Haussmann's demolitions provided material to rebuild the older parts of town. As Loyer puts it, "half of Paris was torn down and used to build the other half."[43]

The alternative was to have the rubble hauled away or disposed of in some way. Roman antiquity favored its use as ship's ballast, but it was of course preferable to find a closer dumping site. The rubble of demolished houses that made room for the Baths of Caracalla was packed into an artificial platform for the monument. The surplus helped cover a cemetery that extended northward between the Via Appia and the Aventine, thus ritually preparing the area for future development. Trajan had done the same a century earlier when he used a graveyard for military men near his Forum as a convenient dumping ground. In the 19th century, debris found a home in railway work. That is where much from the huge site of the Law Courts in London ended up.

THE LIMITS OF HAUSSMANNIZATION

Haussmannization is recurrent at various stages of history. These stages, not surprisingly, correspond with the main episodes of the Grand Manner as I have described them in *The City Shaped*. Thus one of the earliest interventions of this sort was the Roman colonnaded avenue that was run through the length of town in the old cities of the Empire in the East. In Damascus, for example, the new avenue was only a matter of a public front, behind which lay fragments of older buildings dismembered by the inflexible, wide straight line of the cut. In Rome itself, excavations have revealed traces of the fine-grained tissue that was displaced over a period of more than one hundred years for the great complex of the imperial forums. *150* An estimated 3,500 people were made homeless during this vast operation. There is no record that the State made any provision for them, an attitude of non-caring that will become the rule of universal Haussmannization.

The Renaissance and Baroque periods, by and large, avoided destruction, and chose to run modern quarters outside the old fabric. That is why famous cases of Haussmannization like the Via Giulia in Rome and Via Maqueda in Palermo *115* remained modest and exceptional. Napoleon the Great was the first man of power who was willing to countenance radical destruction in the historic cores of the cities of his empire, at least if we are to judge from the hundreds of extravagant projects that were brought to his attention. Napoleon III and in this century Mussolini had the courage, one must grudgingly allow, to go ahead with these grandiloquent visions.

There are degrees between incremental change on the one hand and total Haussmannization on the other. The use of extant "organic" streets as the basis for an imposed formal order is known from instances as farflung as Megara Hyblaea in Sicily, Lorient in Brittany, and 19th-century Sofia in Bulgaria.

Megara, founded according to tradition in 753 BC, did not get its formal layout until the second half of the 7th century BC. As all of the 8th-century houses and the agora line up with the later formal street network, it can be said either that that formal order was prefigured in the 8th-century streets, or that the later streets respected where the early houses were. Since the later grid is not exactly uniform in the agora area, where the early houses were excavated, the latter method may well be the case.[44] Lorient was somewhat similar. It had started as a temporary naval base, and its housing had sprung up spontaneously. The streets the homeowners had inadvertently created were used in a formal plan drawn up by an engineer named Langlade in 1707.[45]

In Roman imperial projects of urban renewal portions of the pre-existing structures, if particularly solid and correctly aligned with the new construction, were routinely incorporated. In the Basilica of Constantine, for example, the walls of an earlier complex of warehouses and shops were re-used as foundations, and in fact predetermined the three-bay division of the Basilica.

274 The practice of slicing off buildings on only one side of a street to be widened was favored as conservative and frugal by Haussmann's predecessor as prefect in Paris, the Comte de Rambuteau. Actually the principle he followed was even older; civil engineers had been using it for about a century for straightening streets. What is involved is that you move back the official building line, in order to straighten or widen a street, and then each time a building on the street is demolished, it has to be replaced by one set on the new building line. Now, of course, buildings being rather long-lived creatures, the process moved very slowly, and for years the street wall remained jagged.

269 In the Rue Rambuteau, a new street in the Halles district, several more expeditious measures were followed: one side of the street would be destroyed and pushed back, instead of both; bits of new roadway would be run through the gardens of the old mansions and monasteries, to minimize destruction; short extant streets coinciding with the new route would be incorporated. But if you were too conservative, you got only small buildings to camouflage the scar, "often little more than closets".[46] Cities then had the thankless task of conducting negotiations to convince owners of fragments left by the new roadway to consolidate their holdings in order to build blocks that were *decorosi*. That is what the current term was in Italy, or at least in Rome, after 1870 capital of the Kingdom of Italy, where a fair amount of Haussmannization was rather gingerly put through. The term abandoned the standard cant that used medical analogies like "urban surgery," and acknowledged the esthetic motivation of the works.

Rome, additionally, had a dense concentration of Renaissance and Baroque monuments precisely in that quarter within the bend of the Tiber where a major artery had to be carved to make access to the Borgo and the Vatican easier. To save as much as possible and exhibit it, the path of the new artery, the Corso Vittorio

276 Emanuele, had to waver, keeping close to the old processional line of the Via Papale, while trying all along to maintain the set width of 20 meters (65 ft.). The monuments

275 found themselves in strange situations. The Palazzo della Cancelleria exposed its hitherto concealed long flank toward the Corso, lessening the importance of its

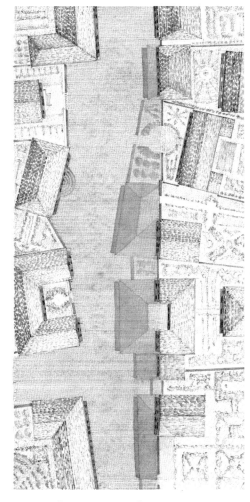

274 *Widening a street by partial demolition of one side. This is the principle often used for the Corso Vittorio Emanuele in Rome* (opposite); *a courtyard may become part of a new façade.*

275 right *Rome, Corso Vittorio Emanuele, looking from the Piazza S. Pantaleo toward the Cancelleria. (In the map below, this is the area at the top just left of center: the Cancelleria, with two colonnaded inner spaces, faced a long square to the left and had a narrow street at its side.) At the left is the Piccola Farnesina, a palace which was mutilated by the new road, leaving its courtyard elevation as part of a pastiche High Renaissance façade.*

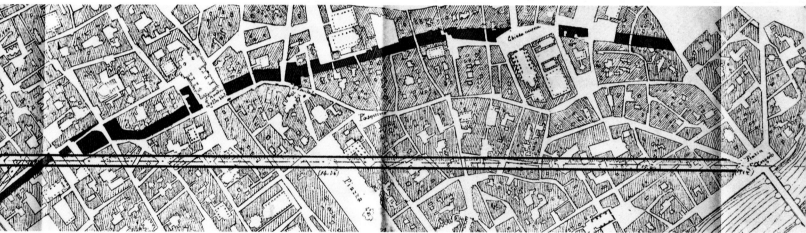

276 above *Rome, alternative routes for the new Corso Vittorio Emanuele, 1881. The map is oriented with southwest at the top. Ponte S. Angelo leading across to the Borgo appears bottom right, the Gesù bottom left. The line of the artery as planned in 1873 and implemented after 1880 is shown in black. From the Gesù to Piazza S. Pantaleo (left of center) it followed the Via Papale; after that it often cut through blocks. Goffredo Narducci proposed instead a straight east–west street between the Campidoglio and the bridge.*

original façade on the Piazza della Cancelleria. Some palaces, having lost their original façade to partial demolition, were given new façades which repeated the formula of the flanks or even of the courtyard (Palazzo Regis or Piccola Farnesina), 275 or else adopted a free interpretation of Renaissance motifs (as with Pio Piacentini's remodeling of the Palazzo Sforza-Cesarini). What is more, the modern buildings played with some of these same motifs, blurring the distinction between old and new, and with their uniform scale canceled any particular dominance the historic buildings originally might have had in their visually subordinate neighborhoods.

HAUSSMANN OUTSIDE EUROPE

That Europe would be swept by the excitement of Second Empire Paris goes without saying. French provincial capitals like Montpellier were first in line—and then the rest of the Continent. Hundreds of seemingly interchangeable plans with sharp straight lines drawn over the twisted streetscapes of history were produced by the civil engineering departments of city halls without so much as the bother of a contour map. But they were of course hardly interchangeable. The lines cut through physical tangles that represented centuries of ownership and often painstaking appropriation of a piece of the urban artifact. The draftsman's straight lines meant destruction of serviceable building stock—and of something even more valuable, the social weave of entire communities.

The influence of Paris on the Muslim world went along with the general Francophile mood on the part of nations that had begun to feel left behind and were making efforts to catch up. A culture that knew no municipal planning as such, and did not even have a municipal government structure until the 19th century, caught the fever as part of its Westernization movement. One of the first conflicts came when this culture which gave no strong primacy to street façades but internalized the architectural experience had to accept a formal curtain of some sort on either side of its broad new avenues, with continuous frontages and houses that faced the street.[47]

In the Mediterranean, Haussmannization took two different forms: what the colonial powers did to Islamic cities, and what Muslims inflicted on themselves. In the French North African colonies in the late 19th century, an initial faith in coexistence brought the army engineers into the medinas to rend asunder what seemed magically, emblematically interlocked. The more enlightened colonial administration of General Lyautey a generation later would lament the physical and social ravage, as he in his turn laid down a program of separate cultures/separate environments, with the medinas "safe" for the indigenous population, and adjacent districts for colonists on the other side of a broad *cordon sanitaire* (see "Urban Divisions," above, pp. 111–12).

Self-inflicted Haussmannization found an early victim in Egypt. In the Exposition Universelle of 1867 in Paris, the "Haussmannized" city was introduced to the world, and one impressed visitor was the Khedive Ismail, who toured the city with the Baron as his guide. Ismail hired a French architect who had had a hand at the planning of the Fair, and in two furious years, in time for the opening of the Suez canal, Cairo was given a Western facelift. Actually, this was less a case of *éventrements* and *percées* within the old city: it consisted rather in the laying out of a vast new quarter, Ismailiyah; extending the newer business center at Azbakiyah and giving it an opera house and a French park on the filled lake; and landscaping roads that led from Cairo to the pyramids.

The same is true of Teheran in the 1870s under Nasr-ed-Din Shah. He had been to Paris and loved it. Upon his return he had the old walls of the city pulled down, and a new set erected further out on the plain, more than doubling the urban area. Between the two walls a new "European" quarter was planned, complete with French-style parks. On the western half was a huge square, an embassy row, and a promenade, Lalehzar Street.[48]

More to the point is Mithat Pasha's work in Ottoman Sofia in the 1860s which defined the five radial streets within the town that started the highways linking Sofia with Istanbul, Kyustendil, Belgrade, Lom and Ruse. He widened two streets whose intersection had been the center of town since Roman times. The destruction was considerable, but the episode has not yet been studied.

Haussmann's influence reasserted itself in the 1920s and '30s. The Frenchman could have had no more enthusiastic disciple than Benito Mussolini. In the Muslim world, Reza Shah's Iran in the 1930s, Beirut, and Kuwait in the 1950s bring

277 *Mashhad (Iran), detail showing the traditional Islamic street pattern cut through by straight avenues and roundabouts.*

Haussmann into the 20th century. In Kuwait the old city was virtually destroyed, and wide streets introduced. Beirut was equally ruthless; there too "a relatively insignificant, although extremely old, historic centre was ruthlessly converted and modernized."[49]

Reza Shah (1925–41) attempted to modernize major cities by driving a network of long straight roads (or *khiabans*) through the heart of the urban fabric, and *Pl.25* articulating crossroads with large roundabouts where he set up statues of himself. This new option led to many commercial activities moving out of the old city. Two intersecting main axes were cut through Teheran, and there were similar *percées* in Isfahan, Mashhad and Yazd, as well as attempts to isolate mosques and shrines. *277*

We have a related example in Baghdad, since 1921 capital of Iraq, in the 100-foot (30-m.) wide al-Keefah Street leading to the Al-Gaylani shrine. More recently Saudi Arabia, and from another political sphere the Rumania of the infamous Ceaucescu, should remind us that Haussmannization will always appeal to regimes that have power and money, or are willing to pawn the future of their nation for the obliteration of indigenous environments and the announcement of the coming Western "progress."

The case of Robert Moses, spectacular and hubristic, is germane to our interests here for the later part of his career as New York City's planner. In his brilliant early years, he was engaged with beaches, parks and expressways rather than the city proper; but when he undertook the Cross-Bronx Expressway, cutting through the borough's center, he condoned destruction at a malicious pace and scale. After his steam shovels and bulldozers had done their work, pounding at the old neighborhoods and streets for ten years in the late 1950s and early '60s, the Expressway was installed but the Bronx was doomed. With its thousands of abandoned buildings and roving gangs, the borough became the symbol of all urban ills. Yet Moses found plenty of admirers, and Sigfried Giedion, who thought Moses had the "energy and enthusiasm of a Haussmann," anointed him as the father of the city of the future, the city of parkways—the first planner to understand the new "space-time continuum" in which old streets and neighborhoods were supremely irrelevant.[50] Haussmannization, which assigned itself the task of modernizing the city, now was given license to replace it altogether in what we might want to see, in our own context, as "terminal process."

URBAN RENEWAL WESTERN STYLE

"Urban renewal" now has a grim sound to it; we think of the rape of Bath, the *284,* quintessential setting of Georgian urbanity, of Metz, where a destroyed quarter *285* had houses going back to the 13th century (one critic called it "Haussmannisme attardé");[51] we think of dozens of American cities gutted needlessly in the name of slum clearance, and left with huge barren parking lots, a glitzy shopping center, or highrise redevelopment projects for blacks, unlandscaped and instantly menacing, which doom the city centers to genuine decay.

But at the time this was the new gospel of salvation. There were even those who saw the slum clearance and urban renewal activity in the United States as the equivalent of war reconstruction. Urban blight worked slower, but the net result was the same as the damage of bombs. "This is blight," a brochure of the National Real Estate Board explained,

> This is what blight does. . . . The blockbusters going off in our cities . . . disintegrate slowly in the space of years, and generate decay and rot around them . . . But every disintegrating building . . . is just as truly a blockbuster as a four

thousand pound bomb that tumbles from a four-engined bomber. The effect is exactly the same.[52]

The turning point in America was the Housing Act of 1949, and its amended version of 1954, which saw the Federal Government for the first time energetically exercise eminent domain for massive slum clearance projects in the downtowns. The way it worked was that the city in question would buy the slum land, and the federal Urban Renewal Administration would absorb two-thirds of any loss incurred by the city in the reselling transaction. Typically the land would be completely cleared of structures before it was resold or leased to a local redevelopment agency for an approved project, which need be nothing more than a hospital extension.

Urban renewal was supposed to free the cities "enslaved to the 20- to 25-foot [6–7.6-m.] lot; to enlarge the street system; and to run highways into the CBD [central business district]."[53] It was the perfect vehicle through which to install the Modernist city in American downtowns. Auto commuting, along with vigorous lobbying by a growing highway construction industry, had put enormous pressure on city administrators to plow high-speed expressways into the heart of the metropolis. Urban renewal removed the last impediment for city centers to be tailored to the needs of automotive transit.

278 Brooklyn (New York), Farragut Houses public housing scheme under construction, 1950. The asterisk-shaped towers were spaced at random on land cleared of all pre-existing buildings, and unrelated to the surviving context. Typically for New York State projects in the 1950s, they covered a very small proportion (13.9 per cent) of the site.

279, 280 *The 19th-century American grid transformed by urban renewal. The original big blocks are bordered by numerous individual structures; in the mid-block alleys, garages, sheds or small houses have been set up. With urban renewal, sites are wiped clean and the scale radically changed, as small units are replaced by large monolithic structures (including parking garages) and open spaces.*

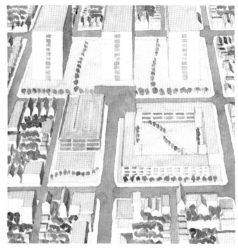

281–283 *The American grid transformed into automobile territory. The blocks are gradually thinned out to provide parking lots, punctuated by fragments of the old structures and widely-spaced new skyscrapers. The diagonally-placed building upper left in the last image is a drive-in bank.*

The long-term erosion of built-up areas through their conversion into "auto- *281–* mobile territory"—land dedicated to the movement, storage, and servicing of *283* cars—has been studied in the U.S. by urban geographer Ronald Horvath. In an initial phase of urban land development, that of low-density districts of single-family residences, streets, driveways, and garages typically occupied 25 per cent of the overall area. As these neighborhoods are redeveloped at increasing densities autos demand an ever greater proportion of the ground surface, and are given it by zoning regulations. The higher-density residential areas in Horvath's study devoted about 50 per cent of the ground to parking and circulation.[54] Urban renewal's remorseless demolitions in the central business district, the oldest precinct in most cities, sacrificed as much as 70 per cent of the surface area to automobile territory. In Detroit, Houston, and Los Angeles, among other American cities, swaths of *Pl.39* centrally located real estate were transformed into asphalt plains: a holding pattern for properties awaiting highrise development. It was Modernist urbanism, but not of the sort envisaged by Le Corbusier. His iconic *ville verte*, a vision of towers in a park, became in America a *ville grise* of towers in a parking lot.

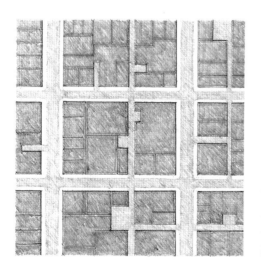

In Europe too we find the same pattern of condemning downtown blocks as insanitary and beyond repair, and replacing them with what the French called *centres directionnels*—administrative and private offices, with shopping arcades and luxury apartments. *The Rape of Britain* by Colin Amery and Dan Cruickshank records the story there. It is a passionate indictment of urban renewal through a detailed inventory of thirty towns that suffered its ravages, from Aberdeen to Wisbech—towns that "have lost their old hearts and received in return transplants of vacuity."

284, 285 The "sack of Bath" is particularly heartrending because much of the ravage was not at all necessary. There was no pressing need for housing or redevelopment, and the volume of traffic hardly overwhelmed the historic town. An ambitious corporation anxious to escape the 18th century found in the grading system of historic buildings as first established in an Act of 1947 license to destroy row upon row of artisan cottages for dubious replacements. Areas of town, southwestern Bath for example, were cut off from the cohesive fabric of the historic city and isolated. Almost no attempt was made to integrate the new buildings with the old.[55]

Finland was not exempt. Nearly all of its old gridded towns received so-called carpet plats, i.e., a completely new plat was superimposed on the wooden city, requiring the demolition of the town and its replacement with apartment buildings and open blocks. Most of the middle-sized towns—Turku, Hameenlinna, Jyväskylä, Kuopio, Oulu—lost the last phase of their historic past to urban renewal. Only in some small coastal towns, renewal did not get started promptly, and by 1970

306 sentiment had shifted toward preservation, defended now on the basis of economic factors, not history alone.[56]

In France the "Loi Malraux" of 1962 established the concept of the *secteur sauvegardé* with the aim of preserving the historic cores from the onslaught of urban renewal. The law was the forerunner of England's Civic Amenities Act of 1967

Comprehensive redevelopment in Bath, England:

284 above left Ballance Street, one of several rows of artisan houses built in the 1770s west of the Circus.

285 above The area in 1972. Portland Place, on the left, survived because it was listed Grade I. The new apartment blocks have the mansard roofs deemed appropriate for historic areas by Bath City Council.

which spawned the notion of "conservation areas." And in America the National Historic Preservation Act of 1966 espoused similar conservative policies, with the Federal Government conceding that an alternative to slum clearance was rehabilitation. In West Berlin, it was disgust with American style urban renewal and urban freeways that led in the 1980s to policies of *Stadtneuerung* and *Reparatur*— incremental repairs of the old building stock.

In fact the most tangible result of this change of heart on either side of the Atlantic was a phenomenon the British named "gentrification." A private process of rehabilitating rundown property, this constitutes a middle-class invasion of lower income districts by students, artists and design professionals, typically single people or couples without children, who want to live in interesting mixed neighborhoods. London's Islington has felt its impact, as have Trastevere in Rome and some frayed *286* working-class areas at the edges of American downtowns which would once, not so long ago, have been targets of slum clearance. Traditionally the well-off sought respite from the center by moving outward and creating new neighborhoods for themselves; those less affluent moved and colonized their houses. Now the prodigal sons return to repossess the houses they abandoned and take their place once again in the center.

286 Gentrification in London, 1970. Cloudesley Square, Islington, started life in the early 19th century as a comfortable middle-class area. Fashionable London moved west, and it went down in the world until the trend was reversed in the 1960s.

INCREMENTAL CHANGES

With the invasions of gentrifiers we enter our third and final theme. Haussmannization and urban renewal, not to mention disasters and wars, are in a way disruptions of urban process—if in the fundamental sense we define the term to mean the daily shifts and changes in the urban fabric that know no beginning and no end. These are likely to be to a large degree autonomous acts—that is, not subject to formal city-planning devices, although they may be reined in by building ordinances; and they take a long time, sometimes decades or even centuries, to have a visible effect on the city form. There has always been a prejudice against this natural way cities have of adjusting to circumstance, because the net result is often untidy, even anarchic.

THE "MEDIEVALIZING" OF ROME

This prejudice shows in a famous example—the treatment of "medieval Rome."[57] Shabby and unglamorous, it has always been contrasted unfavorably with the Rome of the emperors, a city of heroic monumentality and formal adherence to Classical *150* group design at least in the non-residential area of the Campo Marzio; and we talk of the "recovery" of imperial Rome by the Renaissance in a surge of enlightened humanism. This melodramatic myth has long deprived us of a tremendous story of conservative urban process.

First of all, the term "medieval Rome" designates one thousand years in the city's history, from the slow disintegration of the Empire beginning in the 4th century to the return of the popes from their self-imposed "Babylonian captivity" in Avignon in the 14th century. Now medieval Rome in the 6th century was doubtless very different from medieval Rome in the 8th, 10th or 14th century. There were surges of rallying along the way, and reverses; the pace and nature of physical readjustment varied according to events and the rhythms of a one-time world capital determined to survive under reduced circumstances; and this readjustment was, therefore, an on-going and profoundly conservative act of becoming—moving in erratic, unpredictable stages from the megalopolis of the Mediterranean to the Seat of Peter.

This long passage entailed a loss of population from close to 1,000,000 people in the 2nd century to an average in the Middle Ages of 50,000 to 100,000. It entailed a cultural revolution, set in motion by the Emperor Constantine the Great when he adopted the periodically persecuted Christianity as a State religion in the early 4th century. His baptism meant that the great artifacts of imperial bounty—the lavish baths and theaters and amphitheaters through which the State assuaged and pampered an unproductive, idle, restless citizenry—were rendered extinct like species of mastodons. For one thing, the new religion did not tolerate the sometimes lewd and bloody rituals that were staged in these buildings for the masses. For another, with the all-powerful government and its huge resources on the wane, this massive stone landscape could not physically be maintained, even were its rituals to be allowed to continue.

But unlike mastodons, amphitheaters and baths do not disappear or their corpses decay with obliging dispatch. They have to be dealt with through a minimum of effort, and to the extent possible made to serve new contingencies. Building materials would be re-used; exterior arcades turned into shops and squatter settlements; collapsed sections would be accepted as the new ground level and built upon. Those buildings that were not central to the new urban topography (the Baths of Diocletian, for example) would be abandoned, or taken over by fringe-belt activities like monasteries.

None of this was likely to happen as long as there was an active city administration, and the enforceable presumption of public ownership of monuments. For medieval Rome the critical centuries were probably the 6th and 7th. With the final retirement of the imperial presence even in its late Byzantine guise, and the near-disappearance of the *praefectura urbana*, the municipal offices that had final responsibility for services and public monuments, the citizenry were more or less free to turn into scavengers, or else, put in terms of my own bias, to start the redesign of their city until the authority of the Bishop of Rome was able to assert itself in civic matters.

URBAN PROCESS

In cities only change endures. Patterns of habitation are provisional, transformed by the ebb and swell of residency and subject to forces that work with the sluggishness of the millennial erosion of stone, or with the speed of a stray spark. The spatial order cast by houses, monuments, and solid city walls is gradually subverted by generations of seemingly innocuous tinkering, as in the case of Rome, or is deliberately revamped through massive interventions, like those of Haussmann's Paris. In recent times, modern warfare's generous capacity to destroy has been seized as an opportunity to experiment with the latest trends in urban design: lacking a war, mass demolitions can be legislated to similar ends. Even towns in which history is preserved in brick and mortar are the products of urban process, here made self-conscious and painstakingly negotiated.

Pl. 31 Oulu was destroyed by fire in 1822, a common fate for the wooden towns of Finland. Even the stone church, left, was scorched; Jakob Wallin's watercolor shows inhabitants piling their belongings by the shore, as their houses are reduced to a forest of brick chimneystacks. Subsequently the town was rebuilt on a new square-gridded plan.

Pl. 32 The 1889 flood that destroyed Johnstown (Pennsylvania) was the most devastating in American history. Over two thousand people died when a vast earthen dam burst and swept away houses, factories, church, and railroad. Much of the debris stuck on a great stone bridge, exploded, and burned. Seven months later Johnstown was restarted with a new charter.

Pl. 33 After the fall of the Empire, Rome gradually decayed. Citizens squatted in and around the ruins, in small single-family houses, burrowing in and recycling what they found. William Pars's view of the western end of the Forum, painted c. 1778–80, shows the platform and portico of the Temple of Saturn (left of center) encrusted with dwellings, and laundry drying above the site of its lofty flight of steps. On the extreme right, a ramp leads up to the Campidoglio, past structures built over the Tabularium. The Arch of Septimius Severus, deep in rubbish and debris, had been transformed in the Middle Ages into a fort; thanks to the conservative "medievalizing" of Rome, it survived 1,600 years, to be excavated and restored in 1803.

Pl. 34 opposite *Change both incremental and violent is recorded in Adolf Menzel's 1869 view of Paris. Old buildings have been heightened; a new stone-faced block in a more elaborate style stands on the corner. To the left, drastic change is under way. The scene is thought to be near the Opéra, an area that was radically remodeled under Haussmann.*

How to rebuild after the Second World War?

Pl. 35 *The Stalinallee (1952–60) was the showpiece of Communist East Berlin, part of a scheme to plant huge residential blocks with social amenities in the city center. Their material is stone, the style an abstract classicism deemed to be native to Berlin; in a traditional manner they follow the street (later renamed Karl-Marx-Allee).*

Pl. 36 *The Hansaviertel in West Berlin was rebuilt from 1954 as skyscrapers in a park, following pre-war avant-garde housing ideals, and, above all, reacting against the Neoclassicism of the Reich and the Socialist Realism of East Berlin. Planners were Kreuer Jobst and Schiesser.*

Pl. 37 *Gdańsk (Poland) chose like Warsaw to recreate its historic center. The restorers worked with immense care, drawing on photographs and architectural pattern-books, and re-using salvaged materials. New ideas about housing, however, made them thin out the fabric and introduce garden courts. Across the river, the old patterns were completely abandoned.*

Pl. 38 Early evening on deserted Brush Street in downtown Detroit, Michigan, 1990. Since the riots of 1967, the once-prosperous city has lost almost half of its population, as those who could afford to fled to the suburbs. The center has become a wasteland. Each year around Devil's Night (30 October), inner-city dwellers take to the streets and set fire to abandoned buildings. It seems an ironic twist on the "slash and burn" urban renewal by city governments in the 1950s and '60s.

Pl. 39 Houston, Texas, has come to represent the automobile-oriented city in its purest form. With a vast growth in area and a steady increase in automobile commuting to ever-higher office buildings (95% of Houstonians depend on cars for all their transportation), up to 70% of the central business district is now taken up by roadways and parking. The lots also form a holding pattern for properties awaiting development.

Pl. 40 Process manipulated. After a major earthquake in 1925, Santa Barbara (California) decided to enforce strict controls on the style of buildings, landscaping, and street furniture in the old center and on the ocean front, in an attempt to create a tidy townscape with a sense of local identity. A theme was consciously chosen: "New Spain in America." The County Courthouse of 1929, by the W. Mooser Company, is a landmark of the "Pueblo Viejo Historic District." In the city's design guidelines it is described as "graceful, sensitively sited and impressively landscaped," and praised for its "consistency" in massing and details. In the background several recent apartment complexes can be seen emulating its Spanish/Moorish character.

How was this freedom exercised? How does a city of the size and splendor of imperial Rome disintegrate; and how is it recast as a new city for a different culture and a different set of circumstances? The first half of the process—and the two halves were of course continually intertwined—advanced sporadically, and slowly. Emily Dickinson said it best:

> Ruin is formal, devil's work,
> Consecutive and slow—
> Fail in an instant no man did,
> Slipping is crash's law.

The monuments themselves, built of brick-faced concrete cured into monolithic shells, proved virtually indestructible when abandoned after an initial pillaging. This is why we still have major portions of the Baths of Caracalla and Diocletian and the so-called Temple of Minerva Medica (actually a kiosk in the Licinian Gardens). Once the marble facing and roof tiles were stripped, the structure was exposed to the elements. Vegetation and even trees sprouted in the cracks of the concrete vaults, which were thereby weakened and collapsed in segments, bringing down bits of the walls with them. Rubble filled the rooms and halted further collapse. Other monuments, the Theater of Marcellus for example, were preserved because strong *245* lords took possession of them as family forts. Still others were cut down to size, fragmented, miniaturized, and used up by squatters.

The main shift in residential terms was from the apartment blocks of the eastern valleys and hill slopes to the flat land within the Tiber bend, the Campo Marzio, *4* which had been the region of public monuments and entertainment in the imperial city. This shift had to do in part with the failure of the Roman aqueducts, except for the Aqua Vergine which served the Campo Marzio, the Appia which for a time kept the papal quarter of the Lateran going, and the Traiana on the right bank which fed *287* the Vatican. The presence of the Vergine and the river itself, and the religious magnet of the Vatican just across the river, sufficed to pull the population in this direction.

So a two-sided process was set under way. People began to leave the dense landscape of seven- or eight-story tenement houses or *insulae* (40,000 of them according to the sources), until there must have come a time when the old neighborhoods looked like the South Bronx or Detroit today. Upon descending into the Campo Marzio the people squeezed into the cracks between the great stone monuments or squatted inside and around those that seemed unattended. The small *Pl.33* numbers, and the self-centered concern for one's own family, produced a residential fabric of small single-family houses, no longer oriented toward the public spaces of streets and squares. These houses took their shape from that of their neighbors, and changed constantly as additions were made and contiguous structures bought and incorporated. I would estimate at least two centuries for the infiltration, fracturing and colonizing of Roman monuments like the Theater of Pompey; much less for the disappearance of the *insulae*, where whatever was left after vandalism and the stripping of re-usable materials would have been finished off by earthquakes and fires.

This process of anarchic disintegration, much more frightening because of being concentrated into ten or twenty years, should be familiar to Americans. The Sixties were full of talk of decaying cities. Detroit has not stopped decaying since the riots of *Pl.38* July 1967. The center of town has become a wasteland. The skyscrapers that once marked a prosperous CBD have been abandoned. There are vast empty lots everywhere reverting to rangeland. Every neighborhood has its burnt and boarded houses and crumbling buildings. Since 1986, on "Devil's Night," the evening before Halloween, people set hundreds of fires and try to burn down their own neighborhoods.[58] East St. Louis along the Mississippi, a once prosperous blue-collar town of meat-packing plants, railroads, and nice wooden houses, is in an even more advanced state of decay. It has been described as "a partly inhabited ghost town whose factories and theaters and hotels and auto dealerships and gas stations and half of its schools are mostly burnt out shells." Broke and badly in debt, the city cannot collect garbage or repair sewer lines. Recently it was forced to give away City Hall as part of a court judgment against it.[59]

Which is why we must return to medieval Rome, to the second, constructive part of the process it went through. The tragedy of Detroit and East St. Louis is of course racial; the end came with the flight of the white population taking along its tax revenues. In the Middle Ages people had no such option unless it was to escape into the countryside. You were born in a city and you died there and so did your children. With that kind of long-term commitment, you burrowed in and recycled what you had been left. In the case of Rome, it was monuments, a legendary fame, and the tomb of a saint. And these things were a source of pride. They helped Rome to live on when hundreds of less tenacious cities in the old Roman provinces in fact died.

So the obverse of disintegration for medieval Rome was the creation of new communities around parish churches, the selling of Peter to pilgrims, and the tapping of its own past to restore its faith in the future. Physical squalor was tempered by new construction; destruction and internal fighting were transcended by pomp and ceremony. It is the ultimate triumph of the "medievalizing" of Rome that it changed the urban fabric gently and casually, so that at the end of a thousand years, with the city not at all resembling the self it surrendered to Christianity in 313, it still maintained the memory of that distant past, and could put it to good use to revive its sagging spirit. The Renaissance did not "recover" imperial Rome: it was merely there to receive it. The medievalizing of Rome did not mean "The Destruction of Ancient Rome," as book titles always announce: it was a messy, ill-directed, but ultimately successful effort of conservation. Given the destruction of the thousand-year-old St. Peter's, of the equally ancient palace of the Lateran, of the neighborhoods through which the Via Giulia was cut and the Palazzo Farnese and its spatial constellation installed—and all of this in the span of less than a century— the Renaissance would seem more cavalier of the historic city it inherited and hardly in a position to blame the Middle Ages for wanton disrespect of ancient Rome.

"ORGANIC" CHANGES

Without the special burden of being Rome, all cities are caught in a balancing act between destruction and preservation. As long as the management of this balance has not been formalized, citizens will seek their own advantage within a loose frame of social and economic forces.

Let us touch fleetingly on two of these "organic" changes. The deterioration of the building fabric is of course a constant. The responsibility is the individual owner's, and many are unable or unwilling to meet it. Even with the strictest administrative control, decaying or derelict structures are ever present. This is after all the basis of slum clearance, and though that particular concept may be modern the reality of blight is not.

Within this steady rhythm of disintegration, it is sometimes possible to recognize exacerbating circumstances. A case from the distant past is Fustat, the original settlement of Cairo. Everywhere, documents from the 10th to the 13th century

indicate, there were ruins interspersed among the houses, even in the affluent neighborhoods. It is thought that two economic reasons might account for this peculiar presence of ruins, which were bought and fixed up, bought and given away as gifts, and even rented. One reason is that the houses were held in common partnership; they were divided among the owners not physically, by rooms, but according to nominal shares, 24 of them—a division that was modeled on the 24-part division of the unit of currency, the dinar. It was easy in these circumstances to neglect upkeep. Furthermore the high cost of trained labor made repairs very expensive, whereas rents were comparatively low.[60]

A case from the recent past has to do with programs of development. The 1947 Town and Country Planning Act in England required local and county councils to prepare development plans for their areas, and gave them the power to declare Comprehensive Development Areas or CDAs within which they could compulsorily purchase decaying buildings. But the very designation of a CDA means that no new businesses are started, no maintenance is provided by the local council for the area "on the grounds that such expenditure is wasted if it is to be demolished." Consequently, Charles McKean writes, "the locality can deteriorate into an appalling slum, and thus, in a *post hoc* way, justify the Council's original 284 designation."[61]

The rising of the street level is a second constant phenomenon. It is possible to 245 stand on a street and look down upon excavations several feet below us from an earlier period of the city's history. Some of this rise was fairly direct, especially in times innocent of municipal controls. The practice of throwing refuse into the street has only recently been retired. Rain water found its way through and consolidated the debris, raising the street level continuously, if imperceptibly. In many cultures new buildings are erected over the pile of collapsed old buildings, without the bother of clearing the site. By the time of Constantine some areas in Rome were 4 feet (1.2 m.) higher than the Augustan level. A single story of a Roman house collapsed down to a masonry pile about 6 feet (1.8 m.) deep. With *insulae* that went up five to six stories, the process could produce dramatic transformations of the city's topography.

URBAN INFILL

This is obviously the result of crowding—and crowding comes about in one of two ways. Either you start with a closed urban form into which more and more people try to squeeze, or else you have a situation where, even with an open urban form, center-city sites are so sought-after that they are redeveloped at ever-increasing density. Examples of the latter include both the formation of highrise central business precincts and the emergence of tenement districts inhabited by people of low income who have to be near a center-city job.

Closed form comes about physically—city walls—and legally. By legally I mean injunctions against spread, whether the walls are there or not. Baroque Paris, as we saw, tried to prohibit suburban expansion, as London had since 1580. In both cases there were exceptions in favor of the rich (residential squares), but even the less rich found ways to circumvent the law. In London repeated prohibitions against new building simply led to subdivisions and clandestine construction in the back—to quote Braudel, a

> proliferation of hovels and shanties on land of doubtful ownership. It was no great loss if one or other of these buildings fell victim to the law. Everybody therefore tried his luck, and networks or rather labyrinths of lanes and alleys, houses with double, triple, even quadruple entrances and exits, grew up as a result.[62]

Since government is almost exclusively concerned with the outer, public face of the urban fabric, the most intensive, and least noticed, changes happen within, behind the façade. There, houses are subdivided, rooms altered to suit new functions, whole floors inserted, and so on. The individual revisions made by an owner or tenant to his unit—knocking down a wall, opening or walling up a window—may not be of fundamental import to city form. A general conversion of single-family houses into apartments is.

There are two classic cases of this phenomenon. The American case of center-city residential changes—from middle- and upper-middle-class houses to lower-income apartments—is well rehearsed in the literature. The process here was suburbanization, the abandonment of the center by the middle class, and the subdivision of its houses into rentals for low-income families. But a similar situation can be documented in post-Revolutionary Paris, there caused by the shortage of space in the formerly aristocratic neighborhood of the Marais as it was transformed by merchants and craftsmen into a commercial district. A complete change in housing patterns—from the private house to the apartment building—accompanied this increase in population. What we are concerned with here is the transitional phase when one class succeeds another in the same buildings. Large mansions were now subdivided into "apartments"—a term first used to refer to suites of rooms in aristocratic houses. These arbitrary divisions of rental space had little to do with our contemporary notion of apartments as stacked units, each with a layout derived from that of a traditional residence. The destructiveness of these conversions suggests the contempt newly-empowered artisans held for the former residents of these grand houses.

Urban process represents the adjustment of the urban fabric to a whole variety of changes that are economic and social. These changes are often swifter and more deep-seated than the pace and range of physical change. To be more specific, it is the cadastral framework of building plots as it is shaped early on that resists change, while land use undergoes rapid changes. When the design or scale of the old premises

288, 289

288, 289 *Paris, Hôtel de Sully, by Jean du Cerceau: as it looked when completed in 1629 and as restored after 1951, and as it had been altered in the intervening years. Extra floors had been inserted, and the space above the entrance screen filled with three stories of accommodation.*

can no longer meet changing demands, the building comes down to make room for another generation of construction.

For medieval English towns and their later history, the best accounts are those of geographers like M. R. G. Conzen. His study of Newcastle-upon-Tyne identifies the various stages of urban growth for a mid-sized English town, from the pre-urban nucleus of the Norman castle to the present day.[63] They have obvious application to many others.

The medieval phase is predictable: the Norman castle, overlooking the river and the main land road, early on got an open settlement of the *suburbium* type around the hill, with a market by the river and a parish church toward the plateau. A harbor grew along the river; three roadside extensions developed along the valley roads that crossed the plateau, each with its own market and church; friaries and other religious houses arranged themselves on the periphery. At some point all this was encircled by a town wall. This plan, the result of an additive process, which survived almost intact until the mid-18th century, up to this stage is not germane to our present discussion of urban infill patterns.

But with the Industrial Revolution, the process became one of transformation rather than addition. The inherited outlines were used as the frame within which to inscribe change. This change affected the street system, the design of the plots, and the city edge.

The inherited frame consisted of the town wall; the elongated burgage plots, with the buildings concentrated on the street-fronting "head" of the lot and the "tail" left as yard and garden; the original marketplace, filled in (during the late Middle Ages and after) with tiny houses that had no attached burgages; the medieval stronghold, its grounds overgrown with later public buildings and houses; and the waterfront with merchants' offices and warehouses arranged in tightly built-up yards along alleys or "chares" that ran at right angles to the waterfront (a fashion common to medieval seaports). Each element of this inherited frame underwent change after the advent of the Industrial Revolution.

BURGAGE PLOTS

299 The changes here are of two kinds. First, there is the filling up of the unbuilt tails of the burgage plots; and then, there is the change of the actual plot pattern.

The filling up is fairly obvious—and of course it happens both horizontally over the plot's total area, and also vertically as an increase in building height. The cycle may start with accessory buildings that begin to occupy the burgage tails.[64] The final, modern, stage of this development is the clearing of the by now fully occupied plot by demolishing the buildings upon it, in preparation for redevelopment.

290– Loyer details the process of building up the medieval city in his account of historic
298 Paris. The unchanging habit was to build up the lot's street frontage first, since proximity to the flow of pedestrian traffic with its opportunities for commerce and craft was the original incentive for development. Later, a second structure was
291 placed behind the first, separated from it by an intermediate court, generally used as a workyard by craftsmen. On very deep lots a kitchen garden was located at the core of the block, behind the back building.

292 The intermediate space started out by housing constructions connecting the front and back buildings—staircases, passages—as well as kitchens and bathrooms. In time, in response to overcrowding, the sides of the courtyard were rebuilt as separate housing units. With the sides filled up, what remained was the courtyard itself. This
293 began to get low, one-story buildings like simple sheds and warehouses, reducing it

290–298 Stages of urban infill, on the Parisian model. At first, houses sit on the heads of the plots, with gardens behind (290). In the next stage, the gardens are gradually built over (291–293). From then on, the story is one of heightening, as streetfront and then backlot buildings are raised, and the open spaces are further reduced to gloomy courts and airshafts.

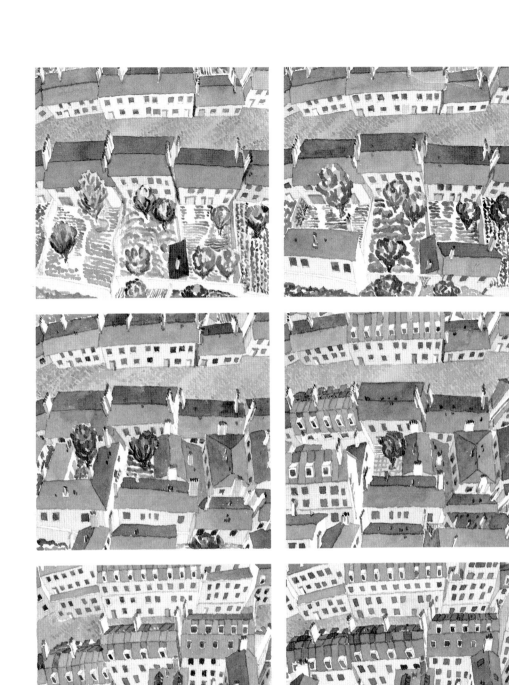

293–295 to a mere passageway. Crafts and small-scale manufacturing found shelter here at a time when there was more and more pressure to drive them out of the city core. This filling-up process was slow; it was still going on in the 1930s in Paris, when a city regulation finally limited the degree to which a lot could be built up.

As for height, "the systematic use of wooden construction," Loyer observes, "allowed buildings to be raised considerably without overloading the foundation masonry."[65] The simplest way to heighten a building was to put a higher roof on it 294–298 and thus change the attic into one or two, or even three floors of living space. Or else Pl.34 you could modify the shape of the roof, from the traditional two-slope roof to a mansard, which with its row of dormer windows made it easier to use an attic as living space. During the Restoration in the early 19th century, the recessed top story—a light structure in wood or a combination of wood and brick, with a little terrace in front—came into fashion; since it was recessed it hardly weighed on the façade, but rather contributed to the building's stability by shifting the weight to the back.

The quest to build up a plot pattern originally suited to a private house eventually reaches its choke point as greater densities are achieved by creating rooms without light and air, without access to the street, or by overloading the foundations of the original structure. In late-18th-century Paris, Loyer tells us, a forced evolution of this old lot pattern was spurred by a new scale of urban development encouraged by big capital. As a reconfiguration of building lots became necessary in larger towns 299 and cities, a common method was to amalgamate burgage plot heads to create lots suitable for larger buildings and then truncate burgage tails for independent lots. The simplest way to accomplish this was to run a mid-block alley through a series of burgages. These changes are most dramatic in the commercial redevelopment of the city center. Plots are intensively developed, combined; new streets are created that force a redistribution of land and a radically altered plot pattern. This obliteration of burgage plots creates a temporary wasteland which Conzen calls "urban fallow." The new blocks are distinguished by shallower building lots with longer frontages, rather than the alignment of many short, deep plots, each with its miserly share of the street, as in the standard configuration of burgages.

THE AMERICAN CASE

The scenario drawn up by Loyer for Paris or by the elder Conzen for English towns does not exist in the United States. The cities were young and brusquely layered. There was no great tradition of burgage plots serially arranged along streets, but 49 rather an early and enduring obsession with the detached house and the grid. The 81, most original urban pattern was the creation of the tall, high-density central 82 business district—the American downtown. American urban process, therefore, has to be explained differently.

With the younger Conzen we have to stress some principal traits of urban America for the 19th century: general low density in the settlement pattern; indistinct urban fringes, consisting of transition zones between rural and urban land use, and a lot of neutral land held off the market in anticipation of development; simple layouts, mostly gridded; frequent stylistic changes, pervasive eclecticism, and an enormous variety of building forms; the pre-eminent role of transport facilities; cheap land turned into a commodity devoid of social meaning; and of course privatism, and the passive role of government in shaping cities.

Extension was hardly orderly, or based on a master plan. The way it happens is something like this. In the urban fringe, large agricultural parcels break down

299 opposite *The transformation of burgage plots. These start out as long narrow fields. First the heads of the plots are built up, then the tails, then the intermediate space. Then adjacent plots are demolished and replaced by larger buildings, and mid-block alleys are run through. The plot pattern has completely changed.*

through exchange to sizes suitable for urban platting. The subdivision of these parcels may take place way ahead of demand—Conzen calls these "abortive plats." 45 The point here is that a free land market system and a municipal government that believed all growth is good made it possible for "any landowner with property in the broad urban fringe . . . to anticipate, institute, and bear the risks of urban growth, regardless of exact location."[66] Result: in 1910 Tacoma, Washington, with 20,000 households, had 74,000 surplus house lots!

Process and economic cycles

To what extent is this 19th-century pattern of urban growth and process linked directly with cycles of the economy? According to the work of Sherry Olson on Baltimore, urban growth is rhythmic, and this rhythm is based on cycles of 300 investment.[67] Every fifteen or twenty years the city built roads, dredged canals, developed new residential areas in a cyclical renewal. This is in accord with the rhythm of eighteen-year "long swings" of urban construction, a phenomenon identified by a number of scholars as a determinant of city-making processes of Western nations.[68]

Looking at successive street-map diagrams of Baltimore, Olson recognizes the rhythm of long swings in new street openings, the amplitude of each building boom

300 *Baltimore (Maryland): ten stages in the city's spasmodic growth. The solid black area is Chesapeake Bay. (After Sherry H. Olson)*

top row, left to right *Streets developed 1745–88; streets developed 1789–1801; streets and turnpike roads developed 1802–21; streets developed 1822–37 and railroads built by 1837 (B&O to the southwest, Baltimore & Susquehanna to the north, Baltimore & Port Deposit to the east).*

center row *Streets developed 1838–64 and railroad extensions toward the waterfront; streets developed 1866–77 and railroad tunnels connecting the Pennsylvania Railroad system, built ca. 1872 (Baltimore & Potomac Railroad to the west, Union Railroad to the east); streets developed 1878–99 and B&O Railroad tunnels and crossover, ca. 1893; streets developed 1900–1918 (chiefly in territory annexed in 1888) and Western Maryland Railroad as developed ca. 1903.*

bottom row *Streets developed 1919–34 in territory annexed in 1918; expressways and waterfront as developed 1935–79.*

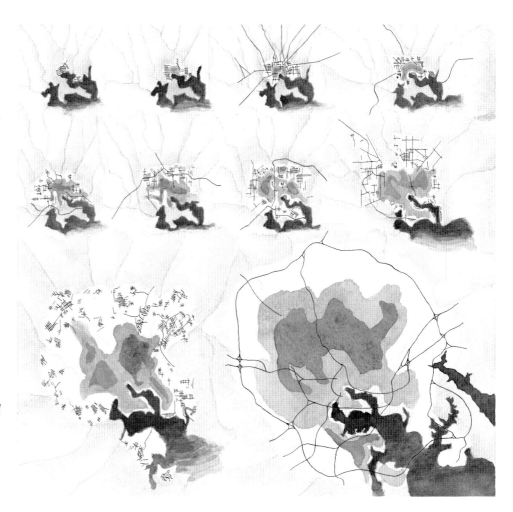

being reflected by the extent of new webbing, and in three dimensions, by façades and streetscapes. As technology changed, so did the pattern of these streets. Eventually, in this century, "the grid of ruler-straight avenues of sixty-six-feet [20-m.] wide and ten-foot [3-m.] alleys gave way to a type of urban contour plowing with a hierarchy of streets of several speeds, slopes, and curvatures, branching out to deadends, and viaducts threaded between earlier-developed paths." The central business district was also rebuilt in accordance with new development models during every building boom.

This cyclic readjustment of the spatial organization of the city maintained the basic structure of inequality. Growth in one part of the city "was always associated with stagnation in another. . . . Each successive suburban fringe corresponded to a reconstruction and expansion of the commercial district and an in-between 'gray area' of disinvestment." Social differentiation developed according to the width of streets—the better-off on main streets, the poor in the alleys. Periods of booming growth overloaded the city's infrastructure, wedding it to expansive new tracts of urban land assembled through the process of annexation.

Prime areas of stress were the city center and the waterfront. Each building boom also involved a spatial redistribution of the population, as new immigrant waves washed in and residents competed for better housing. Olson also notes that buildings, streets, docks, and other capital investments are physically longer-lived than they are useful, considering the brevity of the economic cycle that created them. The dissonance of cyclical investment and its artifacts results in a city built of economically mismatched fragments, insuring, as Olson puts it, "a perennial disequilibrium in spatial organization."

PROCESS AGAINST CONSERVATION: THE LIFE OF URBAN FORM

It is fitting that this chapter on urban process, which concludes the discourse that I began in *The City Shaped*, should come to rest in an unsoothing passage about "perennial disequilibrium." It is fitting, because the one reliable characteristic of urban behavior through history is its unpredictability. Whatever the perfection of its initial form, a city will follow its own rules or rejoice in its lawlessness. Those who see themselves in charge will legislate a built order, turning upon this wilful artifact with stern cures. But always the city has its own mind: it may refuse to go along with what has been prescribed, or find its own mode of obedience that leaves it free to metamorphose without losing track of its idiosyncratic habits.

In a way, to put it quaintly, I have let cities, in these books, tell their own story. Every city has one to tell, and out of many such stories urban form and experience take substance. There has been little theory. I did not wish to set down normative guidelines to the discussion, or generalize to the extent of losing the historical focus on individual cases like Suzhou or Washington, D.C. I have already thereby forfeited the right to a grand conclusion. This is also appropriate in the context of our discussion of urban process, because new cities continue to be built at this moment all over the world, and extant cities are remaking themselves feverishly in big ways and small, advertising their pluckiness and determination to come through and prosper. In their new future exertions, one thing will remain unchanged—their unpredictability. Conclusions deserve more stable subject-matter.

My belief in an urban form that has its own will, as it were, is not a commonly shared viewpoint. With increasing forcefulness those who design and administer cities are seeking ways to tighten their grip, and much of the debate has to do with the "historic fabric." As attitudes harden on one or another side of the issue, the nettlesome questions are glossed over for the comfort of warring parties—civic activists against developers; conservatives against liberals. We must be willing to ask: "Why preserve the old? What is it that an old building stock adds to the urban experience to deserve that it should be retained or perhaps even emulated? Who cares about this elusive entity, 'built heritage', and does what we conserve represent the needs of all of us in this arena?" Can we hold a lovely stretch of historic cityscape in common as a cultural memory, or are our preservation zones monuments to an urban élite?

The trend among urban geographers and others preoccupied with the morphology of cities is toward "townscape management," that is, going beyond conservation of singular structures to the caretaking of entire historical fabrics. James Marston Fitch calls it "curatorial management of the built world" in the title of his comprehensive recent book on historic preservation.[69] But there is no corresponding authority to plan and finance this mammoth operation. What needs managing in a townscape, according to Conzen who first articulated this concept, is precisely its "historicity," which comprises the town plan, the building fabric, and land utilization. This is an expendable quality, as the town plan is altered through the years and the stock of traditional buildings is reduced.

The assessment of historicity is another matter. In the practical world of planning a step in that direction was made thirty years ago with France's *secteur sauvegardé* law of 1962, which made possible the formal designation of conservation areas. Here and in parallel situations in other countries, urban administration, with backing from the national government, was willing to give special status to an area of town whose historic cohesiveness as a whole was considered an object of preservation, rather than isolated "significant" buildings within it. The designation is anything but innocent. It takes the area with its numerous buildings out of the market, or rather imposes strict limits on what is allowed by way of change. That these restrictions on the use of one's property within a conservation area cause hardships to many owners has become quite clear by now. In New York City to date about fifty districts have been granted Landmark status, comprising some 20,000 buildings in all. In the hands of the powerful Landmark Preservation Commission, this vast collection of real estate plays a key role in decisions of land use. The Commission is able to freeze development on prime urban land like the Upper East Side without having to take responsibility for the economic effects of its decisions.

And yet the unexamined and very emotional belief persists that historicity is where we find some visual record of our life as a community with a collective past, that somewhere among the gables and the bay windows is the echo of people who came before us and occupied the place and built these buildings as objects of pride and self-advertisement. At the beginning of this century the Bürgermeister of Hildesheim expressed this point of view at a conference on the care of monuments:

Does a civic administration exist merely for the sake of enabling people to fulfill the needs of daily life as well, as cheaply and as completely as possible? Is the city there for this alone? . . . Is there not something far higher, the spiritual well-being of men, and does it not contribute greatly to this when they feel in close relation to the past, and take delight in realizing . . . how not only the streets, but every single public building, each individual house, even each piece of carved ornament, has

301 *Hildesheim (Germany), the Altstädter Marktplatz in the 1920s, looking toward the House of the Butchers' Guild. The turreted building in the adjacent street, visible in this important view, adopts a free historicist style as advocated by the Bürgermeister at the turn of the century. The public fountain, crowned by a figure of Roland, was erected in 1540.*

grown in the course of time to be what it is? To make this feeling real is the task of the civic authorities.[70]

This task consists of two specific charges: to make sure that the historic crop of buildings is not depleted, and the old street pattern not changed too radically or too fast; and to guard against incongruous new buildings. It is again around 1900, when historic preservation as a movement came of age, that restrictive style regulations surfaced here and there, especially in regions like Bavaria with a strong nationalist fervor. The Bürgermeister of Hildesheim again:

> In the streets and open places . . . those parts of any building which can be seen *301* from any street or public place must be carried out in architectural forms that agree with those previously in use in Germany up to the middle of the 17th century. Further, the new work must as far as possible be in harmony with its nearest surroundings. . . . As a rule, new buildings must be built so that the general appearance of the surroundings is not interfered with. This applies especially to materials, including those used in the roofing and the ornamentation, and to coloring.[71]

The cut-off date, the mid-17th century, with a huge margin of safety, was intended of course to keep "modern" architecture out of the townscape. For the same reason, in restoring Williamsburg, Virginia, Mr. Rockefeller and his advisers stopped at the 1790s to ensure the purity of their version of the colonial town.

Colonial Williamsburg is a historic museum town. People who live there year-round are the managers of the plant and the research, and not a real urban population. But the United States has its Hildesheims too, and two of these prove that what started as a sentimental, moralistic clinging to the past is with us still, but for a different set of reasons: in Santa Barbara, California, out of a desire to create a tidy townscape in the mold of Spain from the disfigured and chaotic small town that was there; in Santa Fe, New Mexico, out of a deeper local tradition, combining something of the strength of the Pueblo Indians and the Spaniards' grudging acceptance of ancient settlement patterns and land-related ritual.

Santa Barbara is a sparkling potpourri of Mediterranean styles, white but for the *Pl.40* splashes of red tile roofs. It was an urban image consciously chosen, for the most part, after a major earthquake in 1925 destroyed the bulk of the business buildings. The City Council set up an architectural board of review immediately which set style ordinances for the historic precinct in the center and the exclusive "Montecito Strip" along the ocean, but not for the rest of town. The "New Spain in America" theme was the fancy of the planning committee; it persuaded the community to go along, and soon there was no turning back. We might be permitted to speak here of an "invented historicity." And it was a brilliant image—the effervescent architectural palette made to work with the incomparable low beaches fringed with palms. It was the city for an élite, and its social cohesiveness was achieved by the imposition of a dominant architectural style—the Spanish Colonial Revival. The city to this day controls all design in the district, including new construction and additions, all landscape changes, all street furniture. The Landmarks Commission's word is final. Little is written down with specificity, though the design guidelines manual does explicitly prohibit such things as metal buildings, aluminum windows, and plastic tiles. The Commission is preoccupied with design and "texture." Decisions are subjective, and architects are admonished about getting "the correct feeling."

Santa Fe, with its sterner, elementarist style, runs a tighter ship. Beyond the main *163* historic district, there is a separate ordinance governing "Townscape," and a "Highway Corridor" ordinance controlling building envelopes along main arteries. Finally the "Terrain Management and Escarpment Ordinance" governs all construction on slopes, hilltops and mesas. A handbook puts in writing, in the no-nonsense tone of the contractor, how the builders and architects are to proceed. It prescribes two different styles—the "Old Santa Fe Style," which is the older and *302* more authentic of the two (real adobe), and the "Recent Santa Fe Style" (adobe *303* look). In the latter the buildings may be higher, and while the flat roofs still rest on

302, 303 Santa Fe (New Mexico): examples of the "Old Santa Fe Style," 1930s, and the "Recent Santa Fe Style," 1950s–60s. Compare Ill. 163.

vigas (exposed beams) there is no pretense that these are structural. The kitschifying of the look in gas stations and motels is always good for a chuckle. But here in the Southwest, where the resonance of historic continuities can still be experienced at Taos and Chimayo and Santa Fe, most buildings still show a proud loyalty to their setting, and the spirit of Pueblo Indians and Franciscans sustains its powerful, uneasy hold. This embalmed historicity in Santa Fe and the chirpy style-consciousness of Santa Barbara set up idols to an ideal past and allow those who live there and those who visit to enjoy their innocent worship.

To the European managers of historic landscapes, these American indulgences are in the nature of theme parks. There is little commonality between the polite

American tinkering with preservation and period styles and the management and development of historic European cities, intensely studied by pioneering workshops like those of Saverio Muratori in Venice and Pier Luigi Cervellati in Bologna. 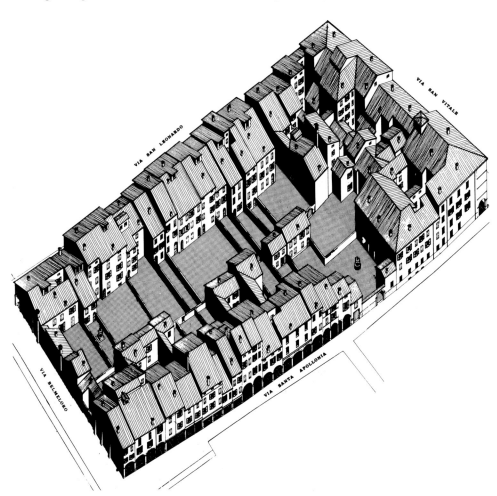 304 Beginning with the belief that these cities cannot be sacrificed on the altar of Modernism, and with the practical agenda that to save history there has to be a strategy of adding on to it lest the cities turn into unproductive museums of memory paid for by tourists, the Italian schools emphasized a scholarly approach to the historic development of fabric. Each began by identifying archetypal specimens of their city's building stock—that is, the original set of built forms out of which the city fabric developed over the centuries. This knowledge was critical in restoring blighted districts. Crowded tenements, instead of being demolished, were stripped of dangerous accretions to reveal the original building type underneath. And where new constructions were inserted into a patch of very old building stock, variety was permitted so long as they maintained traditional bay widths, floor heights, and overall building heights. Restored districts retained their visual consistency and architects their originality, without either incongruous modernism or the disingenuous application of "authentic" façades.

Bologna's experience was unusual for a number of reasons. The most important was the coincident ascendance of a government of the Left, which functioned through neighborhood councils. New housing would no longer be built at the city

304 Bologna (Italy), restoration of one city block on the basis of typological studies; from P. L. Cervellati and R. Scannavini, Bologna: politica e metodologia del restauro nei centri storici *(1973). All the houses in the middle of the block along Via San Leonardo are newly infilled. The façades along the Via Belmeloro were greatly altered and simplified to remove recent additions and renovations. Several flat roofs and roof additions were removed along the Via Santa Apollonia to return the street façade to its typological origins. In addition, the central space has been cleaned up, and new walls separating properties have been suggested.*

305 *Florence (Italy), Borgognissanti, with part of the Palazzo Lenzi-Quaratesi on the left. The palace is an outstanding Quattrocento building (displaying the Florentine arrangement of flat façade to a major space and a jetty only to the side); but it did not escape some alteration in the 19th century, and its 16th-century sgraffito decoration was renewed at that time.*

edge alone: the best undeveloped lands inside the city were acquired through eminent domain, and new housing was raised on them for the working class. Most revolutionary was the concept that conservation should encompass social as well as physical structure. In stabilizing houses, the program was also stabilizing patterns of tenancy. The city expropriated the rundown buildings, renovated them, and then returned them to tenants' cooperatives. The experiment had a lasting effect because it was tied to long-term legal instruments which survived the Communist administration. For most of the emulators there were too many variables to keep such programs going beyond the next election.

Our "historic legacy" is of course a business, too: it brings visitors in, which means much-needed resources. The budget of Athens or Rome comes almost entirely from the wallets of tourists and pilgrims, and almost every town now strives to find a historic angle to the buildings that once simply stood around and served their functions. History is in the old mill or the locks, the stretch of harbor with the old frigate, the rehabilitated warehouse from which the dankness has only just been civilized away.

32

Some of this history is bogus, or at best skin-deep. The thousands who walk the streets of Quattrocento Florence and marvel at the "ambience" are unaware of how 305 much of it is a sanitized pastiche of the 1890s. At the end of Rome's Fascist regime, laws were passed to ensure that nothing within the Aurelian Walls could be altered or destroyed. But it became clear that it was only the street façades that were protected, and those could be pulled down provided they were rebuilt in exactly the same way. The interiors were a free-for-all. Renaissance palaces were repartitioned as banks, Baroque apartment houses condominiumized. Yet we are willing to suspend our disbelief, faced with a sight like the beautiful wooden town of Porvoo in 306 Finland, burnt down and rebuilt several times, because these sets are serviceably evocative despite their progressive remoteness from their origins, and because most of us are content with the joy and quaintness of urban antiquity without needing to fret about historic specificity, the actual moment, the 13th-century hand on the 13th-century finial.

The urge to preserve certain cities, or certain buildings and streets within them, has something in it of the instinct to preserve family records; something of the compulsion to protect a work of art. We can all rejoice that medieval Rome did not scrap the remains of antiquity. But we must not be innocent of urban process as a principle. With pretensions of historical purity to one side, and talk of a scientific approach to urban conservation kept modest and conditional, we can regain the central direction in assessing cities. They are live, changing things—not hard artifacts in need of prettification and calculated revision. Cities are never still; they resist efforts to make neat sense of them. We need to respect their rhythms and to recognize that the life of city form must lie loosely somewhere between total control and total freedom of action. Between conservation and process, process must have the final word. In the end, urban truth is in the flow.

306 Porvoo (Finland). The earliest buildings are the 15th-century cathedral and detached belltower, on the hill to the left. Farther left are the Market Square and Town Hall, rebuilt, like most of the town, after a major fire in 1760. Warehouses cluster on the river bank. The pattern recalls that of Oulu (Pl. 31), where the stone-built church also survived.

NOTES

See also the Bibliography, pp. 311–13.

INTRODUCTION (pp. 7–9)

1. G. Botero, *The Greatness of Cities*, in *The Reason of State* (1588, 1606), transl. R. Peterson (London 1956), 227.

1. THE CITY EDGE (pp. 11–69)

1. Plutarch, *Roman Questions*, as cited in J. Rykwert, *The Idea of a Town* (Princeton 1976), 28.
2. See R. E. A. Palmer, "Customs on Market Goods Imported into the City of Rome," *Memoirs of the American Academy in Rome* 36, 1980, 217–33.
3. See A. Braham, *The Architecture of the French Enlightenment* (London/Berkeley 1980), 191–97.
4. R. E. Dickinson, *The West European City* (2nd ed., London 1961), 147, 149.
5. See N. S. Steinhardt, "Why Were Chang'an and Beijing so Different?," *Journal of the Society of Architectural Historians* 45.4, Dec. 1986, 345, 350.
6. Cited in C. Platt, *The English Medieval Town* (New York 1976), 43.
7. ibid., 41.
8. P. Lampl, *Cities and Planning in the Ancient Near East* (New York 1968), figs. 115, 116.
9. E. A. Gutkind, *Urban Development in Eastern Europe: Bulgaria, Romania and the USSR* (New York/London 1972), 282–87.
10. See Sen-Dou Chang, "The Morphology of Walled Capitals," in G. W. Skinner, ed., *The City in Late Imperial China* (Stanford 1977), 90.
11. G. L. Burke, *The Making of Dutch Towns* (London 1956), 119.
12. Dickinson (n.4 above), 239.
13. Cited by R. Tuttle in "Against Fortifications: The Defense of Renaissance Bologna," *Journal of the Society of Architectural Historians* 41, 1982, 197. I am dependent on Tuttle's essay for this discussion. See also J. R. Hale, "To Fortify or Not to Fortify," in *Essays in Honour of John Humphreys Whitfield* (London 1975), 99–119.
14. See Kostof, *The City Shaped* (Boston/London 1991), 249.
15. Dickinson (n.4 above), 146.
16. See J. Lyle, "The Relevance of Tivoli," *Landscape* 18.2, Spring–Summer 1969, 5–22.
17. J. Heers, *Family Clans in the Middle Ages*, transl. B. Herbert (Amsterdam/New York 1977), 177.
18. L. B. Alberti, *Ten Books on Architecture*, transl. J. Leoni (1755), ed. J. Rykwert (London 1955), VII.ii.
19. M. Aston and J. Bond, *The Landscape of Towns* (London 1976), 105.
20. Burke (n.11 above), 98.
21. M. Bateman and R. Riley, eds., *Geography of Defence* (Beckenham, Kent 1986), 43–44.
22. W. Braunfels, *Urban Design in Western Europe*, transl. K. J. Northcott (Chicago/London 1988), 79.
23. See Chang (n.10 above), 85–86.
24. Dickinson (n.4 above), 18.

25. The best account of the urban geography of New Orleans is by P. F. Lewis, *New Orleans, Making of an Urban Landscape* (Cambridge, Mass. 1976).
26. I am excluding here rare instances in antiquity, the Harappan towns of the Indus Valley for example, where some sort of elementary embankment system did exist to control riverine floods. On Venice and Rome see also "The Street," below, 219–20.
27. J. W. Konvitz, *Cities and the Sea* (Baltimore 1978).
28. See K. G. Holum et al., eds., *King Herod's Dream: Caesarea on the Sea* (New York 1988).
29. J. M. Wagstaff, "Origin and Evolution of Towns: 4000 BC to AD 1900," in G. H. Blake and R. I. Lawless, eds., *The Changing Middle Eastern City* (New York/London 1980), 14, fig. 1.1.
30. See *The City Shaped*, 136.
31. On Berlin's gridded extensions see *The City Shaped*, 238, 258, and figs. 241, 252, 253.
32. On London see J. Summerson, *Georgian London* (London/New York 1946); and D. J. Olsen, *Town Planning in London, 18th and 19th Centuries* (New Haven/London 1964).
33. Quotation in P. Léon, *Paris, histoire de la rue* (Paris 1947), 179.
34. S. J. Watanabe, "Metropolitanism as a way of Life: The Case of Tokyo, 1868–1930," in A. Sutcliffe, ed., *Metropolis: 1890–1940* (Chicago 1984), 412–13.
35. For these instances, see Bateman and Riley (n.21 above), 40; Braunfels (n.22 above), 303.
36. C. E. Schorske, *Fin-de-Siècle Vienna. Politics and Culture* (New York 1961/1980), 33.
37. Cited in L. Mumford, *The City in History* (New York 1961), 427–28.
38. Summerson (n.32 above), 34.
39. See A. Vidler, *Claude-Nicolas Ledoux. Architecture and Social Reform at the end of the Ancien Régime* (Cambridge, Mass./London 1990).
40. See M. Williams, "Parkland Towns of Australia and New Zealand," *Geographical Review* 1.56, 1966, 67–89, for what follows.
41. See D. Thomas, "London's Green Belt: The Evolution of An Idea," *Geographical Journal* 129, 1963, 14–24.
42. Cited by F. J. Osborn in A. Whittick, ed., *Encyclopedia of Urban Planning* (New York 1974), s.v. "Green Belts", 484–86.
43. G. Albers in G. E. Cherry, ed., *Shaping An Urban World* (New York 1980), 154.
44. G. A. Wissink, *American Cities in Perspective: Special Reference to the Development of their Fringe Areas* (Assen 1962), 87ff.
45. B. Ladd, *Urban Planning and Civic Order in Germany, 1860–1914* (Cambridge, Mass. 1990), 226.
46. V. Fournel, *Paris nouveau et Paris futur* (Paris 1865), 232–34. Quoted in N. Evenson, *Paris: A Century of Change, 1878–1978* (New Haven/London 1979).
47. P. C. Papademetriou, *Transportation and Urban Development in Houston: 1830–1980* (Houston n.d.), 69.
48. Watanabe (n.34 above), 404.
49. K. T. Jackson, *Crabgrass Frontier: The Suburbanization of the United States* (New York/Oxford 1985), 36.
50. Ladd (n.45 above), 208.
51. Promotional literature quoted in F. Barker and P. Jackson, *The History of London in Maps* (London 1990), 156–57.
52. Quoted in B. Bobrick, *Labyrinths of Iron* (New York 1981), 91.
53. J. Simmons, "The Power of the Railway," in H. J. Dyos and M. Wolf, eds., *The Victorian City: Images and Realities*, vol. 2 (London/Boston 1973), 297.
54. P. L. Garside, "West End, East End: London, 1890–1940," in Sutcliffe (n.34 above), 230.
55. On land value and use in Chicago, see H. Hoyt,

One Hundred Years of Land Values in Chicago: The Relationship of the Growth of Chicago to the Rise of its Land Values 1830–1933 (Chicago 1933).
56. G. Wright, *Building the Dream* (New York 1981), 252.
57. H. van der Haegen, "The Crisis of the Inner Cities in Belgium," in G. Heinritz and E. Lichtenberger, eds., *The Take-off of Suburbia and the Crisis of the Central City* (Stuttgart 1986), 197–200.
58. The notion of a North Sea culture area of single-household buildings has been expounded in the work of Austrian geographer E. Lichtenberger. See her essay "The Changing Nature of European Urbanism," in B. J. L. Berry, ed., *Urbanization and Counter-Urbanization*, Urban Affairs Annual Reviews, vol.11 (Beverly Hills/London 1976).
59. D. Popenoe, *The Suburban Environment* (Chicago/London 1977), 34.
60. "The French Connection," *Architectural Review* 163:976, June 1978, 351.
61. M. Horsey, "Multi-Storey Council Housing in Britain: Introduction and Spread," *Planning Perspectives* 3, 1988, 168.
62. State-sponsored new towns outside Paris and Stockholm regulated construction of new housing. In both cases the proportion of single-family homes to highrise flats was kept artificially low; that is, far below consumer preference and demand. When these regulations were struck from the books in the 1970s, single-family house construction quickly exceeded that of flats by a factor of two. See Popenoe (n.59 above), 222ff.; Evenson (n.46 above), 336ff.; and P. White, *The West European City. A Social Geography* (London/New York 1984), esp. ch.2.
63. See, e.g., R. J. Ingersoll, "Las Colinas: The Ultimate Bourgeois Utopia," *Texas Architect*, Jan.–Feb. 1989, and also J. Garreau, *Edge City. Life on the New Frontier* (New York 1991), esp. the bibliography.
64. D. Beers, "Tomorrowland," *Image Magazine*, 18 Jan. 1987.
65. R. Fishman, *Bourgeois Utopias: The Rise and Fall of Suburbia* (New York 1987), 185.

2. URBAN DIVISIONS (pp. 71–121)

1. On the Berlin Wall, see D. Cleland, ed., *Post-War Berlin*, AD Profiles (London 1982), esp. 78–83; also A. Balfour, *Berlin. The Politics of Order, 1737–1989* (New York 1990) on the history of the Potsdamerplatz and the Wall.
2. Braunfels (Ch.1 n.22 above).
3. See the chapter "Basel: A Study in Urban Geography," in Dickinson (Ch.1 n.4 above), 63–78.
4. G. Sjoberg, *The Preindustrial City* (New York/London 1960), 111.
5. ibid., 115.
6. Botero (Intro. n.1 above), 261 (Bk. II.11).
7. See F. Braudel, *The Structures of Everyday Life*, transl. S. Reynolds (London/New York 1981), 547.
8. Alberti (Ch.1 n.18 above), V.i.
9. I discussed symmetrical diagrams of princely rule where the ruler puts himself in the middle for very good *symbolic* reasons in *The City Shaped*, 174–89, though cities such as Gur, Baghdad, and the like were surely exceptional.
10. Braunfels (Ch.1 n.22 above), 232.
11. Another example is provided by Vigevano, where Duke Lodovico il Moro commissioned Bramante to redesign the town square and rationalize the dominance of the Sforza castle (see below, p.155 and Ill.151). The Palazzo del Comune was reduced to relative insignificance by its incorporation in the arcading on the opposite side of the square. See A. Bruschi, *Bramante* (London/New York 1977), 64–66, and W. Lotz in *Studi Bramanteschi. Atti del Congresso internazionale*

Milano-Urbino-Roma 1970 (Rome 1974), 205–21.

12. See Kostof, *The Third Rome, 1870–1950* (Berkeley 1973), 10, 12, and "The Drafting of a Master Plan for *Roma capitale,*" *Journal of the Society of Architectural Historians* 35.1, Mar. 1976, 4–20.

13. J. Nolen, "City Making," *The American Architect* 1:1, Sept. 1909, 18.

14. See G. Castillo, "Cities of the Stalinist Empire," in N. AlSayyad, ed., *Forms of Dominance: On the Architecture and Urbanism of the Colonial Experience* (in press).

15. P. Wheatley, "Proleptic Observations on the Origins of Urbanism," in R. W. Steel and R. Lawton, eds., *Liverpool Essays in Geography* (London 1967), 316.

16. G. F. Andrews, *Maya Cities* (Norman, Okla. 1975).

17. F. W. Mote, "The Transformation of Nanking, 1350–1400," in Skinner (Ch.1 n.10 above), 114.

18. Y. Shiba, "Ningpo and Its Hinterland," in Skinner (Ch.1 n.10 above), 422ff.

19. Mote (n.17 above), 115.

20. See G. Kubler, *Building the Escorial* (Princeton 1982).

21. Braunfels (Ch.1 n.22 above), 332.

22. ibid., 55.

23. L. L. Orlin, "Ancient Near Eastern Cities: Form, Function and Idea," in Orlin, ed., *Janus* (Ann Arbor 1975), 35.

24. Braunfels (Ch.1 n.22 above), 15.

25. Dickinson (Ch.1 n.4 above), 255.

26. See also *The City Shaped*, 173–74.

27. Braunfels (Ch.1 n.22 above), 15.

28. Vitruvius, *Ten Books on Architecture*, transl. M. H. Morgan (New York 1914/1960), I.7.1–2.

29. Gutkind (Ch.1 n.9 above), 400.

30. M. Aubrun, *La Paroisse en France: des origines au XVe Siècle* (Paris 1986), 154.

31. ibid., 97.

32. G. W. O. Addleshaw, *The Development of the Parochial System from Charlemagne (768–814) to Urban II (1088–1099)* (London 1954), 4.

33. J. Evelyn, *Diary. London Revived*, ed. E. S. de Beer (Oxford 1938/New York 1959), 38.

34. See *The City Shaped*, 101.

35. ibid., 323–33.

36. J. Jacobs, *The Economy of Cities* (New York 1969).

37. M. Girouard, *Cities and People* (New Haven/London 1985), 257–70.

38. M. Elvin, "Market Towns and Waterways," in Skinner (Ch.1 n.10 above), 469.

39. A. Everitt, "The Market Towns," in P. Clark, ed., *The Early Modern Town* (New York 1976).

40. "Nations" were also formed around pilgrimage sites. The classic case is St. Peter's in Rome. Northern countries, which had a special veneration for the saint, began crowding the Vatican area as early as the 7th century. The defense of Peter by Northern youths is still alive in the presence of the Swiss Guard at the Vatican.

41. A. Voyce, *Moscow and the Root of Russian Culture* (Norman, Okla. 1964) 52–53.

42. Skinner, "Urban Development in Imperial China," in Skinner (Ch.1 n.10 above), 23.

43. Friedman, *Florentine New Towns* (New York 1989), 78.

44. G. L. Gomme, *London in the Reign of Victoria, 1837–1877* (Chicago/New York 1898), 93–108.

45. Everitt (n.39 above), 181.

46. G. A. Sala, *Paris Herself Again* (London 1880), 299; quoted in N. Pevsner, *A History of Building Types* (London/Princeton 1976), 243.

47. Shiba (n.18 above), 409.

48. J. Cramer, "Zur Frage der Gewerbegassen in der Stadt am Ausgang des Mittelalters," *Die alte Stadt* 2, 1984, 96.

49. C. Pythian-Adams, "Ceremony and the Citizen: the Communal Year at Coventry 1450–1550," in Clark (n.39 above), 110.

50. Voyce (n.41 above), 47.

51. J. W. Hall, "The Castle Town and Japan's Modern Urbanization," *Far Eastern Quarterly* 15.1, Nov. 1955, 47.

52. Skinner, "Urban Social Structures in Ch'ing China," in Skinner (Ch.1 n.10 above), 538ff.

53. A. Raymond, *The Great Arab Cities in the 16th–18th Centuries* (New York 1984), 24.

54. E. Giese, "Transformations of Islamic Cities in Soviet Middle Asia into Socialist Cities," in R. A. French and F. E. I. Hamilton, eds., *The Socialist City* (Chichester/New York 1979), 59–62.

55. ibid., 221.

56. J. E. Vance, Jr., "Land Assignment in the Precapitalist, Capitalist, and Post-Capitalist City," *Economic Geography* 47, 1971, 108.

57. See, e.g., T. J. Clark, *The Painting of Modern Life* (Princeton/London 1984), 50ff.; and E. Zola, *Au Bonheur des dames* (Paris 1883).

58. M. Schuyler, *American Architecture and Other Writings*. ed. W. H. Jordy and R. Coe (New York 1963).

59. G. Clay, *Close-Up, How to Read the American City* (Chicago 1980), 87.

60. E. Griffin and L. Ford, "A Model of Latin American City Structure," *Geographic Review* 70.4, Oct. 1980, 398.

61. Yung-Cheng Kao, *The Unit of Place in the Planning of Chinese Cities*, MCP diss., Univ. of California, Berkeley 1981, 30.

62. Wagner in *Architectural Record* 31, May 1912, 492.

63. See also W. M. Bowsky, *A Medieval Italian Commune* (Berkeley/London 1981), 12–14 and *passim*, and notes. He states that the terms *contrade*, *popoli*, and *lire* are often used indiscriminately; his attempt to disentangle them is not quite successful.

64. G. Downey, *Ancient Antioch* (Princeton 1963), 30.

65. See R. I. Burns, *Islam under the Crusaders* (Princeton 1973).

66. C. Morris and D. E. Thompson, *Huanuco Pampa: An Inca City and Its Hinterland* (London 1985), 70–71.

67. Yang Hsuan-chih, *The Temples in Lo-yang*, cited in Ping-ti Ho, "Lo-Yang, A.D. 495–534," *Harvard Journal of Asiatic Studies* 26, 1966, 52–106.

68. Cited in Kao (n.61 above), 52.

69. Clay (n.59 above), 145.

70. Lewis (Ch.1 n.25 above), 38.

71. T. H. Greenshields, "Quarters' and Ethnicity," in Blake and Lawless (Ch.1 n.29 above), 122.

72. See K. Gillion, *Ahmedabad* (Berkeley/London 1968), and A. Desai, "Pre-Industrial Elements in the Industrial City of Ahmedabad," *Ekistics* 295, July–Aug. 1982.

73. Greenshields (n.71 above), 123.

74. Braunfels (Ch.1 n.22 above), 128, 245.

75. W. Bartoszewski, *The Warsaw Ghetto* (Boston 1987), 5.

76. A. Edelson and R. Lapides, *Łódz Ghetto* (New York 1989), 36.

77. See *The City Shaped*, 167, for a discussion of the Nazi concentration camp as a diagram of regimentation.

78. See C. Yip, *San Francisco's Chinatown: An Architectural and Urban History*, PhD diss., Univ. of California, Berkeley 1985.

79. T. G. McGee, *The Southeast Asian City* (New York 1967), 69–70.

80. S. D. Markman, "The Gridiron Townplan and the Caste System in Colonial Central America," in R. Schaedel et al., eds., *Urbanization in the Americas from its Beginnings to the Present* (The Hague 1980).

81. See A. J. Christopher, "From Flint to Soweto: Reflections on Colonial Origins of the Apartheid City," *Area* 15.2, 1983.

82. G. H. Pirie and D. M. Hart, "The Transformation of Johannesburg's Black Western Areas," *Journal of Urban History* 11.4, Aug. 1985.

83. McGee (n.79 above), 56.

84. P. Monelli in *Gazzetta del Popolo*, June 1936.

85. M. Bafile in P. Sica, *Storia dell'Urbanistica, Il Novecento*, vol. 3:2 (Rome 1978), 498, and section V:8 on Italian Fascist colonial planning in general.

86. On assimilation and association in French colonialism, see G. Wright, *The Politics of Design in French Colonial Urbanism* (Chicago/London 1991).

87. British planners declared an agenda of overt subjugation in their choice of a site beside a historic city for the new capital of the Raj: "Delhi is to be an Imperial capital and is to absorb the traditions of all the ancient capitals. . . . It has to convey the idea of a peaceful domination and dignified rule over the traditions and life of India." Delhi Town Planning Committee, *Final Report on the Town Planning of the New Imperial Capital* (London 1913), 2.

88. Wright (n.86 above), 79.

89. ibid., 265–66.

90. ibid., 95.

91. For the best discussion of Lyautey see P. Rabinow, *French Modernism* (Cambridge, Mass./London 1989); also J. Dethier's piece on Morocco 1900–1972 in L. C. Brown, ed., *From Madina to Metropolis* (Princeton 1973).

92. Quoted in Wright (n.86 above), 147.

93. ibid., 153.

94. Hébrard, "L'Urbanisme en Indochine," quoted in ibid., 221.

95. Heers (Ch.1 n.17 above).

96. Alberti (Ch.1 n.18 above), IV.i.

97. P. Hall, *Cities of Tomorrow* (Oxford 1988), 32.

98. White (Ch.1 n.62 above), 49.

99. F. Loyer, *Paris Nineteenth Century: Architecture and Urbanism*, transl. C. L. Clarke (New York 1988), 92.

100. Girouard (n.37 above), 266.

101. F. Engels, *The Condition of the Working Class in England* (London 1845).

102. W. C. Taylor, *Notes of a Tour in the Manufacturing Districts of Lancashire* (London 1842/1968), 92.

103. David Ward, quoted in R. Dennis, *English Industrial Cities of the Nineteenth Century* (Cambridge 1984), 49.

104. F. Trabalzi, "Low-Cost Housing in Twentieth Century Rome," in D. Ghirardo, ed., *Out of Site: A Social Criticism of Architecture* (Seattle 1991), 129–56.

105. K. G. Bristol, *Beyond the Pruitt-Igoe Myth: The Development of American High-Rise Public Housing, 1850–1970*, PhD diss., Univ. of California, Berkeley 1991.

106. N. Lemann, *The Promised Land* (New York 1991), 92–93.

107. M. C. Boyer, *Dreaming the Rational City* (Cambridge, Mass. 1983), 164.

108. E. Szita, "Exclusionary Zoning in the Suburbs: The Case of New Canaan, Connecticut," *Civil Rights Digest* 5:4, Spring 1973, 2–14.

109. Restrictive definitions of the nature of a "household" discriminate against those unable to live alone – e.g., some of the elderly, the physically disabled, the mentally retarded – because they need some continual level of institutional support. See for example the Council of Planning Librarians bibliography by B. A. Shilling, "Exclusionary Zoning: Restrictive Definitions of Family," 31 (Chicago 1980).

110. G. Heinritz and E. Lichtenberger, "Munich and Vienna – A Cross-national Comparison," in Heinritz and Lichtenberger (Ch.1 n.57 above), 1–29.

3. PUBLIC PLACES (pp. 123–87)

1. *Odyssey* IX, 112–15.

2. R. M. Delson, *New Towns for Colonial Brazil*, PhD diss., Syracuse Univ., N.Y. 1979.

3. Cited by C. Dardi in *Agora* 1, July–Aug. 1988, 10.

4. P. Deyon in D. Ozanam, ed., "Plazas ' et sociabilité en Europe et Amérique Latine (Paris 1982), 131–36.

5. J. W. Konvitz, *Urban Millennium* (Carbondale, Ill. 1985), 30.

6. In northern Europe, the revolutionary burden tends to fall on streets; cf. the English expression "to take to the streets" and the French tradition of barricades.

7. Dardi (n.3 above), 9.

8. V. F. Pardo, *Storia dell'urbanistica, dal Trecento al Quattrocento* (Bari 1982), 161–63.

9. Heers (Ch.1 n.17 above), 155–56.

10. G. Gorse, "A Family Enclave in Medieval Genoa," *Journal of Architectural Education* 41:3, Spring 1988, 20–24.

11. A. Safak, "Urbanism and Family Residence in Islamic Law," *Ekistics* 47:280, Jan.–Feb. 1980, 23.

12. N. AlSayyad, *Streets of Islamic Cairo* (Cambridge, Mass. 1981); also his "Space in Islamic Architecture: Some Urban Patterns," *Journal of Architectural and Planning Research* 4.2, June 1987.

13. Cited by L. Alvarez, A. Collantes de Terán and F. Zoido in Ozanam (n.4 above), 81.

14. A. Bazzana in Ozanam (n.4 above), 29–30.

15. J. Sauvaget, *La mosquée omeyyade de Médine* (Paris 1947), 77–78.

16. G. Posner and K. Weil, "Cloister, Court and City Square," *Gesta* 12, 1973.

17. See E. W. Palm, "La place excentrée," in Ozanam (n.4 above), 176.

18. H. Gaube, *Iranian Cities* (New York 1978), 77.

19. Burke (Ch. 1 n.11 above), 81.

20. See L. Cervera Vera, *La Plaza Mayor de Ávila* (Ávila 1982).

21. The *musalla* was especially important in the Islamic cities of Spain. See L. T. Balbas in *Al-Andalus* 13, 1948, 167–80; and P. Chalmeta in Ozanam (n.4 above), 11.

22. Balbas (n.21 above), 177.

23. ibid., 179.

24. Downey (Ch.2 n.64 above), 32.

25. For a far-off example, we might note the *plaza* of a new town for Indians (*aldeia*) in Brazil called São Miguel, from 1765. One side of the *plaza* was left open to face the river, one side had the church, and one side had the houses of the director of the community and the resident priest side by side, and the warehouse for the collection of fruits at the back. See Delson (n.2 above).

26. See A. B. Correa in Ozanam (n.4 above), 69–80. The plaza got its present semicircular shape in a reconstruction of 1856.

27. Orlin (Ch.2 n.23 above), 31.

28. Alvarez et al. in Ozanam (n.4 above), 81.

29. Delson (n.2 above), 105, fig. 11.

30. ibid., 44. Delson illustrates as typical Santo Antonio de Macapa, Amapa, from 1761.

31. Cited by H. Blumenfeld in "Scale in Civic Design," *Town Planning Review* 24:1, Apr. 1953, 41.

32. S. Tobriner, *The Genesis of Noto* (London 1982), 30–31.

33. ibid., 97.

34. P. Zucker, *Town and Square: From Agora to Village Green* (New York 1959), 2.

35. For the following paragraphs, see B. Ladd, "Urban Aesthetics and the Discovery of the Urban Fabric in Turn-of-the-Century Germany," *Planning Perspectives* 2, 1987, 270–86; also Blumenfeld (n.31 above).

36. See Institut Français d'Architecture, *Toulouse, Les délices de l'imitation* (Brussels/Liège 1986), 270–79.

37. Cited in Ladd (n.35 above), 275.

38. H. Maertens, *Der optische Massstab in den bildenden Künsten* (Berlin 1877).

39. *The American Architect and Building News* 27, 15 Mar. 1890, 162.

40. M. Smets, "Reconstruction of Leuven after the Events of 1914," in *Villes en mutation, XIXe–XXe siècles* (Brussels 1980), 506–8.

41. S. Kostof, "His Majesty the Pick: The Aesthetics of Demolition," *Design Quarterly*, 1982, 32–41.

42. Cited by Ladd (n.35 above), 281.

43. S. Kostof, *The Third Rome, 1870–1950* (Berkeley 1973); and by the same author "The Emperor and the Duce: The Planning of Piazzale Augusto Imperatore in Rome," in H. A. Millon and L. Nochlin, eds., *Art and Architecture in the Service of Politics* (Cambridge, Mass./London 1978).

44. See *The City Shaped*, 231.

45. A. Speer, *Inside the Third Reich*, transl. R. and C. Winston (New York 1970/1981), 109; for the description of the Nüremberg Party grounds see 97–111. See also L. Lenzi, "Architettura del Terzo Reich," *Architettura*, Aug. 1939, 477ff.

46. H. Carter, *The Theatre and Cinema of Soviet Russia* (London 1924); repr. in W. G. Rosenberg, ed., *Bolshevik Visions* (Ann Arbor 1984), 445–47.

47. N. Bylinkin in *Architectural Review*, May 1947, 184.

48. F. W. Carter in French and Hamilton (Ch.2 n.54 above), 429.

49. Cited in R. Conquest, *The Harvest of Sorrow* (New York 1986), 208.

50. See Castillo (Ch.2 n.14 above).

51. See De Seta in Ozanam (n.4 above), esp. 141.

52. Gaube (n.18 above), 111–12.

53. The edition used here is the third, published in Leipzig in 1924. For the section on squares, see 140–95. A chapter on esthetics ("Öffentliche Plätze in künstlerischer Beziehung") follows, 196–221.

54. M. Trieb, *Grundlagen des stadtgestalterischen Entwerfens*, Städtebauliches Institut der Univ. Stuttgart, 25, 1977, 24–47.

55. Evelyn (Ch.2 n.33 above), 37.

56. Heers (Ch.1 n.17 above), 174–75.

57. See M. Dennis, *Court and Garden: From the French Hôtel to the City of Modern Architecture* (Cambridge, Mass./London 1986), 79–82.

58. ibid. 50–51. Of the project, only two of the streets were executed.

59. On the agora and the Roman forum, we have the studies of R. Martin. Much of the discussion here comes from a piece of his in R. Chevallier, ed., *Forum et plaza mayor dans le monde hispanique* (Paris 1978), which in turn seems to summarize Martin's *Recherches sur l'agora grecque* (Paris 1951); his *Urbanisme dans la Grèce antique* (2nd ed., Paris 1975); and his "Agora et forum" in the *Mélanges* of the Ecole française de Rome, 84, 1972, 909–33.

60. Pausanias as cited by Martin in Chevallier (n.59 above), 8.

61. J. Burckhardt, *Griechische Kulturgeschichte* (Berlin/Stuttgart 1898), 76.

62. See J. Le Gall in Chevallier (n.59 above), 23–26.

63. R. Chevallier in ibid., 30.

64. Gutkind (Ch.1 n.9 above), 383.

65. Morris and Thompson (Ch.2 n.66 above), 58–59.

66. Bateman and Riley (Ch.1 n.21 above), 45.

67. B. Vayssière and J. P. Le Flem in Chevallier (n.59 above), 48–50.

68. See J. L. Acquaroni, *Bulls and Bullfighting* (Barcelona 1964), 21.

69. See J. Armitage, *Man at Play* (London 1977), 26.

70. See L. Clare, *La quintaine, la course de bague, et le jeu des têtes* (Paris 1983). The quoted passages come from 241 and 94 respectively. Clare includes a document of 1660, in which Louis XIV orders the demolition of some houses for the widening of the Rue Sainte-Catherine opening into the Place Royale (des Vosges), to facilitate tournaments there: see 239–40.

71. J. Stuart [attr.], *Critical Observations on the Buildings and Improvements of London* (Los Angeles 1978), 7.

72. Cited in Girouard (Ch.2 n.37 above), 224.

73. Alberti (Ch.1 n.18 above), VIII.vi.

74. W. A. Eden in *Town Planning Review* 19–20, 1943, 23.

75. See H. Ballon, *The Paris of Henri IV* (Cambridge, Mass. 1991).

76. See J. Summerson, *Inigo Jones* (Harmondsworth 1966), 85–86.

77. J. P. Babelon in P. Francastel, ed., *Urbanisme de Paris et l'Europe, 1600–1680* (Paris 1969), 54 and pl.4.

78. W. Braunfels (Ch.1 n.22 above), 218, points out a parallel in Berlin. There, an equestrian statue of the Great Elector Frederick I by Andreas Schlüter was set up in 1703 on the Lange Brücke, facing downstream in the direction of the royal palace (the Altes Schloss), rather than in the middle of the palace square.

79. W. Herrmann, *Laugier and 18th Century French Theory* (London 1962), 134.

80. Stuart (n.71 above), 8–9.

81. Weale, *London Exhibited in 1851*, 769. Quoted in Olsen (Ch.1 n.32 above), 19.

82. Alvarez et al. in Ozanam (n.4 above), 98.

83. H. Frankfort, "Town Planning in Ancient Mesopotamia," *Town Planning Review* 21.2, July 1950, 103.

84. Cicero, *De Divinatione*, I.101.

85. G. and S. Jellicoe, P. Goode and M. Lancaster, eds., *Oxford Companion to Gardens* (Oxford 1986), 115. Much of what follows is indebted to Lancaster's article there, "Public Parks," 456–61. See also N. T. Newton, *Design on the Land* (Cambridge, Mass. 1971).

86. Ovid, *Ex Ponto*, 1.8.33–38.

87. The classic source for what follows remains S. E. Rasmussen's chapter called "Origin of Recreation Grounds," in his *London: The Unique City* (New York 1937). See also C. Trent, *Greater London* (London 1965).

88. Cited in Rasmussen (n.87 above), 80.

89. ibid., 82.

90. Gomme (Ch.2 n.44 above), 148.

91. Trent (n.87 above), 235. By the 1760s 6,500 keys had been issued. Many had been duplicated and used by hundreds of prostitutes and their clients.

92. Rasmussen (n.87 above), 96.

93. Cited in Newton (n.85 above), 232.

94. M. L. Simo, *Loudon and the Landscape* (New Haven/London 1988), 194.

95. Jellicoe (n.85 above), 296.

96. M. Francis, "Changing Values for Public Spaces," *Landscape Architecture* 78:1, Jan.–Feb. 1988, 57.

97. J. Muntañola-Thornberg in *Places* 4.1, 1987, 75.

98. M. Treib in *Landscape Architecture* 75:4, July–Aug. 1985, 73.

99. H. Dupree, *Urban Transportation: The New Town Solution* (Aldershot, Hants/Brookfield, Vt. 1987).

100. D. Sinz, "Place Royale and Palais Royal in Paris," *Anthos* 27:4, 1988, 24.

101. Muntañola-Thornberg (n.97 above), 75.

102. See, e.g., B. P. Spring, "Evaluation: Rockefeller Center's Two Contrasting Generations of Space," *AIA Journal* 67:2, Feb. 1978, 26–31; R. Ramati, "The Plaza as Amenity," *Urban Land* 38:2, Feb. 1979, 9–12.

103. E. K. Carpenter, "Making Minneapolis Work," *Design and Environment* 6.2, 1975, 39.

104. W. H. Whyte, *City* (New York 1988), 210.

105. "From Minneapolis to Paris," *Shopping Centers Today*, May 1990, 75.

4. THE STREET (pp. 189–243)

1. See *The City Shaped*, 69–89.

2. See J. Rykwert, *The Necessity of Artifice* (London/New York 1982), 105.

3. See *The City Shaped*, 57–62.

4. Frankfort (Ch.3 n.83 above), 111.

5. B. S. Hakim, "Examples of Traditional Housing Design Elements and their Associated Vocabulary from the Tunis Region," *Arabian Journal for Science and Engineering* 7.2, Apr. 1982, 77–79.

6. See *The City Shaped*, 50.

7. Aston and Bond (Ch.1 n.19 above), 97.

8. Regulations quoted in Olsen (Ch.1 n.32 above), 146.

9. Quoted in C. C. Savage, *Architecture of the Private Streets of St. Louis* (Columbia, Mo. 1987), 3.

10. This paragraph summarizes Pythian-Adams (Ch.2 n.49 above).

11. R. J. Ingersoll, *The Ritual Use of Public Space in Renaissance Rome*, PhD diss., Univ. of California, Berkeley 1985.

12. C. Lane, *The Rites of Rulers* (Cambridge 1981), 279–80.

13. W. Vaughan, *Romantic Art* (London/New York 1978), 62. Also *Les Architectes de la liberté*, exh. cat., Ecole des Beaux-Arts, Paris 1989.

14. A. A. Andreev, "Light, color and movement," *Sovetskoe iskusstvo* (Soviet Art) 210, 8 May 1933. Quoted in V. Tolstoy, I. Bibikova, and C. Cooke, *Street Art of the Revolution* (London 1990), 225–26.

15. See *The City Shaped*, 272–74.

16. See the chapter "The Evolution of Architectural Control under the Nazi Regime" in B. M. Lane, *Architecture and Politics in Germany, 1918–1945* (Cambridge, Mass. 1968/1985).

17. Stuart (Ch.3 n.71 above), 24. The specimen that offended the author was Burlington House.

18. For a good picture, see Braudel (Ch.2 n.7 above), 545.

19. For these, see principally W. Braunfels, *Mittelalterliche Stadtbaukunst in der Toskana* (Berlin 1953).

20. See *The City Shaped*, 256–58.

21. Ladd (Ch.1 n.45 above), 112.

22. For modern examples, see C. Rosen, *The Limits of Power* (Cambridge, Mass. 1986), 95–109 on the aftermath of American disasters.

23. Braunfels (n.19 above), 130.

24. Platt (Ch.1 n.6 above), 45.

25. Evelyn (Ch.2 n.33 above), 53.

26. Cited by Gomme (Ch.2 n.44 above), 138–39.

27. Stuart (Ch.3 n.71 above), 5.

28. Cited by Gomme (Ch.2 n.44 above), 139.

29. ibid., 139–40.

30. H. F. Lake, "The Billboard Nuisance," *American City* 3, 1910, 219–24.

31. D. Crouch, *Water Management in Ancient Greek Cities* (in press).

32. J. B. Ward-Perkins, "Early Roman Towns in Italy," *Town Planning Review* 26:3, Oct. 1955, 135.

33. Platt (Ch.1 n.6 above), 69.

34. Evelyn (Ch.2 n.33 above), 53.

35. Quoted by Olsen (Ch.1 n.32 above), 220.

36. Ladd (Ch.1 n.45 above), 52–57.

37. See Loyer (Ch.2 n.99 above), 112. Illustrations of all this can be had in M. F. E. Belgrand, *Les Travaux souterrains de Paris* (Paris 1872–87).

38. See *The City Shaped*, 149.

39. A convenient summary is in M. Girouard, *The English Town* (New Haven/London 1990), 259ff.

40. Ladd (Ch.1 n.45 above), 110, and 103–10 generally for this section.

41. F. L. Thompson, "Width and Allocation of Space in Roads," *Journal of the Town Planning Institute*, 1915–16, 122.

42. N. P. Brooks and G. Whittington, "Planning and Growth in the Medieval Scottish Burgh: The Example of St. Andrews," *Institute of British Geographers, Transactions* 2.3, 1977, 285.

43. Both examples are from Aston and Bond (Ch.1 n.19 above), 97.

44. See Hakim (n.5 above).

45. AlSayyad, "Space in Islamic Architecture" (Ch.3 n.12 above), 116.

46. Loyer (Ch.2 n.99 above), 121, who gets it from Jean Louis Subileau.

47. See J. André, "Les noms latins du chemin et de la rue," *Revue des études latines* 28, 1950, 121ff.

48. Evelyn (Ch.2 n.33 above), 52.

49. Stuart (Ch.3 n.71 above), 5.

50. Gutkind (Ch.1 n.9 above), 81.

51. H. W. Lawrence, "Origins of the Tree-Lined Boulevard," *The Geographical Review* 78.4, Oct. 1988, 370, citing Rambuteau's memoirs.

52. G. E. Haussmann, *Mémoires* (Paris 1890–93), vol. 3, 149.

53. Cited in Olsen (Ch.1 n.32 above), 224–25.

54. J. F. Geist, *Arcades*, transl. J. O. Newmann and J. H. Smith (Cambridge, Mass./London 1983) 62–63.

55. Loyer (Ch.2 n.99 above), 158, n.17.

56. All instances mentioned in Platt (Ch.1 n.6 above), 48–50.

57. The chronicler Rigord, quoted in V. W. Egbert, *On the Bridges of Paris* (Princeton 1974), 26.

58. D. Cruickshank and N. Burton, *Life in the Georgian City* (London 1990), 13–15.

59. Platt (Ch.1 n.6 above), 48–49.

60. In *Letters from England* (London 1807; repr., ed. J. Simmons, London 1951), cited by Ladd (Ch.1 n.45 above), 36.

61. Gutkind (Ch.1 n.9 above), 228.

62. ibid., 217.

63. ibid., 239.

64. L. Woolley, *Excavations at Ur* (London 1965), 177–78.

65. E. D. Very, "Modern Methods of Street Cleaning," *American City* 7.5, Nov. 1912, 435.

66. Ladd (Ch.1 n.45 above), 58–60.

67. The best source for modern paving materials is C. McShane, "A Look at the Revolution in Paving, 1880–1924," *Journal of Urban History* 5.3, 1979, 279–307, based on his PhD diss., *American Cities and the Coming of the Automobile*, Univ. of Wisconsin, Madison 1975.

68. Cited in B. L. Grad, *Visions of City and Country: Prints and Photographs of Nineteenth-Century France* (Worcester, Mass./New York 1982), 200.

69. D. Friedman, *Florentine New Towns* (New York 1989), 207.

70. R. S. Johnston, "The Ancient City of Suzhou," *Town Planning Review* 54.2, Apr. 1983, 206–8.

71. K. W. Forster, "From 'Rocca' to 'Civitas': Urban Planning at Sabbioneta," *L'Arte*, Mar. 1969, 16–17.

72. See R. A. Goldthwaite, *The Building of Renaissance Florence* (Baltimore 1980).

73. Friedman (n.69 above), 207.

74. See *The City Shaped*, 255–61.

75. Gutkind (Ch.1 n.9 above), 257.

76. H. Blumenfeld, "Russian City Planning of the 18th and Early 19th Centuries," *Journal of the Society of Architectural Historians* 4.1, Jan. 1944, 23.

77. R. Krier, *Urban Space*, transl. C. Czechowski (New York 1979), 66.

78. See A. Boethius, *The Golden House of Nero* (Ann Arbor 1960).

79. W. L. MacDonald, *The Architecture of the Roman Empire, I* (New Haven 1965), 27–30.

80. See *The City Shaped*, 142.

81. I. Browning, *Palmyra* (Park Ridge, N.J. 1979), 138.

82. W. L. MacDonald, *The Architecture of the Roman Empire, II. An urban Appraisal* (New Haven/London 1986), 48.

83. Boethius (n.78 above), 181.

84. N. Miller, *Renaissance Bologna* (New York 1989), 38.

85. See F. W. Kent, "The Rucellai Family and Its Loggia," *Journal of the Warburg and Courtauld Institutes* 35, 1972, 397–401. A dissertation of the same year (G. Leinz, *Die Loggia Rucellai, ein Beitrag zur Typologie der Familienloggia*, Rheinische Friedrich-Wilhelms Univ., Bonn) collects all contemporary references to the Florentine family loggia, but fails to distinguish between the street variety and the interior arcades of palace courtyards. I am indebted to Dr. Brenda Preyer for sharing her research on this subject.

86. F. Sullivan, "Passing of the American Front Porch," *House and Garden*, June 1952, 68.

87. For example Donatius, *Ad Ter.*, Ad. 578: "Angiportum, id est angusta et curva via . . ." For this Roman typology, see André (n.47 above), 104–34.

88. See *The City Shaped*, 112.

89. P. J. Edwards, *History of London Street Improvements 1855–1897* (London 1898), 125.

90. Johnston (n.70 above), 197.

91. My main source is Johnston. See also *The City Shaped*, 96 and ill. 103.

92. See Egbert (n.57 above).

93. D. Thompson, *Renaissance Paris* (Berkeley 1984), 73–74.

94. Babelon (Ch.3 n.77 above), 48.

95. See M. Selimonte, *Le Pont Neuf et ses charlatans* (Paris 1980).

96. Evelyn (Ch.2 n.33 above), 51.

97. See *The City Shaped*, 249–52.

98. The designer of the Boston Prado was A. A. Shurcliff, and his account of the project appeared in *Landscape Architecture* 25.4, July 1935, 177–82. The idea is credited to the then mayor, James M. Curley, who had visited Havana and was taken with its Prado.

99. Geist (n.54 above).

100. Pedestrian passages through urban blocks were not confined to Paris. London knew them. James Fenimore Cooper, in his London visit of 1828, described these "private ways, called passages . . . by which one can avoid the carriages and much of the streets, besides greatly shortening the distances." This comment is cited in Gomme (Ch.2 n.44 above), 17–18. In fact, in the late 18th and early 19th centuries, these open London passages included luxurious private streets in the West End, built over the gardens that occupied the interiors of the oversized blocks. Their equivalents in Paris were called *cités* or *passage ouverts*, and were closed off by gates and guarded by porters at each end.

101. According to R. Doisneau and B. Delvaille, *Passages et galeries du 19e siècle* (Paris 1981), which deals with those in Paris.

102. Loyer (Ch.2 n.99 above), 81.

103. D. J. Olsen, *The City as a Work of Art* (New Haven/London 1986), 248.

104. Le Corbusier, *Towards a New Architecture*, transl. F. Etchells (London/New York 1927), 59–61.

105. Le Corbusier, *The City of To-morrow*, transl. F. Etchells (London 1929/1971), 167.

106. A. E. Bongard and I. C. Bongard, "Die Ausbildung von Fahrlehrern in der Bundesrepublik Deutschland," *Unfall-und Sicherheitsforschung, Strassenverkehr* 43, 1983, 1–21; quoted in C. H. Klau, *The Pedestrian and City Traffic* (London 1990), 38.

107. Le Corbusier (n.105 above), 179.

108. ibid., 177–78.

109. S. D. Adshead, "Camillo Sitte and Le Corbusier," *Town Planning Review* 14.2, Nov. 1930, 85–94.

110. Cited in Gomme (Ch.2 n.44 above), 153.

111. See P. L. Garside, "Unhealthy Areas: Town Planning, Eugenics, and the Slums, 1890–1945," *Planning Perspectives* 3, 1988, 26.

112. Wright (Ch.1 n.56 above), 125.
113. Le Corbusier, *The Athens Charter*, transl. A. Eardley (New York 1973), 57.
114. Le Corbusier, *The Radiant City*, transl. B. P. Knight et al. (New York 1933/1964), 121.
115. R. Mallet-Stevens, "L'influence de l'architecture sur la population des villes," *Tekné*, 21 Sept. 1911, 307; quoted in R. Becherer, "Monumentality and the Rue Mallet-Stevens," *Journal of the Society of Architectural Historians* 40.1, Mar. 1981, 46.
116. E. Mendelsohn, "Dynamics and Function" (lecture), 1923, in U. Conrads, ed., *Programs and Manifestos on 20th Century Architecture* (Cambridge, Mass. 1970).
117. F. Choay, *Le Corbusier* (New York 1960).
118. Quoted in P. Wolf, *The Future of the City* (New York 1974), without a source.
119. See articles by C. Rowe and S. B. Warner, Jr., in *Design Quarterly* 129, "Skyways" (Cambridge, Mass./London 1985).
120. See *The City Shaped*, 276–77.
121. A. Duany, E. Plater-Zyberk, C. E. Chellman, "New Town Ordinances and Codes," in *Prince Charles and the Architectural Debate* (New York 1989), 71.
122. M Culot and L. Krier, "The Only Path for Architecture," *Oppositions* 14, Fall 1978, 42.

5. URBAN PROCESS (pp. 245–305)

1. The following account is substantially based on T. F. Reddaway, *The Rebuilding of London after the Great Fire* (London 1940), still unsurpassed after half a century. J. N. Hearsey, *London and the Great Fire* (London 1965), deals only with the progress of the fire itself based on eyewitness accounts.
2. The following account is based on J. A. Franca, *Una città dell'Illuminismo: La Lisbona del marchese di Pombal* (Rome 1972). T. D. Kendrick's *The Lisbon Earthquake* (London 1956), being "concerned mainly with the related themes of eighteenth-century earthquake theology and the end of optimism," is not germane to my argument.
3. H. Stephan, "Rebuilding Berlin," *Town Planning Review* 29.4, Jan. 1959, 216.
4. H. Lilius, *The Finnish Wooden Town* (Rungsted Kyst 1985), 172. The fire of 1681 that ravaged Trondheim (Norway) surely compares.
5. The best account is in L. Richardson, Jr., *Pompeii, An Architectural History* (Baltimore/London 1988), 18–27.
6. See especially S. Tobriner, "Three Cases of Seismic Disaster and Reconstruction: Sicily (1693), Calabria (1783) and San Francisco (1906)," in C. Latina, ed., *Vulnerabilità ai terremoti e metodi per la riduzione del rischio sismico* (Noto 1984), 63–71; also his *Genesis of Noto* (Ch.3 n.32 above); an essay on the Calabrian *casa barracata* in *Journal of the Society of Architectural Historians* 42.2, May 1983; and a forthcoming book on safety and reconstruction in San Francisco after earthquakes and fires 1849–1915, *Fate of the Phoenix*.
7. W. H. Coaldrake, "Order and Anarchy: Tokyo 1860 to the Present," in M. Friedman, ed., *Tokyo: Form and Spirit* (Minneapolis/New York 1986), 68–69.
8. See C. Winters, "Traditional Urbanism in North Central Sudan," *Annals of the Association of American Geographers* 67.4, Dec. 1977, 500–520.
9. See A. Verhulst, "The Origins of Towns in the Low Countries and the Pirenne Thesis," *Past and Present* 122, 1989, 20.
10. P. Hughes, "The Great Galveston Hurricane," *Weatherwise* 32.4, Aug. 1979, 155.
11. Heers (Ch.1 n.17 above), 104.
12. Loyer (Ch.2 n.99 above), citing B. Rouleau, *Le Tracé des rues de Paris* (Paris 1967).
13. Heers (Ch.1 n.17 above), 175.

14. N. S. Steinhardt, "The Plan of Khubilai Khan's Imperial City," *Artibus Asiae* 44.2–3, 1983, 148.
15. K. Hewitt, "Place Annihilation: Area Bombing and the Fate of Urban Places," *Annals of the Association of American Geographers* 73.2, June 1983, 259.
16. S. Jankowski in J. M. Diefendorf, ed., *Rebuilding Europe's Bombed Cities* (London 1990), 79.
17. See Hewitt (n.15 above), 257–84.
18. M. Hastings as cited in ibid., 275.
19. ibid., 267–73.
20. D. Irving, *The Destruction of Dresden* (London 1963), 39.
21. Hewitt (n.15 above), 267.
22. What follows is based on K. von Beyme, *Der Wiederaufbau, Architektur und Städtebaupolitik in den beiden deutschen Staaten* (Munich 1987), esp. Ch.5.
23. Quoted by N. Gutschow and H. Beseler, *Kriegsschicksale deutscher Architektur*, vol. 1 (Neumünster 1988), p.ix.
24. Cited in R. Miller, "Chicago's Spectacular Apocalypse: The Great Fire and the Emergence of the Democratic Hero," in J. Zukowsky, ed., *Chicago Architecture 1872–1922* (Munich/Chicago 1987), 34.
25. Cited in Smets (Ch.3 n.40 above), 501.
26. Quoted by F. Fischer in Diefendorf (n.16 above), 141–42.
27. M. Smets, "Belgian Reconstruction after World War I: a Transition from Civic Art to Urban Planning," *Planning Perspectives* 2, 1987, 20. See before-and-after pictures of the marketplace in Leuven, p.24, to appreciate the point.
28. ibid., 21.
29. ibid., 23.
30. For these details, see P. Bieganski, "How Warsaw Arose out of the Ashes," *Built Environment* 1.5, Aug. 1972, 313–17.
31. Jankowski (n.16 above), 84.
32. J. F. C. Fuller, *The Decisive Battles of the Western World* (London 1954).
33. A. Wheatcroft, *World Atlas of Revolution* (London 1983), 74–77.
34. Bateman and Riley (Ch.1 n.21 above), 27.
35. See M. Lacave, "Stratégies d'expropriation et Haussmannization," *Annales: Economies, sociétés, civilisations* 35.5, 1980, 1015 and *passim*.
36. G. B. Ford, ed., *City Planning Progress in the U.S. in 1917* (Washington, D.C. 1917), 140.
37. Cited in Léon (Ch.1 n.33 above), 53–54; he gives no source, but from the context it seems to be Du Breul.
38. R. González de Clavijo, cited in Gutkind (Ch.1 n.9 above), 407–8.
39. S. A. Al-Hathloul, "Codes and Regulations in Arab Muslim Cities. The Effect of Muslim Law on the Traditional Physical Environment," in I. Serageldin and S. El-Sadek, eds., *The Arab City* (Arlington, Va. 1982), 75; this essay is based on Al-Hathloul's PhD diss. (MIT, Cambridge, Mass. 1981) entitled *Tradition, Continuity, and Change in the Physical Environment: The Arab-Muslim City.*
40. ibid., 75.
41. See Z. Celik, *The Remaking of Istanbul* (Seattle/London 1986), 61–62.
42. "Demolition by Dynamite," *Architectural Forum* 108:4, Apr. 1958, 136–37.
43. Loyer (Ch.2 n.99 above), 55.
44. J. B. Ward-Perkins, *Cities of Ancient Greece and Italy: Planning Classical Antiquity* (New York/London 1974), figs. 34, 35.
45. Konvitz (Ch.1 n.27 above), 118ff.
46. Loyer (Ch.2 n.99 above), 17.
47. See K. Scharlau, "Moderne Umgestaltungen im Grundriss iranischer Städte," *Erdkunde* 15.3, 1961, 180–91.
48. Details in M. Alemi, "The 1891 Map of Tehran. Two Cities, Two Cores, Two Cultures," *AARP Environmental Design*, Jan. 1985, 74–84.

49. R. I. Lawless, "The Future of Historic Centres: Conservation or Redevelopment?" in Blake and Lawless (Ch.1 n.29 above), 179.
50. This in the 1939 Harvard lectures which became the famous book *Space, Time and Architecture*. On Moses, the one indispensable piece in a vast body of literature remains the chapter in M. Berman, *All that Is Solid Melts into Air* (New York 1982).
51. See D.I. Scargill, *Urban France* (New York/London 1983), 122–24.
52. Quoted by Fischer in Diefendorf (n.16 above), 133–34.
53. C. Rifkind, *Main Street* (New York 1977), 236.
54. R. J. Horvath, *The Origin and Functional Structure of Santa Fe Springs, California*, MA diss., Univ. of California, Los Angeles 1961.
55. A. Fergusson, *The Sack of Bath* (Salisbury, Wilts. 1973).
56. Lilius (n.4 above), 187.
57. What follows derives from the Charles T. Mathews lectures I delivered at Columbia Univ., New York, in 1977, which remain unpublished.
58. See Z. Chafets, "The Tragedy of Detroit," *The New York Times Magazine*, 29 July 1990, 20ff., with a most remarkable set of images, including the one reproduced here as Pl.38; also by Chafets, *Devil's Night and Other True Tales of New York* (in press).
59. On East St. Louis see I. Wilkerson, "Ravaged City on Mississippi Floundering at Rock Bottom," *The New York Times*, 4 Apr. 1991, 1ff.
60. See S. D. Goitein in I. M. Lapidus, ed., *Middle Eastern Cities* (Berkeley/Los Angeles 1969), 80–96.
61. C. McKean, *Fight Blight* (London 1977), 13–14.
62. Braudel (Ch.2 n.7 above), 548.
63. See Conzen's essays in J. W. R. Whitehand, ed., *The Urban Landscape: Historical Development and Management* (London 1981), esp. "The Plan Analysis of an English City Center," on Newcastle-upon-Tyne.
64. See *The City Shaped*, 148.
65. Loyer (Ch.2 n.99 above), 54.
66. See M. P. Conzen, "Analytical Approaches to the Urban Landscape," in K. W. Butler, ed., *Dimensions of Human Geography* (Chicago 1978), 128–65.
67. S. Olson, "Baltimore Imitates the Spider," *Annals of the Association of American Geographers* 69.4, 1979, 557–74; also "Urban Metabolism and Morphogenesis," *Urban Geography* 3.2, 1982, 87–109; and *Baltimore, The Building of an American City* (Baltimore 1980).
68. See, among others, W. Isard, *Location and Space Economy* (Cambridge, Mass./New York 1956) and his *Methods of Regional Analysis* (Cambridge, Mass. 1960) on the transport-building cycle; also R. A. Easterlin, *Population, Labor Force, and Long Swings in Economic Growth: the American Experience* (New York 1968); M. Abramovitz, *Evidence in Long Swings in Aggregate Construction since the Civil War* (New York 1964); and H. Hoyt, "The Urban Real Estate Cycle – Performances and Prospects," *Urban Land*, June 1950 (repr. in a self-published volume, *According to Hoyt: 50 Years of Homer Hoyt*, which is a compendium of all of his work), and Hoyt's dissertation on land values in Chicago (Ch.1 n.55 above).
69. See J. M. Fitch, *Historic Preservation. Curatorial Management of the Built World* (Charlottesville, Va./London 1990).
70. A. von Oechelhäuser, ed., *Denkmalpflege. Auszug aus den stenographischen Berichten des Tages für Denkmalpflege*, vol. 1 (Leipzig 1910), 328.
71. ibid.

BIBLIOGRAPHY

The following is a very limited selection from the extensive literature consulted in the writing of the text. Further specific sources will be found in the chapter notes.

Abbreviated references are to the notes ("Ch.1 n.2") and to paragraphs within the chapter bibliographies here ("Ch.3 para.1 above").

The surveys used in writing *The City Assembled* are essentially the same as those used for *The City Shaped*; for an extensive list, see that volume, p. 341 ("Introduction").

1. THE CITY EDGE

A convenient source for ancient foundation rituals is Rykwert (Ch.1 n.1). On Hindu delimitation and circumambulation, see N. Gutschow and T. Sieverts, eds., *Stadt und Ritual* (Darmstadt 1977), 11, 17, 26.

On ancient customs boundaries, see Palmer (Ch.1 n.2). On Ledoux, see now Vidler (Ch.1 n.39), 209–35. On general issues of early citadels and walled suburbs, see I. Acaroglu, *The Evolution of Urbanization from the Beginning of the Sedentary Life until the Fall of the Roman Empire, 8000 B.C. to 400 A.D.*, diss., Cornell Univ., Ithaca 1970. For twin cities in China, see Sen-Dou Chang, "Some Observations on the Morphology of Chinese Walled Cities," *Annals of the Association of American Geographers* 60.1, Mar. 1970, 63–91, and Ch.1 n.10.

The standard works on Cairo include J. Abu-Lughod, *Cairo: 1001 Years of the City Victorious* (Princeton 1971); C. J. R. Haswell, "Cairo, Origin and Development," *Bulletin de la Société Royale de Géographie d'Egypte*, Mar. 1922; W. B. Kubiak, *Al-Fustat, Its Foundation and Early Urban Development* (Cairo 1987); N. AlSayyad, *Cities and Caliphs* (New York/London 1991), 135–51; and O. Grabar's essay on the history of Cairo's form in the Aga Khan symposium proc., ed. A. Evin, *The Expanding Metropolis: Coping with Urban Growth in Cairo* (Singapore 1985). On Cracow, see K. Dziewonski, "The Plan of Cracow," *Town Planning Review* 19.1, 1943, 29–37.

Standard sources on fortifications include H. de la Croix, *Military Considerations in City Planning* (New York 1972); Bateman and Riley (Ch.1 n.21); F. E. Winter, *Greek Fortifications* (Toronto/Buffalo 1971). On bastioned walls, see H. de la Croix, "Military Architecture and the Radial City Plan in Sixteenth Century Italy," *Art Bulletin* 42.4, 1960, 263–90; and the cat. *Vauban et ses successeurs en Franche-Comté* (Besançon 1981). On the defences of Constantinople, see A. Van Millingen, *Byzantine Constantinople, The Walls of the City and Adjoining Historical Sites* (London 1899).

On fringe belts, the most important sources are essays by M. Barke, J. Vilagrasa and B. von der Dollen in T. R. Slater, ed., *The Built Form of Western Cities* (Leicester/London 1990); and M. R. G. Conzen (Ch.5 n.63). Also

J. W. R. Whitehand, "Urban Fringebelts: development of an Idea," *Planning Perspectives* 3, 1988, 47–58. Wissink's *American Cities in Perspective* (Ch.1 n.44) contains an excellent summary of fringe belt history throughout the world.

On city gates, see K. A. C. Creswell, *The Muslim Architecture of Egypt* (Oxford 1952–59); for Rome I. A. Richmond, *The City Wall of Imperial Rome* (London 1930/College Park, Md. 1971), and M. Todd, *The Walls of Rome* (London 1978). Also E. B. Smith, *Architectural Symbolism of Imperial Rome and the Middle Ages* (Princeton 1956); E. H. Kantorwicz, "King's Advent and the Enigmatic Panels in the Doors of Sta. Sabina," *Art Bulletin* 26, Dec. 1944. On the U.S., H. J. Nelson, "Walled Cities of the United States," *Annals of the Association of American Geographers* 51.1, Mar. 1961, 1–22.

On river towns, see P. Kramer, "River Cities: 1800–1850," in Kramer and F. L. Holborn, eds., *The City in American Life* (New York 1970, 1971); L. Harris, *Canals and their Architecture* (London 1969/1980); Le Gaulle's work on the Tiber Island; and Girouard's "The Waterside" in *The English Town* (Ch.4 n.39). Konvitz (Ch.1 n.27) is the best source for ports. On specific ports, see Gomme (Ch.2 n.44); C. van Traa, ed., *Rotterdam. Der Neubau einer Stadt* (Rotterdam 1957); R. Bartoccini, *Il Porto Romano di Leptis Magna* (Rome 1958); Holum et al. (Ch.1 n.28).

On modern projects for waterfronts, see the special issue of *Process*, 52, Nov. 1984. On Adelphi Terrace, see D. Yarwood, *Robert Adam* (London 1970), 143–47. On the 19th-century promenade and waterfront in Algiers, see F. Cresti, "The Boulevard de l'Impératrice," *AARP Environmental Design*, 1985, 54–59. H. Kirker's *The Architecture of Charles Bulfinch* (Cambridge, Mass. 1969), 188–93, is the best work on Bulfinch's India Wharf in Boston. On mills and mill towns, see J. Coolidge's classic account, *Mill and Mansion* (New York 1942); S. Dunwell, *The Run of the Mill* (Boston 1978); D. Macauley, *Mill* (Boston 1983), with its wonderful pictures of mill construction; T. K. Harevan and R. Langenbach's *Amoskeag* (London 1979) gives a complete picture of life and work in one of these mill towns, down to the present day. See D. H. Burnham and E. H. Bennett's *Plan of Chicago* (Chicago 1909, repr. New York 1970) for the magnificent renderings and superb explanations of the proposed Chicago harbor. On the warehouses in St. Louis, L. Eaton, "Warehouses and Warehouse districts in Mid-American Cities," *Urban History Review* 11.1, June 1982, 17–26; and the useful architectural guide to Laclede's Landing by H. C. Toft and O. Overby (St. Louis 1977). Also R. Karson, "Battery Park City Takes Manhattan," *Landscape Architecture* 75:4, July–Aug. 1985, 64–69, and his "South Cove," *Landscape Architecture* 76:3, May–June 1986, 48–53.

For Pirenne and his thesis, see his *Medieval Cities* (Princeton 1925); the critique by A. Verhulst (Ch.5 n.9); T. Hall, *Mittelalterliche Stadtgrundrisse* (Stockholm 1980); E. Ennen, *The Medieval Town*, transl. N. Fryde (Amsterdam/New York 1979). For the development and growth of the German city, see K. Gruber, *Die Gestalt der Deutschen Stadt* (Munich 1952/1976).

For an introduction to the suburbanization of the industrial city, see H. Carter, *An Introduction to Urban Historical Geography* (London 1983), 130–48. For U.S. suburbanization the best accounts are Jackson (Ch.1 n.49), J. R. Stilgoe, *Borderland: Origins of the American Suburb, 1820–1939* (New Haven/London 1988), and S. Warner, *Streetcar Suburbs, Process of Growth in Boston 1870–1900* (2nd. ed., Cambridge, Mass. 1978);

see also J. Archer, "Country and City in American Romantic Suburbs," *Journal of the Society of Architectural Historians* 42:2, May 1983; W. Creese, *Search for Environment, the Garden City Before and After* (New Haven 1966); and the bibliography in Kostof, *America by Design*, 355. For more recent U.S. suburbs, see R. A. Miller, "Exurbia's Last Best Hope," *Architectural Forum*, April 1958, 92–188; "The City's Threat to Open Land," *Architectural Forum*, Jan. 1958, 87ff. C. S. Sargent, Jr., "Land Speculation and Urban Morphology," in J. Adams, ed., *Urban Policymaking and Metropolitan Dynamics: A Comparative Geographical Analysis* (Cambridge, Mass. 1976) is crucial. Also see C. Tunnard and B. Pushkarev, *Manmade America: Chaos and Control* (New Haven/London 1963). On land values and their morphological implications see the classics by Hoyt (Ch.1 n.55); R. M. Hurd, *Principles of City Land Values* (New York 1903/1924); and W. Firey, *Land Use in Central Boston* (Cambridge, Mass. 1947). On the Lakewood plan in Los Angeles, see J. Hulpke, *The Lakewood, or Contract, Plan of Municipal Government* (Sunnymead, Calif. 1962).

For the English picture, see A. M. Edwards, *The Design of Suburbia* (London 1981); on early London, F. M. L. Thompson, ed., *The Rise of Suburbia* (Leicester 1982). On the suburbs of Turin, see D. Jalla, "Belonging Somewhere in the City–Social Space and Its Perception-The 'Barrière' of Turin in the Early 20th Century," *Oral History* 13.2, Autumn 1985, 19–34. On Munich and Vienna, see G. Heinritz and E. Lichtenberger (Ch.1 n.57); also C. Schorske's classic work (Ch.1 n.36). On European suburbs in general, see A. Clementi and F. Perego, eds., *Eupolis. La riqualificazione delle città in Europa* (Rome 1990). Popenoe (Ch.1 n.59) provides a useful comparison of U.S. and Swedish suburbs.

On greenbelts see Ch.1 nn.40–43. For the greenbelt concept, besides the classic text of Ebenezer Howard, *Garden Cities of Tomorrow* (London 1902), and the promotional text of F. J. Osborn, *Green-Belt Cities* (London 1945), see D. R. Mandelker, *Green Belts and Urban Growth* (Madison, Wis. 1962), and P. G. Hall, *Urban and Regional Planning* (London 1975). On Ottawa's greenbelt, see R. Wesche and M. Kugler-Gagnon, eds., *Ottawa-Hull: Spatial Perspectives and Planning* (Ottawa 1978).

For information on master plans see Kostof, "The Drafting of a Master Plan for *Roma Capitale*," *Journal of the Society of Architectural Historians* 35.1, Mar. 1976, 4–20. Also A. Sutcliffe, *Towards the Planned City. Germany, Britain, the United States and France 1780–1914* (Oxford 1981), and his *The Rise of Modern Urban Planning* (London 1980). On London, see Summerson and Olsen (Ch.1 n.32); on Cologne, see H. Kier and W. Schaefke, *Die Kölner Ringe* (Cologne 1987).

On new towns, see F. J. Osborn and A. Whittick's *The New Towns. The Answer to Megalopolis* (New York 1963), and a more recent case study, G. Anstis, *Redditch: Success in the Heart of England* (Stevenage 1985). For France see J. Tuppin, "New Towns in the Paris Region," *Town Planning Review* 50:1, Jan. 1979; J. M. Goursolas, "New Towns in the Paris Metropolitan Area," *International Journal of Urban and Regional Research* 4:3, Sept. 1980; F. Torres, ed., *Marne-la-Vallée* (Paris 1991). On the U.S., see most recently Garreau (Ch.1 n.63), with an extensive bibliography.

2. URBAN DIVISIONS

On the Berlin Wall, see Ch.2 n.1 and R. L. Merritt, "Infrastructural Changes in Berlin," *Annals of the*

Association of American Geographers 63.1, 1973, 58–70. On the Speer Axis, see S. Helmer, *Hitler's Berlin: The Speer Plans for Reshaping the Central City* (Ann Arbor 1985); L. O. Larsson, *Albert Speer, Le Plan de Berlin 1937–1943* (Brussels 1983; publ. in German 1978); *The City Shaped*, 272–74.

On American civic centers, see J. Draper, *The San Francisco Civic Center*, PhD diss., Univ. of California, Berkeley 1979; E. Johannesen, "Cleveland's Group Plan," *Inland Architect* 31.6, Nov.–Dec. 1987, 30–36. Also the exh. cat. *The American Renaissance 1876–1917* (Brooklyn 1979). On the special publication by the A.I.A. Committee on Town Planning, see G. B. Ford, ed., *City Planning Progress in the United States* (Washington, D.C. 1917), a study of Grand Manner cities from Akron to Zanesville.

For material on holy cities, see *The City Shaped*, "City as Diagram" chapter; also Wheatley (Ch.2 n.15), 315–45. On episcopal cities, see W. Braunfels, "Cathedral Cities" and "Monastic Republics, Cities and Citadels," in his *Monasteries of Western Europe* (London/Princeton 1972). On parishes, see Addleshaw (Ch.2 n.32); C. N. L. Brooke, *London 800–1216, The Shaping of a City*, Berkeley/Los Angeles 1975); Aubrun (Ch.2 n.30). On American parishes, see S. M. Tomasi, *Piety and Power: The Role of the Italian Parishes in the New York Metropolitan Area* (New York 1975); J. Dolan, ed., *The American Catholic Parish, A History 1850–Present* (New York 1987).

For general views of Old Jerusalem, see A. Kutcher, *The New Jerusalem, Planning and Politics* (London 1973); A. Kashtan's conference paper, "Architectural Confrontations on the Old City of Jerusalem" (Rome 1967); F. Maraini, *Jerusalem, Rock of all Ages* (New York 1969); A. S. Kaufman, "Where the Ancient Temple of Jerusalem Stood," *Biblical Archaeology Review* 9.2, Mar.–Apr. 1983, 40–60. For specific details on some holy buildings, see O. Grabar, "The Umayyad Dome of the Rock," *Ars Orientalis* 3, 1957, and the excellent bibliography in his *The Formation of Islamic Art* (New Haven/London 1973).

On market towns, see Elvin (Ch.2 n.38) and Everitt (Ch.2 n.39). For a discussion on *suqs*, see E. Sims, "Trade and Travel: Markets and Caravanserais," in G. Michell, ed., *Architecture of the Islamic World* (London 1978); and for an in-depth survey of Near Eastern bazaars M. Scharabi, *Der Bazar* (Tübingen 1985). Also R. Fonseca on Old Delhi in *Ekistics* 31.82, Jan. 1971, 72–80; J. Naji and Y. N. Ali, "The Suqs of Basrah," *Journal of the Economic and Social History of the Orient* 24.3, 298–309.

For general works on the department store see S. P. Benson, "Palace of Consumption and Machine for Selling: The American Department Store, 1880–1940," *Radical History Review*, Fall 1979, 199–221; monographs on department stores include M. B. Miller, *The Bon Marché: Bourgeois Culture and the Department Store* (Princeton 1981); M. L. Clausen, "La Samaritaine," *Revue de l'art* 32, Oct. 1976, 57–77. See also M. Trachtenberg, *The Incorporation of America* (New York 1982).

On the central business district (CBD), see H. Carter, *An Introduction to Urban Historical Geography* (London 1983), Ch.8; H. Carter and G. Rowley, "The Morphology of the Central Business District of Cardiff," *Institute of British Geographers: Transactions* 38, June 1966, 119–34; J. E. Vance, "Six Forces in the Life of Downtown," most recently included in his *Scene of Man: Role and Structure of the City in the Geography of Western Civilization* (New York 1977); T. J. Baerwald,

"The Emergence of a New 'Downtown,'" *The Geographical Review* 68.3, July 1978, 308–18; R. E. Preston, "The Zone in Transition: A Study of Urban Landuse Patterns," *Geographic Review* 70.4, Oct. 1980. For an impressionistic account of the American strip with good photographs, see R. P. Horwitz, *The Strip* (Lincoln, Neb./London 1985).

For works on urban spatial structure both residential and social in China, see Yung-Cheng Kao (Ch.2 n.61); F. W. Mote, "A Millennium of Chinese Urban History: Form, Time and Space Concepts in Soochow," *Rice University Studies* 59.4, Fall 1983; H. D. R. Baker, "Extended Kinship in the Traditional City," in Skinner (Ch.1 n.10); J. Needham, *Science and Civilization in China* 4:III (Cambridge 1971), 67, 71ff.; P. Miao, "Seven Characteristics of Traditional Urban Form in Southeast China," *Traditional Dwelling and Settlements Review* 1.11, Spring 1990, 35–47; A. Boyd, *Chinese Architecture and Town Planning* (Chicago 1962), 49–60.

On Islamic city structure see the works cited above on *suqs* (para.5) and on Cairo (Ch.1 para.3 above). Also Greenshields (Ch.2 n.71); Raymond (Ch.2 n.53); Lapidus and English in *From Madina to Metropolis* (Ch.2 n.91); AlSayyad (Ch.1 para.3 above); Lapidus, ed. (Ch.5 n.60).

A selection on the structure of 19th-century European cities includes J. H. Johnson and C. G. Pooley, eds., *The Structure of Nineteenth Century Cities* (New York 1982), esp. the chapters by Pooley, Dennis and Cannadine; P. Sica, *Storia dell'urbanistica, L'Ottocento* (Rome 1977), Pt. I, 32ff., 50ff. On Birmingham see J. E. Vance, "Housing the Worker: The Employment Linkage as a Force in Urban Structure," *Economic Geography* 42.4, Oct. 1966, 294–325, and "Housing the Worker: Determinative and Contingent Ties in Nineteenth Century Birmingham," *Economic Geography* 43.2, Apr. 1967, 95–127. On Paris, see Loyer (Ch.2 n.99).

For America, see D. Ward, *Cities and Immigrants. A Geography of Change in Nineteenth Century America* (London/Toronto 1971), and his "The Emergence of Central Immigrant Ghettoes in American Cities: 1840–1920," *Annals of the Association of American Geographers* 58.2, June 1968, 343–59; Kramer (Ch.1 para.7 above); D. Schuyler, *The New Urban Landscape* (Baltimore/London 1986), 149ff.

On squatter settlements, see *The City Shaped*, 64, 69; H. Dietz, "Urban Squatter Settlements in Peru: A Case History and Analysis," *Journal of Inter-American Studies* 11, 1969, 353–70.

On colonial cities, see A. D. King, *Colonial Urban Development* (London/Boston 1976), and his *Urbanism, Colonialism and the World Economy* (London/New York 1990); R. Ross and G. J. Telkamp, eds., *Colonial Cities* (Dordrecht/Boston 1985); McGee (Ch.2 n.79). For India, see N. Evenson, *The Indian Metropolis, A View Toward the West* (New Haven/London 1989); P. P. Karan, "The Pattern of Indian Towns: a Study in Urban Morphology," *Journal of the American Institute of Planners* 23, 1957, 70–75. On Islam, see works cited in Ch.2 nn.54, 81, 86, 91; and J. L. Abu-Lughod, *Rabat. Urban Apartheid in Morocco* (Princeton 1980).

On segregation and residential differentiation, see Dennis (Ch.2 n.103). On American residential segregation and zoning, see Boyer (Ch.2 n.107); Wright (Ch.1 n.56); J. Jacobs, *Death and Life of Great American Cities* (New York 1961). Very useful are the Council of Planning Librarians (Chicago) bibliographies nos. 13, 15, and 96 on discrimination in housing. On housing

estates as cities of the poor, see A. R. Hirsch, *Making the Second Ghetto. Race and Housing in Chicago 1940–1960* (Cambridge, Mass. 1983); Hall (Ch.2 n.97); and *Wonen in Wenen: Sociale Woningbouw met Vise* (Antwerp 1987) on the Viennese proletarian Ringstrasse. An excellent overview is provided by White (Ch.1 n.62).

3. PUBLIC PLACES

General works include C. Sitte, *City Planning According to Artistic principles*, in G. R. and C. C. Collins's masterful analysis and translation (New York 1965/1985); A. E. Brinckmann, *Platz und Monument* (Leipzig 1908); J. Stübben, *Der Städtebau* (Leipzig 1924 ed.), esp. Chs.6, 7; Zucker (Ch.3 n.34).

More recent works include R. Krier (Ch.4 n.77); E. Bacon, *The Design of Cities* (London 1967); Trieb (Ch.3 n.54); M. Webb, *The City Square* (London 1990); A. Hecksher, *Open Spaces. The Life of American Cities* (New York 1977). *Places* 6.1, Fall 1989, "The Future of Urban Open Space," contains several relevant articles. See also *Agora*, a magazine issued in relation to a major study of Italian piazzas, first issue July–Aug. 1988.

For the social content of public places, classic studies are R. Sennett, *The Uses of Disorder: Personal Identity and City Life* (New York 1970) and *The Fall of Public Man* (New York 1970); Jacobs (Ch.2 last para. above); L. A. Lofland, *A World of Strangers: Order and Action in Urban Public Space* (New York 1973). See also "The Public Realm" in Kostof, *America by Design* (New York 1987); J. Sanders, "Toward a Return of Public Places: A Survey," *Architectural Record* 173.4, Apr. 1985, 87–95; Francis (Ch.3 n.96). Also see M. C. Cunningham and D. F. Savoie, "Is the Piazza Unamerican? Its Uses in Italian Urban History," *Ekistics* 39, Mar. 1975, 172–76.

The standard works on French squares include those of Dennis, Ballon, and Babelon (Ch.3 nn.57, 75, 77). See also R. Cleary, *The Places Royales of Louis XIV and XV* (in press).

On Islam and public places, see Ch.3 nn.11, 12, 21.

For a host of informative essays on the Spanish *plaza mayor*, see the colloquium proceedings *Forum et plaza mayor* (Ch.3 n.59); also Cervera Vera (Ch.3 n.20); and P. Sica, *Storia dell' Urbanistica, Il Settecento* (Rome 1976), 146–52. On Palermo's serial squares see C. De Seta and L. Di Mauro, *Palermo* (Rome 1980).

A selection on games in public places includes Armitage (Ch.3 n.69), esp. on tournaments; V. Bartlett, *The Past of Pastimes* (Edinburgh 1969), on the pall mall; on bullfighting Acquaroni (Ch.3 n.68) and N. Lujan, *Historia del toreo* (Barcelona 1954); on the palio in Siena, L. Harris in *The New Yorker*, 5 June 1989.

On disencumbering, see the works by Ladd cited in Ch.1 n.45 and Ch.3 n.35.

For the squares of St. Petersburg, see I. A. Egorov, *The Architectural Planning of St. Petersburg: Its Development in the 18th and 19th Centuries*, transl. E. Dluhosch (Athens, O. 1969). Sica (above, para.6) deals with St. Petersburg (392–99), the Forum Bonaparte in Milan (317ff.), and a similar project in Florence (323ff.).

On Nazi public places and spectacle besides the works cited in Ch.3 n.45, see the classics by Lane (Ch.4 n.16); R. R. Taylor, *The Word in Stone* (Berkeley 1974); and H. Frank, ed., *Faschistische Architekturen. Planen und*

Bauen in Europa 1930 bis 1945 (Hamburg 1985); also D. Bartetzko, *Zwischen Zucht und Ekstase. Zur Theatralik von NS Architektur* (Berlin 1985).

On parks, see the works cited in Ch.3 nn.85, 87; G. Cranz, *The Politics of Park Design: A History of Urban Parks in America* (Cambridge, Mass. 1982); and M. Tafuri et al., *The American City* (London 1980).

On some modern squares, see M. Treib, "Fragments on a Void, Tsukuba Center," *Landscape Architecture*, July–Aug. 1985; on the Pershing Square competition in Los Angeles, see *Urban Design International* 10, 1989, 1.1–27, and *Progressive Architecture* 72, Dec. 1991, 20, for the revised decision; on Williams Square, Las Colinas, *Landscape Architecture*, Sept.–Oct. 1985, 64–67, and Ingersoll (Ch.1 n.63); on the Piazza d'Italia in New Orleans, "Place Debate: Piazza d'Italia," *Places* 1:2, Winter 1984, 1–31. On M. Trieb's work, see his *Stadtgestaltung. Theorie und Praxis* (Düsseldorf 1974), *Stadtbild in der Planungspraxis* (Stuttgart 1976), and Ch.3 n.54.

On corporate plazas, see Ch.3 n.102, and S. Hasegawa and S. Elliott, "Public Spaces by Private Enterprise," *Urban Land* 42.5, May 1983, 12–15. On suburban shopping malls, see B. Maitland, *Shopping Malls* (New York 1985), and the periodical *Shopping Centers Today*.

4. THE STREET

General works include S. Anderson, ed., *On Streets* (Cambridge, Mass. 1978); Rykwert (Ch.4 n.2); J. Robertson, "Rediscovering the Street," *Architectural Forum* 140:4, Nov. 1973, 24ff. Also Z. Celik, D. Favro, and R. Ingersoll, eds., *Stadivarius: Categorical Streets of the World. Essays in Honor of Spiro Kostof* (in press).

On Khirokitia, see S. Kostof, *A History of Architecture* (New York 1985), 48–50; A. Le Brun, ed., *Fouilles récentes à Khirokitia (Chypre) 1977–1981*, 2 vols. (Paris 1984, 1989). On streets in the ancient Near East, see Frankfort (Ch.3 n.83) and Lampl (Ch.1 n.8).

On the Strada Nuova in Genoa, see E. Poleggi and P. Cevini, *Genova* (Rome 1981); L. Benevolo, *The Architecture of the Renaissance* (Boulder 1978); and E. Poleggi, *Strada Nuova* (Genoa 1968).

On street pageants, see Ingersoll (Ch.4 n.11); R. Trexler, *Public Life in Renaissance Florence* (New York 1980); E. Muir, *Civic Ritual in Renaissance Venice* (Princeton 1981). On festivals themselves, see N. Z. Davis, *Society and Culture in Early Modern France* (Stanford, Calif. 1975); P. Burke, *Popular Culture in Early Modern Europe* (1978/2nd ed. Aldershot, Hants/Brookfield, Vt. 1988); S. Anglo, *Spectacle, Pageantry, and Early Tudor Policy* (Oxford 1969). On urban space and ritual in Southeast Asia, see Gutschow and Sieverts (Ch.1 para.1 above).

On arcades, Geist (Ch.4 n.54) is indispensable; but see also Doisneau and Delvaille (Ch.4 n.101). On porticoes in Bern, see A. Guegg, ed., *Materialien zur Studie Bern* (Zurich 1975). On Bologna, see the exh. cat. ed. F. Bocchi, *I portici di Bologna e l'edilizia civile medievale* (Bologna 1990), and Miller (Ch.4 n.84). On the American porch, see P. West, "Rise and Fall of the American Porch," *Landscape* 20:3, Spring 1976, 42–47, and Ch.4 n.86.

On signs, see W. H. Wilson, "The Billboard: Bane of the City Beautiful," *Journal of Urban History* 13:4, Aug. 1987, 394–425, and most contemporary books of the City Beautiful movement such as C. M. Robinson's *Modern Civic Art* (New York 1903). On pavements, see McShane (Ch.4 n.67), with an extensive bibliography. On the Maestri delle Strada, C. Allan, *The Quartiere de' Banchi: Urban Planning in Rome in the First Half of the Cinquecento*, PhD diss., Univ. of Pennsylvania, Philadelphia 1977.

On the Parisian boulevard, see *The City Shaped*, 249–52, as well as Loyer's essential book (Ch.2 n.99). On the American boulevard, see D. R. Suisman, *Los Angeles Boulevard* (Los Angeles 1989). On the *paseos* of Spain, see E. M. Prellwitz, "The Paseos of Spain," *Landscape Architecture* 14:2, Jan. 1924, 81ff; and for their influence in America Ch.4 n.98.

On the Fascist street, see D. Y. Ghirardo, "Architecture and Theatre: The Street in Fascist Italy," in *"Event" Arts and Art Events* (Ann Arbor 1987), 175–99; and Ch.3 para.10 above.

On the Modernist street, besides the cited works by Unwin (*Town Planning in Practice*, London 1909) and Le Corbusier (Ch.4 nn.104, 105, 113, 114), see F. Choay, *The Modern City: Planning the Nineteenth Century*, transl. M. Hugo and G. Collins (London 1977), and R. Fishman, *Urban Utopias in the Twentieth Century* (Cambridge, Mass./London 1982). On Ernst May, see the cat. *Ernst May und das Neue Frankfurt 1925–1930* (Frankfurt 1986). On the Gläserne Kette, see I. B. Whyte, ed., *The Crystal Chain Letters* (Cambridge, Mass. 1985).

On linear cities, see *La Ciudad Lineal*, a journal pub. 1897ff.; G. R. Collins, "The Ciudad Lineal of Madrid" and "Linear Planning throughout the World," *Journal of the Society of Architectural Historians* 18:2, May, 18:3, Oct. 1959; G. R. Collins and C. Flores, *Arturo Soria y la Ciudad Lineal* (Madrid 1968) which includes most of Soria y Mata's writings.

On pedestrians and traffic, see J. A. Proudlove, "Traffic in Towns: A Review of the Buchanan and Crowther Reports," *Town Planning Review* 34:4, Jan. 1964. On the pedestrian mall, see R. Brambilla et al., *American Urban Malls: A Compendium* (New York 1977); R. Brambilla and G. Longo, *For Pedestrians Only: Planning, Design and Management of Traffic Free Zones* (New York 1977); D. Carlson and M. R. S. Carlson in *Urban Land* 33, May 1974, 19; G. Eckbo, "Fresno Mall Revisited," *Landscape*, Nov.–Dec. 1986, 54–57. For Europe, see M. R. Wulfe, "Shopping Streets," *A.I.A. Journal*, May 1962, 33–42; R. Monheim, "Pedestrianization in German Towns," *Built Environment* 12:1–2, 1986, 30–44; R. Brambilla and G. Longo, *Rediscovery of the Pedestrian: 12 European Cities* (Washington 1977). On *woonerfs* and creative ways of organizing the street, see J. H. Kraay, "Woonerfs and Other Experiments in the Netherlands," *Built Environment* 12.1–2, 1986; also articles by P. Bosselmann and R. Monheim in the same issue.

For a review of Duany and Plater-Zyberk, see "Our Towns," *Architectural Record*, Oct. 1991, 110–19. On a related planning idea, see P. Calthorpe, *The Pedestrian Pocket Book: A New Suburban Design Strategy* (Princeton 1989).

5. URBAN PROCESS

On disasters, see generally J. Cornell, *The Great International Disaster Book* (New York 1976). On subsequent reconstruction, J. E. Haas, R. W. Kates and M. J. Bowden, eds., *Reconstruction Following Disaster* (Cambridge, Mass. 1977) on Rapid City, Anchorage, Managua, and San Francisco; C. Rosen, *The Limits of Power* (Berkeley 1986) on Boston, Chicago and Baltimore; I. Davis, "Skopje Rebuilt," *Architectural Design*, Nov. 1975, 660–63. Also P. Degan, *The Johnstown Flood of 1889* (New York 1984).

On the destruction of war, see Hewitt (Ch.5 n.15); Gutschow and Beseler (Ch.5 n.23). On reconstruction in Europe, see Diefendorf (Ch.5 n.16); L. Grebler, *Europe's Reborn Cities*, Technical Bulletin 28, Urban Land Institute, Washington, D.C., Mar. 1956. On England, see L. Esher, *A Broken Wave. The Rebuilding of England 1940–1980* (London 1981). On Rotterdam see Van Traa (Ch.1 para.7 above); and P. Johnson-Marshall, *Rebuilding Cities* (Chicago 1966), Ch.7. On Warsaw, see S. Dziewulski and S. Jankowski, "The Reconstruction of Warsaw," *Town Planning Review* 28.3, Oct. 1957, 209–21; and A. Ciborowski, *Warsaw, A City Destroyed and Rebuilt* (Warsaw 1969). On Germany, see N. Gutschow and W. Durth, *Träume in Trümmern* (Brunswick 1988).

On self-inflicted Haussmannization, esp. Islamic, see Ch.5 nn.47, 48. On America's City Beautiful movement and Philadelphia, see D. B. Brownlee, *Building the City Beautiful* (Philadelphia 1989), W. H. Wilson, *The City Beautiful Movement* (Baltimore 1989), and *The City Shaped*, 233ff. and bibliography.

On urban renewal in the U.S., see M. Anderson, *The Federal Bulldozer* (New York 1964), and C. D. Ellis, *Vision of the Urban Freeway*, PhD diss., Univ. of California, Berkeley 1990. Specific studies include those of R. Lubove, *Twentieth Century Pittsburgh* (New York 1969), R. Plunz, *A History of Housing in New York City* (New York 1990), and Chafets (Ch.5 n.58). In England, see Fergusson and McKean (Ch.5 nn.55, 61). For London, Amsterdam and Berlin, see H. Bodenschatz et al., *Schluss mit der Zerstörung* (Giessen 1983), as well as the vast literature on the I.B.A. show in Berlin as an end to the destructive forces of urban renewal and slum clearance.

On American morphology, see M. P. Conzen, "The Morphology of Nineteenth Century Cities in the United States," in W. Borah et al., eds., *Urbanization in the Americas* (Ottawa 1980); see also Conzen's *Making of the American Landscape* (Boston 1990) for the cultural evolution of the American landscape. On English burgage plots and M. R. G. Conzen, see Ch.5 n.63. On cycles, see Ch.5 nn.67, 68. On the formation of the American CBD, see Ch.2 para.7 above.

On design legislation in Santa Barbara, see the cat. by D. Gebhard, *Santa Barbara – The Creation of a New Spain in America* (Santa Barbara 1982), and *Guidelines. El Pueblo Viejo District*, pub. by the city (1987). On Santa Fe see *Design and Preservation in Santa Fe* (1977) and three handbooks, *Historic District* (1986), *Architectural Design Review* (1990), and *The Business Capitol District* (1990), all pub. by the city. For some critical insights see "Change and the Changeless in Santa Fe," *Historic Preservation*, Jan.–Mar. 1974, 4–11.

On Bologna and the Italian experience, see I. Samuels, "Architectural Practice and Urban Morphology," in T. R. Slater, ed., *The Built Form of Western Cities* (Leicester/London 1990); F. Bandarin, "The Bologna Experience: Planning and Historic Renovation in a Communist City," in D. Appleyard, ed., *The Conservation of European Cities* (Cambridge, Mass./London 1979); and P. L. Cervellati and R. Scannavini, *Bologna: politica e metodologia del restauro nei centri storici* (Bologna 1974).

ACKNOWLEDGMENTS FOR ILLUSTRATIONS

Sources of photographs and locations of images illustrated, in addition to those mentioned in the captions, are as follows:

Aerofilms 70, 75, 162, 247 – *Al Araby* magazine 68 – Alinari 99, 224, 275 – VVV Amersfoort 2 – Musée Royal des Beaux-Arts, Antwerp (photo ACL, Brussels) 78 – *Architectural Review* (photo Dan Cruickshank, courtesy The Architectural Press) 285 – Associated Press 122, 181, 252 – Avon County Library (Bath Central Library) 284 – E. A. Bauer 301 – By kind permission of the Marquess of Tavistock and the Trustees of the Bedford Estates 179, Pl. 33 – Beijing Palace Museum 189 – Raffaello Bencini 305 – Roloff Beny Pls.18, 25 – in Berlin: Berlin Museum (photo Hans-Joachim Bartsch) 36, 165; Landesbildstelle 46; Staatliche Museen Preussischer Kulturbesitz (Kupferstichkabinett) 287; Staatsbibliothek Preussischer Kulturbesitz (Kartenabteilung) 16 – © Presse und Informationsamt der Bundesregierung, Bundesbildstelle, Bonn 55, 267 – University of California at Berkeley (Bancroft Library) 90 – courtesy of the Bostonian Society, Old State House, Boston 31 – Bournville Village Trust 198 – Camera Press (UK) Ltd (photo R. Meigneux, © Imapress) Pl.20 – Greg Castillo 14, 27, 41, 53, 54, 63, 67, 74, 84, 166, 228, 238, 244, 257, Pls. 8, 23, 24, 29, 35, 36 – Chicago Historical Society (neg. ICHi–04192) 81 – The Library of the Royal Danish Academy of Fine Arts, Copenhagen 24, 245 – Kölnisches Stadtmuseum (photo Rheinisches Bildarchiv), Cologne 51, Pl.6 – Colorific! (Christopher Morris/Black Star) Pl.38 – Pascal Costa 229 – Staatliche Kunstsammlungen, photo Sächsische Landesbibliothek: Abteilung Deutsche Fotothek, Dresden Pl.28 – Kunstmuseum, Düsseldorf 34 – *Drum* magazine 91 – Randall Eveleigh 173 – Museo di Firenze com'era, Florence (photo Scala) Pl.27 – William Garnett 50 – Kai Gutschow 169 – Landesgalerie, Hanover 124 – The Hulton Picture Company 223 – Martin Hürlimann 26 – Ilmavoimat 306 – A. F. Kersting 212, 256 – Jean Knöss 1 – KLM Luchtfotografie 243 – Bundesarchiv, Koblenz 89 – courtesy Léon Krier 98, Pl.30 – courtesy Rob Krier 126–31 – Landslides Pls. 5, 39 © 1991, Alex S. MacLean) – Emily Lane 28, 286, Pls. 12, 37 – Biblioteca e Arquivo Histórico do Ministério da Habitação e Obras Públicas, Lisbon 248 – Photo Löbl 61 – in London:

photo courtesy Travel Alberta 174; Barbican Estate Office 241; British Library (Map Library) 17, 148, 246, (India Office Library) 92; British Museum (Prints and Drawings) 195; Courtauld Institute of Art (Conway Library) 61, 77, 151, 178; The Danish Tourist Board 242; The Guildhall Library 191, 192; courtesy of Hampstead Garden Suburb Archive Trust 231; Imperial War Museum 258; London Transport Museum Pl.7; Museum of London 161, 164, Pl.21 – Professor Amedeo Maiuri 249, 251 – Eric de Mare 48 – Arxiu Mas, Barcelona 154, 255, Pl.3 – Compania Mexicana Aerofoto, S.A. 254 – Collection Centre Canadien d'Architecture/Canadian Centre for Architecture, Montreal 49 – Landeshauptstadt, Munich 62 – in New York: Fiorello H. LaGuardia Archives, F. H. LaGuardia Community College 278; Museum of the City of New York 47, 234 (photograph by Jacob A. Riis, Jacob A. Riis Collection); Courtesy The New-York Historical Society Pls. 13, 22 – Courtesy, The Oakland Museum History Department 218 – Collections of Pohjois-Pohjanmaan Museo, Oulu Pl.31 – in Paris: Archives d'Architecture Moderne 236; Archives Photographiques 288, 289; Bibliothèque de l'Institut de France 239; Bibliothèque Nationale 5 (photo Bulloz), 25, 158, 160, 225, 226, Pl.14; Musée Carnavalet 38 (Photo Lauros-Giraudon), Pl.17; Musée des Arts Décoratifs (Cabinet des Dessins) 182–85; Musée de la Marine (photo Bulloz) Pl.4 – Philadelphia City Archives, courtesy of Philadelphia Museum of Art 271 – Private Collection 250 – Archivio e Studio Folco Quilici, Rome Pl.16 – Roger-Viollet 30, 199, 270 – in Rome: Biblioteca Vittorio Emanuele (photo GFN) 180; Museo della Civiltà Romana 150; Museo de Roma (photo Scala) Pl.19; Musei Vaticani 3 – Laclede's Landing Redevelopment Corporation, St. Louis 32 – Department of Public Works, Bureau of Architecture, City and County of San Francisco. Photo: Ben Blackwell, courtesy San Francisco Museum of Modern Art Pl.15 – courtesy of the Museum of New Mexico, Santa Fe 101, 163 – Scala, Florence Pls. 1, 2, 19, 26, 27 – Werner Schumann for Guggenheim Productions Pls. 9, 32 – Palazzo Pubblico, Siena (photo Scala) Pl.1 – Edwin Smith 200, 230 – reconstruction by Alan Sorrell 114 – W. Tillig 64 – Richard Tobias 7–12, 20–22, 44, 56, 58–60, 65, 66, 71, 73, 80, 83, 85, 86, 93, 103, 106–9, 112, 115, 120, 123, 125, 132–47, 156, 170–72, 176, 188, 190, 204–11, 213–16, 219–22, 233, 264–66, 269, 274, 277, 279–83, 290–300, Pl.11 – Royal Ontario Museum–Canada, Toronto 149 – Marc Treib 168, 302, 303, Pl.40 – Galleria Sabauda, Turin (photo Scala) Pl.2 – in Vienna: Bildarchiv der Österreichischen Nationalbibliothek 69; Historisches Museum der Stadt Wien 116 – Accademia, Venice (photo Scala) Pl.26 – Muzeum Narodowe, Warsaw 175 – in Washington, D.C.: Library of Congress (LC-USF 342–8057A) 194; Pennsylvania Avenue Development Corporation 203 – Baron Wolman Pl.10.

AMC (Architecture Mouvement Continuité) (Dec. 1984) 97 – C. A. Boethius and J. B. Ward-Perkins, *Etruscan and Roman Architecture* (Harmondsworth 1970) 187 – L. Cervera Vera, *La Plaza Mayor de Ávila* (Ávila 1982) 111 – K. Gruber, *Die Gestalt der Deutschen Stadt* (Munich 1952/1976) 35 – W. Hegemann, *Civic Art, The American Vitruvius* (New York 1922) 159 – after J. Herrmann, *Die Slawen in Deutschland* (Berlin 1970) 201 – K. Hoffmann, R. Lodders and A. Sander, *Die Hochhäuser am Grindelberg* (Stuttgart 1959) 261–63 – Institut Français d'Architecture, *Toulouse, Les délices de l'imitation* (Brussels/Liège 1986) 118, 119 – D. Kobielski, *Warsaw from a Bird's-Eye View* (Warsaw 1971) 259 – after C. Morris and D. E. Thompson, *Huanuco Pampa* (London 1985) 153 – Le Corbusier, *La Maison des hommes* (Paris 1942)/*The Home of Man* (London 1948) 235; *Oeuvre complète 1910–1929* (Zurich 1964) 232; *Oeuvre complète 1946–1952* (Zurich 1961) 240 – K. Nishi and K. Hozumi, *What is Japanese Architecture?* (Tokyo 1985) 87 – after S. H. Olson, *Baltimore, The Building of an American City* (Baltimore 1980) 300 – T. Özgüç, "An Assyrian Trading Outpost," *Scientific American* (Feb. 1963) 34 – E. Poleggi and P. Cevini, *Genova* (Rome 1981) 102 – A. Ravaglioli, *Roma la capitale* (Rome 1971) 272 – P. Ricard, *Le Maroc*, Guide Bleu (Paris 1925) 94 – A. Ricard de Montferrand, *Plans et détails du monument consacré à la mémoire de l'Empereur Alexandre* (Paris 1836) 152 – C. Ruano Llopis, *Impresiones* 155 – U. Vogt-Göknil, *Turquie ottomane* (Fribourg 1965) 72 – R. Willis and J. W. Clark, *Architectural History of the University of Cambridge* (Cambridge 1886) 177 – J. Wulf, *Die Bildenden Künste im Dritten Reich* (Gütersloh 1963) 186.